Latin American Neostructuralism

Latin American Neostructuralism

The Contradictions of Post-Neoliberal Development

Fernando Ignacio Leiva

University of Minnesota Press
Minneapolis
London

Portions of chapters 6 and 9 draw from "Neoliberal and Neostructuralist Perspectives on Labor Flexibility, Poverty, and Inequality: A Critical Appraisal," *New Political Economy* 11, no. 3 (September 2006): 337–59. Portions of chapters 8 and 9 draw from "From Pinochet's State Terrorism to the Politics of Participation," in *Democracy in Chile: The Legacy of September 11, 1973*, ed. Silvia Nagy-Zekmy and Fernando Leiva (Brighton and Portland: Sussex Academic Press, 2005), 73–87.

Published by the University of Minnesota Press
111 Third Avenue South, Suite 290
Minneapolis, MN 55401–2520
http://www.upress.umn.edu

Library of Congress Cataloging-in-Publication Data is available from the Library of Congress.

Printed in the United States of America on acid-free paper

The University of Minnesota is an equal-opportunity educator and employer.

15 14 13 12 11 10 09 08   10 9 8 7 6 5 4 3 2 1

For Karen, Camila, and Elisa

The power of capital is now so drearily familiar,
so sublimely omnipotent and omnipresent,
that even large sectors of the left have succeeded in
naturalizing it, taking it for granted as such an
unbudgeable structure that it is as though they hardly
have the heart to speak of it.

—TERRY EAGLETON, *THE ILLUSIONS OF POSTMODERNISM*

Contents

List of Acronyms

AFPs: *Administradoras de Fondos de Pensiones* (Pension Fund Management companies)

ALBA: *Alternativa Bolivariana para América Latina y el Caribe* (Bolivarian Alternative for Latin America and the Caribbean)

ASEXMA: *Asociación de Exportadores de Manufacturas* (Manufactures Exporters Association)

BBVA: *Banco Bilbao Viscaya Argentaria*

BNDES: *Banco Nacional de Desenvolvimento Econômico e Social* (Brazilian Development Bank)

BPO: Business Processing Outsourcing

CAFTA: Central American Free Trade Agreement

CED: *Centro de Estudios para el Desarrollo* (Center for Development Studies)

CEPAL: *Comisión Económica para América Latina y el Caribe* (Economic Commission for Latin America and the Caribbean)

CIE: *Comité de Inversiones Extranjeras* (Foreign Investment Commitee)

CIEPLAN: *Corporación de Estudios para Latinoamérica* (Corporation of Latin American Studies)

CORFO: *Corporación de Fomento de la Producción* (State Development Corporation)

CPPSE: Changing Production Patterns with Social Equity

DESAL: *Centro para el Desarrollo Económico Social de América Latina* (Center for the Economic and Social Development of Latin America)

DOS: *División de Organizaciones Sociales* (Social Organizations Division)

ECLAC: Economic Commission for Latin America and the Caribbean

ENE: *Encuesta Nacional de Empleo* (National Employment Survey)

EO: export-oriented

ENTEL: *Empresa Nacional de Telecomunicaciones* (National Telecommunications Company)

FDI: foreign direct investment

FGV: *Fundaçao Getulio Vargas*

FLACSO: *Facultad Latinoamericana de Ciencias Sociales* (Latin American Social Sciences Faculty)

FOSIS: Fondo de Inversión y Solidaridad Social (Social Investment and Solidarity Fund)

FRS: French Regulation School

FTAA: Free Trade Area of the Americas

GCI: global competitiveness index

GDP: gross domestic product

HDI: human development index

ICOR: Investment Concentration Ratio

IDB: Inter-American Development Bank

IEDI: *Instituto de Estudos para o Desenvolvimento Industria* (Industrial Development Research Institute)

ILPES: Instituto Latinoamericano de Planificación Económica y Social (Latin American Institute for Economic and Social Planning)

ILO: International Labour Organization

IMF: International Monetary Fund

IPEA: *Instituto de Pesquisa Económica Aplicada* (Institute for Applied Economic Research)

ISI: import substitution industrialization

ISIC: International Standard Industrial Classification

IT: inflation targeting

ITS: Index of Technological Specialization

LCRCE: Office of the Chief Economist for the Latin American and Caribbean Region

LOCE: *Ley Orgánica Constitucional de la Enseñanza* (Constitutional Organic Law for Education)

MEA: *Municipalidades en Acción (Municipalities in Action)*

MERCOSUR: *Mercado Común del Sur* (Southern Common Market)

MIDEPLAN: *Ministerio de Planificación* (Planning Ministry)

NAFTA: North American Free Trade Agreement

NGO: nongovernmental organization

NTEG: nontraditional export growth

OAS: Organization of American States

OECD: Organisation for Economic Co-operation and Development

OMP: other manufactured processing

PDOE: Productive Development in Open Economies

PNR: processed natural resources

PPA: *Plan Pluri-Anual* (Multi-Year Plan)

PPP: purchasing power parity

PSDB: *Partido da Social Democracia Brasileira* (Brazilian Social Democracy Party)

PT: Partido dos Trabalhadores (The Workers' Party)

SBR: structural balance rule

SEGEGOB: *Secretaría General de Gobierno*

SI: Socialist International

SNO: supranational organization

SSA: Social Structures of Accumulation

SSC: shared service center

SUDENE: *Superintendencia do Desenvolvimiento do Nordeste* (Agency for the Development of the Northeast Region)

TIMSS: Trends in International Mathematics and Social Science

TNC: transnational corporation

TRIMs: Trade-Related Investment Measures

TRIPs: Trade Related Aspects of Intellectual Property Rights

UDI: *Union Demócrata Independientes*

UFRJ: *Universidade Federal de Rio do Janeiro*

UNCTAD: United Nations Conference on Trade and Development

UNICAMP: *Universidade Estadual de Campinas* (State University of Campinas)

UNIDO: United Nations Industrial Development Organization

UNDP: United Nations Development Program

USAID: United States Agency for International Development

VAT: value-added tax

WTO: World Trade Organization

YPFB: *Yacimientos Petrolíferos Fiscales Bolivianos* (State Petroleum Corporation of Bolivia)

Acknowledgments

Economic ideas and theories of development become powerful for many different reasons. They can inspire visions of a better future or conceal inequalities and naturalize an unjust status quo; they can beckon forth creative effort, new forms of cooperation and collective action, and even dreams of liberation. They interact in complex and changing ways with political struggles and existing class interests. Yet economists, economics, and development economics have remained, for the most part, resistant to self-criticism and to examinations of how our own "truth claims" are constructed and how economic ideas interact with existing social relations.

My interest on the power of economic ideas is rooted in history and my own biography. I belong to that generation of Chileans who turned seventeen a few weeks before President Allende was democratically elected in September 1970. The Allende government and its attempts to build a Chilean road to socialism along with the military coup and ensuing military regime—during which dogmatic laissez-faire policies operated in tandem with state terror, leading to a negotiated transition and eighteen years of Concertación administrations promising "growth with equity"—provide in condensed form an example of what has been happening in the rest of Latin America and the Caribbean: the interaction of economic ideas and social power under shifting historical circumstances.

In writing this book—an antidote to the seductions offered by the latest development paradigm and a call for greater awareness of how economic ideas interact with power relations—I have drawn inspiration and support from many people and institutions. Edmundo Jiles, Patricio García, Rosa Quintanilla, and the educational work among *pobladores* and workers during the second half of the 1980s and early 1990s (by the now defunct Taller PIRET) taught me more about the "embeddedness" of economics than did years of university studies. I started my economics training at Instituto de Economía of the Universidad Católica in Santiago, the home of Chile's "Chicago Boys." I finished at the Department of Economics of the University of Massachusetts at Amherst, where I found professors such as Carmen Diana Deere, Nancy Folbre, David Kotz, Richard Wolff, Steve Resnick, James Crotty,

Sam Bowles, and Jim Boyce who are not afraid to challenge mainstream ways of thinking with intellectual fearlessness and rigor that I still try to emulate today, a decade later.

At the University at Albany in New York, thanks to the Nuala Drescher Diversity Fellowship and a Faculty Research Award, I obtained the release time and resources necessary to complete the basic research and write the first draft of this book. Throughout this process, professors Edna Acosta-Belén, Chris Bose, José Cruz, and Glyne Griffith encouraged and supported me directly and indirectly beyond what I expected. Other colleagues and my graduate students in the Department of Latin American, Caribbean, and U.S. Latino Studies continually challenged me through their commitment to an interdisciplinary and transnational hemispheric approach. My friends Brian O'Shaugnessy, Maureen Casey, and Elizabeth Grob generously allowed me into their "homes away from home" to write. None of these friends and colleagues bear any responsibility for the concepts or possible shortcomings in these pages.

I thank Jason Weidemann, Adam Brunner, Laura Westlund, Mike Stoffel, and Alicia R. Sellheim at the University of Minnesota Press as well as Rosemi Mederos for copyediting the initial manuscript. Special thanks to Marcelo Montecino for allowing me to use one of his photographs. My extended family in Chile and the United States put up with my "partial presence" during visits to Santiago, Washington, D.C., and the lake in Minnesota. Most of all I am indebted to Karen and our daughters, Camila and Elisa, without whose love, patience, and good humor (did I say patience?) this book would not have been possible.

Latin America's Post-neoliberal Turn

A "new breed of pragmatic leftists" dedicated to combining "the left's traditional warm-hearted social goals with a new found appreciation for cold economic calculus" is now occupying key economic posts in Latin America according to the *Wall Street Journal* (Luhnow 2005). Whether one agrees with this interpretation or not, the election after 2000 of leftists presidents and progressive governments in Chile, Brazil, Argentina, Uruguay, Bolivia, Venezuela, Ecuador, Nicaragua, Guatemala, and Paraguay, as well as the continued presence of powerful social movements, suggests that a historically significant political and intellectual realignment seems indeed under way.

The emergence and rise to predominance of a new, more pragmatic approach to economic development known as Latin American neostructuralism is an important factor, though clearly not the only one, behind Latin America's "post-neoliberal" turn. A creation of the United Nation's Economic Commission for Latin America and the Caribbean (ECLAC), the hemisphere's most influential economic think tank headquartered in Santiago, Latin American neostructuralism informs much of the politico-economic frameworks and policy formulation of the region's center–left political parties and governments. Latin American neostructuralism was officially launched in 1990 with ECLAC's publication of *Changing Production Patterns with Social Equity*, and from its inception it sought to replace "market fundamentalism" and humanize the "savage capitalism" imposed by decades of laissez-faire neoliberal dogmatism in the region. ECLAC and Latin American neostructuralism claim to have successfully combined economic growth, social equity, and political democracy in such a way that Latin America can fully take advantage of the opportunities offered by twenty-first-century globalization.[1] As a result, an array of observers and pundits asserts that a triumph of "a more pragmatic approach, a political economy of the possible" has become the dominant trend in the Latin American continent, a direct result from the definitive defeat both of 1960s "good revolutionaries" and 1980s "well-intentioned free-marketeers" (Santiso 2006, 8).

Warm Hearts + Cold Economic Calculus?

Neostructuralism's displacement of neoliberal free-market dogmatism raises key questions not yet adequately addressed in previous literature: What are the chief strengths and weaknesses of the emerging paradigm? What scope of transformations can Latin American neostructuralism enact? What does the ascendance of this new set of economic ideas mean for Latin American politics and society? Does Latin American neostructuralism constitute a genuine alternative to neoliberalism?

This book aims to answer these questions by systematically examining Latin American neostructuralism's key concepts, modes of theorizing, and politico-economic outcomes while locating its ascendance within the current historical context, a time of profound restructuring of Latin American capitalism and the world economy. Since its debut in 1990, Latin American neostructuralism has garnered widespread intellectual and political influence, moving from the margins to the very center and becoming a key player in the formulation of economic development and social policy, as well as contemporary political discourse. Over the course of its ascent, it has recast conceptualizations about the relationship between economy, state, and society; introduced a new development lexicon increasingly embraced by international development institutions, such as the World Bank and the Inter American Development Bank; and advanced a program of action for establishing a new relationship among institutional reform, modernity, social cohesion, and globalization in the twenty-first century. Rather than trusting celebration, Latin American neostructuralism's ascendance as the latest development discourse calls for an incisive investigation into the "politics of possibilism" and resulting interactions between policies promoting social consensus and existing hierarchies of power. In this spirit, two major themes organize the intellectual journey proposed:

- Where lie the roots of Latin American neostructuralism's strengths and weaknesses?
- What is the impact of Latin American neostructuralism upon the trajectory of Latin American development, broadly defined?

Beyond addressing these crucial questions, this book's broader ambition is to contribute to the revitalization of Latin American critical thinking in the tradition of radical political economy. Pragmatism has lulled many into contentment with short-term, descriptive rather than explicative, modes of inquiry. The analysis presented in the following chapters is an effort to formulate an effective antidote for those who, seduced by the ostensible coherence of this ascending post-neoliberal paradigm, shy away from a sharper examination of the structure and dynamics of power constituting contemporary Latin American capitalism.

What Is Latin American Neostructuralism?

Latin American neostructuralism is the first fully articulated development discourse to directly challenge the hegemony of neoliberal ideas. Even before Anthony Giddens, Britain's New Labor Party, or European social democracy had formulated the "Third Way," Latin American neostructuralists working at ECLAC laid the intellectual foundations for contending neoliberalism's supremacy (Giddens 1998).[2] Understanding the nature and trajectory of the first counterdiscourse to confront neoliberal dogmatism and to surface in the wake of the profound processes of capitalist restructuring experienced over the past decades should be of interest to Latin Americanists and non-Latin Americanists alike.

What is Latin American neostructuralism, then? As we will see, this question has at least has four complimentary answers; Latin American neostructuralism's discursive potency derives from simultaneously being (1) an alternative vision to neoliberal dogmatism; (2) a comprehensive development strategy; (3) an integrated policy framework; and (4) a grand narrative about the path toward modernity that the twenty-first century offers Latin American and Caribbean societies. Reducing it to only one of these dimensions is to misrepresent and underestimate it. Precisely because it is more than just an approach to economic development, Latin American neostructuralism has been able to influence policy planners and international development agencies and suffuse the discourse of center–left coalitions, such as those presently governing in Chile, Brazil, and Uruguay.

An Alternative Vision to Neoliberal Market Dogmatism

Latin American neostructuralism is the response by thinkers at ECLAC headquarters to the intellectual offensive of neoliberalism and perceived deficiencies of structuralism and the state-led industrialization development strategy it had supported from the late 1940s to the 1960s. Whereas during the second half of the 1970s and 1980s neoliberals insisted that market and price signals alone remained the fundamental tools for reforming Latin American economies and achieving international competitiveness, neostructuralists countered that, although market forces continued to be primary, politics and governmental intervention were imperative for constructing the society-wide "systemic competitiveness" necessary to successfully compete in world markets (ECLAC 1990). Political and institutional intervention, they argue, are essential for generating the synergy, levels of coordination and social harmony indispensable for fluid and speedy integration into the globalization process.

By replacing the market dogmatism of the 1970s and 1980s with a more holistic approach that restored the political, institutional, and cultural dimensions to economic development, Latin American neostructuralism promises to transform Latin America. To recouple economic growth with social equity under the new historical context, ECLAC argues, intellectual and political leadership, not just laissez-faire policies, are needed.

A Development Strategy Offering Growth, Equity, and Democracy

In contrast to the traumas and sufferings brought on by laissez-faire economics and dictatorial rule during the "lost decade" of the 1980s, Latin American neostructuralism hoists the highly seductive notion that international competitiveness, social integration, and political legitimacy can synergistically be attained by swimming along, not against, the swift currents unleashed by globalization. Through a conceptual and policy framework where economic growth, equity, and democracy mutually reinforce one another, Latin American neostructuralism offers the region a new path through which it is possible to remake the countenance of globalization: without having to challenge the power of transnational corporate capital but by relying upon a lucid policy and political intervention, it is possible to fashion a new "globalization with a human face."

Neostructuralists argue that if Latin America and the Caribbean are to travel down this more desirable path toward globalization, a broader vision of economic development is required; governments, institutions, and political systems must prepare themselves to play a qualitatively different leadership role in ensuring international competitiveness. Productive development policies, in addition to social pacts and explicit initiatives to sustain social cohesion, must become part of an integrated menu of development policies.

Through this more holistic approach, individual export enterprises as well as entire economies can be transformed into radiating hubs propagating globalization's economic, technological, and social benefits. Chile after 1990 has been the launching site, testing ground, and, arguably, the showcase for this new post-neoliberal development approach.

An Integrated Policy Framework Supportive of the "Post-Washington Consensus"

Latin American neostructuralism has also been called a "package" of economic measures that will help remedy the crises spawned by neoliberalism through policies that "will prove viable politically and socioeconomically but also promote democratic regimes and greater social justice" (Meller 1991, 1). Its main premise is that through a different set of economic policies—more attentive to institutional, political, and cultural factors too long excluded by free-market reductionism—countries can attain the "high road" to globalization. Instead of radical reforms, Latin America's massive problems of poverty, inequality, and disappointing economic growth rates can be better addressed by ensuring a more dynamic entry into world markets. On the basis of "reforming the reforms" and improved policy design, international competitiveness, economic growth, social equity, political democracy, and legitimacy can be made to mutually reinforce one another in an ever-expanding virtuous circle.

Latin American neostructuralism represents an important change in policy design inasmuch as it represents an explicit recognition that if market forces are to operate effectively, they need to be complemented by non-market-based forms of coordination. Economic policies must be conceived with an explicit awareness about the role that institutions, culture, and social capital play in economic coordination. Economic growth, social equity, and democratic governance and governability require a much expanded policy mindset and palette therefore. The main characteristic of the neostructuralist policy framework, then, is the *active promotion of new forms of social coordination beyond those offered by market forces alone*. Neostructuralist policies acknowledge the importance of institutional intervention, civic–state alliances, and trust-based networking to overcome market imperfections, asymmetrical information, and transaction costs.

In terms of economic policies, neostructuralists consider that without active export-promotion policies, exports would concentrate on a few firms and products vulnerable to fluctuations in international demand, trapping a country's exports in a tranche of raw materials with low levels of processing. Among policies considered in this area, neostructuralists call for supporting technical innovation through partial subsidies for innovation and the promotion of strategic alliances between local and transnational firms, as well as programs aimed at training the labor force and improving their skill levels through firm-specific training programs (ECLAC 1994). As discussed in greater detail in the following chapters, such a framework represents a significant departure from neoliberalism's market reductionist laissez-faire approach.

A Narrative about "Progressive Modernity" in the Twenty-first Century

However, it is as a grand narrative about how to reach that always elusive goal of modernity where Latin American neostructuralism displays its greatest discursive potency and enacts its most relevant political practices. Latin American neostructuralism and ECLAC have constructed a discourse and operational guidelines aimed at promoting modernization (the means) to achieve modernity (the goal) at a time when other paths, such as those offered by socialist revolution in the 1960s and neoliberalism in the 1980s, have shown themselves as seriously flawed, particularly in light of the technological and cultural transformations and challenges brought about by globalizing capital.

The thrust of neostructuralism's efforts is to midwife the region's transition to a "progressive modernity," one in which "macroeconomic equilibrium, [and] productive modernization, coincide also with macrosocial and macroenvironmental equilibria" (Rosales 1995, 99). To achieve it, one needs to understand that "a solidarity-based modernization will be possible only in so far as it emanates from solid social accords, supported by institutions that promote informed debate among those social actors who are most representative and have a greater technical component in their proposals, engaged both in the diagnosis, but also in the solution, with a culture of shared compromises and of negotiated solution to conflicts" (Rosales, 1995, 98–99; my translation). ECLAC argues that a progressive or solidarity-based modernity requires a new pragmatism that places social cohesion as the essential core of international competitiveness and, ergo, as the beacon guiding the design of social policy (ECLAC 2007). Rather than redrawing property rights or redistributing the economic surplus, this framework displaces the center of gravity of policy intervention from economics to the realm of subjectivity, symbolic politics, and the cultural dimension. The actions of the state and political institutions have to create a new type of expectations, new citizens, and new ways of understanding citizenship—that is, a new political culture—as well as those attitudes and behaviors congruent with this new master narrative and system of domination. Policies are thus increasingly displaced to operate at the symbolic, socioemotional, and subjective levels.

Probing the New Paradigm, Reversing Its Imposing Tapestry

To use Terry Eagleton's apt figure of speech, this book aims to reverse neostructuralism's "imposing tapestry" to "expose in all its unglamorously disheveled tangle the threads constituting the well-heeled image it presents to the world" (Eagleton 1986, 80). For too long Latin American neostructuralism was able to fend off critical scrutiny on the basis of two arguably unassailable lines of defense.

First, Latin American neostructuralism claims to be the only viable extant "alternative" to neoliberal policies. Two astute observers of Latin American development—Cristóbal Kay and Robert Gwynne—assert that "neostructuralism should not be interpreted as caving in to neoliberalism nor as an indication that structuralism was wrong but rather as an attempt to come to terms with a new reality. . . . Despite the shortcomings of neostructuralism it is *the only feasible and credible alternative to neoliberalism* in present historical circumstances—at least for the time being" (Kay and Gwynne 2000, 62; emphasis added). Indeed in a context characterized by the crisis of state-led inwardly oriented development, the downfall of statist socialism, weakening of the labor movement, and major transformations in the world economy brought about by globalizing capital, a neostructuralist approach initially appears to be the only viable alternative. As Osvaldo Rosales, director of ECLAC's International Commerce Division, has stated, "In a world marked by globalization and technological change, the old playbooks are no longer useful," consequently, "The challenge of progressives is to achieve the old ideals of equity, social justice and participation in a world that requires to grow economically by exporting, that clearly requires competitiveness, innovation and flexibility, in a democratic framework. To achieve such goals, neither the market fundamentalist option, nor the authoritarian societies of 'actually existing socialism' constitute efficient alternatives" (Rosales 1995, 126).

Second, neostructuralists argue that their pragmatic stance leaves ample room for deploying a wide range of public policies capable of effectively coping with the colossal problems left in the wake of neoliberal restructuring and the policies of liberalization, privatization, and deregulation that it promoted. Along these lines, Osvaldo Sunkel, a key figure in the history of Latin American structuralism and neostructuralism, depicts the prevailing pragmatic mindset pointing out, "if the critics only limit themselves to condemnation, I respond that I am not interested in denouncing, I am interested in proposing. Thus, neostructuralism is *the only neosocial–democratic alternative* that I can envision. With it, one seeks to accept an economy broadly based on the market, privately owned capital, foreign capital and a reduced but effective role for the state" (Treviño 2000). If these are the parameters for policy making, then for Sunkel and other planners at the new ECLAC, "the issue then just becomes what are the possible and necessary tasks in such a context" (Treviño 2000). It is this second line of defense that presently has proved more effective, surrounding Latin American neostructuralism with a seemingly invulnerable protective armor: entertaining more radical alternatives that challenge the power of transnational capital is not only unwise and unfeasible but also ultimately unnecessary for achieving growth with equity.

Indeed, despite the far-reaching reforms announced by President Hugo Chávez of Venezuela and Evo Morales of Bolivia, no fully articulated theoretical or political alternative yet exists to Latin American neostructuralism.[3] Though gaining momentum, the emergence of fully formed and more radical alternatives to neostructuralism, as well as the constitution of those social and political forces capable of supporting such alternatives, has proven so far to be a slow, fragmented, and uncertain process. This book's contribution to critical inquiry, then, is to advance a method for assessing Latin American neostructuralism at a time when it enjoys widespread intellectual and political support, and its lines of defense have so far proved impregnable.

"Deconstructing" Latin American Neostructuralism

To reverse its imposing image, the study of Latin American neostructuralism presented in this volume combines political economy with elements of literary theory. I choose this hybrid approach, because mainstream economics and the field of economic development in particular remain methodologically ill-equipped to perform a basic act of theoretical self-awareness that should be part of any discipline: a critical self-analysis of its own modes of theorizing and constructing meanings.[4] In contrast to trends in other social sciences, economics still lacks the will as well as the tools to explore the way it uses language in constructing its claims to truth (Henderson et al. 1993). Much less is the discipline willing or prepared to explore how these constructs interact with existing social power either to legitimize or undermine existing hierarchies and structures. As a result, the small but growing number of economists interested in exploring these issues have turned to literary theory, hermeneutics, rhetoric, and the sociology of science for understanding how knowledge claims and meanings are socially negotiated and constructed within the discipline.[5]

The following chapters therefore braid together two very different strands of contemporary thought—political economy and literary theory. Political economy, broadly influenced by Marxism, feminism, critical theory, post-structuralism, and current debates on capitalist globalization, explores the interaction between power relations and economic outcomes, a concern traditionally excised from consideration by neoclassical economics. At the same time, literary theory's concept of deconstruction, and its insight that every text is the outcome of specific acts of exclusion and opposition, studies the rhetorical and linguistic forms used in the production of texts and discourses. To couple political economy and the deconstructive techniques of literary theory, I follow Terry Eagleton's lead in the sense that for "deconstruction" to triumph over its often sterile, self-referential excesses, the *historical* relationship between *discursive* and *material practices* has to be firmly planted at the center of analysis. By understanding economic ideas as "bod[ies] of meanings and values *encoding certain interests relevant to social power*" (Eagleton 1991, 45 [emphasis added]), development paradigms like neoliberalism and neostructuralism can be examined in a qualitatively more revealing manner.

Comparisons between competing economic paradigms usually entailed either assessing the predictive power of opposing theoretical models or attempting to empirically evaluate the outcomes of economic policies endorsed. Cast in the mold of the "conventional approach," much of the literature discussing Latin American neostructuralism (Bitar 1988; Ffrench-Davis 1988; Meller 1988; Sunkel and Zuleta 1990; Colclough and Manor 1991; Green 1995), engages in extended comparison of policy dichotomies (short-term versus long-term, markets versus institutions, export-promotion, etc.). It rarely investigates the modes through which these contending claims are produced. Such a conventional approach allows for a preliminary (and useful) taxonomy; however, insufficient attention is paid to the nature of the overall project of economic and societal restructuring promoted, to the role of economic discourse in transforming or legitimizing existing power relations, or to how such efforts, in turn, transform these very discourses and the action-oriented beliefs they engender.

Main Argument: Appeal and Contradictions

More than just as a post-neoliberalism development discourse emphasizing equity, social cohesion, and institutions, I look at Latin American neostructuralism through a lens that focuses on how it interacts with existing social power. The main thesis put forth in these pages is that Latin American neostructuralism's appeal (i.e., its discursive strengths) and inherent contradictions (i.e., its incoherencies) have the same common root: a sanitized analysis of Latin American economy and society scoured clean of conflict and power relations.[6] By abjuring to key tenets from its structuralist past and embracing the defense of the current export-oriented (EO) regime of accumulation, neostructuralism proceeds to hyperbolize the purported harmonious nature of Latin America's actually existing capitalism. My starting point, then, is that Latin American neostructuralism's mode of theorizing marginalizes power relations from the analysis of the economy and society.[7] These "acts of omission" give rise to Latin American neostructuralism's own "inconsistency syndromes" (Stallings and Peres 2000).[8] Neostructuralist discussions about productivity and technical change, for example, neglect class, gender, and labor control from consideration. The gendered nature of the economy and social reproduction in countries that have undergone drastic, and many times violent, transformations of social arrangements at the level of the household, workplace, and community are also ignored, as is the growing power of transnational and financial capital over the global as well as each Latin American country's economy. By tracing these acts of omission and their repercussions, we can gain insight into the limitations of neostructuralism as a development paradigm and assess the changing historical role of the new ECLAC.

I argue that Latin American neostructuralism's mode of theorization gives rise to contradictions in three interconnected realms. First, because its political economy perspective marginalizes power relations, inconsistency continually *undermines the internal coherence of Latin American neostructuralism's core foundational ideas.* By renouncing to structuralism's methodological legacy—namely a focus on how economic surplus is produced, appropriated, and distributed within a single, world capitalist economy—Latin American neostructuralism becomes *analytically impotent in adequately explicating the scope of the qualitative transformations experienced by Latin American capitalism over the past decade.* The transnationalization of economic, social, and political structures, the informalization of capital–labor relations accompanying EO capitalist development, and the growing financialization of the economy are three mutually supporting dynamics decisively shaping socioeconomic and politico-cultural developments in the region. A third contradiction of ECLAC's post-neoliberalism paradigm manifests itself in what I call the "heterodox paradox," namely, how progressive public policies designed to promote international competitiveness and participatory governance excised of categories sensitive to existing power relations, led to the *politico-economic consolidation, legitimization, and furtherance of the process of capitalist restructuring initially set in motion by neoliberal ideas and policies.* Each one of these inconsistencies can be traced to the conceptual and discursive innovations and methodological retreats Latin American neostructuralism enacted as it molted from its formerly structuralist skin. As a result, instead of being a coherent all-encompassing alternative, Latin American neostructuralism's shortcomings leave ample theoretical and political space for revitalizing critical or radical political economy.

Structure of the Book

If we are to explore how the production of meanings—a development discourse such as Latin American neostructuralism—unfolds in a concrete historical context of social and political struggles, a mechanistic approach will not do. Rather, the investigation presented in this volume entails a series of connected analytical steps, which can be described as (1) identifying its core concepts; (2) historicizing Latin American neostructuralist economic discourse; (3) revealing acts of omission; (4) studying how economic discourse interacts with existing power relations; and (5) tracing efforts to prolong the "shelf-life" of neostructuralist concepts. These steps, not necessarily followed in a linear fashion, constitute the backbone connecting each of the book's chapters.

Identifying Core Concepts

Latin American neostructuralism's ability to formulate a development framework, a set of action-oriented beliefs and policies, and a narrative about modernity in the twenty-first century is the product of a process that combines conceptual innovation with intellectual retreat. I begin by identifying those concepts that give specificity to the emerging paradigm and those rhetorical forms that constitute the new discourse through a series of conceptual ruptures and continuities with its neoliberal predecessor. Chapter 1, "Conceptual Innovation: Combining Growth, Equity, and Democracy," explores how neostructuralism's grand development vision rests on deploying innovative notions that challenged neoliberal orthodoxy with the concepts of systemic competitiveness, technical progress, proactive labor flexibility, concerted action, and virtuous circles. Chapter 2, "Methodological Retreats," explores the itinerary and content of the intellectual retreat enacted by Latin American neostructuralism, evident in three crucial aspects of the "new ECLAC's" economic thinking: (1) the replacement of the concept of economic surplus with that of international competitiveness; (2) the jettisoning of a systemic approach along with the core-periphery model that examined Latin American economies within the development of a single world capitalist economy; and (3) the restoration of politics and institutions to development thinking in a manner that decouples them from capitalist accumulation and struggles over the distribution of economic surplus. It is this simultaneity in conceptual innovation and retreat, the amalgam of rupture and continuity, which gives Latin American neostructuralism its discursive specificity and makes it a distinct contribution in the universe of economic development theories.

Historicizing Latin American Neostructuralism

To "historicize" Latin American neostructuralism means to inscribe its emergence within a specific historical and economic juncture, namely the transition from import substitution industrialization (ISI) to the current EO regime of accumulation in Latin America, and to show how its signifying practices interact with such a process. In chapter 3, "Historicizing Latin American Neostructuralism," I review the contending yet complementary roles played by neoliberal and neostructuralist ideas in enabling such a transition by offering four different angles from which to examine the neostructuralist discourse–capitalist restructuring relationship. After a broad overview of how different theories of development—structuralism, dependency theory, neo-liberalism, and neostructuralism—relate to the evolution of Latin American capitalism over the past six decades, I focus more on the trajectory of the region's recent EO regimes. Emphasis is placed on the how neostructuralism must provide the means for channeling and regulating economic, social, and cultural conflicts under the new order. Chapter 4, "Neostructuralism in Chile and Brazil," continues to historicize the emergence of the new paradigm by studying how Latin American neostructuralism moved from the margins to the center of policy formulation in these two emblematic countries. These two case studies highlight that historical periodization, though necessary, is by itself insufficient to explain Latin American neostructuralism's different degrees of influence in each one of these countries. Other factors, such as the conduits through which ECLAC's economic thinking influences economists and policymakers, the size and export-profile of the economy, and the political juncture must also be considered. The comparative analysis of neostructuralism's influence during Chile's governments (1990–2006) and Brazil's *Partido dos Trabalhadores* (PT [The Workers' Party])-led administration (2002–6) shows that the interplay of structural and conjunctural elements shapes Latin American neostructuralism's differentiated influence in each country.

Revealing Acts of Omission

Drawing on the notion that every discourse commits certain exclusions in its construction, the following two chapters identify the specific acts of omission enacted by neostructuralist discourse. As chapter 5, "Foundational Myths, Acts of Omission," illustrates, the marginalization of power relations from economic analysis unwittingly undermines the coherence of Latin American neostructuralism's own core ideas or five foundational myths: (1) the necessity for off-ramping onto the "high road" to globalization; (2) the promotion of "open regionalism"; (3) the possibility of de-linking distribution from accumulation and therefore delivering "changing productive structures with social equity" within the confines of the existing regime of accumulation; (4) the purported dichotomy between "spurious" versus "genuine" competitiveness; and (5) the imperative of deliberately designing public policies that foster consensus and concerted action to improve the speed and adaptability of workers, firms, and societal subsystems to the requirements of international competitiveness and the global economy. Each one of these initially seductive ideas proves to be built upon feet of clay. Recalcitrant realities that are inherent to an increasingly transnationalized Latin American capitalism, periodically short-circuit the virtuous circle through which neostructuralists promise that international competitiveness, social integration, and political stability will become mutually supportive.

Perhaps one of the most surprising conclusions presented in this volume is that, despite wielding a more "holistic" development approach than neoliberalism, Latin American neostructuralism remains incapable of fully understanding the strategic transformations experienced by Latin American capitalism over the past decade. In chapter 6, "Effacing the Deep Structure of Contemporary Latin American Capitalism," I show how the systematic excising of power and power relations from economic analysis and its proclivity to mollify conflicts, seriously dulls Latin American neostructuralism's analytic edge. When confronted with the task of explaining different phenomena, such as the continuous reorganization of the social and technical basis of production, the transnationalization and financialization of the region's economy, the increasing informalization of labor–capital relations and precariousness of employment that accompany the expansion of globally integrated production systems, Latin American neostructuralism displays an advanced case of myopia. As chapter 6 demonstrates, three recent qualitative transformations—transnationalization, financialization, and precarization—are inextricably linked to one another and increasingly undermine the possibility of achieving economic development with social equity and democracy in the region.

Interactions with Existing Social Power

Based on the premise that every discourse directly participates in conflicts of power by either (a) proposing lines of action and the imaginary resolution of real contradictions existing in society through its economic and social policies or (b) masking or suppressing social conflicts that arise through its politics, Latin American neostructuralism has had and will continue to have a profound influence on power relations in the region.[9] Both chapter 7 ("The Politics of Neostructuralism and Capital Accumulation") and chapter 8 ("Erecting a New Mode of Regulation") focus on the wide array of policies deployed to manage social and economic conflict that, according to *Social Cohesion and a Sense of Belonging in Latin America and the Caribbean* published by ECLAC in 2007, constitutes the Pole Star for contemporary public policies.

The analysis presented in both of these chapters shows that neostructuralism neither "caves in" to neoliberalism nor brings about a sharp rupture with the existing regime of accumulation ("economic model"). On the contrary, thanks to its discursive and policy innovations, it contributes to consolidate, legitimize, and regulate the EO regime of accumulation. Whereas neoliberal policies gave rise to the *orthodox paradox*—namely that "economic policy reforms aimed at expanding the role of markets *appear to strengthen the power of the core of the state*" (Bates and Krueger 1993, 463; emphasis added), Latin American neostructuralism in turn begets what I call the *heterodox paradox*, namely, that economic and social policies aimed at expanding the role of "participatory governance" and "civil society" result in deepening the subordination of the public sphere and society's noneconomic realm to the logic of transnational capital. The outcome is a weakening of popular sovereignty and citizenship and the consolidation of capitalist hegemony. Chapters 7 and 8 illustrate how the type of "participatory politics" promoted by neostructuralists contributes to capital accumulation by propping up the profit rate and the establishment of a new mode of regulation that allow for the reproduction of the new system of domination.

Chile has been heralded as the country where Latin American neostructuralism reached its highest levels of influence and greatest success. Chapter 9, "Chile's Evanescent High Road and Dashed Dreams of Equity," brings the assessment of how economic discourse interacts with existing power relations back to Latin American neostructuralism's birthplace. Jumping off from the June 2006 uprising by Chilean high school students, chapter 9 studies the twin failures of neostructuralism and Chile's *Concertación*[10] governments: after more than a decade and a half, the "high road to globalization" and "growth with equity" are nowhere to be found. The chapter compares and contrasts those indicators used to portray Chile as the region's "success story" with the often ignored and more "toxic" politico-economic outcomes of Chilean development. The extent to which the uncontested power of transnational capital has forced Chilean neostructuralists to successively revise their notion of the "high-road" to globalization—to the point where it has become a caricature of its original formulation—is underscored. From a "second-phase" of the export-model based on manufactured exports defended in the early 1990s, a tortuous road has led to the present, where the center–left government has no other alternative but to offer Chile as a dependable "springboard" (*país plataforma*) for transnational capital's regional expansion in the financial, telecommunication, and service sectors. Such a path chokes off the possibilities for "growth with equity." As Chile's youth have recently shown, two mechanisms used by the "Asian Tigers" to reach the "high road," providing a high-quality educational system and investing the fiscal surplus in "human capital," lie outside the realm of possibilities in Latin America's most highly rated economy, which is not surprisingly the one most firmly under the control of transnational finance capital.

Tracing Efforts to Prolong Neostructuralism's "Shelf-life"

Chapters 10 and 11 consider economic discourses as being continually forced to negotiate and resolve their internal contradictions. Just like perishable commodities stamped with a clearly visible sell-by date, economic discourses also possess a comparable "shelf-life," that is, a span of time after which they exhibit a declining ability to perform their role. This shelf-life is determined by the interaction of a complex set of conflicting factors, not the least of which is each discourse's ability to negotiate its own internal inconsistencies and timely adapt to changing circumstances. For this reason, Latin American neostructuralism must be seen not as a fixed unchanging set of ideas or guidelines but rather as being in a constant state of flux as it is strives to resolve its inconsistencies and patch up the crevices between its rhetoric and socioeconomic reality.

Chapter 10, "Neostructuralism and the Latin American Left" reviews the conceptual innovations introduced by neostructuralism after 2004—the characterization of Latin America as a "three-speed model," "segmented trans-nationalization," and a renewed emphasis on producing social cohesion—in a vain attempt to present itself as the only modern and viable progressive alternative for the region. In contrast to the simplistic and flawed framework that presents Latin America as a battlefield between a "modern–cosmopolitan" versus a "retrograde" Left, the chapter compares neostructuralism's "globalization with a human face" strategy with Venezuela's "twenty-first century socialism" and Bolivia's quest for an "Andean-Amazonic capitalism." Chapter 11, "The Future of Latin American Neostructuralism," brings together the previous strands of inquiry from previous chapters to ask: What are the prospects for this ascending development paradigm in the coming years? Even though it has displayed a significant capacity to adapt and reinvent itself as it changed from "early" neostructuralism (1990–98) to middle neostructuralism (1999–2007), the chapter explains why Latin American neostructuralism finds itself at a crossroads. Either it engages in a profound self-criticism of its mode of theorization and reconnects with the best traditions of critical political economy and Latin American critical thinking, or, conversely, it becomes more irretrievably trapped within a short-term, descriptive framework, binding itself even more firmly to its present role of defending a status-quo increasingly dominated by transnational finance capital. In light of neostructuralism's idealized version of a high road to globalization, the book concludes by explaining why a renewal of debates about alternative development models is in order. Latin America's post-neoliberal turn, hence, is not characterized by the definitive triumph of pragmatism, but it remains still to be shaped by the reemergence of a more a radical and critical political economy.

Three Caveats

From the outset I want to offer the reader three words of caution. First, the book deals exclusively with Latin American neostructuralism, that is, with the intellectual and policy production of ECLAC as presented over the past two decades in its institutional publications and those authored by key staff members (see Figure 1). It does not consider the work of U.S. or European structuralists and neostructuralists, such as Lance Taylor, Joseph Stiglitz, or Dani Rodrik, among others, whose ideas also inform the post-neoliberalism development debate.[11] I have attempted to faithfully capture both ECLAC's initial production from the early 1990s as well as the evolution of neostructuralist thinking as it appears in its latest documents (early 2007), with a focus on the intellectual production at ECLAC's Santiago headquarters, which to a great extent reflects the objectives and perspectives of the Commission's Executive Secretariat. Even though ECLAC has regional offices in Argentina, Brazil, Colombia, Mexico, the Caribbean, and Washington, D.C. and the research and policy concerns at these other sites is often more grounded on emerging dynamics, I focus on the official, institutional discourse of ECLAC headquarters. The evident risk has been neglecting important undercurrents, nuances, and debates gathering momentum in the periphery of the institution.

The second caveat refers to the notion of "neoliberalism." The term has become omnipresent, employed with vastly different meanings in the literature to denote alternatively (1) a set of economic ideas; (2) a policy regime; (3) an "economic model"; and (4) the all-encompassing mode of experiencing the economic, political, and cultural existence under the current era of

Year	Author–Title

Passage from Structuralism to Neostructuralism (1983–89)

1983	Fajnzylber, "La industrialización trunca de América Latina"
1986	Ffrench-Davis, "Neoestructuralismo e inserción externa"
1988	Fajnzylber, "Industrialización en América Latina: de la "caja negra" al "casillero vacío." Comparación de patrones contemporáneos de industrialización"

"Early" Neostructuralism (1990–98)

1990	*Changing Production Patterns with Social Equity*
1991	*Sustainable development: changing production patterns, social equity and the environment*
1992	*Education and Knowledge: Basic Pillars of Changing Production Patterns with Social Equity*
1992	*Social Equity and Changing Production Patterns: An Integrated Approach*
1993	*Population, social equity and changing production patterns*
1994	*Open Regionalism in Latin America and the Caribbean: Economic Integration as a Contribution to Changing Production Patterns with Social Equity*
1994	*Latin America and the Caribbean: Policies to Improve Linkages with Global Economy*
1996	*Strengthening Development: The Interplay of Macro- and Microeconomics*
1998	*The Fiscal Covenant: Strength, Weaknesses, Challenges*

"Middle" Neostructuralism (1999–2007)

1998	Ocampo, "Beyond the Washington Consensus"
1998	Ocampo, "Our agenda"
2000	*Equity, Development and Citizenship*
2000	*The Equity Gap: A Second Assessment*
2002	*Globalization and Development*
2004	*Productive Development in Open Economies*
2005	Machinea and Hopenhayn, *La esquiva equidad en el desarrollo latinoamericano: una visión estructural, una aproximación multifacética*
2007	Ottone and Sojo, *Social Cohesion: Inclusion and a Sense of Belonging in Latin America and the Caribbean*

Figure 1. The main documents of Latin American neostructuralism. ECLAC is the author, unless specified otherwise. Source: ECLAC, institutional books prepared for Commission Sessions and other publications by key ECLAC headquarter staff members.

globalization. I use neoliberalism in a tightly restricted sense of denoting a particular set of economic ideas and policies. I employ the term of "EO regime of accumulation" when referring to the "new economic model" that replaced ISI in most countries in the region. Making such distinction has important analytical consequences. First, it enables me to explore how different, even contending, sets of economic ideas contribute to consolidate (or undermine) a given set of power relations embedded in the EO regime of accumulation. This is particularly relevant for assessing center–left governments in the region. Without a clear distinction between economic ideas and a regime of accumulation, debates about the role of the center left have become increasingly muddled, leading analysts to make two equally untenable claims. Either, unbeknownst to them, Latin American socialists and progressives have converted ideologically to neoliberal ideas and this "conversion on the road to Damascus" explains their support for the "neoliberal model," or Latin American socialists and progressives have remained true to their transformative convictions, and by deploying a wider set of equity-enhancing social and productive modernization policies, they have been able to significantly reform the previous "neoliberal model" de facto transforming into a different yet unnamed economic model or models (e.g., social liberalism, neostructuralist regimes). By claiming that Lula or Ricardo Lagos have become neoliberals, the real nature and scope of their historical role is obscured and minimized. In contrast to such a claim, the clear separation that I propose between neoliberalism understood as a set of economic ideas and the EO regime of accumulation, in whose establishment and consolidation *both* neoliberal *and* neostructuralist ideas and policies play critical but different roles, allows for a more grounded assessment. Above all, it enables us to engage in the discussion of whether Latin American neostructuralism is really an "alternative" to neoliberalism with a longer range and more fruitful perspective.

The third and final clarification refers to calling Latin American neostructuralism a paradigm. It is clear that ECLAC and its "economic thinking" are not an academic creation produced to inhabit the safe confines of the ivory tower. As in the past, ECLAC's intellectual production combines vision with policy orientations developed "on the go" to assist governments in the formulation of economic and social policy to resolve concrete and pressing problems. Despite such instrumental characteristics, Latin American neostructuralism displays the defining traits of a paradigm (Fine 2002): it represents the defense of a particular world vision, it has a body of professionals engaged in producing and renewing that world vision, and it upholds an exemplar of what is desired for the region. I have tried to represent the core ideas and foundational myths that undergird such vision as best as possible, respecting neostructuralist logic without sacrificing my own critical voice. I leave it to the reader to determine whether I have succeeded or not.

1

Conceptual Innovation:
Combining Growth, Equity, and Democracy

"Here is the solution to all of our problems!" announced Fernando Fajnzylber when he arrived in Rio de Janeiro to present the founding manifesto of Latin American neostructuralism (Bresser-Pereira 1992, 6; my translation).[1] Written under his leadership and published in 1990, *Changing Production Patterns with Social Equity* seemed to solve three pressing challenges confronting the United Nation's Economic Commission for Latin America and the Caribbean (ECLAC) as it sought to craft a credible response to neoliberalism's laissez-faire counterrevolution in development thinking. After years of hard work during the 1980s, economists at ECLAC finally managed to (1) identify the weakest chinks in the discursive armor of the then-dominant neoliberal paradigm; (2) renew ECLAC's conceptual apparatus, erasing the stigma of obsolescence attached to its earlier support for state-led industrialization; and (3) formulate a new set of attractive foundational ideas and action-oriented propositions seemingly capable of addressing the problems faced by Latin American countries in the era of globalization. Armed with this new vision, Latin American neostructuralists would march on to challenge and ultimately defeat dogmatic neoliberalism's stranglehold over the hemisphere, blazing the trail and clearing the obstacles for the rise to predominance of a new discourse extolling Latin America's possibilities for reaching a "progressive modernity" through the high road to globalization.

After enduring wrenching social, economic, and political restructuring under neoliberal policies and the military regimes of the 1980s, political leaders and public opinion eagerly welcomed neostructuralism's discursive innovation: Latin America's dynamic integration into a changing global economy did not have to continue being a politically, socially, and economically traumatic affair. Transformation of productive structures imposed by globalization could be achieved via a different path from that offered by neoliberalism's "savage" capitalist route: productive transformation could take place with social equity. The tantalizing fruits of modernity offered by global

1

markets and media could be reaped while simultaneously preserving solidarity, social cohesion, and deepening democratic forms of governance. Like a salve on open sores, the region welcomed neostructuralism's new discourse promising social harmony with open global markets and flows.

Altering the economic and ideological trajectory imposed by neoliberalism rested on a double movement that entailed both innovation and retreat from preceding development theories, innovation in relation to regnant neoliberalism of the 1970s and 1980s, and conceptual retreat with respect to status-quo transformative structuralism of the 1950s and 1960s. The new neostructuralist development paradigm was anchored on the five key concepts: (1) "systemic competitiveness"; (2) technical progress; (3) "proactive labor flexibility" to elicit workers' cooperation; (4) concerted action; and (5) virtuous circles to be engendered by reshaping the links between economics, society, and politics. Neostructuralism's originality lies not in crafting each one of these separate components but in combining them in a seemingly coherent whole capable of offering a new politico-economic imaginary, a corresponding set of action-oriented guidelines along with a grand narrative about how Latin America could climb back on the train to modernity during the closing moments of the twentieth century and early years of the twenty-first century.[2]

The Discursive Allure of Neostructuralism

Embedded within each of Latin American neostructuralism's interlocking notions, one finds both its discursive strengths and its inconsistencies. A brief analysis of each of these notions offers insights into what sets it apart from its neoliberal predecessor and the extent to which its success is also linked to this contradictory double movement. Such a comparison reveals that neostructuralists pay much greater attention to social, political, and cultural variables and not just a "cold-hearted" devotion to the rule and magic of the market. In this chapter I examine the first aspect of neostructuralism's double movement, namely the discursive innovations that lie at the very heart of its appeal. Such innovations allowed neostructuralism to directly challenge the then-predominant neoliberal paradigm and define itself as a distinctly new approach to development.

Understanding the ambivalence and contradictions embedded in its core conceptualizations is the key for unlocking how Latin American neostructuralism has managed to achieve success as it rises to become the prevalent development paradigm in the region (see Figure 2).

Innovations with Respect to Neoliberalism	Core Concepts	Foundational Myths
1. Mode of insertion into world economy must be purposeful, cannot only be left to market forces 2. Technical progress 3. Equity is of parallel importance as economic growth; no growth-equity tradeoff 4. Role of the State: articulates market-based initiatives and productive sectors; complement market with non-market forms of coordination 5. Open regionalism 6. Active promotion of strategic public–private sector partnerships	1. Systemic Competitiveness 2. Technical Progress 3. Proactive Labor Flexibility 4. Concerted Action 5. Virtuous Circle	1. Off-ramping from low to high-road to globalization is both possible and necessary 2. Promotion of open-regionalism makes WTO and regional based initiatives compatible 3. Distribution can be de-linked from accumulation (Greater equity is achievable through productivity-led export-led growth) 4. Dichotomy exists between spurious and genuine competitiveness 5. Concerted action to improve speed and adaptability of workers, firms, and societal subsystems to requirements of international competitiveness

Figure 2. Innovations, core concepts, and propositions. Constructed by author on the basis of Fajnzylber (1994), Leiva (1998), and Rosenthal (2000).

Systemic Competitiveness

Throughout the 1970s and 1980s, wielding the concept of "comparative advantage," neoliberalism formulated policies that sought to make markets and competition at the local and international levels the only acceptable forms of economic and social interaction. During this period, the International Monetary Fund (IMF) and World Bank-promoted stabilization and structural adjustment policies of liberalization, deregulation, and privatization were instrumental in promoting the neoliberal agenda across Latin America and the Caribbean. In the search for a politically and economically viable alternative to regnant laissez-faire dogmatism, ECLAC economists embraced the concept of "systemic competitiveness" (Fajnzylber 1988; ECLAC 1990). With this notion, they asserted that what competed in the world market were not *commodities* per se but *entire social systems*. Brandishing this concept and voicing support for "changing productive structures with social equity," neostructuralists argued that changes in productivity and the absorption of technical progress were overwhelmingly determined by institutional, political, and even cultural factors. In their view, an economy's technological performance and degree of international competitiveness depended "to a much greater degree on the presence of whole series of differing types of synergy and externalities than it does on the optimization efforts of individuals [*sic*] firms in response to changes in the price system" (ECLAC 1990, 71). In counterpoint to the economicist and reductionist approach of neoliberals, Latin American neostructuralists held that in order to tap the dynamic trends existing in the world economy and change the structure of production, effective policies "must include the *entire system* within which the enterprises operate: the technological, energy and transport infrastructure; the educational system; relations between workers and employers; the whole apparatus of public and private institutions, and the financial system" (Lahera et al., 1995, 8 [emphasis added]).

As previously mentioned, one of the main proponents of the new ECLAC strategy was the late Fernando Fajnzylber, who served as Director of the Joint ECLAC/UNIDO (United Nations Industrial Development Organization) Industry and Technology Division. Fajnzylber is to be credited for stealing neoliberalism's rhetorical fire, an act that allowed neostructuralists to take the intellectual offensive and gain the discursive high ground. Retracing Fajnzylber's footsteps as he developed the analysis underpinning the notion of "systemic competitiveness" is highly illustrative.

Albeit with some reservations, Fajnzylber was swept along by the new intellectual current of "flexible specialization," which by the late 1970s and early 1980s postulated that a new "technical economic paradigm" was emerging from the midst of a restructured world economy.[3] Based on this core notion about the changing and increasingly "systemic" nature of international competitiveness, Fajnzylber and Latin American neostructuralists mounted an effective counterattack to neoliberal claims regarding the infallibility of market forces and price signals.

Technical Progress and Dynamic Entry in Global Markets

Fajnzylber's point of departure was to contrast the lag existing between industrial restructuring programs in industrialized countries and those in Latin America (Fajnzylber 1988). Whereas in advanced countries industrial restructuring sought to secure improved competitiveness—"understood as a country's capacity to expose itself to the external market and to maintain or raise its people's living standards"—in Latin America, by contrast, he observed that neoliberal-inspired restructuring programs sought to "generate a sufficient trade surplus to service the enormous foreign debt" (Fajnzylber 1988, 7). These two contrasting types of restructuring engendered differences "between competitiveness based on technological progress, which is what industrialized countries seek, and competitiveness based on reduction of incomes" (Fajnzylber 1988, 7).

Neoliberal policies, he concluded, were leading Latin American countries down the wrong path. At a time when a new technological paradigm was emerging in the global economy, Latin America once again was being left behind by the departing train of progress. According to Fajnzylber, the new paradigm imposed by globalization was characterized by

i) reduced importance of economies of scale based on mass production using capital-intensive techniques; ii) greater integration within a company of the functions of design, production, purchasing, and research and development; iii) the capacity rapidly to change [sic] products and processes; iv) coordination of integrated networks of suppliers of parts and components, assembly plants, distributors and research and development laboratories, with major saving of capital; and, v) emergence of new service activities associated with production (software, design, technical information) which can be carried out by companies. (Fajnzylber 1988, 8)

Fajnzylber's main concern arose from his disturbing awareness of what these transformations implied for Latin America's ability to compete in international markets.[4] Whereas for neoliberalism, societal restructuring was dictated by the need to unleash the principle of comparative advantage, for Fajnzylber this imperative was based on technical grounds: the need to participate in the transition between two technical paradigms taking place at a global scale. From such an analysis, Fajnzylber drew two conclusions that became the central planks of the neostructuralist discourse and of the "changing productive structures with social equity" strategy officially endorsed by ECLAC in 1990. First, competitiveness depends in the medium- and long-term on a country's capacity to sustain and expand its share of international markets *at the same time* that it improves its people's standard of living. This requires increased productivity and incorporation of technical change. Second, exchange rate devaluation as practiced by neoliberals indeed increased the relative position of the business sector in the short-term, but by itself such a market-based policy was incapable of increasing productivity or encouraging technical change. On the contrary, such narrowly conceived policies led instead to the erosion of social cohesion as real wages declined and profits of exporting firms rose, illustrated clearly during the early 1980s under Pinochet in Chile.

In contrast to the prevalent IMF–World Bank vision, Fajnzylber and later on ECLAC argue that whatever progress Latin America accomplished during the 1980s in terms of its international competitiveness had been "spurious" in nature. "Genuine" increases in international competitiveness, he argued, stem from rising productivity created through incorporation of technical advances, not on account of "phony" increases in competitiveness gained through artificial devaluation and forced reduction in real wages. Consequently, Fajnzylber came to understand that in the medium and long run, the international engagement of countries depended much more on a broad range of structural factors, such as rates of investment, adequate institutions for allocating resources, a smooth functioning of the labor market, the nature of industrial relations, business organization, and the degree of infrastructure for education, research, and development, which were systematically ignored by neoliberal formulations. Therefore, he concludes, "it is not only companies which compete in the international market. It is also a field of confrontation between production systems, institutional structures and social organs, in which business is an important element but one integrated in a network of relations with the education system, the technological infrastructure, management-labor relations, the public and private institutional apparatus, the financial system, etc." (Fajnzylber 1988, 36). As a result Fajnzylber developed an analytical framework highlighting the links between four mutually reinforcing variables: equity, austerity, growth, and international competitiveness (Jenkins 1992, 451). The aspiration to spark and tap into the virtuous circle connecting economic growth, equity, and international competitiveness, will remain a distinct characteristic of Latin American neostructuralist discourse.

Contrasting Conceptions of Competitiveness

In the same fashion as neoliberals, neostructuralists consider that the imperative of international competitiveness requires major societal transformation. This involves not only creating new economic structures but also, and just as importantly, producing a new culture, a whole mindset and way of life also require transformation. According to Sunkel, what needs to be overcome is "the whole syndrome derived from national industrial and consumer oriented (populist) strategy that the crisis of the 1930s and World War II and its aftermath forced upon Latin America, and that persisted because it brought good profits" (Sunkel 1990, 155). Breaking with the past will not be as easy as neostructuralists point out. Laying the foundations for successfully competing in world markets goes

> beyond simply liberalizing domestic markets, it is necessary to undertake a wide-ranging overhaul, nothing less than an overall development strategy based on the conquest of world markets, with all the profound and complex implications that this carries for a country's international relations, and, in the domestic sphere, for inter-sectoral relations, for standards and patterns of consumption, for the reallocation of investments, for the creation of innovation capacity, for technological adaptation, for the reorientation of credit from fostering consumption to fostering exports, as well as for the more obvious and elementary aspects that affect the exchange rate, tariffs and others economic policy tools. (Sunkel 1990, 155)

This marks a critical difference between neoliberal and neostructuralist conceptualizations of international competitiveness: while neoliberals restrict its achievement to the realm of the market, neostructuralists see it as societywide phenomena, where cultural change is an essential component.

In its original formulation, the material basis for "changing productive structures with social equity" is achieving an international insertion via "dynamic exports of increasing complexity" (CEPAL 1992, 21). Latin American neostructuralists therefore do not disagree with neoliberals in their call for an export-led growth model. On the contrary, the inextricable connection between increasing exports and social equity is reinforced time and time again in the neostructuralist literature. Export-led growth "seems to be the most promising way of ensuring that productive employment and the wage bill increase in a rapid and sustained manner, thereby contributing both to economic growth as well as to equity" (CEPAL 1992:21).

Based on such convergent analysis, ECLAC during the 1990s considered that exports should be increased in terms of volume and value, placing special emphasis on changing a country's export profile. In the majority of Latin American countries, exports continue to be concentrated on natural resources with low levels of transformation, precisely those products with the least growth potential in international markets. Hence, policies that encourage manufactured exports and the incorporation of more value-added products in a country's export profile are to be actively pursued.

Neostructuralists therefore do not disagree in principle with the "outward-oriented" development strategy imposed by neoliberalism, but they criticize the fact that neoliberals "attribute export and output success to a fairly narrow set of policy instruments being manipulated in a tightly defined way. Their analysis takes account of very little else" (Colclough and Manor 1991, 11). According to Sergio Bitar, neoliberals emphasize fiscal, monetary, tariff, and tax instruments *but neglect structural, institutional, and political factors* (1988).

Whereas neoliberals see markets and undistorted prices as the prime levers for ensuring efficient resource allocation and international competitiveness, neostructuralists consider that "getting the prices right" is not enough. They strive for a smooth and synergetic interface between political and social institutions and the market, since, in their view, this "systemic approach" is a fundamental prerequisite so that economic restructuring takes place with the required speed imposed by global markets. Only such a systemic approach can succeed in moving Latin American economies beyond low cost–cheap labor-based competitiveness that traps countries in the slowest growing niches of the international economy (raw materials with low levels of processing). In the neostructuralist view, the competitiveness of Latin American exports under neoliberal policies was achieved through either drastic reduction of wages or devaluation of the exchange rate. Avoiding this form of "spurious" competitiveness and accessing the "high road" to globalization demands highly coordinated trade, financial, productive development, and exchange rate policies (see Figure 3). Only through such coordination, neostructuralists argue, can linkages with international markets beget a process of technical change that spreads from the export sector to the rest of the economy.

Consequently, the state is seen also with very different eyes: neoliberals envisage the state's primary role as guaranteeing the functioning of market through the protection of property rights, the enforcement of contracts, the collection of data, and the provision of limited social services for the destitute. Neostructuralism's conception of "systemic competitiveness," on the other hand, assigns the state an important auxiliary role in the search for international

	Neoliberalism	Neostructuralism
Operative Notion	"Comparative Advantage"	"Systemic Competitiveness"
Root of Competitiveness	Prices	Incorporation of technical progress
Realm of Competitiveness	The Market	Society as a Whole: (interface between market, institutions, mindset)
Role of the State	• Guarantee adequate conditions for the market to function; • Protect property rights; • Enforce contracts; • Collect data; • Provide limited social services	• Generate social and political consensus around national drive for exports; • Complement the market; • Promote exports • Enable private/public partnerships • Foster civil society/ state alliances
Social Conflict	• Repress and disarticulate collective social actors • Targeted subsidies • "Trickle down"	• Channel/Subordinate to "common goal" of competitive insertion in world economy • Actively promote social cohesion

Figure 3. Comparison of neoliberal and neostructuralist conceptions.

competitiveness. Through what ECLAC calls an "integrated approach," fusing macro, meso, and microeconomic policy initiatives (CEPAL 1992) with political intervention to construct a broad social consensus, neostructuralists support the export drive in ways that seek to capture and endogenize technical progress. Likewise, social conflict must be addressed in a completely different manner. Whereas neoliberalism, in practice, represses and disarticulates collective social actors, neostructuralism recognizes the legitimate existence of such actors while actively trying to channel and subordinate the logic of collective action to the "national effort" behind the export drive. Politics and political action, not coercion or market competition alone, also need to be tapped in order to shape individual and social behaviors so that they conform to the new economic realities.

Proactive Labor Flexibility

The core neostructuralist concept of "systemic competitiveness," calling upon the state to generate a consensus behind the export drive to improve the interface between society's different subsystems with private exporters, boosts the importance of labor. Neoliberal policies implemented by military regimes of the 1980s sought to drastically lower real wages and repress labor at the national and workplace levels. "Systemic competitiveness," on the contrary, requires policies that promote worker involvement in production. Within individual firms, "vertical and hierarchical structures should gradually be replaced with more horizontal and flexible systems which permit the intensive exchange of information and stimulate cooperation" (Lahera et al. 1995, 10).

Neostructuralism's view of globalization as the driving force for technological innovation and its goal of changing Latin America's export profile toward manufactured goods with greater value-added will succeed to the extent that worker consent and their active involvement are forthcoming. Moving toward differentiated and better quality products requires replacing vertical and hierarchical labor relations with more horizontal and flexible ones, "characterized by an intensive exchange of information, so that the initiative, creativity and responsibility of the labor force can be taken advantage of" (CEPAL 1992, 23).

As we shall see below, passage from "vertical" to more "horizontal" labor relations advocated by neostructuralism confronts numerous obstacles at all levels. In addition to institutional mechanisms for generating consensus behind the export drive among employers and workers, neostructuralist propose three addtitional lines for state action: (1) the need for a new type of labor movement; (2) reliance on a new type of wage system that emphasizes increases in productivity; (3) and policies that promote a new type of labor flexibility or adaptability of workers.

The need for a "new" type of labor movement. State and political initiatives must be undertaken to create a labor movement that supports "systemic competitiveness." This assumes the existence of a "technically-informed labor movement, conscious that its 'adversary' was not the employer as such, but competition, and, therefore, that the movement's objectives should also include improving productivity" (CEPAL 1992, 23; my translation). Recasting the labor movement with such an orientation requires that it renounce what neostructuralist consider outdated classist and conflict-based traditions.

Variable wages linking payment to performance. Such a shift toward cooperation, not confrontation, can be facilitated by a wage system that makes use of "participatory wages": the neostructuralist *bon mots* for a variable wage system. By paying a portion of wages in variable form (as a function of profits, sales, or analogous arrangements), this type of wage system fosters not only improvements in productivity but more importantly stabilization, and it even increases the level of employment: "Therefore, even though its application is just beginning in the region, this mode of payment should be explored further since it has already generated great interest" (CEPAL 1992a, 23; my translation).

Expand and improve labor flexibility. Finally, state action must be oriented to ensure the transition from "defensive" to "offensive" or proactive policies to achieve labor flexibility (Lagos 1994). Neoliberal policies encouraged only the former by emphasizing reduction in labor and nonlabor costs, making it easier for employers to lay off workers and adjust the number of workers to fluctuating market and technical conditions. Neostructuralist policy goes beyond such a limited vision, actively supporting a proactive form of flexibility. Without discarding the need to increase labor market flexibility, this more proactive approach questions many of the assumptions on "rigidity," emphasizing the need to provide training and new skills to the labor force so as to facilitate its adaptability to changes in the productive process (Lagos 1994, 91; my translation).

To implement such policies, the state must play a crucial political role, actively building consensus between the public and private sector, between worker and employer organizations, and between enterprises from the same sector. This type of state involvement is justified for the sake of "guaranteeing flexibility and ability to adapt to an extremely changing dynamic of techno-logical change" (Zuleta 1992, 311; my translation). An inkling of the changing role of the state in terms of ensuring labor flexibility arises out of the Chilean case. One analyst points out that

> if, the key element to labor flexibility during the 1980s was wage cost flexibility, given the competitive requirements faced by the economy, other components of flexibility should become more prevalent in the decade of the 1990s. Flexibility of employment via increases in labor supply confronts the limitation of having to rest upon the incor-poration of female labor, which is limited by legislation, costs and traditional practices within enterprises. Thus, once again functional flexibility, linked to training and management systems, becomes potentially more fruitful. (Romaguera 1996, 12; my translation)

Implicit in such formulation is the belief that, just as "spurious" forms of competitiveness would have to give way to more "genuine" forms, a tran-sition would take place in the realm of labor relations. The more harmful forms of labor flexibility—that is, wage flexibility, external numerical flex-ibility, and subcontracting—had to give way to "superior" forms, namely functional flexibility, purported to be less deleterious to workers.

"Virtuous Circles": Competitiveness, Equity, and Social Cohesion

Discarding a dogmatically market-centric vision and now armed with a "ho-listic" policy framework along the lines already described, neostructuralists went on to proclaim that the "high road" to globalization was feasible, and it would engender virtuous circles endowed with far-reaching healing powers both at the macro and micro level. By choosing the high road, a sequence of mutually supportive feedback loops linking international competitiveness, social equity, and political legitimacy could be triggered and their curative effects, like expanding and self-sustaining waves, would wash over ever-increasing realms of Latin American society.

At the macro level, neostructuralist policies promised to generate a syner-gistic relationship between three dimensions (the simultaneous achievement of international competitiveness, greater social integration, and increased democratic political stability) that have stubbornly eluded neoliberals and the Washington Consensus (see Figure 4). With the new macroeconomic concept of systemic international competitiveness, it was presumed that Latin America would increase participation in the world market through exports with greater value added, which at the same time would increase living standards for workers. Export competitiveness would no longer rely mainly on cheap labor but would also rely on increasing technical innovation and raising labor productivity. Democratic stability and institutions promoting consensus and social dialogue (*concertación social*) became both a necessary condition and an outcome of "systemic competitiveness." Improving and intensifying the interface between the different subsystems that generate conditions for systemic competitiveness requires levels of consensus-building that can only flow from democratic institutions. At the same time, improved living standards resulting from genuine competitiveness reduce social conflicts enhancing political stability and legitimacy. Thus a mutually supportive and self-expanding virtuous circle between economic competitiveness, social integration, and political stability would be forged by the fires of globalization.

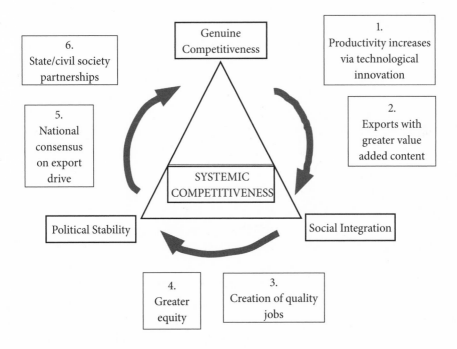

Figure 4. Virtuous circle and potential short-circuits.

This macrosocial "virtuous circle" is also to be mirrored at the enterprise level. Competition via increases in productivity will lead to higher wages as well as other benefits for workers. By linking the wage level to changes in labor productivity, workers would have an incentive to improve their performance. Benefits could be reaped both by the firm as well as the individual worker. Conflictive labor–management relations would transmute into cooperative ones, since both management and workers now would share in the common interest of ensuring entrepreneurial success in the never ending race for international competitiveness.

Economic Policy

From the strictly economic policy point of view, Latin American neostructuralism represents a significant change in perspective. Whereas neoliberals relied on market signals alone, neostructuralists endorsed selective and active export-promotion policies. Without such policies, countries would be trapped into exporting raw materials with low levels of processing and their export sector would be dominated by relatively few firms and products, making them highly vulnerable to fluctuations in international demand. Countries therefore should apply an active export-promotion policy due to a number of reasons, such as positive externalities generated by export activity, market failure in capital markets to finance exports, economies of scale and learning process surrounding exports (ECLAC 1994, 18).

Neostructuralists additionally support the *selective promotion of exports* based on close and systematic collaboration between the private and public sector. Neoliberals' blind belief on market forces is unjustified, because by themselves, they are incapable of ensuring sustained export growth. An effort truly national in scope is required to achieve dynamic comparative advantages; such an effort requires the government to play an active role supporting exporters and creating conditions for the vast array of nonmarket coordination underpinning systemic competitiveness.

Neostructuralist export promotion places a priority on the development of manufactured exports for it is understood that these goods are doubly endowed with positive characteristics. On the one hand, their international demand is expanding, and, on the other hand, they can most effectively ensure that technical change is transmitted from the export sector to the rest of the economy.

Neostructuralist export-promotion policies can be understood therefore in four coordinated levels: trade, exchange rate, export-promotion policies, and productive-development policies (CEPAL 1994).

Trade policy. Neostructuralists call for "integral trade reform," criticizing neoliberals for relying only on tariff reduction. Agreeing with the need to eliminate the antiexport bias, low tariffs, and nontariff barriers, neostructuralists believe in the adoption of transitory policies selectively biased in favor of nontraditional exports (Ffrench-Davis 1988; CEPAL 1994; Lahera et al. 1995). But these policies need to be articulated with other institutions and instruments of macroeconomic policy, namely policies that guarantee exporters easy access to inputs (temporary internment of inputs for export production free of duties) and that generate improved coordination between exporters and domestic firms supplying them. Trade policy has to be coordinated with exchange rate policies, productive development, and financial policies at the macro, meso, and microeconomic levels (CEPAL 1992, 1994; Lahera et al. 1995).

Exchange rate policy. Neoliberal policy of sharply devaluating the exchange rate to improve the competitiveness of exports is only of short-run usefulness in the neostructuralist view. Recognizing the important role that the exchange rate plays in promoting exports, neostructuralists believe that gradual devaluation that takes into account the behavior of the external sector and the economy is preferred. Exchange rate lags (as in Chile in the late 1970s) should be avoided and close attention should be placed on the relationship between exchange rate policies and macroeconomic stability (a scorecard where neoliberals have done poorly). Some neostructuralists consider the possibility of having more than one exchange rate (Ffrench-Davis 1988). This approach has to be complemented with an active strategy of integration to world markets seeking to sign regional and bilateral agreements that will gain greater market share for a country's exports. For these reasons, ECLAC has been an active promoter of the North American Free Trade Agreement (NAFTA) and the policy of "open regionalism."

Other export promotion policies. Neostructuralists provide a wider and more detailed menu of export promotion policies than did neoliberals in the 1980s. In part, this is due to being able to draw from more than a decade of neoliberal policies, but it is also consistent with the integrated approach seeking to establish "systemic competitiveness." Provision of adequate fiscal incentives to exports (drawbacks on imported raw materials and tax exemption on domestic value added), financial incentives, and support for "pioneer" exporters form part of an array of policies to be coordinated by a central body entrusted with export promotion to be created in each country.

Government and government-supported institutions should act as a clearinghouse of information, allowing for improved coordination among the different actors taking part in the export drive: disseminating requirements of export firms to local producers; promoting the use of leading-edge technology (microelectronics, telecommunications, satellite-based technologies); and informing on the quality and volume of natural resources economically available to investors. In general, neostructuralists call for public support for information, financing, export insurance, administration, and the promotion of export goods and services.

Productive development policies. Perhaps the most significant difference with neoliberalism is neostructuralism's call for "productive development" policies in support of export promotion and for ensuring a more beneficial relationship with the international economy. Supporting technical innovation through partial subsidies, the promotion of strategic alliances between local and transnational firms and programs aimed at training the labor force and improving their skill levels through firm-specific training programs are among the policies recommended.

These programs replace "industrial policy" promoted by the state under import substitution industrialization (ISI). This shift is in line with new competitiveness policies that have moved from sectoral policies toward policies of "entrepreneurial competitiveness," seeking to increase efficiency in the allocation of resources rather than to generate new sectors (Peres 1994). In this new view, macroeconomic stability, trade liberalization, privatization, and deregulation conform the basic context and necessary conditions that need to be complemented by additional policies. Guiding these initiatives is the notion that it is necessary to "improve the offer of systemic supports to competitiveness." In the words of Wilson Peres, ECLAC's specialist on the new generation of industrial policies, "among these contributions, one finds that the supply of electricity, telecommunications and transport infrastructure, have a growing importance because . . . the producers of raw materials that make intensive use of capital and economies of scale have an increasing greater weight in the region's output and exports" (Peres 1994, 53; my translation). Rather than a new set of policies, "systemic support to competitiveness" often sounds like a repetition of the rationale for export-processing zones.

One revealing component of productive development policies is neo-structuralists' active support for the formation of strategic alliances between large national enterprises and "international leaders in technology," which is the phrase neostructuralists use to refer to transnational corporations and transnational capital. In this sense, neostructuralists pretend to go beyond what neoliberals have done:

Even though governments have traditionally supported large national enterprises and have eliminated most all of the regulations that formerly hindered foreign investment, only a few have out rightly supported alliances between both types of [national and transnational] firms that lead to the transfer of technology. Recent experiences such as those of Chile and Mexico illustrate the extreme importance of those alliances to shape the industrial pattern that will predominate in the future. A clear commitment by policymakers with the task of pushing for entrepreneurial alliances constitutes one of the most important mechanisms to achieve a better insertion in the international market. (Peres 1994, 53)

The menu of initiatives to promote competitiveness at the level of the enterprise include programs to: massively disseminate the diffusion of best technologies in use; continue improving systems and networks of technological information; improve conditions for financing technological development of firms; direct fiscal incentives for reasearch and developtment for those firms that introduce innovations; improve the alliance among enterprises by simplifying procedures; and access information and fiscal stimulus, among others (Peres 1994). Finally, neostructuralists assign a special role to the development of long-term capital markets that can finance investment programs geared to export markets (CEPAL 1994). The striking difference is that neoliberals basically rely only on market forces for comparative advantage to kick in. Neostructuralists, on the other hand, for a number of reasons (e.g., incomplete and imperfect markets, the systemic nature of competitiveness) see the need to draw upon a broader arsenal of instruments, developing selective policies that, without violating the primacy of the market, foster export growth, particularly in manufactures, by creating a closer and more functional interaction between the public and the private sector.

Neostructuralism's Meteoric Rise

On the basis of these discursive innovations, Latin American neostructural-ism steadily expanded its intellectual influence in the hemisphere after 1990, when ECLAC published *Changing Production Structures with Social Equity*. By the mid-1990s, the dogmatic neoliberal imprint to economic policy in the region began to give way to a more neostructuralist orientation.[5] By 2007, more than a decade and a half after the appearance of its founding manifes-to, neostructuralist development discourse originally launched in Santiago could display three impressive achievements.

First, neostructuralist concerns about the importance of politics, institu-tions, culture, and equity for the smooth functioning of markets and friction-less integration into the global economy successfully penetrated and modi-fied the market-centric discourse of development institutions. Hence, by the end of the 1990s, international development agencies talked about the emer-gence of a "post–Washington Consensus" that celebrated the synergy and not the trade-offs between increasing equity and economic growth (Ocampo 1998; Birdsall et al. 1998). Development economists at the World Bank and IMF turned their attention to the role of institutions and the importance of ensuring greater social equity to maintain support for the program of eco-nomic reforms (World Bank 1997; IMF 2003). Many began to question the validity of trade-offs between rapid economic growth and reduced income inequality, as they envisioned that increased equality could help enhance economic growth through a number of channels, such as increasing political and macroeconomic stability, boosting the saving capacity and investment opportunity of the poor, promoting higher education levels, and boosting aggregate demand (Solimano et al. 2000). The World Bank's 2006 *World De-velopment Report: Equity and Development*, for example, argues that "equity, not just as an end in itself, but because it often stimulates greater and more productive investment, which leads to faster growth."

By the first years of the twenty-first century, the sanctity of neoliberalism's universal cure-all recipe of privatization, liberalization, and deregulation at-tached to the Washington Consensus had lost much of its intellectual allure. Though generally recognized as successful in eliminating hyperinflation, achieving fiscal balance, promoting exports, and reducing the productive and regulatory role of the state, neoliberal reforms failed to achieve the cen-tral goals of delivering significant economic growth rates, poverty reduction, and greater levels of equity (Stallings and Peres 2000; Reinhardt and Peres

2000; Rodrik 2002). Mediocre gross domestic product (GDP) growth rates of 2.4 percent between 1990 and 2002, and only 1.5 percent during the last five years, along with regressive distribution of income and the appearance of ten million more poor over the last decade, further dented economists' blind confidence on the neoliberal recipe.[6] Disillusionment became so wide-spread that the Washington Consensus came to be seen as a damaged brand: "Instead of prosperity, the consensus now emits the poisonous odours of a recipe concocted in Washington by a cabal of inept technocrats who are out of touch with the realities of poor countries or, even worse, are in the pockets of Wall Street. Widely derided as 'market fundamentalism' or 'savage neo-liberalism,' the concoction is accused of making the poor poorer and the world unacceptably inequitable and dangerously unstable" (Naim 2002).[7]

Neostructuralism's second achievement was to extend its growing influence over progressive Latin American intellectuals and the region's renovated Left parties, who embraced neostructuralist notions that a more "human" road to globalization was both possible and necessary (Castañeda 1998; van Deijk 2003). In a June 1999 meeting, the Socialist International (SI) launched its "Buenos Aires Consensus," calling for structural reforms that went beyond the market and placed emphasis on social integration.[8] As some analysts have indicated, such a shift contributed to the surfacing of a new political platform that not only stemmed "reform fatigue" but also placed "the restoration of poverty and inequality to a place of prominence in debates about the future of Latin American development . . . [offering] new opportunities for bridging the yawning conceptual and programmatic chasm that have divided policy-makers in supranational organizations (SNOs), local governing elites, academics, center-left political parties, organized labor, social movements, and nongovernmental organizations (NGOs)" (Korzeniewicz and Smith 1999, 2). Thus, one additional outcome of such an intellectual shift was the foundation for a new type of political discourse. The new political projects launched throughout the region, influenced by debates within European social democracy and the conceptual innovations behind "Third Way," discursively and programmatically prized consensus building and social cohesion. Thus, neostructuralism became an important force that reshaped economic development discourse and the political landscape in the region by offering "the hopeful possibility" for the "rise of polycentric development coalitions" and a political agenda that seeks "to deepen and effectively extend democracy beyond the electoral arena to include basic issues related to the construction of more just societies in the hemisphere" (Korzienewicz and Smith 1999, 2).

Given the continent's experience of the 1980s—a "lost decade" in economic terms and the prevalence of brutal military regimes—such a formulation inherently possessed tremendous powers of attraction.

Nonetheless, despite this more holistic shift, welcomed by scholars, intellectuals, and voters, each one of the key concepts differentiating it from neoliberalism also represents a significant conceptual retreat from the economic thinking of the 1950s and 1960s. The result has been that power and power relations are excised from economics, politics, and culture precisely at the historical moment when a focus on power relations seems to be most needed in political economy.

2

Methodological Retreats

No, it is not like that at all. What has happened is that ECLAC still lives under the stigma of the stance taken during the 1950s and 1960s, which was a very strong epoch for the institution. Therefore, people remain stuck with that image without really knowing the work that has been done in the last ten years.

—José Antonio Ocampo, ECLAC Executive Secretary

Despite its initial discursive potency and recent political triumphs, Latin American neostructuralism carries within itself profound contradictions. To an important extent, these stem from the methodological and intellectual shifts enacted during the 1980s that gave rise to Latin American neostructuralism and the "new ECLAC" (Economic Commission for Latin America and the Caribbean). Though many have seen these changes as a necessary adaptation to new conditions created by the demise of the import substitution industrialization (ISI) regime of accumulation, changes in the world economy and the growing influence of U.S.-based economic theories—such as new endogenous growth theory, neo-Schumpeterian evolutionary models,[1] and new institutionalist economics (Hounie, Pittaluga et al. 1999; Kuntz Ficker 2005; Love 2005)—they can also be interpreted in an altogether different light: as encompassing a profound intellectual and methodological retreat from the best traditions of Latin American critical thinking inasmuch as they excise power relations from economic discourse and theorization. Thus, in the passage from structuralism to neostructuralism, in the transition from Raúl Prebisch's and Celso Furtado's "old" CEPAL (Comisión Económica para América Latina) to Fernando Fajnzylber's, Gert Rosenthal's, and José Antonio Ocampo's "new" CEPAL, neostructuralism has implemented far-reaching changes in its methodological approach and framework. Although such modifications have allowed neostructuralism to regain policy relevance, they have also exacted a high price: realigning ECLAC solidly behind the status quo and dulling its capacity to probe the "deep structure" of twenty-first-century Latin American capitalism. In what follows, I reverse the tapestry of its imposing rhetorical and conceptual innovations to reveal the major strands of such intellectual retreat.

Adaptation, Renewal, or Intellectual Retreat?

Headquartered in Santiago, ECLAC economists and planners witnessed firsthand neoliberalism's ascent to hegemonic status. Bent on refounding Latin American capitalism, neoliberalism's victory in the region was inextricably linked to the violent 1973 military coup in Chile. The brutal overthrow of President Allende became a turning point for the entire continent. The intellectual leadership, which since the late 1940s ECLAC exercised over generations of Latin American policy planners, economists, and intellectuals, violently ended due to the alliance between neoliberal economists and military regimes that seized power in the mid-1970s. The coupling of market forces and state terrorism in the Southern Cone and Andean region of the Americas resolved the prolonged crisis of the ISI regime of accumulation and consolidated both a "neoclassical counterrevolution" in the realm of economic ideas as well as in class relations.

After more than a decade of confusion and disarray, ECLAC economists led by Fajnzylber began formulating in the mid-1980s the outlines of what would become a response capable of challenging the hegemony of neoliberal ideas. Such a rejoinder (i.e., Latin American neostructuralism) combined a critique of neoliberalism's price and market reductionism with a farewell to core tenets of the structuralist approach established during the 1950s by ECLAC's intellectual founders, Prebisch, and other structuralist pioneers like Furtado and Aníbal Pinto. Different authors have welcomed Latin American neostructuralism's conceptual innovations, celebrating them as evidence of ECLAC's capacity for adaptation: "Neostructuralism should not be interpreted as caving in to neoliberalism nor as an indication that structuralism was wrong but rather as an attempt to come to terms with a new reality. In this sense structuralism is showing an *ability to adapt to changing historical circumstances* rather than *remain frozen* in the past" (Gwynne and Kay 2003, 27; my emphasis). Other authors, mostly current or former staff members of ECLAC, on occasion of the fiftieth anniversary of ECLAC's founding also asserted that the transition from structuralism to neostructuralism maintained continuity both in the basic "historical–structural" methodological approach originally laid down by Prebisch and in the basic economic concerns of the past (the distribution of "technical progress"). Thus, neostructuralists' self-image is one of successful and successive adaptation to new circumstances while preserving an unbroken line linking the present with the original structuralist concerns of Prebisch (Bielschowsky 1998; Di Filippo 1998; CEPAL 2000). In fact, ECLAC economists have gone to great pains to stress that neostructuralism should be conceived as "a continuation of the basic posture of structuralism, with some adjustments derived from new realities both internal as well as international" (Treviño 2000). Is there a basis for such a claim beyond the vigorous declaration to that effect? Has passage from structuralism to neostructuralism and adaptation to the "new historical circumstances" enabled leaps forward in ECLAC's analytical sharpness? Or rather, as I argue in this chapter, has it meant an important methodologically retreat that severely weakens Latin American neostructuralism's capacity for understanding the nature of Latin American capitalism at the present historical juncture?

Indeed change in economic ideas, doctrines, and paradigms constitutes part and parcel of the history of ideas and of societal development itself. What becomes important to determine however is not that economic ideas change but rather the nature of such shifts and their resulting historical and political consequences. Intellectual changes enacted by Latin American neostructuralism, its rupture with its structuralist past, and its critique of neoliberalism have to be analyzed in the historical context of the ongoing restructuring of Latin American capitalism itself. Within such a framework, Latin American neostructuralism's conceptual shifts and rupture with its structuralist past represent an important intellectual and political retreat that enfeebles rather than updates it.

Steeped in the language of pragmatism, upholding a dehistoricized "technical progress" and celebrating an international competitiveness sanitized from actually existing power relations, the methodological retreat of Latin American neostructuralism is evident in three crucial aspects of the "new ECLAC's" economic thinking: (1) replacement of the concept of economic surplus with that of international competitiveness; (2) throwing out a systemic approach along with the core-periphery model; and (3) the incorporation of politics and institutions in a manner that delinks them from accumulation and struggles over the distribution of economic surplus. Each one of these renunciations was essential for the construction of neostructuralism's core concept of "systemic competitiveness" and its strategy of "changing productive structures with social equity" with which it has successfully contested neoliberal ideas.

Replacing Economic Surplus with the Quest for "International Competitiveness"

Toward the end of his long and productive life, Raúl Prebisch underscored that

> the root cause of the incapacity of neoclassical thinking to interpret peripheral capitalism lies above all in its failure to take into consideration the economic surplus, which is the hub of this system's basic characteristics. It disregards the structural heterogeneity which possibilitates the existence of a surplus; it bypasses the structure and dynamics of power which explain how the surplus is appropriated and shared out; it shuts its eyes to the monetary mechanism of production which allows the surplus to be retained by the upper strata; and it underestimates the waste involved in the ways in which the surplus is currently used. (Prebisch 1981b, 153)

Paradoxically, Presbisch's well-aimed criticism of neoclassical economics, a body of thought he was never afraid to challenge, can also today be leveled against Latin American neostructuralism. Along with Celso Furtado, Raúl Prebisch located the question of the production, appropriation, and distribution of economic surplus as the key element in their framework for explaining Latin America's underdevelopment. In his book, *Capitalismo Periférico: Crisis y Transformación*, published more than three decades after *The Economic Development of Latin America 1949* and fully aware of the unfolding "neoclassical counter-revolution," Prebisch reaffirms the necessity of structurally transforming Latin American capitalism because, "at its core, peripheral capitalism is based on inequality. And inequality has its origins, as we have said, in the capturing of economic surplus mainly by those who concentrate in their hands the majority of the means of production. Economic surplus plays a primary role in my interpretations. It is essentially a structural phenomenon. It is also a dynamic one" (Prebisch 1981b, 15; my translation). In contrast, Latin American neostructuralism has abandoned any approach that even vaguely locates the production, appropriation, and distribution of economic surplus as a central concern.

For Prebisch, increasing the efficiency in the social use of the surplus was central (Welters 2004). In this regard he states, "The solution to the problem consists above all in ensuring that the surplus perform its dynamic role with the greatest efficacy possible; that is, that it raises the pace of accumulation and provide employment with rising productivity and incomes, for the new members of the labor force as well as for those sectors of it that have been relegated to the bottom of the social structure with inferior productivity. The social use of the economic surplus is a must" (Prebisch, 1985, 67; my translation).

In contrast to such an analysis, Latin American neostructuralism holds attaining of international competitiveness as the ultimate goal of both economics and politics. In so doing, Latin American neostructuralists erase economic surplus as an important analytical category. Consequently, they ignore power relations embedded not only in the economy but also in the production and distribution of "international competitiveness" itself. In fact, by renouncing to this theoretical heritage that emphasized the centrality of economic surplus, Latin American neostructuralists excises the analysis of power relations from three critical dimensions of society in which power relations are deeply embedded: (1) the international economy; (2) labor-capital relations in production and technical change processes; and (3) in the articulation between production and social reproduction. The result is a utopian view of Latin American economies.

The Role of Economic Surplus in Structuralist Analysis

Many observers were surprised by Raul Prebisch's explicit embrace of the concept of surplus as central to his critical analysis of peripheral capitalism (Di Filippo 1984; Hodara 1977, 1998). Some incorrectly attribute Prebisch's shift as a sign of his adoption of elements of dependency theory and a distancing from structuralist thought and the economic thinking of ECLAC. After all, structuralism's analytical emphasis lay on the differential capture of "technical progress" between core and periphery countries due to declining terms of trade and the different income demand elastisticities existing between them. My contention that neostructuralism represents an intellectual retreat because it abandons the concept of economic surplus would then be baseless or, at best, conflate Prebisch's own thinking in the latter stages of his life, with structuralism, and with the original economic thinking of ECLAC.

Despite the fact that ECLAC never mentioned economic surplus in its major official publications, enough evidence exists to make a strong case that, despite never officially endorsed by ECLAC, the concept of economic surplus became an integral part of the intellectual apparatus used by ECLAC staff to analyze the obstacles to Latin American underdevelopment. Either because there was no other concept at the time or because it acknowledged it as a useful tool, the concept of economic surplus plays an important explicative and formative element in the in the training manuals of ECLAC and the *Instituto Latinoamericano de Planificación Económica y Social* (ILPES, Latin American Institute for Economic and Social Planning), through which thousands of economists and government planners were exposed to ECLAC's thinking and structuralist conceptions in Santiago and Brazil (ILPES 1962). Between 1956 and 1989, 2,388 professional from Brazil alone had gone through such programs (Santiago 1990).

Aníbal Pinto, José Echeverría Medina, Osvaldo Sunkel, and Celso Furtado, all of whom played an important role in shaping the structuralist paradigm and in developing the first training texts, designing the curriculum, and heading ILPES at different times, used the concept of economic surplus as a key explicative tool.[2] Aníbal Pinto, best known for developing the concept of "structural heterogeneity" as part of the structuralist's analytical toolset, uses it in his early intellectual production.[3] Writing in 1961, Pinto asks a key question: Why is it that in Latin American countries, we are only able to copy the form but not the dynamism and structure of capitalism, as in the central countries? (Pinto 1961, 34). After a detailed analysis of economic, political, and cultural factors and acknowledging the work of Paul Baran, Pinto answers this question by using the case of Chile, which he knew well:

> Only partial research has been carried out on the volume of resources extracted from Latin American economies by foreign investors, but it would be very hard to arrive at an adequate measure of this bleeding. As an example, one can point to the case of Chile, which still in the decade of the 1920s for each dollar of copper exported, the return to Chile under the item of internal costs and taxes was less than 25 cents. On top of this direct and heavy extraction, one should add that derived from trade and financial control by foreign individuals and firms. Undoubtedly, through such mechanisms, a great percentage of the "surplus" that could have been theoretically used to accelerate the growth of dependent economies leaked out, in fact, strengthening the position of the industrialized countries. (Pinto 1961, 39; my translation)

José Medina Echevería, a sociologist who was director of ILPES, a key producer of these texts that were to be part of the CEPAL/ILPES Training Program, and who contributed to the early development of ECLAC's interdisciplinary approach to development, also relies on this concept. In one of the key texts used in the CEPAL/ILPES training program, he defines economic development in terms of use of the surplus. Medina defines economic development as "a continuous process whose essential mechanism consists in repeated application of the surplus through new investment, that leads likewise, in the incessant expansion of the productive unit under consideration" (Medina Echeverría 1967, 12; my translation).

Osvaldo Sunkel, another key contributor to the structuralist paradigm and one of the first directors of the CEPAL/ILPES training program, also cites Paul Baran's *The Political Economy of Growth*, published in 1956, and applies the concept of economic surplus to the analysis of Latin American underdevelopment. In another core text of the CEPAL/ILPES curriculum, Sunkel poses a critical question: What factors explain why the economic surplus generated by the export sector were not destined in greater amounts to benefit other geographical areas of the country, other social groups, and other economic activities (Sunkel 1967)? Like Pinto, Furtado, and others, Sunkel's answer revolves around the issue of the economic surplus. According to him, economic and political factors gave Latin American societies a dual character, "which ensured, on the one hand, full participation in the international economy, and on the other, allowed the maximum extraction of surplus from internal productive activities" (Sunkel 1967, 46; my translation).

When Prebisch was finally free from "executive responsibilities" at ECLAC and UNCTAD (United Nations Conference on Trade and Development), he entered what he called the "fifth stage" of his career and was able "for the first time in many years, to review and systematically develop [his] thinking" (Prebisch 1996, 771–72; my translation). Part of that revision was to once again pose and seek a coherent answer to the question of why the development process was accompanied by rising income and wealth inequality. As he himself acknowledges, that search led him "to review with a critical spirit my earlier ideas. There were valid elements in them, but they were far from constituting a comprehensive theoretical system. I concluded that it was necessary to develop a framework that looked beyond just economics" (Prebisch 1996, 782; my translation). Such a quest led him to identify the analytical centrality of the economic surplus. His efforts did not represent, however, a great innovation or a paradigmatic break; rather it merely revalued a conceptual category that, as we have seen, had been already incorporated and extensively used by his closest collaborators. As Nora Lustig points out, "although no version of the term exploitation appears explicitly in any of the structuralist literature, the notions of surplus generation and appropriation do emerge—along with the identification of the losers in this process: the periphery versus the center, workers versus capitalists, *campesinos* versus the urban sector, and finally, the very poor versus the rest of society" (Lustig 1991, 28).

Yet, the notion of the production, appropriation, and distribution of surplus has completely vanished from neostructuralist literature at a time when transformations in the world and Latin American economies make it analytically more necessary than ever.

Jettisoning a Systemic Approach and the Core-Periphery Model

The originality of the structuralist paradigm lay in conceiving that "the process of development and underdevelopment is a single process: that the center and periphery are closely interrelated, forming part of one world economy" (Kay 1989, 26). By locating the problems of development within the context of single world economy, Latin American development thinkers of the structuralist and dependency schools were able to analyze trade, investment, and technology patterns with a systemic perspective. Challenging mainstream approaches of the time, they conceived "development" as a holistic process characterized by profound inequalities rooted in the development of capitalism itself on a world scale. One outcome of such a framework was the center-periphery model, which explained Latin American underdevelopment on the basis of an international division of labor that reserved manufactured goods and capture of technological progress by the center, while the majority of Third World countries specialized in the production of raw materials. Despite its often cited shortcomings—a focus on circulation, not production (or rather on the all the circuits encompassing the accumulation of capital)—this mode of framing the problems of Latin American development as part of single world economy and capitalist system gave rise to a rich and diverse intellectual tradition that shaped both the official pronouncements of ECLAC, the thinking of its staff, and the formation of generations of economists and government planners during the 1950–75 years. It generalized the use of what Prebisch and others called "peripheral capitalism" to underscore the historical specificity of Latin American economic underdevelopment. It could be said, then, that "according to the original ECLAC conception specialization is the underlying reason for external imbalance, while heterogeneity lies at the root of structural underemployment. This conception also holds that these two structural conditions give rise, together, to a third tendency: deterioration in the terms of trade" (Hounie et al. 1999, 10).

In discarding the "center-periphery" model,[4] Latin American neostructuralists have thrown out the baby with the bathwater; the "center-periphery" has been replaced by a short-term perspective that examines only the macroeconomic role of the "external sector" but no longer places Latin America's trade, investment, and other external links within the framework and structural dynamics of the capitalist world economy (Osorio 2002).

In the same way that the crisis of the ISI regime of accumulation led to abandoning the concept of economic surplus, changes in the international division of labor during the 1960s and 1970s set off a sequence of events that led to rebuffing structuralism's systemic approach and disowning the notion that the particularities of Latin American underdevelopment were anchored on the region's unique peripheral status, its historically based structural heterogeneity, and declining terms of trade. Armando Di Filippo, a long time ECLAC staff member, in an article titled "The Center-Periphery Framework Today," published in the Spanish-only special 1998 issue of *CEPAL Review* to commemorate the fiftieth anniversary of ECLAC, asserts that the growing role of intrasector, intraindustrial, and intrafirm trade of goods and the expansion of trade in services in international trade rendered the old geographical notions of center-periphery model obsolete (Di Filippo 1998). New mechanisms for the international distribution of increases in productivity had emerged. ECLAC's historic preoccupation with understanding the way increases in productivity derived from technical changes were distributed needed to be thoroughly reconceptualized. Consequently, Di Filippo argued, "the issue of the terms of trade between manufactured for primary products has become a topic of decreasing economic importance" (Di Filippo 1998, 117; my translation). The old view that conceived a systemic pattern of unequal exchange between center and the periphery of the world capitalist economy had to be discarded, because in the new global economic context, "foreign direct investment transfers to the periphery high productivity technology" that, combined with peripheral real wages lower than those from the center, "generate profits from productivity gains in the periphery that are transnationally appropriated to be either invested in the peripheries themselves or remitted in the form of profits or repatriated as equity to the head offices in the central countries" (Di Filippo 1998, 117; my translation). Within this new context, Latin American neostructuralism "assumes that for products of equivalent quality, there will be sufficient increases in labor productivity so as to be able to compete via a reduction in international prices and, at the same time, will allow for increasing the real wages of the labor force in the periphery that contributes to produce them" (Di Filippo 1998, 118; my translation).

These two questionable assumptions—that foreign direct investment (FDI) acts as a diffuser of technical progress and that the sustained increase in the productivity of labor engaged in the production of international commodities will *simultaneously* lead to lower international prices and rising wages—are at the heart of the jettisoning of the historico-structural analytical approach. ECLAC's neostructuralists retain the labels of "center" and "periphery" but now only as empty shells, as vestiges of an intellectual past best forgotten.

Such a shift is defended on the basis of two assumptions. First, the new mechanisms for the distribution of labor productivity increments in the reshaped world economy, "will lead to the convergence in the living standards between developed and developing countries"(Di Filippo 1998, 118; my translation). Consequently, the nature of the main conflict facing countries has been drastically redrawn and is no longer pitting the center against the periphery over the appropriation of technical progress or the surplus. A new international distribution of the increments of labor productivity has emerged in which, thanks to its high mobility, transnational productive capital becomes the bearer of high technology and innovation, basically favoring "knowledge workers." Thus the "center-periphery" model ceases to be analytically relevant. For peripheral countries, the key to development has become how to capture the benefits of globalization: "It is no longer, therefore, national frontiers between centers and peripheries that delimit the distribution from the increments in productivity, but it is the frontiers of the knowledge acquitted between non-skilled and skilled workers. The forces that drive this new world context are those of technological and productive globalization based on the quest of competitive advantages on the part of transnational corporations" (Di Filippo 1998, 118; my translation).

By erroneously equating the distribution of technical progress with the reorganization of production, ECLAC analysts such as Di Filippo see a rosy picture. Technical progress is no longer captured by the center in detriment of the periphery. On the contrary, now the "center" becomes the main source and distributor of technical progress worldwide. As the "center" no longer refers to a geographic region, the new bearers of progress are transnational capital and the multinational corporation who, like a Rostowian *patrón*, dispense technological progress throughout the globe: "Technical progress is transferred from the centers towards the peripheries through two essential mechanisms. On the one hand, the export of computer and telecommunications equipment through which the advances of informational technology is realized; on the other hand, direct investment in the production of goods and services in which the installation of subsidiaries by transnational corporations implies the transplant of technological processes, frequently endowed with productivity comparable to that of the centers themselves" (Di Filippo 1998, 123; my translation).

Based on this biased reading of the transformations and forces driving economic globalization, Latin American neostructuralism buries the core contents of structuralist thought. Toward the mid-1990s, Peter Evans asked, "Are positions in the International Division of Labor structurally determined or is there room for agency? Put more simply, can countries deliberately change the position they fill in the international division of labor?" (Evans 1995, 8). By jettisoning the center-periphery model, neostructuralists seemed to lean toward defending the role of agency and the notion that, through an act of political will, such positions could be transformed if "developmentalist" replaced "predatory" states.[5] The difference between structuralist and neostructuralists defense of agency is significant. In the structuralist imaginary, the collective will of the nation represented by the national-developmentalist state took the form of the state's involvement in steering the process of capital accumulation. In the neostructuralist imaginary, the defense of agency involves two important differences. First, transnational capital and transnational corporations have been annointed as the crucial actors in the diffusion of technological progress and development itself. Second, political agency has been redefined essentially as an act of "romancing capital," that is, into displaying leadership and levels of coordination that ensure that all subsystems, social energies, and sectors will be harnessed to serve foreign investors' demands. Political agency is no longer conceived an exercise of political will over the use of social surplus, which under the ISI-regime of accumulation took the form of state-led industrialization, public enterprises, and protected markets.

In abandoning a systemic approach, Latin American neostructuralists discarded notions about the specificity of peripheral capitalism and moved toward accepting an enlightened version of modernization theory. Hence, the second act of intellectual retreat was consummated when Latin American neostructuralism also disposed the "historico-structural" approach that framed the problems of Latin American development within the context of the development of the capitalist system on a world scale.

A Domesticated Notion of Politics

Neostructuralism's advantage over neoliberalism is that it reincorporates politics, institutions, and culture into development discourse and the formulation of economic policy. Understanding that all economic activities are embedded within a broader set of social, political, and cultural relations enables neostructuralists to politically challenge neoliberals as to who is better equipped to manage globalizing processes. As Hoff and Stiglitz have stated, these efforts form part of a welcomed restorative thrust, for "in leaving out institutions, history, and distributional considerations, neoclassical economics leaves out the heart of development economics" (Hoff and Stiglitz 2000, 390).

Such restoration, however, is misleading as an important act of legerdemain is carried out: politics and institutions are given a central role but are no longer analytically linked to the process of the accumulation of capital and struggles over the appropriation or distribution of economic surplus. On the contrary, politics has been safely penned within the parameters prescribed by the United States' new institutionalist economics: overcoming market failure, reduction of transaction costs, coordination, and risk management in the context of globally integrated markets. Politics and institutions are given a role insofar as they become subordinate and complementary to the dictates of the market, facilitate a dynamic entry into global markets, and ensure governability of globalization processes within the existing status quo. Paraphrasing Hoff and Stiglitz, neostructuralists transplant politics and institutions back into the body of economics but in a manner such that this new post-neoliberal heart is prevented from pumping question of class, power, and structural change.[6]

This particularly sanitized modality of conceiving the role of politics and institutions partially explains the contradictory nature of neostructuralism, an ambivalence that both enhances and limits its historical role. By incorporating politics and institutions, it is able to displace neoliberal economists from their post of state managers, arguing that, unlike them, they do not ignore the institutional context in which markets operate and "by which the costs of market transactions are determined" (Cameron 2004, 98). Additionally, at a time of increasing contagion and vulnerability produced by the integration of markets, neostructuralists can claim to be on the leading edge of what the World Bank and the International Monetary Fund (IMF) have belatedly discovered, namely that "good macroeconomic policy is not enough; good institutions are critical for macroeconomic stability in today's world of global financial integration" (Burki and Perry 1998, 5).

This mode of incorporating politics and institutions (increasingly influenced both by new institutionalist economics and the Third Way) explains the conundrum presented by Latin American neostructuralism, namely how one of its defining characteristics, that is, its attention to politics and institutions, coexists and is covalent with the marginalization of power from economic analysis.

The old "ECLAC" of Prebisch and Furtado, criticized justly so for lacking a coherent analysis of the capitalist state, for underestimating the role of class struggle in shaping economic development, or for not paying enough attention to the production of surplus, at least had a much more grounded understanding of the role that power played in socioeconomic development and preserved a clear analytical link between institutional change and socioeconomic power relations. Under the influence of new institutional economics and the Third Way, Latin American neostructuralism restricts the role of institutions and politics to (1) allocating costs and risk in markets; (2) facilitating processes of technological innovation and productivity increases; (3) ensuring governability, governance, and legitimacy by promoting nonmarket and voluntary forms of coordination; and (4) shaping behaviors and subjectivity by operating at the symbolic and socioemotional levels. Though this approach allows neostucturalists to successfully dispute leadership posts in national and transnational state apparatuses, it also deeply embeds unsolvable contradictions within neostructuralism's political economy, discourse, and historical action.

In abandoning ISI policies and the ISI regime of accumulation (clearly in crisis from the mid-1960s onward), Latin American neostructuralists also abandoned the theoretical and methodological approach that in the 1950s had won structuralists international acclaim. In the process, they intellectually severed links with those traditions within political economy that have long examined the predominant role that power plays in economics.[7] Significant aspects of economic relationships—the organization of work, international trade and financial relations, the operation of markets, and distribution between wages and profits—"involve power, coercion, hierarchy, subordination and authority" (Bowles et al. 2005, 54). As Latin American economies experienced far-reaching process of restructuring, ECLAC emptied out its analytical arsenal. By sacrificing the centrality of economic surplus and power relations during the transition from structuralism to neostructuralism, ECLAC gouged out the vision, enabling it to see beyond the immediate and the short-term. The crisis of ISI and transformations in the world economy brought about by globalizing capital, as vast as they might seem, do not provide a convincing and logical explanation for such methodological retreats.

Reversing Key Structuralist Tenets

Spurred on by these interconnected methodological shifts—discarding the centrality of the economic surplus, abandonment of a systemic approach represented by the center-periphery paradigm, marginalizing power relations by delinking of politics and institutions from accumulation and distribution—the gateway opened to reverse the founding proposition of structuralist thinking and Latin American political economy (see Petras and Leiva 1994, 64–73).

First, instead of being the root and propagating mechanism for economic underdevelopment, the internationalization of productive and commercial structures was now welcome and seen as the main route to achieve productive modernization. Previously conceived as mechanisms for deepening underdevelopment, foreign capital and transnational corporations now became the key levers for productive modernization and technical change. Achieving systemic competitiveness and a "dynamic" entry into global markets now depended on enticing private transnational and domestic capital to fulfill its neo-Schumpeterian role attributed by Fajnzylber and the "new ECLAC."

Second, private capitalists, private firms, and markets (not the state or its role in socializing economic surplus to ensure its social efficiency as Prebisch's analysis of peripheral capitalism argued) were transformed into the key agents of economic development. The state and public policy were no longer conceived as organizing societal capabilities to ensure that collective interests about the use of society's economic surplus were fulfilled. The "new ECLAC" reconceptualized the role of public policy and the state as that of safeguarding macroeconomic balances, ensuring greater coordination among private producers and better articulation of private and public initiatives, managing conflicts arising from globalization, and above all, harnessing social energies and societal systems to the quest for international competitiveness.

Third, the logic of distribution was seen as detachable from the logic of export-oriented (EO) accumulation. Greater equity would not be the result of social reforms but would flow from increased exports and economic growth. The main obstacles to greater economic justice were not the concentration of urban and rural productive assets in a few hands or the concentration of income and conspicuous luxury consumption of Latin America's richest decile concentrating more than 40 percent of national income. The obstacles to development were now those barriers preventing dynamic entry into global markets.

Trajectory of an Intellectual Retreat

A methodological retreat of the scope already described was bound to have powerful aftershocks. Indeed, it turned ECLAC's development strategy upside down and realigned the institution politically and intellectually behind the expansive logic of transnational capital. The reversal of structuralist notions repositioned ECLAC from being an entity oriented by the transformative and reformative zeal of structuralism seeking to overcome Latin American underdevelopment through state-led industrialization to being an institution promoting status-quo friendly policies that placed private transnational capital as the main agent of economic and social development.

Neostructuralism's retreat has been a two-faced process consisting both of conceptual renewal and compression. It is observable before 1990, during the passage from structuralism to neostructuralism, but it has continued after neostructuralism's official launching. The renewal and gutting of structuralism's transformative ambition and its conversion into a status-quo enhancing paradigm can be seen as unfolding in three distinct stages: (1) Passage from Structuralism to Neostructuralism (1983–89); (2) "Early" Neostructuralism (1990–98); and (3) "Middle 'Neostructuralism'" (1999–2007).

Passage from Structuralism to Neostructuralism: Mea Culpa (1983–89)

Throughout the 1970s and early 1980s, prior to the publication of neostructuralism's founding document, ECLAC was unable to articulate a coherent proposal capable of challenging the neoliberal policies supported by the World Bank and the IMF, which partly thanks to the repressive power of

Latin America's military, imposed comprehensive programs of structural reforms. As the then Secretary General of ECLAC, Gert Rosenthal, recalls that "the institution was frankly on the defensive, both in terms of the collective imaginary as well as in the academic world" (Rosenthal 2000, 74; my translation). Caught between the onslaught of neoliberal orthodoxy and structuralism's policy proposals supportive of the failing ISI-model, the leadership of ECLAC confronted a daunting question: What development paradigm could be offered to the region? Facing increasing pressure to provide an answer, ECLAC found itself intellectually disoriented and theoretically disarmed for responding to the new challenges and historical conditions. Again, Gert Rosenthal describes the intellectual climate amid the staff he directed during this period: "Some staff members leaned toward defending the *cepalino* message of yore, while others were finding certain merits to the theoretical winds that were starting to blow, specially in the Southern Cone" (Rosenthal 2000, 74).Buffeted by these crosswinds, ECLAC found itself lacking a theoretical compass for a good part of the 1980s. According to Rosenthal, "For many years, there was no synthesis of the internal debate into a renovated and coherent message, but rather different proposals that offered ambiguous and even contradictory signals regarding the institutional stance" (2000, 75).

It was not until under the intellectual leadership of Fernando Fajnzylber, when ECLAC published "Changing Production Patterns with Social Equity" (1990), that the defensiveness, perplexity, and internal disarray could be overcome. The new ECLAC proposal *Changing Production Patterns with Social Equity* (CPPSE) was produced under constraints and designed specifically to overcome a defensive posture. Former ECLAC secretary General Gert Rosenthal identified the main components of this context as (1) the resurgence of orthodox economics; (2) the "incipient phenomenon" of the internationalization of the economy; (3) the response to the deep economic crisis faced by the region after 1982; (4) the predominance of short-term economic policy as opposed to medium and long-term proposals "given the conjunctural obsession of the moment was simply to survice" (Rosenthal 2000, 77; my translation); and lastly (5) the mounting evidence that the import-substitution strategy reached its limits and was exhausted.[8]

When ECLAC finally was able to articulate the proposal contained in CPPSE, ECLAC economists had undergone an intellectual transformation. First, to their dismay, they realized that the banner of structural transformation had been wrested from their hands by their former neoliberal monetarists adversaries. Second, they offered what I have called a "public mea culpa" for supporting the ISI strategy. Different authors (Ffrench-Davis 1986; Rosales 1988; Bitar 1988; Lustig 1988; Sunkel and Zuleta 1990; Bertholomeiu et al. 2005) have catalogued the errors of the past that would have to be exorcised in order to lay the foundations for neostructuralism. These included the following:

1. Weak handling of short-term macroeconomic policies
2. Faulty understanding and attention to monetary and financial aspects of development
3. Excessive trust on the value of state intervention and distrust of the market
4. Complacent attitude toward inflation and fiscal deficits
5. Utilization of price setting of key commodities as a distributive mechanism
6. Omission of external constraint considerations
7. Attention to only demand-side and ignoring of supply side considerations in the design of income distribution policies
8. Underestimating the role of expectations in the evolution of macroeconomic aggregates
9. Allowing a political management of state enterprises
10. Export-pessimism

In sum, this comprehensive catalogue of publicly acknowledged policy mistakes can be interpreted in many different manners. Either ECLAC economists finally saw the light and learned a lesson about the importance of sound macroeconomic management, or, alternatively, they theoretically surrendered to the main criticisms leveled against them by neoclassical and neoliberal economists. Independent of the interpretation, this mea culpa in the realm of economic policy making was coupled to their recognition that efforts to bring about social transformation ended in what one ECLAC economist called the "Greek Tragedy of social change" (Rosales 1991, 5). The setting was then established for the contradictory double movement that, combining conceptual innovation and retreat, was to lead to the formulation of Latin American neostructuralism.

Early Latin American Neostructuralism (1990–98)

During "early" neostructuralism, ECLAC deployed the CPPSE framework and expanded it so that all realms of economic and public policy would become conceptually subordinated to the logic of achieving "systemic competitiveness." The initial CPPSE approach was expanded to include the environment (1991), educational policy (1992), public and social policy (1993), international trade and economic policy (1994), economic policymaking (1996), and fiscal policy (1998) through a series of institutional books prepared for the sessions of the Commission. Through these publications, the new neostructuralist paradigm sought to both critique and demonstrate its superiority over the neoliberal approach. Achieving these twin goals depended on convincingly arguing that Latin American neostructuralism paid attention to market social, political, and institutional variables and, by so doing, conceived policy design as a much more integrated process, encompassing micro, meso, and macro levels of intervention.

The "early" period is thus marked by a sort of blind confidence on the benefits that Latin American countries will reap from the high road to globalization. Such optimism wanes as a result of the Asian financial crisis, a period of financial instability and contagion that coincided with the replacement of Gert Rosenthal with the former Finance Minister of Colombia, José Antonio Ocampo, as the new Executive Secretary of ECLAC. With the publication, *The Fiscal Covenant: Strength, Weaknesses, Challenges* (ECLAC 1998), Latin American neostructuralism shifts its attention more and more to questions of macroeconomic policy management. The definitive proof of capacity to exercise leadership over society begins now to be measured not just by displaying a balanced budget achieved in many countries during the 1980s through drastic cutbacks in social services, but also through exercising political leadership over the different actors so as to be able to construct a consensus around the "fiscal covenant."

A compromise among different social actors as to how State resources are to be used becomes essential for ECLAC because, as it explains in its 1998 publication,

> the success of the profound transformation of the economy that
> is now taking place . . . will falter if the State is not in a position to
> make its essential contribution. Privatization of public utilities, for
> example, must be accompanied by effective regulation; accumulated
> human capital and quality infrastructure are essential to economic
> growth; and equity in the distribution of the fruits of development
> is necessary to the political and social stability required for stable
> growth. But the State cannot systematically and efficiently carry out

its functions if the fiscal covenant is not operative. There is a tremendous need, then, to reconstruct and renew the fiscal covenant. This is undoubtedly an enormous task politically and technically; but, as this analysis attempts to show, the elements required to undertake it are at hand, and it is therefore not only necessary but possible. (ECLAC 1998, 11)

The key phrases for this new fiscal covenant are (1) consolidation of the existing reforms; (2) promotion of a stable macroeconomic environment; and (3) commitment of the government to using resources efficiently. Having set these objectives, the fiscal covenant must also ensure transparency, equity, and strengthening of democratic institutions. Such a covenant "is a prerequisite if the region is to make further progress toward its goal of changing production patterns with social equity" (ECLAC 1998, 11).

Middle Latin American Neostructuralism (1999–2007)

The Asian financial crisis and similar experiences of financial contagion produced a shift in neostructuralist discourse. The Asian financial crisis punctured neostructuralism's initial optimism about the "high road" along with dramatically illustrating that countries already on it, showing "sound macroeconomic fundamentals," could be seriously affected by the underestimated ugly underside of globalization. ECLAC economists began to pay growing attention to the vulnerability of countries caused by international capital flows, propelling them into debates about the necessity of creating a new global financial architecture and global institutions to produce "global public goods" for addressing the negative aspects of globalization. Whereas *Changing Production Patterns* offered new vistas and possibilities, the message of ECLAC's central document for this new period, *Productive Development in Open Economies* (ECLAC 2004), has the stale tone of Washington-based development institutions of old in the midst of the unraveling of the Washington Consensus. The message becomes "Keep to the same course despite failures and high costs; design palliative measures to address difficulties." As the approach promoted by *Productive Development* states, "ECLAC contends that the region must build upon the progress it has already made, but it also has to close existing gaps and address unresolved issues. The inroads made in these areas may play a vital role in consolidating the region's fuller integration into the world economy and in ensuring that the social, economic and political costs of the economic reform process have not been incurred in vain" (ECLAC 2004, 13).

To successfully confront these problems, ECLAC proposes more of the same:

> In order to accomplish this, the "more market and less State" approach that guided the economic reform process must give way to an emphasis on properly functioning markets and quality in governance. This new approach, which entails the use of active public policies capable of overcoming both market and government failures, can prove to be more market-friendly than the line of reasoning that was the driving force behind the initial reforms. These active public policies must be backed by the political legitimacy afforded by democratic institutions and must be founded upon public transparency as well as efficient, effective government programmes subject to strict oversight and evaluation. (ECLAC 2004, 13–14)

Thus, after 1998 instead of rethinking their assumptions, neostructuralists retreaded their discourse away from "changing productive structures with social equity" toward an emphasis on "managing globalization" through better public policies. After 1998, evidence about the shortcomings of neoliberal policies mounted with unparalleled speed. Pushed by these events, mainstream economists and international financial institutions like the World Bank and the IMF abandoned their dogmatic neoliberal approach of the 1980s and increasingly accepted the importance of equity and of institutions and politics in economic policy making.

By 2002, with the publication of *Globalization and Development*, ECLAC realized it could no longer remain blind to the asymmetries and mounting number of "losers" generated by globalizing processes. Even though, during the 1990s, Latin America and the Caribbean could show stellar figures in terms of FDI and export growth, ECLAC's commitment to modernization via internationalization failed to deliver the promised outcomes. Neoliberal meltdown in Argentina and rising popular discontent reaffirmed neostructuralism's critique of neoliberalism but did not lead toward questioning the failed assumptions embraced by the new ECLAC. On the contrary, during this period, the intellectual retreat that began in the late 1980s was further consolidated.

Despite sophisticated analyses, ample availability of data, and increased emphasis on the quality of governance, ECLAC's *Productive Development in Open Economies* reaffirms neostructuralism's commitment to the existing development strategy:

> In seeking to highlight the link between the external constraint and the production structure, the former is defined as a balanced trade account or a sustainable trade deficit. . . . Within this framework, as the economy's relative productivity rises, it will become more competitive, and its export capacity will therefore increase. This will permit it to finance a larger volume of imports, thus generating a virtuous circle of growth that will, in its turn, spur future productivity gains. In the opposite case—i.e., if the economy's relative competitiveness declines—then the smaller volume of exports will create a need for a higher volume of capital inflows to finance the economy's larger trade imbalance. The region's past experience demonstrates that when external financing requirements are on the rise, the situation becomes untenable and usually ends up triggering recessionary adjustments. This analysis underscores the importance, within the context of open economies, of achieving productivity gains, since this is what ultimately drives export growth. If domestic productivity is determined by aggregate demand and the production structure's ability to absorb, generate and diffuse knowledge and innovations, then production policies should be designed to fortify these factors. (ECLAC 2004, 162)

The four type of policies encouraged within such a framework by *Productive Development in Open Economies* are (1) policies to better position the region within the international economy; (2) technological development and innovation policies; (3) policies for enterprise development and job creation in the formal sectors; and (4) policies that strengthen productive structure by fostering and consolidating strategic sectors. These policies contribute to further intensify the three intellectual retreats previously discussed and further subordinates public policies to the requirements of transnational capital and the local conglomerates that dominate most Latin American economies.

3

Historicizing Latin American Neostructuralism

The rise to predominance of a new school of thought, such as Latin American neostructuralism, does not take place in a historical vacuum or instantaneously once it demonstrates a purported conceptual superiority over the dominant paradigm.[1] Hence, if we are to understand Latin American neostructuralism's seductive power (as well as its limitations), we must go beyond taxonomic comparisons of concepts, policy bundles, or predictive prowess of contending models. If we are to deconstruct Latin American neostructuralism by bringing to the center of analysis the historical relationship between its *discursive* and *material practices*, then we should explain how we are going to do it. How can neostructuralist discourse and policy initiatives be placed within a historical framework? How can we explain the historical role of different and contending economic visions? What is the societal impact of policies grounded on neoliberalism's emphasis on the magic of the market and "comparative advantage"? What will be the impact of policies based on neostructuralism's notion of systemic competitiveness and role attributed to political leadership?

To "historicize" Latin American neostructuralism means, at the very least, to provide plausible answers to the following questions: Why does Latin American neostructuralism arise and gain ascendancy when it does? What alteration of social and economic structures does neostructuralism propose and why? Why do its main propositions resonate so powerfully among policymakers and voters? Such questions stem from an understanding that economic ideas and economic policies are conditioned by, and modify, the social and political context in which they are put into practice: "Economic policies, therefore, are introduced *in order* to alter social structures" (Letelier 1976, 137).[2]

This chapter offers four complementary approximations on how to "historicize" Latin American neostructuralism and its role. First, this chapter presents a stylized sequence or stages that Latin American economies traverse as they are force-marched through the transition from an import substitution industrialization (ISI) to the current export-oriented (EO) model. With such a map in hand, we can better assess the nature of the historical tasks undertaken by neoliberal and neostructuralist ideas in the region.[3] A second approach for historicizing Latin American neostructuralism borrows from the French Regulation School (FRS): its concepts of "regime of accumulation," "mode of regulation," and "mode of socialization" help us to comprehend that economic ideas must operate beyond the strictly economic realm if societal structures are to be successfully altered in a lasting manner. Economic ideas must also provide means for channeling and regulating social and cultural conflicts arising from the new order; in other words, neoliberalism and Latin American neostructuralism must not only ensure capital accumulation but also actively contribute to the legitimization of the new system of domination. The third tack compares Latin American capitalism under the ISI to the EO regimes of accumulation offering a highly schematic characterization of the way both capital accumulation and social reproduction unfold under these two different "economic models." Finally, this chapter offers a broad overview of the relationship between development theories of the past sixty years (structuralism, dependency theory, neoliberalism, and neostructuralism) and capitalist development in Latin America. This analysis underscores that debates about theories of development have a close dialectical relationship with the patterns of capital accumulation and underlines the historically embedded nature of Latin American neostructuralism.

By tracing the intertwined trajectories of development theories and patterns of accumulation, this chapter highlights the interaction between economic discourse and capitalist restructuring. Such analysis shows that Latin American neostructuralism enters the historical stage contending neoliberal economic ideas when the process of capitalist restructuring or "economic reform" is well under way. Thanks to its differences with dogmatic neoliberalism, Latin American neostructuralism plays, as we will see, a complementary and key role in completing the process of capitalist restructuring experienced in the region in past decades.

Stages of the Restructuring Process

For a long time policymakers followed the World Bank's recommendation to distinguish between the *initiation*, *implementation*, and *consolidation* of the reforms (World Bank 1993). Such differentiation was supported initially by the necessity of clearly identifying the economic constraints involved in the timing and sequencing of different economic policy initiatives.[4] Over time, particularly during the 1990s as military regimes were replaced by civilian elected governments, the emphasis shifted toward political factors. Thus, from an initial emphasis on the economic necessity of privatization and the sequencing of deregulation, the focus was displaced toward understanding the necessary procedures for building coalitions capable of overcoming rising discontent and opposition to maintain the momentum behind the reform process.[5]

According to Marcelo Selowsky, who in 1990 was the World Bank's Chief Economist for Latin America and the Caribbean, in order to successfully restructure their economies, all countries of the region had to follow a logical sequence of three stages (Selowsky 1990). This sequence—studied and later enriched by others (Haggard and Kaufman 1992; World Bank 1993, Bates and Krueger 1993)—was presented as the sine qua non for achieving positive growth rates in an increasingly competitive international context. Not surprisingly, Chile was touted then, as now, as the one Latin American country that pioneered and progressed further along in this process.[6] The blueprint for economic reform outlined for the World Bank consisted of three stages (see Figure 5).

First Stage: Adjustment, Stabilization, and Initiation

During this stage, World Bank–endorsed policies seek to reestablish basic macroeconomic balances in the arena of fiscal, monetary, and balance of payments, bringing inflation under control. This is the period of "shock treatment" and "austerity measures," experienced by Latin American countries in the 1970s and 1980s. Policies prescribed for this stage appear as having a single historical objective: imposing the implacable logic of the market on the economy, thereby clearing the way so that the market can operate without the multiple "distortions" introduced by previous ISI-inspired government policies and political commitments. These encompassed a long list of state-fixed and subsidized prices for basic necessities and key productive inputs, as well as the establishment of multiple government-controlled interest and exchange rates. According to its neoliberal promoters, economic policies of this stage require "political courage" and decisiveness to impose unpopular measures that will liberate prices and market forces from undue political intervention. Though deregulation and liberalization will have a

Stage	Objectives	Policies
First Stage: **Stablization/ "Shock Therapy"** (1973–78 for Chile)	• Re-establish macroeconomic equilibrium • Markets operating without "distortion"	• Control inflation • Fiscal equilibrium • Trade balance • Pay external debt
Second Stage: **Deep Structural Reforms** (1978–89 for Chile)	• Increase internal and external competitiveness • "Rationalize" the institutional system • Expand the logic of the market to every area of society	• Privatize public enterprises • Reform labor legislation • Liberalize foreign investments • Privatize social services (social security, health, education) • Municipalization
Third Stage **Consolidate Reforms/ Restore Investment Levels** (1990–present for Chile)	• Complete process of opening up the economy and society • Legitimize privatization, liberalization, and deregulation	• Liberalize capital markets • Promote "second generation" reforms (public administration, judicial system, infrastructure, etc.)

Figure 5. Stages of capitalist restructuring. Compiled by author on basis of Selowsky (1990).

strong negative impact on family income in the short run, it is alleged that these will turn out to be healthy for the economy in the long run. Justification was often couched with medical terminology: "sometimes one must cut off a limb to save a patient," or "prosperity through pain." The metaphor of neoliberal economists as surgeons capable of healing an ailing economy and body politic through bitter medicine or painful surgery was abundant during this stage. In the case of Chile this first stage lasted from 1974 to 1978 and coincided with the beginning protracted influence of the "Chicago Boys," the disciples of Milton Friedman, under most of Augusto Pinochet's dictatorship.

Second Stage: Deep Structural Reforms and Implementation

The purpose of this second stage is "to increase internal and external competitiveness in the goods, input and financial markets, along with the rationalization of the entire institutional system" (Selowsky 1990). This is achieved through intensifying the privatization of state enterprises and social services, the full liberalization of trade and foreign investment among other institutional reforms.

Again from the perspective of the transition from an ISI to EO regime of accumulation, the goal of this second stage was to expand the logic of the market to the totality of institutions and social relations. Success of this stage is measured by the extent to which government policies facilitated the logic of the market and private profit to permeate every interstice of social life, corroding and undermining all remnants of previous solidarity-based and market regulating institutions. This is a stage when basic social services—such as health, education, and the social security system—are privatized, new regulations covering foreign investment are passed, public goods such as water and other natural resources are commodified, and labor legislation is comprehensively revamped to create the conditions for a restructured and weakened labor force, with reduced expectations and demands. No significant area of socioeconomic existence can remain sovereign from the rule of commodity relations. In Chile, this stage lasted from 1979 to 1989, which was the end of the military regime.

Third Stage: Consolidation of Reforms and Recuperation of Investment Levels

The purpose of this stage is to provide broad social legitimacy to the previous processes of privatization, deregulation, and liberalization. It is a stage characterized by the political and institutional consolidation of the reforms and "a new understanding of the role of the state and the public sector" (World Bank 1993). During this stage, the basis for renewed economic activity along a new, open, and export-oriented pattern of growth is established. From an economic point of view, once private investors come to recognize the scope and steadfastness of the reform process, they become willing to invest, which in turn leads to a recuperation of investment levels and a rise in output. The success of this third stage, according to Selowsky depends, among other factors, upon the full liberalization and deepening of capital markets. This "mature phase" is achieved once there is society-wide recognition that reforms have provided tangible results, and that a broad-based coalition of political parties explicitly supports the reform process. In Chile, the opening of this stage corresponds also to the transition from a military to a civilian-elected regime, described as the negotiated transition to democracy. In the Chilean case, there is a perfect synchronization between the exit of neoliberal economists (Chicago boys) from governmental posts and policy formulation and the beginning of this third stage. Enter Latin American neostructuralism and a new set of economists committed to economic growth and social equity known as the "CIEPLAN monks" (Silva 1991).

Salient Features

On the basis of such sequencing, we can deduce certain features that will impinge upon the role of economic discourse and particularly upon the changing function of the state throughout the long restructuring process. State intervention will be shaped by factors, such as the politico-economic objectives of each stage; the degrees of coercion necessary to achieve them; the extent to which economic ideas can perform their ideological role[7]; and the nature of the social costs and levels of popular resistance associated with each stage. The two contending discourses—neoliberalism and neostructuralism—propose different approaches for addressing each one of these aspects.

Politico-economic Objectives of Each Stage

Each stage has a certain politico-economic objective whose achievement is crucial for maintaining continuity of the reform process. Completion of the historical objectives of each stage creates the conditions for moving on to the next.

As Latin American countries traversed through the restructuring process, the historical record shows marches and countermarches, indicating that—with few exceptions, Chile among them—a neat and seamless sequence is not likely. Nevertheless, independent of such twists and turns, it is possible to observe how the state's role and the very profile of the state apparatus is influenced by the objectives set for each stage. The launching of an austerity package, for example, requires that the executive, and economics, and finance ministries have the capacity to resist pressures that would divert them from implementing the stabilization program. In light of mounting social resistance to International Monetary Fund (IMF) and World Bank sanctioned austerity measures, it is not surprising that this stage corresponds to a greater reliance on the repressive apparatus of the state and on regimes of exception, as was the case in the Southern Cone.

As a society advances from the initial stage of market deregulation to the stage of structural reforms, the role of the state as the organizer of the privatization of social services implies a different deployment of the state apparatus and use of state power. In addition to the threat of direct coercion, it must prevent opposition to reforms from coalescing into powerful movements capable of tapping into widespread discontent. As public assets and services are privatized, the state must also have the capacity to set some agreed-upon ground rules (at least among private economic actors) for the transfer of such resources to private hands. Finally, during the third stage, the center of gravity of state action shifts toward rearticulating the links between national and international capital, particularly transnational finance capital, as well as toward strengthening coalitions that will sustain and consolidate the reform process. In the 1990s, for example, as Latin America moved from military to civilian-elected regimes, concerns shifted toward addressing "reform fatigue" through political means and innovative social policies. The Inter-American Development Bank (IDB), warned that "if the policymakers vacillate and yield to the growing adjustment fatigue, confidence could be quickly destroyed, the resource transfer interrupted, and the recovery short lived. The political challenge in the 1990s consists therefore of generating broad-based social support for the reform process by spreading the benefits of renewed growth more equally overall groups of the population" (IDB 1992, 1).

During this third stage, one of the tasks of those at the helm of the state apparatus is to build support for the reform process by paying greater attention to distributive concerns, but they must do so without losing sight of or undermining the ultimate purpose of reform policies: the creation of an investment friendly environment that will raise capitalist profit rates. In the words of the IDB, "the challenge for Latin American policy-makers therefore consists of creating and maintaining a stable macropolicy environment with clear and transparent rules of the game that *minimize uncertainty for foreign investors*" (IDB 1992, 13; emphasis added). Simultaneously satisfying international investors while maintaining support for the reform process requires a much more sophisticated political intervention by the State apparatus. "Shock therapy," austerity measures, and belt-tightening *paquetazos* must give way to a greater sensitivity toward acknowledging the role of civil society in economic policy design and of the possibilities offered by the cultural realm for constructing hegemony and new subjectivities supportive of the new system of domination.

A Changing Mix of Coercion and Consent

This stylized three-stage process of transition from the ISI to the EO regime of accumulation provides a useful general framework for discussing the role of neostructuralism in Latin America. It can also be used to contrast the different degrees of influence achieved by neostructuralism in Chile and Brazil, analyzed in chapter 4. Chile is not only the region's pioneer in neoliberal restructuring, but it is also unique because, as mentioned earlier, there is a clear cut coincidence between the transition to a civilian-elected regime in 1990 and a transition into the third stage of the restructuring process. No other country in the region offers such clear congruence. The 1989 electoral victory of the Coalition for Parties for Democracy or Concertación in the wake of years of massive anti-dictatorial mobilizations meant the arrival of a new set of economists strongly influenced and linked to Latin American neostructuralism. The new set of Concertación economists calling for revamping the Pinochet economic model and for an export drive built on democracy and consensus, not authoritarianism and coercion, displayed an admirable capacity to exploit the historical opportunity and political moment. The problem, as we will see in later chapters, is that this happy coincidence unfolded in a country that was successfully integrating into the world economy via the export of natural resources with low levels of processing, produced by a precariously employed and super-exploited labor force. In Chile, neostructuralism's call for the high road to globalization based on passage to a second phase of the export model, with greater reliance on manufactured exports would turn out to be a failed proposition, a caricature of what was initially confidently promised.

The above framework is equally useful for understanding the trajectory of neostructuralism in Brazil, which unlike Chile was the late and reluctant reformer of the continent. In Brazil, Latin American neostructuralism's influence was hampered by the unfinished business of capitalist restructuring. Instead of neat, clearly demarcated stages in which different economic schools and ideas could play their historic role, Brazilian capitalism faced the task of implementing the first and second stages of neoliberal restructuring from the mid-1990s in a very different political and intellectual climate from that of the continent's early (Chile) and mid (Bolivia) reformers.

This is one of the major reasons, though not the only one, why Brazil has witnessed a process that defies easy categorizations. As we will see in chapter 4, the premier intellectual associated with structuralism and reformist strain of dependency theory, and someone who was linked for decades to the work of the Economic Commission for Latin America and the Caribbean (ECLAC), Fernando Henrique Cardoso, became the promoter of the first two stages of capitalist restructuring in Brazil, turning into the chief architect and cheerleader of those policies that in Chile were linked to dogmatic neoliberalism. Thus, the Cardoso government, intellectually linked at the hip with ECLAC and neostructuralism, carried out those destructive tasks and restructuring of the relations of class power better suited for neoliberalism. But for the Cardoso government to do so with the political acumen and sensibility to the discursive and rhetorical dimensions fostered by neostructuralism gives rise to what some analysts called "pseudo-neoliberalism." It is also the reason President Inácio da Silva's economic program and policies have come under so much criticism from the left and the social movements. His commitment to complete the unfinished stage of structural transformations initiated by Cardoso (privatization of social security for example) have not allowed him to fully deploy a discourse concordant with the third stage of the restructuring process.

As the analysis that follows shows, understanding the stages of capitalist restructuring in each country, though important, does not fully account for the role of economic ideas or of Latin American neostructuralism in each country.

Regime of Accumulation, Mode of Regulation, Mode of Societalization

Since its inception in the 1970s, the FRS (and to a lesser extent its U.S. counterpart, the Social Structures of Accumulation (SSA) school), has provided political economy with tools for analyzing the structure and development of capitalist economies and societies.[8] In particular, the FRS seeks to explain long-run patterns of capital accumulation "by analyzing the relation between the capital accumulation process and a set of social institutions which affect that process" (Kotz 1994b, 86). In the exploration of the historical relationship between capitalist accumulation and institutions, the FRS has advanced three useful analytical categories—regime of accumulation, mode of regulation, and mode of societalization—that are helpful for assessing the role of Latin American neostructuralism. These categories focused on the "historically-contingent ensembles of complementary economic and *extra-economic* mechanisms and practices which enable relatively stable accumulation to occur over relatively long periods, despite the fundamental contradictions, crisis tendencies and conflicts generated by capitalism" (Jessop 1997, 503). These three categories are particularly suitable for historicizing Latin American neostructuralism, helping to demystify the restoration of institutions enacted by neostructuralism and the relinking between "democracy and development" supported by the international development establishment over the past decade.

The concept of "regime of accumulation" describes "the stabilization over a long period of the allocation of the net product between consumption and accumulation; it implies some correspondence between the transformation of both the conditions of production and the conditions of the reproduction of the wage earners. It also implies some form of linkage between capitalism and other modes of production" (Lipietz 1986, 19). Recalling some of Prebisch and Furtado's concerns, the central analytical category deployed by FRS is built around the historical forms taken by the production, appropriation, and distribution of surplus. Envisioned as a historically concrete allocation of social surplus that enables the reproduction of capitalist production and wage earners over a long period of time, a *regime of accumulation* requires at the same time "a set of norms, habits, laws, regulating networks and so on, that ensure the unity of the process, i.e. the approximate consistency of individual behaviors with the schema of reproduction. This body of interiorized rules and social process is called the mode of regulation" (Lipietz 1986, 19). A *mode of regulation*, therefore, is "a set of mediations which ensure that the distortions created by the accumulation of capital are kept within limits which are compatible with social cohesion within each nation" (Aglieta 2000, 391).

To the notions of regime of accumulation (comprised of a macroeconomic regime that supports a structurally coherent pattern of growth in capitalist production and consumption) and mode of regulation (constituted by the ensemble of norms, organizational forms, social networks, and patterns of conduct that supports and guides a given accumulation regime) some analysts have added a third component, a *mode of societalization*, which is understood as "a pattern of institutional integration and social cohesion that complements the dominant accumulation regime and its mode of economic regulation, thereby securing the conditions for its dominance in the wider society" (Jessop 2002, 56).

With a theoretical production spanning more than three decades, the FRS has explored how the trajectory of the capital accumulation process has been the outcome and, at the same time, has stimulated the supporting role of a specific set of social institutions. Time and again, FRS analysts have emphasized that prescripted outcomes do not exist and that the relationship between *regime of accumulation, mode of regulation*, and *mode of socialization should not be understood in mechanistic or functionalist terms*. Regimes of accumulation and modes of regulation are the historical products of human struggles and they co-constitute one another, so that "a regime of accumulation and forms of regulation get stabilized together, because they ensure the crisis-free reproduction of social relations over a period of time" (Lipietz 1986, 20).

Armed with an understanding of the stages of capitalist restructuring and the insights offered by Regulation Theory, we can begin to historicize Latin American neostructuralism. In a nutshell, the eighteen-year-old trajectory of Latin American neostructuralism shows how—in the new historical stage of a restructured society—its "holistic" conceptualizations and public policies overcome obstacles and create more favorable conditions for both the accumulation of capital as well as for the construction of a new mode of regulation for the export-oriented economic model structured in the region since the mid-1970s.[9] In the process, Latin American neostructuralism's vision about the importance of politics and of its intersection and inseparability with economics enable the far-reaching reorganization, recalibration, and reorientation of the state (Jessop 2002), which is fundamental for erecting new modes of regulation and societalization supportive of export-oriented accumulation.

From Iron Fist to Velvet Handshake

Using the categories of FRS, we gain insight on how neoliberalism and neostructuralism measure up against the tasks of structuring the three interconnected regime of accumulation, mode of regulation, and mode of societalization that ensure that capitalist restructuring will be successful and enduring. Neoliberalism, particularly in its more dogmatic register, calls for unleashing the market from its societal and political fetters, regardless of short-term pains and protests; neostructuralism on the other hand, calls for consensus-building so that the new export-oriented and transnational market forces can be supported by newly designed societal and political arrangements. The changing role of the state in the different stages of such passage partly explains such difference. We remarked on the way, during the initial stage, the state had to exercise its full coercive power to destroy the institutional and class foundations of the old ISI regime of accumulation, using its monopoly over the instruments of violence to clear the way for laying down the foundations for the current export-oriented regime of accumulation. At the same time, in order to consolidate and legitimize the process of restructuring, coercion had to give way to consent. Neostructuralist discourse and policies thus enable a shift in the state's role, replacing the iron fist with the velvet handshake.

In what follows, I bring in the scope offered by the FRS to explore the way politics of Latin American neostructuralism contributes to create the vast range of institutions necessary to regulate the new regime of accumulation. Latin America's neostructuralist political task is not just that of replacing authoritarian politics and market centric economics; it must also develop the gamut of institutions that allow the restructured capitalist state to promote both accumulation and legitimization under the present historical conditions. The functions of the state are neither simple nor clearly defined in Latin America and the Caribbean under the present conditions (see Figure 6). Along with securing the general conditions for capital accumulation and the right of capital to control labor power, the state must also carry out other functions, including defining and modifying the boundaries and links between the economic and extraeconomic spheres to ensure capital accumulation. The state must also address and manage the wider spectrum of dilemmas and contradictions that arise from capitalist development, including producing ideologies of social well-being and belonging with enough verisimilitude so as to stabilize a system based on socialized and internationalized production with private appropriation of surplus labor (Jessop 2002). In order for Latin American societies and political systems to tackle these new state functions, Latin American neostructuralism has to successfully displace neoliberalism as the predominant economic discourse.

Comparing the Import-substitution and the New Export–oriented "Model"

The massive fracture of economic and social processes recently experienced by Latin America can be illustrated by contrasting the previous ISI model of development with the current EO economic model.

If we examine the differences between the process of accumulation of capital (investment, production, and realization) and the reproduction of labor (wage, indirect wage, and domestic labor) under the ISI and EO regimes of accumulation presented in Figure 7, we can visualize some of the major

Functions	Type of activities
1. Secure the general external conditions for capitalist accumulation	Preserve the legal order Protect property rights
2. Secure fictitious commodification of land, labor, money, and knowledge and modulate resulting conflicts	Manage supply of labor and employment Titles over natural resources
3. Secure the right and capacity of capital to control labor power in the production process and capitalist labor relations in terms of employment	Labor legislation and labor courts Labor reforms enabling different forms of labor flexibility
4. Define the boundaries between economic and extra-economic sphere, modifying the links between them as a preconditions for capital accumulation	Privatization of public resources and assets WTO-rules
5. Promote provision of general conditions of production, capital-intensive infrastructure with long-turnover time.	Financing of roads, power, ports, construction, and other transport systems
6. Manage the contradiction between the increasing social nature of production and the private appropriation of surplus labor	Produce ideologies of social good and belonging
7. Articulate interlinked processes of de- and re-territorialization and de- and re-temporalization associated with remaking of spatio-temporal fixes for relatively stable periods of capital accumulation	Address issues of overproduction, over accumulation, falling rate of profit, balance between consumption, and accumulation
8. Address the wider political and social repercussions of capitalist contradictions and dilemmas	Poverty alleviation, social protection, maintain social order

Figure 6. Functions of the capitalist state. Source: Jessop (2002, 45 [box 1.2]).

differences in the way Latin American capitalist societies have reorganized over the past decades.

If we first examine the process of capital accumulation, we can see how production for global markets binds both the accumulation of capital and social reproduction to decision-making and the material interests of very different social sectors. The investment decision is now controlled overwhelmingly by the private sector, so that the impact of capitalists' decision about what to do with the surplus, whether to invest or consume it, is intensified. Even more so, when such decisions are made by a handful of transnational conglomerates who dominate the export sector and whose expansion increasingly comes under influence of shareholder expectations and the logic of speculative investments. Production no longer is organized along the lines of vertically integrated division or sections, grouping hundreds and even thousands of workers in the same work site where a shared space of socialization provide them with possibilities for the construction of collective identities and interests, as was the case in many of the industrial and mining concerns under ISI. Today, production is organized in much more flexible and fragmented terms, heavily relying on two and three-tiered workforces, where only a small nucleus enjoys stable employment, benefits, and job security. The sale or realization of production of the most dynamic sectors of Latin American economies is now carried out in external markets. The result is that workers in the export sector are not the consumers of what they produce. Consequently, wages and working conditions can be depressed without significantly affecting profits. More importantly, the shared interest between capitalists and labor unions in expanding the internal market, which for decades served as the basis for the multiclass support for the national-developmentalist project, has vanished. The outcome of all of these transformations is that under the EO model, distribution becomes even more tightly bound to accumulation, creating a new set of structural constraints for "growth with equity."

If we now look at the sphere of social reproduction and contrast the ISI and the current EO regime of accumulation, we can also notice major structural differences. The main distinction is that in the past the costs of reproduction of labor were shared by workers, the state, and employers. Today under the EO regime, the search for international competitiveness, regardless of whether it is carried out by neoliberal or neostructuralist policies, seeks to transfer the costs of reproduction of labor onto the shoulders of workers and their families, thereby liberating capitalists and the state from having to shoulder such costs. Wages are no longer indexed to inflation or defended by collective bargaining agreements. Public provision of social services shrank significantly, along with the declining role of indirect wages in helping proletarian families ensure access to collective consumption. Unpaid domestic labor continues falling mostly on the shoulders of women, many of whom have entered in the labor market, expanding the mass of low-paid, flexible, and disposable workers required under the current export-oriented regime.

As result of these previously described structural transformations, poverty and inequality become firmly anchored in the functioning of labor markets and in the expansion of informalized labor-capital relations demanded by transnational productive capital and domestic conglomerates. A structurally different relationship between wages and consumption is established under the current export regime of accumulation, as workers in the most dynamic export sectors are no longer the consumers of the commodities they produce. This means that those structural limitations on the downward pressure on wages and labor conditions that existed under the ISI regime, where capitalists and the state were interested in expanding worker incomes, has disappeared. The most dynamic sectors of the capitalist class and the state now are interested in ensuring flexible, malleable, cheap labor, willing to accept the prerogatives of employers in the organization of the production process to suit their quest for profits in globally competitive export markets. Labor control and extraction of labor effort become the pillars of the new labor regime being consolidated under the EO regime of accumulation.

The structural differences between the ISI and EO models of Latin American capitalism underscore the structural limits that allegedly "progressive" post-neoliberal approaches to development will presently face if they remain committed to the export-oriented regime of accumulation. The reproduction of the current export-oriented regime concentrates the investment decision in the hands of private capitalists; to compete successfully, not only must a flexible force be guaranteed but also the costs of reproduction of labor are to be borne by workers and their families. These are the ironclad limits inherent to the self-expansion of Latin American capitalism that are placed upon economic policy makers. Neoliberals understood this and did not care about the social consequences with the tragic results that we have seen in Latin America. Neostructuralists on the other hand, also understand this, but attempt to manage the contradictions of the new system, deploying progressive policies that do not dare challenge the pillars sustaining the current export-oriented regime of accumulation.

	Import Substitution Industrialization Model (1930s–1970s)	Export-Oriented Model (1975–present)
Capital Accumulation	**Investment => Production => Realization (SALE)**	
1. Investment	• State (75%) • Private (25%)	• Private (75%) • State (25%)
2. Production	• Centralization of capital with vertical integration • Development of large industrial concerns • Concentration of workers	• Centralization of capital with horizontal integration (Grupos económicos) • Fragmentation of production processes (outsourcing) • Precarious work contract • Two/three tier workforce
3. Realization	*Internal Market* 1. Limit to rate of exploitation (urban workers contribute to realization of surplus-value [sale]) 2. Fraction of capital interested in expanding the buying power of urban middle, proletariat and popular sectors	*External Markets* 1. Workers do not consume exports (no built-in limit to exploitation) 2. International competitiveness forces a never-ending race to lower production costs 3. International prices are not controlled by individual firm; imperative to prevent wage increases over increases in productivity.
Reproduction of Labor	**Direct Wage + Indirect Wage + Unpaid Domestic Labor**	
	Costs of reproduction are shared by workers, their families, employers and the State	Costs of reproduction are shifted from the State and employers onto workers and women

Continued on next page

Figure 7. Comparison of import substitution industrialization (ISI) and export-oriented (EO) regimes of accumulation.

	Import Substitution Industrialization Model (1930s–1970s)	Export-Oriented Model (1975–present)
Reproduction of Labor (continued)	Direct Wage + Indirect Wage + Unpaid Domestic Labor	
1. Wage (direct)	• Wages are readjusted to keep with inflation • Stable contracts • Job stability • Collective bargaining	• Wages are reduced • Firm level bargaining • Precarious employment • Wage, external, internal, functional flexibility
2. Social Benefits (indirect wage)	State guarantees access to: • Health • Education • Social Security • Other benefits • Notion of "social rights"	• Social benefits are eliminated • State no longer guarantees "rights" • Market criteria prevail • Notion of "user pays"
3. Domestic Labor	1. Carried out by women 2. Roles within working class family 3. Access to collective consumption goods	1. Carried out by women 2. Roles change as men are laid-off, women join the remunerated labor force 3. Deterioration of access to collective consumption goods.

Figure 7. (Continued) Comparison of import substitution industrialization (ISI) and export-oriented (EO) regimes of accumulation.

Latin American Capitalism and Theories of Development

To further probe the nature of Latin American neostructuralism, I examine the connections between the major development theories of the past decades—structuralism, dependency theory, neoliberalism, and neostructuralism—with the evolution of Latin American capitalism. I want to highlight a simple idea that seems to have been lost amid positivist pretensions and postmodernist paroxysms: the rise, predominance, and decline of economic ideas and theories of development, such as neoliberalism or Latin American neostructuralism, are historically embedded processes. I am not arguing here that economic ideas are a mechanical expression of the development of the productive forces. On the contrary, I want to insist that a more complex relationship exists that needs to be revealed. Historicizing development theories—for example, exploring their complex interaction with the evolution of Latin American capitalism—can help us better understand not only the internal dynamics of each theory but also gain greater theoretical self-awareness about how they interact with existing power structures and relations.

Following Eagleton, economic discourses and theories of development like structuralism, dependency theory, neoliberalism, and Latin American neostructuralism can be understood by examining the way their signifying activities and theoretical constructs contribute to (1) chart a new course for societal development; (2) maintain and recreate the unity of the dominant classes or bloc in power; and (3) dissolve the acts of oppositional forces that resist the direction and character of the societal transformation espoused (Eagleton 1991).

If we take the case of structuralism and dependency theory, we can see how these approaches were eminently entwined with the rise and crisis of the ISI model of development, while neoliberalism and Latin American neostructuralism find their roots in processes of creative destruction of the old ISI economic model and in the establishment of the new export-oriented regime of accumulation (see Figure 8).

Such a perspective reinforces the notion that by raising the banners of comparative advantage, liberalization, privatization, and deregulation, neoliberalism sought to destroy the institutional arrangements that was the foundation for inward-oriented import-substituting industrialization under state capitalism that, since the late 1930s, expanded in many countries of the region. With its dogmatic and fundamentalist commitment to unfettering market forces, neoliberalism not only destroyed the old ISI model but, in many countries, was also able to set down the basis for a new model of development. Latin American neostructuralism, with its emphasis on consensus-building and its initial unsinkable optimism about the bounty of genuine globalization, makes its contribution to altering social structures by providing an adequate conceptual framework for complementing market-based coordination with those coordinating mediations afforded by command and state as well as trust and network-based forms of coordination. In such a fashion, a broader set of mechanisms can be brought to bear toward ensuring productive modernization as well as social cohesion in the context of

Regime of Accumulation	Import Substitution Industrialization Model (1930s–1970s)		Export-Oriented Model (1980s to present)	
Phases/Stages	"Easy ISI Phase"	"Crisis of ISI"	Stabilization and structural reform stages of capitalist restructuring	Consolidation and legitimization stage of capitalist restructuring
Approximate Years	1938–late 1950s	1967–73	1973–89	1990–present
Development Theory	Structuralism	Dependency Theory	Neoliberalism	Neo-structuralism
Motto	Modernization via industrialization	Modernization via authentic national sovereignty	Modernization via privatization	Modernization via internationalization
Root of Problem	Declining terms of trade center-periphery structural heterogeneity	Extraction of surplus; unequal exchange	Prices and market not allowed to operate as allocative mechanism	Insufficient incorporation of "technical progress"
Realm of Action	Internal market, domestic productive structure	Capitalist world economy	The market	Society as a whole: (interface between market, institutions, mindset)
Task 1: Chart a new course for societal development	Provide justification and impel forward the process of industrialization	Explain the exhaustion of ISI model; provide for a popular-democratic	Restructure–overhaul Latin American capitalism; destroy the foundations of the ISI model	Consolidate and create mechanisms to regulate the new regime of accumulation

Continued on next page

Figure 8. Development theories and regimes of accumulation.

Regime of Accumulation	Import Substitution Industrialization Model (1930s–1970s)		Export-Oriented Model (1980s to present)	
Task 1: Chart a New Course for Societal Development	already underway as a result of the crisis of the primary export model (1860–1929) and liberal policies of Latin American oligarchies	solution to the crisis of the ISI model	realign class forces to set the foundations of the new regime of accumulation	
Task 2: Contribute to Unity of Bloc in Power	Legitimize role of industrial entrepreneur as bearer of nationhood	Construction of an anti-imperialist and anti-capitalist popular social block	World market ultimate determinant of economic efficiency and social rationality; only "fittest" survive.	Enhances market, state, and network–trust-based coordination, supportive of globalization processes
Task 3: Dissolve Oppositional Acts	State-led national development praised as essential for nationhood; multi-class coalitions including industrialists, urban middle classes and unionized workers to oppose landlords and oligarchy	National sovereignty and anti-imperialist revolution through armed struggle if necessary	Resistance to liberalization painted as "rent-seeking" behavior and "populism" resistance overcome through State terrorism and strengthening State authoritarianism	Construction of broadly based national consensus behind export sector and quest for international competitiveness

Figure 8. (Continued) Development theories and regimes of accumulation.

export-oriented and globalized economies. Thus, it is not a particular policy component per se nor specific concepts alone that allow us to deconstruct these theories; it is rather their historical embeddedness as they seek to alter societal structures that provides us with the key for understanding them.

A Glimpse into Neostructuralism's Role

We can now bring together the different strands of analysis to historicize the relationship between neostructuralist economic discourse and capitalist restructuring in an attempt to answer the questions posed at the beginning of this chapter.

When does neostructuralism manage to take flight, soaring into discursive and policy relevance? Latin American neostructuralism emerges as a convincing economic discourse and development framework in the transition from an ISI to an EO regime of accumulation. More specifically, it is able to rise to predominance in a country once the first two stages of capitalist restructuring—"stabilization" and "structural transformations"—have been completed. Neostructuralism can display the full range of discourse potency when a country is ready to enter into the third stage of "legitimization of the reforms and restoration of investment levels." It is at this stage when neostructuralism's concern for the role of institutions, politics, culture, and its emphasis on consensus-building can resonate most powerfully.

What historical role is Latin American neostructuralism called to play? Based on the insights drawn from the FRS, we can see that neostructuralism is better prepared conceptually and politically to establish mechanisms that will enable the regulation of conflicts within limits compatible with social cohesion. Despite the rich palette of policies and instruments Latin American neostructuralism deploys toward this end, such an effort is not exempt of contradictions, as we will see in the following chapters.

Under what conditions and constraints does Latin American neostructuralism carry out its role? Latin American neostructuralism carries out its Herculean task of reorganizing, reorienting, and recalibrating[10] the role of the state and political culture under the constraints imposed by the new export-oriented regime of accumulation (Jessop 2002). The structural characteristics of export-oriented accumulation and social reproduction, in which economic surplus is produced and appropriated by an ever smaller transnationalized minority, undermines both the coherence of an essentially nonantagonistic development discourse as well as the margin of maneuver for equity and social cohesion-enhancing policies. These cannot step over clearly delimited property rights or transnational flows, but they must attempt to fulfill their objectives by tapping into the social capital and resources from the noneconomic realm. In other words, effective social policy rests more on operating at the symbolic, subjective, and socio-emotional levels than in just producing a significant reallocation of resources or assets.

The insights gleaned from this first approximation at historicizing Latin American neostructuralism are very general. A more richly textured vision is to be accomplished by examining the concrete experience of Latin American neostructuralism's emergence in Chile and Brazil, as well as by reviewing how its core concepts and foundational myths enable it to perform the historical task it has set for itself in the region.

4

Neostructuralism in Chile and Brazil

The March 1990 inauguration of Patricio Aylwin marked a turning point for Latin American economic development theory and Chilean politics. While for Chileans it brought the long-sought end to almost seventeen years of Augusto Pinochet's military regime, for Latin America and the Caribbean Aylwin's election heralded the hemispheric debut of a new development discourse—Latin American neostructuralism. With the return of civilian rule in 1990, Chile became the birthplace, the testing ground, and arguably the showcase for neostructuralism in the Americas. Economists and planners from the United Nation's Economic Commission for Latin America and the Caribbean (ECLAC), headquartered in Santiago, have influenced and shaped economic and social discourse and policy during three consecutive Chilean administrations—Aylwin (1990–93), Frei (1994–89), and Lagos (2000–2005)—occupying key cabinet posts and economic policy making positions.

Coinciding with the publication of *Changing Production Patterns with Social Equity* by ECLAC, the inauguration of Chile's first *Concertación* administration provided neostructuralism with its first opportunity to prove its mettle. After being shut out for almost two decades, ECLAC economists found in Chile's Aylwin government a breach in the neoliberal wall; ECLAC's ideas once again could contribute to formulate public policies and shape economic development discourse in the region. Aylwin's 1990 inauguration, thus, contributed to launch into the public sphere of economic ideas and thinking that, up until then, only had circulated within the narrow confines of ECLAC insiders. Chile provided the first opportunity for emergent Latin American neostructuralism to influence public policy in Latin America. Emerging from a decade of defensive postures, perplexity, and internal disarray, the year 1990 became a critical turning point for ECLAC in its efforts to restore its prestige and regain intellectual leadership in Latin American political and economic development debates. By gaining a governmental toehold in Chile's nascent Concertación administration, Latin American neostructuralists initiated a sustained process that over the coming decade and half would successfully dispute the intellectual terrain from an ailing neoliberal orthodoxy; the experience in Chile would contribute to expand neostructuralism's stature and legitimacy within the international economic development establishment.

Twelve years after Aylwin's election, on January 1, 2003, an equally momentous presidential inauguration unfolded in Brazil. For the first time in Latin America's history, a worker, a militant trade-unionist and founder of the Workers' Party (Partido dos Trabalhadores [PT]), was sworn in as president of the world's ninth largest economy. Latin American neostructuralism then faced the unique opportunity of exercising its influence over the largest and most important country in the region. In Brazil as in Chile, the electorate supported a candidate promising to lead the country down a different post-neoliberal path. José Genoíno, president of PT, assured that the hopes for a new model of development were to be realized through a gradual transition "without ruptures or traumas" (Genoíno 2004).

This chapter compares and contrasts Latin American neostructuralism's influence in these two emblematic but markedly different countries. Such analysis highlights important traits of Latin American neostructuralism's ascending trajectory, probing some of the strengths and weaknesses evidenced when it has had to face real world demands. The comparative analysis undertaken in this chapter accomplishes four important tasks. First, it locates historically the appearance of Latin American neostructuralism's discourse of changing productive structures with social equity in a specific stage of capitalist restructuring during the transition from the import substitution industrialization (ISI) model to the current export-oriented (EO) model. Such a framework is used then to contrast the role of neostructuralism in Chile, the pioneer of a restructuring process initiated in the mid-1970s by the military, with the role played in Brazil, the region's latecomer to neoliberal reforms in the 1990s. Second, it gauges the ability of Latin American neostructuralism to address the challenges of export-led growth and social equity in two very different contexts: a small resource-intensive highly liberalized economy in the case of Chile, and a huge, complex, and manufacturing EO economy in the case of Brazil. Third, the comparative analysis of these two countries highlights the similarities and differences in the mechanisms and channels through which ECLAC's new ideas and development approach influenced governments and policy making. Finally, the analysis presented in this chapter illustrates how in both countries the passage from the margins to the center entailed significant concessions leading to a hollowing out of neostructuralist discourse at least as originally formulated. In other words, when confronted with the recalcitrant realities of class power, neostructuralist discourse in Chile and Brazil followed a similar route: subordination of its avowed commitment to equity to the ironclad requirements of defending the capitalist profit rate and a transnationalized EO economic growth.

It behooves us then to define the social and political situation existing in both Chile and Brazil at the time of neostructuralism's emergence and its efforts to expand its influence and take the center stage. Historicizing Latin American neostructuralism by placing it in the context of the process of capitalist restructuring allows us to link its ascent and influence to the particular timing and sequencing of the restructuring process in each country. This approach enables us to solve one of the great conundrums emerging from neostructuralism's trajectory in Latin America: its overwhelming influence in Chile and its rather limited impact in Brazil so far. Given the economic disparities (small resource economy vs. industrial powerhouse) and political differences (timid center-left, no significant social movements, powerful legacy of the military regime vs. ascending left, powerful social movements, and popular mandate for change) separating Chile and Brazil, one would expect a much different result. Such a surprising outcome is partly explained by the dissimilar pace and trajectory of the restructuring of the ISI regime of accumulation in each country.

Neostructuralism and Chile's Concertación Administration

Latin American neostructuralism's path from outcast to influential player was blazed first in Chile, and this has influenced the subsequent trajectory of Latin American neostructuralism in a number of ways. By 1990, when both Latin American neostructuralism and Chile's first civilian-elected government emerged, Chile had already completed the first two stages of the restructuring process required to make the transition from an ISI to an EO regime of accumulation. Serving as the intellectual wellspring for a government coming into office after a military regime, capitalizing on a wave of a democratic mobilizations and a negotiated transition to civilian rule, Latin American neostructuralism was thrust into the public arena in a country where the bulk of neoliberal structural reforms were already carried out. In the following years, Chile provided neostructuralism with valuable lessons about the possibilities and constraints for economic change in a post-neoliberal era.

Having its headquarters in Santiago and nurturing close contacts with opposition leaders to Pinochet, ECLAC senior staff became acutely aware of the importance of signaling a clear break with dogmatic neoliberalism and the authoritarian past. At the same time, as front-row observers both to the export-led boom experienced by the Chilean economy after 1985 and the negotiated transition from civilian to military rule, ECLAC policy makers were equally sensitive to the importance of providing adequate assurances and guarantees to Chile's *poderes fácticos*, the powerful alliance of transnational investors, exporters, conservative leaders of the Chilean conglomerates or *grupos económicos*, and the military high command that had risen to predominance in previous decades under Pinochet. The conditions under which the transition from military to a civilian regime took place in Chile underscored one important fact: though enrobed with a genuine concern for social equity, neostructuralist and Concertación policies could not appear as threatening the underlying economic status quo, a favorable climate for foreign investment, or any of the other basic determinants of capitalist profits in the open economy hewn by the Pinochet regime. To the contrary, success hinged upon demonstrating that the incoming neostructuralist-aligned economic team could provide political stability and greater access to global markets for the alliance of transnational productive and financial investors and the domestic conglomerates that then (and more so now) dominated the Chilean economy.

Thus, despite its relatively small-sized economy and resource-intensive export profile, Chile provides an excellent case study for assessing the impact of neostructuralism in the region. In fact, for the past decade and a half (1990–2005), neostructuralist notions and policy makers closely linked to ECLAC have played a decisive role in shaping the economic and social policies of the first three Concertación governments and their attempts to deliver "growth with equity" while promoting increased opening of the economy to international trade and capital flows. As during much of the twentieth century, today Chile is a laboratory where contending political projects and development paradigms are first launched and tested before being exported to the rest of the region. Macroeconomic success, political stability, export dynamism, and reductions in poverty levels have transformed Chile into a model of policies to be followed elsewhere. International financial markets have repeatedly bestowed praise upon Chile's post–Pinochet policy planners, rating Chile with one of the lowest country risk indicators in the world (see Table 1).

TABLE 1

Chile: Selected macroeconomic and social indicators

YEAR	GDP	FIXED GROSS CAPITAL FORMATION AS % OF GDP	EXPORTS	INFLATION	COUNTRY RISK EMBI**	UNEMPLOYMENT NATIONAL	POVERTY INDIVIDUALS BELOW POVERTY LINE (%)	INEQUALITY RATIO OF AVERAGE HOUSEHOLD INCOME 10 TH DECILE/ DECILES 1–4
1990	3.3	23.1	8.6	26.0	–	7.8	38.6	18.2
1991	7.3	19.9	12.4	21.8	–	–	–	–
1992	10.8	22.4	13.9	15.4	–	–	–	–
1993	6.9	24.9	3.5	12.6	–	–	–	–
1994	5.0	23.3	11.6	11.6	–	–	27.6	–
1995	9.0	23.9	11.0	8.2	–	7.4	–	––
1996	6.9	24.9	11.8	7.6	–	6.4	23.2	18.3
1997	6.7	26.4	11.2	5.9	–	6.1	–	–
1998	3.3	27.1	5.2	5.1	–	6.4	23.3	–
1999	-0.5	26.1	7.3	3.3	145	9.8	–	–
2000	4.5	20.8	5.1	3.8	228	9.2	20.2	18.7
2001	3.5	20.7	7.2	3.6	176	9.1	–	–
2002	2.0	21.6	1.6	2.5	168	9.0	–	–
2003	3.3	21.2	6.5	2.8	86	8.5	18.7	18.8
2004*	6.2	22.2	11.7	2.4	68	10.0	–	–
2005*	6.3	25.8	3.5	3.7	77	9.2	–	–
2006*	4.4	–	4.2	2.1	87	7.9	–	–

Source: ECLAC: *Statistical Yearbook of Latin America and the Caribbean 2005*
* 2004-2006 Data from CEPAL, *Balance Preliminar de la Economía Latinoamericanas y del Caribe 2006* (December)
** JP Morgan, *Emerging Market Bond Index*

Of course some might argue that my analysis unjustly places on neo-structuralism's shoulders shortcomings specific only to the Chilean case. Though such risk evidently exists, the launching and later evolution of Latin American neostructuralism are inextricably linked to the Chilean experience. There are three main reasons why Chile is essential for understanding neostructuralism discursive potency and, at the same time, for gaining insight into the inherent weaknesses of this new "post-neoliberal" development discourse. First, ECLAC economists and ECLAC affiliated intellectuals have had an inordinate level of influence on Chile's Concertación governments. Aylwin himself acknowledged the pivotal role of neostructuralism in providing his 1990–93 government (and the two subsequent Concertación administrations) with a key plank of its program: "the policy of *growth with equity* that constituted one of the pillars of my administration was inspired by ECLAC and I believe that we implemented with a high degree of success" (Fromin 2001). Second, as the region's pioneer in neoliberal restructuring, Chile was also at the forefront in illustrating the exhaustion both of dogmatic neoliberalism as a politico-economic discourse and the natural resource EO regime of accumulation; in other words, no other country offered neostructuralism a better opportunity to display its ability to fill those discursive and policy voids evidenced by neoliberalism. Third, Chile's political, economic, and public policy experience has contributed to the conformation of a unique, symbiotic relationship among Chilean economic policy makers, party-affiliated think-tanks, and international development agencies, such as ECLAC, Inter-American Development Bank (IDB), the World Bank, the International Monetary Fund (IMF), and the International Labour Organization (ILO). This veritable epistemic community, and the intense exchange of ideas within it, has created a dense transnational public policy apparatus where economic and public policies are designed, tested, assessed, repackaged, and circulated as *le dernier cri*, the latest product to grace the stalls of the international development bazaar.[1]

ECLAC's Invisible Hand in Chile

Chile's progressive and Left economists, those who were not assassinated, disappeared, or exiled by the Pinochet regime, found in the Santiago offices of UN agencies like ECLAC and the ILO an intellectual and material haven to weather the combined forces of the market and state terrorism, the twin forces that profoundly restructured Chilean society and people's daily life during the 1973–89 period. As Chilean economist Alejandro Foxley, Finance Minister under Aylwin and Foreign Minister under Bachelet, points out, it would not be an exaggeration to state that "in Chile, every economists who does not fully accept orthodoxy in one way or another, has either worked in or will end up working for the International Labor Organization." (Foxley 2003, 22; my translation). Either through direct employment, consulting services, or working relationships established with the various nongovernmental research centers, such as the *Corporación de Estudios para Latinoamérica*

(CIEPLAN, Corporation of Latin American Studies), the *Centro de Estudios para el Desarrollo* (CED, Center for Development Studies), and Chile Siglo 21, among others, ECLAC and the ILO offices in Santiago contributed to ensure the continuity of intellectual work critical to the Pinochet regime. Given that heterodox economics departments were closed by the military and heterodox economists were fired from the Chilean university system, institutions like ECLAC and the ILO offered an essential space for their personal and professional survival. Economists and social scientists critical of the neoliberal Chicago boys could find employment only in UN-sponsored agencies or externally funded nongovernmental institutions that, in the midst of a conceptual and political counterrevolution, looked to ECLAC as a beacon of alternative thinking.

It is not surprising therefore, that ECLAC and neostructuralism held a high level of influence in the first three of the *Concertación* governments after the end of the military regime. When at the end of 1997, a Chilean right-wing weekly magazine interviewed José Antonio Ocampo, Colombia's former Finance Minister who was newly appointed as the Executive Secretary of ECLAC, and asked him to provide concrete evidence that the "new ECLAC" had fully exorcised its state *dirigiste* past, he replied, "Simple things like the fact that the last three Presidents of the Chile's Central Bank—Andrés Bianchi, Roberto Zahler, and Carlos Massad—have all come from the ranks of ECLAC" (Soza 1998; my translation).

The migration of ECLAC functionaries to *Concertación* ministries has been an important and ongoing process during the first three Concertación administrations (see Figure 9). If the data included short-term or project-based consultants, the scope of ECLAC's influence and the overlap with high-level cadre occupying Concertación government posts would be significantly larger.

During the Aylwin government, a first wave of ECLAC functionaries swept into government posts, including Andrés Bianchi, Ricardo Ffrench-Davis, Carlos Massad, Sergio Molina, and Roberto Zahler, taking over key posts in the Central Bank and social ministries. It is perhaps during president Ricardo Lagos's administration, with the shifting of the coalition's center of gravity from Christian Democratic to the Socialist Party–Party for Democracy axis that the flow between ECLAC and the Concertación government expanded most significantly. Under President Lagos, ECLAC functionaries like Ernesto Ottone and Eugenio Lahera moved into the Moneda presidential palace, becoming key advisors on strategic political and public policy

Name	ECLAC Post	Concertación Government Posts
Concertacion I: Aylwin (1990–93)		
Andres Bianchi	• Deputy Executive Secretary of ECLAC (1988-1989) • Director Economic Development Division (1981–88)	• Central Bank Governor (1989–91) • Ambassador to the United States (2000–2005)
Ricardo Ffrench-Davis	• Principal Regional Advisor (1992–present)	• Director of Research, Central Bank (1990–92)
Carlos Massad	• Consultant, Project Coordinator, Adjunct Executive Secretary (1974–92)	• Minister of Health (1993) • Central Bank President, Governor (1996–2007)
Sergio Molina	• Project Director Poverty in Latin America (1975–83)	• Minister of Planning (1990–93)
Roberto Zahler	• Chief Regional Advisor for Monetary and Financial Policy (1984–89) • ECLAC/UNDP Projects (1978–84)	• Central Bank President, Governor(1991–96)
Concertacion II: Frei (1994–99)		
Nicolas Eyzaguirre	• Expert on Monetary and Financial Policy (1985–90)	• Director of Research Central Bank (1990–97)
Concertacion III: Lagos (2000–2005)		
Nicolas Eyzaguirre		• Minister of Finance (1999-2005)

Continued on next page

Figure 9. The revolving door: migration from ECLAC to Chile's Concertación government posts. Compiled by author from various news sources.

Name	ECLAC Post	Concertación Government Posts
Concertacion III: Lagos (2000–2005)		
Eugenio Lahera	• Advisor on Public Policies (1987–2000) • Technical Secretary for CEPAL Review (1987–2000)	• Chief Advisor to the President for Public Policies (2000–2005)
Ernesto Ottone	• Secretary of the ECLAC Commission	• Chief Advisor to the President for Strategic Planning (1999–2005)
Osvaldo Rosales	• Officer Economic Affairs (1990–2000) • Adjunct Director for Training ILPES (1990–2000)	• Director General for External Economic Relations, Ministry of Foreign Relations (1999–2005) • Co-Coordinator of the Economic Program for Frei Campaign (1993) • Coordinator Economic Program Lagos Campaign (1999)

Figure 9. (Continued) The revolving door: migration from ECLAC to Chile's Concertación government posts. Compiled by author from various news sources.

Note: Andres Bianchi and Roberto Zahler also held top post in important transnational private banks. Bianchi was Chairman of the Dresden Banque Nationale de Paris in Chile (1996–2000) and Chairman of Credit Lyonnais Chile (1992–96). Roberto Zahler is a Board member of Banco Santander-Chile, and Chairman of the Advisory Board of Deutsche Bank Americas Bond Fund (New York). Ricardo Ffrench-Davis, Ernesto Ottone, and Osvaldo Rosales have returned to ECLAC after serving on the Lagos administration.

issues to the Chilean president. Nicolás Eyzaguirre took over the Ministry of Finance, and Osvaldo Rosales played a key role in negotiating free trade agreements with the United States and other countries. Rosales, Ottone, and Lahera each played an important role in fashioning ECLAC's research agenda and neostructuralist development discourse during the late 1980s and 1990s. As a result of this migration of high-level functionaries, the mutual influence between the Concertación and Latin American neostructuralism became much more intense in Chile after 2000, inextricably linking their successes and failures. It is probable that such bonds will continue in the future as Ffrench-Davis, Ottone, and Rosales have returned to ECLAC, where they will inject Chile's Concertación experience into the dissemination of neostructuralist discourse in the region.[2] Paradoxically, this relationship ended, weakening the progressive character of Latin American neostructuralism.

Symbiotic Relationships, Epistemic Community, and Hegemony

The design and application of economic and social policies in a context of profound societal transformations under the military and civilian regimes has produced in Chile a battle-hardened cadre of state managers and technocrats with a vast wealth of experience. As a result, a symbiotic relationship between Chile's state managers and those from the international development establishment formed. Growing coordination, mutual support, circulation of staff, joint publications, consultancies, and training programs have established solid linkages among Chilean economic policy makers, party-affiliated think-tanks, and international development agencies, such as ECLAC, IDB, the IMF, the ILO, the Organization of American States (OAS), and the World Bank. During the past eighteen years of Concertación administration, Chile's political elites and progressive economists influenced by Latin American neostructuralism have become the consumers and producers of development discourse and policies. After being tested in Chile, these are enthusiastically circulated and hawked in the international development marketplace supported by the Chilean narrative of successfully combining growth, political stability, and equity.[3] Prominent Concertación technocrats and policy makers have risen to occupy the highest leadership posts in key international agencies. Eduardo Aninat, former Finance Minister under Eduardo Frei, became the IMF's Managing Deputy Director from 1999 to 2003; Juan Somavía is the current Director General of the ILO; and José Miguel Insulza, a cabinet member under both Eduardo Frei and Ricardo Lagos, is the current Secretary General of the OAS. Below these prominent figures, one can find dozens of midlevel international staff members that circulate between employment in international development agencies, high level positions in Concertación administrations and private consulting activities, and the directorships of domestic and transnational conglomerates.

Neostructuralism in the Tropics

The Case of Brazil

Beginning in the 1950s, structuralism and *cepalismo* shaped generations of Brazilian economists and policy makers, achieving in Brazil a degree of influence unparalleled in other countries of the region. Nonetheless, by the 1990s and especially during the first five years of the twenty-first century, the influence of Latin American neostructuralism and of the new ECLAC has been much weaker in Brazil than in Chile. At first glance, this seems like a surprising outcome. After all, the size, level of development, complexity, and extensive manufacturing base of the Brazilian economy, along with the existence of a progressive administration led by Luis Inácio da Silva and the Workers' Party or PT, would seem like an ideal environment for the neostructuralist paradigm to take root and flourish. Yet fathoming the reasons behind the meager influence of ECLAC's new paradigm in Brazil provides important insights about the role of Latin American neostructuralism itself, the restructuring of Brazilian economy and society, and the interrelationship between economic ideas and policy formulation.

Structuralism's Weight in Brazil

The power exercised by structuralism in Brazil during bygone decades can be explained by two major factors. Undoubtedly the first of these is the towering influence of Celso Furtado, one of the pioneers of ECLAC who from the very beginning was a close collaborator of Raúl Prebisch. Furtado's work, *Formação Econômica do Brasil (The Economic Growth of Brazil)*, published in 1959 contributed to the fleshing out of the nascent structuralist paradigm, helping to overcome two of its principal weaknesses at the time: "(1) the structuralist analytical framework was insufficiently articulated and organized and (2) it was essential to demonstrate that the historical evolution of those countries that in the mid-twentieth century continued being underdeveloped, was necessarily different from that of developed countries" (Bielschowsky 1989, 39; my translation). Furtado is credited by economic historians, like Bielschowsky, with producing the first structuralist interpretation of Brazilian underdevelopment, highlighting how it could be traced to the absence of a dynamic domestic entrepreneurial class, the relation between the composition of employment, income distribution, and the development of the internal market. Furtado played a key role in providing structuralism with a more coherent analytic framework. His work during the 1950s and 1960s gave an added coherence to structuralism by (1) incorporating a long-run historical perspective; (2) showing that underemployment was a structural result of the difficulties of modern urban sectors to absorb a growing labor force leaving the countryside, so that increases in output could coexist with persistent low wages and an unequal distribution of income; and (3) focusing on the indissoluble relationship between economic growth and income distribution, arguing that "the concentration of income and property predetermined the sectoral composition of investment and technology choice" deepening structural heterogeneity of the economy and society (Bielschowsky 2006, 10; my translation).

Beyond Furtado's indisputable intellectual influence, structuralism took root in Brazil mainly because it provided a coherent discourse, analytical tools, and a set of policies to guide and propel forward the process of industrialization already under way since the 1930s. Structuralism offered a rationale and a narrative for a national-developmentalist project of state-led industrialization that captured the interests of a broad array of classes, particularly the emerging manufacturing bourgeoisie that supported the idea of industrialization. Close contacts between structuralists and the Brazilian business class were established through a series of consulting activities carried out by structuralists for leading industrial business federations and confederations throughout the 1950s and 1960s (Mantega 1989). Brazil's business associations also supported structuralist ideas, because structuralism's national development discourse provided the ideological foundations for making the specific interests of the industrial bourgeoisie appear as the universal interests of the nation (Mantegna 1989).

Coherence, timeliness, and ability to respond to the needs of the moment created the conditions for the rise to predominance of the structuralist discourse in Brazil. Economists and social scientists schooled in Prebisch and Furtado's "historico-structural" approach and commitment to a national development project based in ISI gained important institutional toeholds in the state bureaucracy as well as in academia.

In Brazil, the joint group Comissão Econômica para a América Latina-Banco Nacional do Desenvolvemiento Econômico e Social (CEPAL-BNDES, Economic Commission for Latin America and National Bank for Economic and Social Development) was created in 1953 under the directorship of Celso Furtado and with the participation of economists like Roberto Campos and Cleantho de Paiva Leite. During the 1960–64 period, the Center for Economic Development CEPAL/BNDES was led by prominent Chilean structuralists Aníbal Pinto and Osvaldo Sunkel. In addition to collecting data supporting the preparation of the annual survey published by ECLAC, the Center also carried a training program first in Rio and later in the north and south of Brazil (Figueiredo 1990). The center has been recognized as playing an important role in the formation of influential economists, who to this day have remained faithful to the visions of structuralists, such as Maria Conceição Tavares, Carlos Lessa, and Antonio Barros de Castro (Tavares 1996).

The influence of ECLAC and of structuralist thinking reached not only state institutions, like the Banco Nacional de Desenvolvimento Econômico e Social or Brazilian Development Bank (BNDES), the Superintendencia do Desenvolvimiento do Nordeste (SUDENE, Agency for the Development of Brazil's Northeast), and the Instituto de Pesquisa Econômica Aplicada (IPEA, Institute for Applied Economic Research) linked to the Ministry of Planning, but structuralist ideas also played an important and instrumental role in the creation of economic departments such as the Economics departments at the State University of Campinas (Universidade Estadual de Campinas [UNICAMP]), Universidade Federal de Rio do Janeiro (UFRJ) and the Universidade Fluminense (Tavares 1996). Due in part to structuralism's influence in earlier decades, heterodox economic thinking finds institutional support in spaces provided by the state bureaucracy and academia.

Structuralism's declining influence has received different interpretations. Within Brazil, Luiz Bresser-Pereira has claimed that over time structuralism became severely distorted "on account of the populist conversion that it suffered at the hands of incompetent politicians and second level propagandists" (Pereira 2001, 9). As we will see, this seems like a flimsy explanation for the eclipse of the structuralist economic paradigm and the abandonment of Prebisch's "historico-structural" approach and the "historico-regionalist-structuralist" approach developed by Celso Furtado for Brazil (Mendes and Teixera 2004). A more convincing explanation is necessary, particularly since it was economists and sociologists like Fernando Henrique Cardoso, Carlos Serra, and Luiz Bresser-Pereira who worked in the structuralist and dependency traditions and who, in the 1990s, would become the architects of the destruction of the ISI model and of the neoliberal inspired restructuring of Brazilian capitalism.

Even though many economists and social scientists influenced by structuralist thinking sought exile in Chile after Brazil's 1964 military coup, the nature of the Brazilian military regime differed markedly from Chile's. Unlike the Chilean junta led by Pinochet, the Brazilian military did not seek to refound Brazilian capitalism along neoliberal lines. On the contrary, Brazil's military governments were a last ditch and ultimately failed attempt to relaunch the state-directed national development project by replacing a national–popular class alliance as its social base with a new alliance of transnational corporations, local elites, and the state. As one Brazilian analysts points out, "if the 1980s continued being a decade of crisis and undefinition over the paths of our national development, it is indisputable that, during the second half of the 1970s, the Geisel government, going against the prevailing ideological tide and an unfavorable national economy, it was the last of Latin America's developmentalist governments, and certainly, the most representative of the dreams of Prebisch and ECLAC from the end of the 1940s" (Fiori 1992, 80).

Paradoxically, this lack of historical simultaneity between military regimes, neoliberalism, and capitalist restructuring in Brazil, as opposed to the synchronicity in Chile, becomes critical for understanding the Brazilian puzzle and the still feeble influence of Latin American neostructuralism "in the tropics." Whereas in Chile the military regime brought about a profound restructuring of class relations and created conditions so that the most dynamic fractions of the bourgeoisie could impose their domination and later hegemony over Chilean society, expelling heterodox economic thinking from academic and state institutions in the process, in Brazil realignments in the patterns of capital accumulation and in the structure and functions of the state were to be attempted long after the military had returned to their barracks. Unlike the Chilean military closely advised by the disciples of Milton Friedman known as the "Chicago boys," for the Brazilian military purging heterodox economic thinking from all aspects of social life never became the prime of objective of national security. Neoliberal restructuring in Brazil was to begin in earnest after 1990, the year in which ECLAC launched its neostructuralist paradigm. The late nature of capitalist restructuring in Brazil led to a veritable dance of masks and discursive transformations: the strategic interests of the Brazilian capitalist class in restructuring Brazilian society were not represented *manu militari* or by its traditional political and intellectual representatives of old. The unfinished task of establishing the new basis for capital accumulation, a new hegemony, and the corresponding state institutions could not find its expected protagonists. In comparison to Chile's experience, the casting director of the Brazilian drama, seemed to have scrambled the script: the military are entrusted with extending the exhausted ISI regime of accumulation, not with destroying its foundations. An internationally acclaimed dependency theoretician such as Fernando Henrique Cardoso is entrusted with bringing about neoliberal stabilization and neoliberal structural reforms, replaced later in that role by *Lula*, Latin America's first worker and trade unionist elected to office.

This staggered (and to some staggering) manner in which the political representation of the historical requirements for restructuring Brazilian capitalism has unfolded creates a challenging context in which to evaluate the influence and role of economic ideas there. Heterodox and anti-neoliberal economists in Brazil have not embraced Latin American neostructuralism in part because, as Ricardo Bielschowsky points out, "they have been unwilling to accept ECLAC's compromise with trade liberalization and privatization, or at least they were not until such process had been concluded."[4] In short, unlike Chile, economists have not had to abjure from their heterodox past (Marxist, structuralist, institutionalist, post-Keynesian) nor has consensus about the future path for Brazil's development been forthcoming. Different observers explain the absence of such a consensus by pointing to the current system of institutional incentives that render both right-wing and social democratic forces as "too weak, too disorganized, and too unimaginative to envision an alternative to neoliberalism" at the same time that "the conservative periphery and its clientelist networks have thrived under current institutions and, in so doing, have made themselves an indispensable political ally" of the governing coalitions (Schneider 2003, 96). Yet such problems in the political realm must also be explained by considering the lack of renewal on the level of economic ideas and the weak catalyzing role that the sluggish expansion of the Brazilian economy has played in encouraging such convergence. The best path for the future expansion of Brazilian capitalism remains unclear and still contested. Unlike Chile, where the center–left's embrace of neostructuralist ideas enabled it to play a key historical role in consolidating and legitimizing the new EO regime of accumulation, in Brazil center–left intellectuals like Fernando Henrique and many in the PT were saddled with the historical task of implementing rather than legitimizing neoliberal restructuring. Hence, more progressive economists have not engaged in the intellectual and methodological retreats that would lead them into the arms of neostructuralism; those in policy positions in the state apparatus have found little worth, at least so far, in the full scale adoption of neostructuralist formulations.

Constraints on Neostructuralism

To probe the reasons for neostructuralism's current weak influence in Brazil we need to review the interaction between the stage of capitalist restructuring, the institutional basis of heterodox economists, and the Politico-economic context and their interplay specific to the Brazilian case.

1. *Stage of restructuring.* The completion in Chile of the first and second stage of capitalist restructuring enabled toward the mid-1980s the emergence of a consensus about the future direction of the Chilean economy. Alejandro Foxley and other critics of the Chicago Boys acknowledged that neoliberal reforms had finally woken up the "animal spirits" of Chilean capitalists. In light of high economic growth and export rates posted in the second half of the 1980s, many former critics of neoliberalism became celebrants of the economic model. In the case of Brazil, however, which only started sustained neoliberal restructuring in the 1990s, the process of structural reforms of the Brazilian economy has not been successfully completed yet, and the consensus about the future path that could be engendered in part by a record of sustained economic growth of the Brazilian economy has not been forthcoming (Pinheiro 2003). No long-term consensus or widespread political commitment to a development model exists in Brazil from business associations, political leaders, and economists. Consequently, because consensus among elites and the political class is nonexistent, the traction, appeal, and political advantages to be gained from deploying ECLAC's neostructuralist discourse is not at all clear.

2. *Institutional basis of heterodox economic thought.* In Brazil the nature of the military coup and the ability of heterodox economists to retain an institutional basis both in the state apparatus, as well as academic settings, meant that opposition to neoliberal ideas did not have only a neostructuralist repertoire through which to express itself. Over the two past decades heterodox economists in Brazil became neo-Keynesian, neo-Schumpeterian, or Marxists, and their institutional basis of support were not reduced only to what ECLAC or ECLAC-related think tanks could provide. In stark contrast to Chile's traumatized intellectuals and economists, for whom ECLAC headquarters in Santiago served both as beacon and life raft during the Pinochet dictatorship, the influence of neostructuralism in Brazil followed a very different path. Instead of exercising its influence through the migration of key individuals from ECLAC offices to cabinet posts as in Chile, the ECLAC office in Brazil was able to establish long-term institutional relationships with key agencies of the state as well as with academia. The unwillingness of heterodox and anti-neoliberal economists to

fully and uncritically embrace Latin American neostructuralism therefore has many reasons: the timing of neoliberal reforms, the lack of neoliberal hegemony and subsequent disavowal of structuralist ideas, and the diversity in the academic formation, career paths, and political connections available to Brazilian economists. In sum, ECLAC and Latin American neostructuralism did not become the intellectual magnet, personal lifeboat, and fountainhead that it did in Chile.

3. *The Politico-economic context.* A final element behind the weak attractive force exercised by Latin American neostructuralism in Brazil is found in the politico-economic context. Despite encouraging signs at the beginning of the Plano Real in 1994, most economic indicators show that, on balance, Brazil achieved dismal economic results during the 1990s. In fact, during the 1997–2003 period, Brazil only grew at an annual average of 2.2 percent, and the rate of investment measured by the Gross Fixed Capital Formation as a percentage of GDP declined from 20.7 percent in 1994 to 17.8 percent in 2003, while unemployment steadily climbed from 4.6 percent to close to 12 percent over the same period (see Table 2).

The exhaustion of the ISI model of development and of the developmentalist state became clearly evident in the 1980s as a crisis of military rule. However, clarity about the path out of that dual crisis has been slow and confusing. Thus two important differences from the Chilean experience are of note. First, unlike Chile, structuralist economists in Brazil have not completely and fully converted into neostructuralists, renouncing to a national development project in which the state plays a decisive role in steering the accumulation process.[5] Second, the discourse of "growth with equity," though present in Brazilian debates, unfolds in a society lacking a broad-based elite consensus and whose transnational finance capital, unlike Chile's, is still struggling to impose the framework, rules, and overarching logic under which conflicts between growth and equity will always be resolved in its favor. These two elements—the survival of unconverted structuralists and the lack of elite consensus—have shaped economic discourse and policy formulation under two Cardoso administrations (1995–2002) as well as during the first Lula da Silva government (2003–7).

TABLE 2

Brazil: Selected macroeconomic and social indicators

YEAR	GDP 1990 CONSTANT PRICES	GROSS FIXED CAPITAL FORMATION/ GDP	EXPORTS ANNUAL GROWTH RATE*	INFLATION	UNEMPLOYMENT	INEQUALITY RATIO OF POVERTY INDIVIDUALS BELOW POVERTY LINE (%)	AVERAGE HOUSEHOLD INCOME TENTH DECILE/ DECILES 1–4
1990	-4.6	20.7	-8.6	2 862.4	4.3	48.0	31.2
1991	1.0	18.1	0.7	429.9	–	–	–
1992	-0.3	18.4	13.2	981.8	–	–	–
1993	4.5	19.3	7.7	1 936.3	–	45.3	–
1994	6.2	20.7	12.9	2 111.6	–	–	–
1995	4.2	20.5	6.8	66.0	4.6	–	–
1996	2.5	19.3	2.7	15.4	5.4	35.8	32.2
1997	3.1	19.9	11.0	6.1	5.7	–	–
1998	0.2	19.7	-3.5	3.7	7.6	–	–
1999	0.9	18.9	-6.1	5.0	7.6	37.5	32.0
2000	3.9	19.3	14.7	6.2	7.1	–	–
2001	1.3	19.5	5.7	6.8	6.2	37.5	–
2002	1.5	18.3	3.7	8.5	11.7	–	–
2003	0.6	17.8	21.1	14.7	12.3	38.7	27.9
2004**	4.9	18.0	32.0	7.6	11.5	–	–
2005**	2.3	17.9	22.6	5.7	9.8	–	–
2006**	2.8	18.5	–	3.0	10.1	–	–

Source: ECLAC *Statistical Yearbook for Latin America and the Caribbean 2005* (unemployment data is for 6 metropolitan regions)

* Export Data: *Ministerio de Comercio Exterior Evolução do Comércio Exterior Brasileiro e Mundial–1950 / 2005*

** ECLAC, *Preliminary Overview of the Economies of Latin American and Caribbean 2006*

Neostructuralist Influence after 1990

Despite differences in the stages of capitalist restructuring and trajectories in each country's EO regimes, in the institutional basis for heterodox economic thinking, and in political and economic contexts between these two countries, one should not conclude that Latin American neostructuralism has had no influence whatsoever either on the Cardoso or Lula da Silva administrations. On the contrary, neostructuralist themes and strands of policy initiatives have been present throughout the 1990s and during the first half of the 2000s. In fact, a 1992 publication by the *Instituto de Estudos para o Desenvolvimento Industrial* (IEDI) of Sao Paulo, which groups the main national manufacturing firms of the country, echoed many of the themes of the initial neostructuralist agenda (IEDI 1992). Rejecting statism and laissez-faire, it called for drawing from the experience of successful countries in the global economy. In IEDI's view, these showed two specificities: (1) prioritizing of objectives, so that the search for competitiveness appears as the highest priority that subordinates all other goals and policies, and (2) the articulation and cooperation among different actors, a process to which state intervention gives consistency and concreteness to policies transmitting signals primarily through market mechanism to the relevant economic actors (IEDI 1992, 138). As the IEDI report states,

> The dynamism and creativity of private initiative; nimble and flexible entrepreneurial planning; engagement of the labor force in the search for gains in the productivity of labor (proportionally distributed in the form of wage increments); high levels of education and training of workers; structured and prioritized R&D activities' intense and frequent cooperation between firms and technological institutes; excellence in the infrastructure for basic and applied research; are all, the current characteristics of countries that are leading the current industrial revolution. By that set cannot consolidate, and mainly, cannot articulate itself without the coordination role exercised by the State (IEDI 1992, 139; my translation).

Similar themes have also been incorporated into the 2004–7 the Multiyear Plan (*Plan Pluri-Anual* or PPA), a statement on the country's development objectives that, according to the 1988 constitution, each government must submit to Congress for approval. The main objectives of the 2004–7 PPA, "Brazil for All" presented as the strategic development goals of the PT government are reflected in the PPA's three core "macro" objectives: (1) enhanced social inclusion and reduction of inequality; (2) economic growth (5 percent target for 2007) that is environmentally sustainable and reduces regional inequalities; and (3) promoting citizenship and participation, that contributes to better governance and public sector management. The PPA's long-term strategy consists of promoting social inclusion and deconcentration of income with growth of output and job creation, an environmentally sustainable development, a reduction of regional disparities fueled by a rise of mass consumption, investment and increases in productivity, and the clearing for the competitive expansion of activities that overcome external vulnerability. "The five dimensions of the strategy (social, economic, regional, environmental and democratic) represent the macro objectives to be pursued" during the 2004–7 period (*Plano Brasil*).

In the preamble to the Cardoso administration and in the strategic objectives of Lula's 2004–7 Multiyear Plan, neostructuralist themes and ideas therefore are present, though not articulated by neostructuralists themselves. According to Matias Vernengo, "the main economists of Cardoso's *Partido da Social Democracia Brasileira* (Brazilian Social Democracy Party [PSDB]) or Lula's PT with close connections to ECLAC, José Serra in the case of the PSDB and Conceição Tavares in the case of the PT for example, were not key in the policy decisions made after 1994, when the PSDB/PT began dominating Brazilian politics."[6]

Neoliberalism and the Cardoso Administration (1995–2002)

In Chile, a clear divide exists between the predominance of neoliberal and neostructuralist ideas, and there also exists a clear-cut correspondence of these ideas to distinct phases of capitalist restructuring. This is a tribute to the capacity of the Chilean ruling class to rely on Pinochet, the officer corps of the Armed Forces, and economists trained in the image of Milton Friedman to conceptualize and execute the destruction of the ISI model and set the foundations for the new EO regime. Many of the key planks of this transformation were clearly formulated in May 1973 in *El Ladrillo* (*The Brick*), a CIA-funded economic blueprint by conservative Chilean economists, four months before the military coup. In the case of Brazil, such a task, still uninitiated throughout the 1980s, fell in the 1990s on the shoulders of former dependency theorists and structuralists like Fernando Henrique Cardoso.

Cardoso's intimate relationship with ECLAC and neostructuralism allows him to state, "I began and ended my eight years in government in close contact with ECLAC, and this is very important for someone who has always drawn inspiration from that organization's determination to comprehend the reality of Latin America on its own terms" (Cardoso 2004, 8). His invitation to present the Third Annual Raúl Prebisch Memorial Lecture at ECLAC headquarters in Santiago suggests that such feelings of admiration are mutual.

Despite this reaffirmed intellectual affinity with ECLAC, it was up to Cardoso as the minister of finance and later as president to implement neoliberal reforms in Brazil. Even though financial and trade liberalization began in the late 1980s under Collor de Mello, it was not until the adoption of the Plano Real in 1994 that Brazil embraced the neoliberal agenda and the Washington Consensus *tout court* (Vernengo 2003a). Not only was stabilization through a fixed exchange system and the structural surplus rule enforced, but also by opening up the economy it was hoped that exposure to international competition would have toning effects on the Brazilian productive structure resulting from its new exposure to greater competition from imports and an increase in foreign investment in the economy.

It is this hybrid character—neoliberal reforms with neostructuralist discourse—that has led some to describe Cardoso's administration as "pseudo-neoliberalism" or "neoliberalism dressed as the Third Way." In the 1990s, the neoliberal reform program in Brazil was not implemented under the leadership of Chicago-style dogmatic neoliberals but rather under the direction of Fernando Henrique Cardoso. The Plano Real implemented in 1994 while Cardoso was Finance Minister was not just a stabilization attempt, but also one that sought to create an attractive environment for transnational capital (Rocha 2003). For the Cardoso government as for the new ECLAC, transnational capital was considered the key force for restoring investment rates to historic levels and reenergizing economic growth rates. "FDI would perform multiple services to the country: it would help finance balance-of-payments deficits, modernize industrial structures, develop advanced technology, promote productivity and boost the international competitiveness of Brazilian exports. In fact, a central section of the stabilization plan advocated modernization of the economy with the help of foreign capital. To this end, Cardoso recommended elimination of the barriers to foreign companies in the exploitation of natural resources, and to enable multinational corporations to participate in the privatization of strategic state enterprises in the infrastructure sector" (Rocha 2002, 7). Fernando Henrique boasted that in the task of transforming Brazil, "we have something that neither Marx nor Weber nor anyone else imagined—they couldn't have done: capital has internationalized rapidly and is available in abundance. Some countries can take advantage of this excess of capital, and Brazil is one of them" (Rocha 2002, 8).

From the outset, Cardoso's central premise was that only if inflation was slashed would multinationals find Brazil attractive for investment and be able to take advantage of "this excess of capital"; only massive inflows of such productive capital from abroad could provide a new and sound basis for long-term domestic growth. According to this view, foreign direct investment (FDI) flows would provide multiple benefits for Brazil: finance balance-of-payments deficits, modernize industrial structures, develop advanced technology sectors, promote productivity, and boost the international competitiveness of Brazilian exports. To this end, Cardoso implemented a vast program of privatization that eliminated barriers to foreign companies in the exploitation of natural resources and enabled multinational corporations to participate in the privatization of strategic state enterprises in the infrastructure sector (Rocha 2002, 7).

Early evaluations of the Plano Real by Cardoso's team emphasized the beneficial results of compressing stabilization and structural reforms, the first two stages of capitalist restructuring, into the same time period and in triggering a dynamic industrial restructuring process (de Barros and Goldstein 1997). The role of politics in this endeavor of structural transformation was to ensure transparency and build a broad consensus behind such measures. What is also clear is that, in order to take advantage of what "neither Marx nor Weber" imagined, Cardoso and his team had to abandon the concept of economic surplus and the understanding that Brazil's underdevelopment, like his teachers once taught him, had to be understood within the context of the development of capitalism on a world scale.

Neostructuralism, the PT, and Lula (2003–5)

Lula's election in 2002 raised great expectations and hopes that a new course for Brazil's development strategy and entire continent was close at hand. With the support of more that fifty-three million votes, Brazilians expected that Lula would bring about a change in economic policy, establish a new form of more participatory politics, and reorient the economy. Progressive analysts saw the possibility of a new historical reencounter between progressive political parties (such as the Workers' Party), powerful social movements, and an alternative economic policy, which would follow very different lines from the technocratic economics and politics espoused by Fernando Henrique. International financiers and speculators did not expect Lula to win, promoting a vast fear campaign about the tragic consequences voting Lula would bring. In the months preceding the elections, as Lula climbed in the polls, international financier George Soros predicted that if Lula won, the Brazilian Plano Real would face devastating speculative attacks. If elected, Lula would be forced to declare a moratorium on Brazil's debt, thereby precipitating a much larger version of the catastrophe that has been played out in Argentina during 2001. Soros believed that such a prospect would dissuade Brazilians from electing Lula. It was tough, he said, but: "In the Roman empire, only the Romans voted. In modern global capitalism, only the Americans vote. Not the Brazilians" (Hilton 2002).

Proving international speculators wrong, the majority of the Brazilian electorate deposited their hopes for change on Lula. However the first sign that the Lula administration was going to dramatically distance itself from the interests of its popular base arose when practically no economists from the PT or the Left were named to government posts, certainly none closely linked to structuralism or neostructuralism. Government posts went to economists linked to Rio's Fundaçao Getulio Vargas (FGV), "such as Joaquin Levy, Marcos Lisboa, considerably more conservative and who never had connections with ECLAC."[7] The presidency of the Central Bank was given to Henrique Meirelles, a former director of Fleet-Boston and a member of Cardoso's outgoing political party. Continuity with Cardoso's economic policy became evident as the Lula administration moved forward with a proposal to reform social security, going against the wishes of the trade union and social movements like the MST and even expelling PT Congress members that refused to go along.

During 2003 and 2004, the progressive mantle of Lula's economic policy was severely questioned in a series of public statements signed by progressive economists. In late 2003, over three hundred economists linked to the PT, published a manifesto titled *A Agenda Interditada: Uma alternativa de prosperidade para o Brasil*, which calls for a complete reversal of the conceptual matrix guiding Lula government's policy. They suggested adopting policies such as control on capital flows and exchange rates, a gradual reduction of the primary fiscal surplus, an expansion of public expenditures prioritizing job-creating sectors, and a reduction of the base interest rates, exactly the opposite of what the Lula government was doing (Folha de Sao Paulo 2003). Among those signing the manifesto were Luiz Gonzaga Belluzo, Ricardo Carneiro, Reinaldo Goncalves, Plinio de Arruda Sampaio Jr., and Theotonio dos Santos. A year later, PT economists again expressed their criticisms in a document titled "E Nada Mudou" ("And Nothing Changed"). Even more critical than the previous manifesto, the same group of economists indicated that "the slight signs of economic growth do not change the exclusionary and immiserating character of the current economic policy" (*Gazeta de Alagoas* 2004; my translation), going on to add that "the adoption by the Lula government of the same economic policy adopted during the second term of the FHC government—and with the purpose of maintaining the economic model inaugurated by Collor—proves that the desire for change, clearly expressed by the people in the 2002 elections, has been usurped by the same economic power, that wants to preserve its privileges at all cost" (Alia2, 2004; my translation)[8] As in Chile, a progressive discourse that drew on popular aspirations ended being co-opted by a political project ultimately subordinate to the power and requirements of transnational capital.

Conclusion

This chapter has offered an overview of how, after 1990, Latin American neostructuralism moved from the margins to becoming a central player in the construction of development discourse and economic policy formulation in the region. In Chile and Brazil such passage was decisively patterned by the characteristics and timing of capitalist restructuring in each country.

In the case of Chile, the crossover of functionaries from ECLAC to Chilean ministries and cabinet posts began in 1990 and continued over the entire span of the 1990–2005 period. The symbiotic relationship between ECLAC headquarters, the Concertación Governments, and high-level staff at the World Bank, IMF, and other development institutions (IADB, ILO, and OAS among others) has had, as one of its outcomes, the consolidation of a veritable "epistemic community" within which the different schools of thought were able to converge. It has also facilitated the establishment of the Chilean experience as the benchmark of sound macroeconomic management, intelligent political leadership, and effective social policies.

Brazil, on the other hand, during the much shorter 2003–5 period, though offering a much broader material base and better political conditions for the deployment of neostructuralist policies (the existence of a political coalition with a broad mandate and the initial support of the country's powerful social movements), faced severe constraints imposed by its high level of international indebtedness and leverage in the hands of transnational financial capital. Here the influence of a neostructuralist perspective on policy makers has been much more restricted to the social policy arena, as the first two stages of capitalist restructuring have not been fully completed. Likewise, the institutional basis available for heterodox economists has been much broader in Brazil than in Chile, and heterodox economists have not embraced Latin American neostructuralism.

The experience of both of these countries offers a preview of contradictions neostructuralist discourse will face in the rest of the Americas. Brazil and Chile, particularly the latter, provide an excellent case study for assessing the power, performance, shortcomings, and evolution of neostructuralism in the region. The influence of neostructuralism on government discourse and policy design, which is limited in Brazil and extensive in the case of Chile, seems to be determined by (1) the stage of the restructuring process in which each country finds itself; (2) the economic and political context and the opportunities it offers for deploying a discourse promising the "high road" to globalization; and (3) the institutional basis from which neostructuralists as outsiders exercise their influence. These common threads should be attentively followed in neighboring countries where Latin American neostructuralism has gained influence. From the cases of Chile and Brazil examined in this chapter, some salient trends emerge. First, in both countries there has been a retreat from the original claims and promises; neostructuralism proved incapable of offering a status-quo transformative path for overcoming important obstacles in the socioeconomic development of both countries. When push came to shove, the promise giving equal weight and simultaneity to economic growth and social equity, socialists Lagos and Lula did not waver in placing economic growth first. A second trend is the hyperbolization of discourse on citizenship and the role of civil society at the same time that neostructuralist policies reveal their inability and unwillingness to reform the material basis of the existing regime of accumulation or enact any initiative that could be construed as threatening to the profitability of transnational investors. Third, despite a more holistic approach to policy design and the promotion of participatory governance, in both countries, clear limits have been placed to mass participation, ensuring that it is institutionalized and channeled through conduits that do not threaten the status quo.

In the subsequent chapters we explore in greater detail how Latin American neostructuralism's mode of theorizing and acts of omission with respect to power relations deepen its contradictory nature and widen the gaps between its rhetoric and reality. These crevices offer points where the apparent solidity and coherence of Latin American neostructuralism can be pried apart to reveal its weakness and inconsistencies.

5

Foundational Myths, Acts of Omission

Every discourse is the outcome of certain acts of omission and Latin American neostructuralism is no exception. This insight provides us with a valuable entry point for studying neostructuralism and encourages us to formulate the following question, what are the consequences of excising power relations from economic analysis for the internal coherence of neostructuralist discourse? This chapter explores this question by examining the "acts of omission" embedded in five central notions that constitute the very foundations of Latin American neostructuralism. These are (1) the promise of favorable prospects for moving onto the high road to globalization; (2) the promotion of "open regionalism"; (3) the possibility of achieving "changing productive structures with social equity" within the confines of the current export-oriented (EO) regime of accumulation; (4) the purported dichotomy between "spurious" versus "genuine" competitiveness at the firm as well as the country level; and (5) the benefits of achieving international competitiveness through consensus building behind the export drive among different actors.

Studying neostructuralism's foundational myths can also throw light on contemporary debates on Latin American development. How viable are post-neoliberal development strategies such as the "high road" to globalization and "managed openness" that have gained support in Latin America and elsewhere? (See, for example, Weiss 1999). Furthermore, how can a critical political economy perspective that does not eschew power relations contribute to development economics and the formulation of economic development strategy and policies for Latin America? Each of neostructuralism's five foundational myths is assessed in terms of its omissions and the crevices these present through which a critical economy perspective can pry open its rhetorical armor and expose its limitations.

Low and High Roads

A key neostructuralist tenet is that Latin American countries can off-ramp from the "low road" onto the more promising lanes of the "high road" to globalization. Such a switch, neostructuralists claim, would allow countries to break from specialization in natural resource-intensive and cheap-labor exports condemning them to the least dynamic niches of world trade; they could then begin to compete via technological innovation, productivity gains, and higher value-added exports. This shift would transform entire economies and individual export enterprises into radiating hubs that propagate the economic, technological, and social benefits of globalization to the rest of society. If Latin America and Caribbean societies are to travel down this more desirable path, a broader vision of economic development is necessary. Government, institutions, and political systems must be prepared to play a qualitatively different leadership role than in the past. To move onto the high road and achieve "systemic competitiveness," it becomes imperative to transform each firm into a privileged space of cooperation. Cooperation between labor and capital and among different firms, along with the active commitment of the trade unions and business associations to export promotion, innovation, and technological change must complement the inexorable forces of market competition. Social pacts and explicit initiatives to sustain social cohesion, along with productive development policies, must become part of an integrated menu of policies aimed at establishing the type of modern competitiveness associated with setting foot on the high road to globalization (ECLAC 2004).

Such a quest entails embracing "open regionalism," the clunky moniker used by the Economic Commission for Latin America and the Caribbean (ECLAC) to denote the combination of unilateral liberalization with the adoption of a vast range of free trade agreements. Productivity-led export growth and open regionalism would improve the external insertion of Latin American countries and foster the emergence of a productive structure capable of generating productive employment, reducing structural heterogeneity, improving income distribution, and reducing poverty levels. Latin American neostructuralism, therefore, transforms the high road to globalization and the construction of systemic competitiveness into the Holy Grail of economic development; it is the trusty compass that orients the design of public policy and also the foundation for neostructuralism's political discourse for the era of post-neoliberalism. The high road to globalization is, in sum, the overarching narrative offered about Latin America's struggle to reach modernity in the twenty-first century; it is ECLAC's yellow-brick road to the Emerald City.

Latin American neostructuralism's adoption of the low road–high road dichotomy for framing the economic choices faced by Latin America and the Caribbean has been a powerful device for successfully confronting neoliberalism and forging an alternative to the so-called Washington Consensus. This dichotomous low road–high road conception has enabled Latin American neostructuralism to "steal neoliberalism's thunder" by promising the attainment of rapid economic growth, the region's insertion in global economic flows and *at the same time* delivering equity, democracy, and participatory forms governance.

Neostructuralism's rhetoric regarding the high road to globalization allows it to engage in two other important discursive maneuvers. On the one hand, it enables neostructuralism to rescue from oblivion, the role of agency, politics, institutions, consensus-building, and political leadership in shaping a country's placement in the international division of labor. Additionally, the idea that a productivity-led path to globalization can be attained *without major transformations* in the status quo or property relations is implicit. Consensus building and democratic governance are presented not only as outcomes flowing from but also as essential means for gaining passage onto the high road. On the other hand, the high road can be reached only through wise and judicious public policies and changes in social relations (greater trust, cooperation, reliance social capital) that, entailing cultural change and new subjectivities, do not require radically transforming the existing class structure or redistribution of material assets. The historical experience of the "Asian Tigers" (as the fast growing economies of South Korea, Taiwan, Singapore, and Hong-Kong were dubbed) or of Scandinavian countries like Finland and Norway, which successfully transited from natural resource to higher valued-added exports, are extolled as examples Latin America should emulate.

Latin American neostructuralism takes full advantage of the performative potential that the low road–high road dualistic framework offers—we can do better, only small but significant cultural changes (greater adaptability, horizontality, synergy, self-regulation, etc.) inherent to globalization's modernity are required. However, as we saw in chapter 2, such a framework entails a methodological shift away from the historico-structural approach that characterized earlier structuralism. In the low road–high road framework, the obstacles to development nest in the absence of the right set of policies, not in the appropriation of the economic surplus by an elite and its use in ways counter to social needs, as Raúl Prebisch, Celso Furtado, and other structuralists argued.

Despite these shortcomings, the notion of a high road to globalization powerfully resonates among the region's political leaders and economic policy makers. Capitalist restructuring of the Latin American and world economy has given rise to rapidly and still unfolding changes in the region's participation in the international division of labor. The evolution of the region's export profile shows significant changes over the past two decades (see Table 3). In 1987, primary products represented 50.9 percent of the $ 92.2 billion exported that year. By 2000, primary products had declined to only 27.5 percent of total exports, while manufactures represented almost 71 percent of the $ 348.1 billion exported. During the first years of the twenty-first century, the available data shows that, although manufactured exports represent the overwhelming majority (67.9 percent) of the region's exports, primary exports seem to have staged a slight comeback from their 2001 low point when they only accounted for less than 27 percent of total merchandise exports from the region. Aspirations to the high road to globalization thus are anchored not only to discursive performance but also to important changes in the region's export profile. This important shift in the region's export profile seems to offer uncontestable evidence that the high road lies within reach.

However the rising proportion of manufactures within the structure of the region's merchandise exports conceals a more complex story. If we accept, as ECLAC suggests, that the measure of an economy's competitiveness can be measured by its capacity to maintain and, more importantly, increase its market share of world trade, then a much more nuanced and troubling picture surfaces. When the share of international trade is broken down into different zones within Latin America, a tale of two different trajectories of international insertion emerges. In effect, whereas Mexico and the Caribbean Basin have been able to increase their overall market share by 40.2 percent from 1985 to 2000, creeping from the still meager 2.39 percent to 3.35 percent of world trade during the period, the trend for South America is quite the opposite. Over the same 1985–2000 period, South America, saw its share of world trade *decline* from 3.4 percent to only 2.62 percent, a fall of almost 23 percent (see Table 4). Most worrisome is the starkly divergent trajectories followed by nonnatural resource-based manufactures considered to be the most dynamic niche of world trade. Whereas Mexico and the Caribbean saw

TABLE 3

Latin America and the Caribbean: Structure of merchandise trade, by category, 1987, 1990, 1995, 2000–2003 (Billions of U.S. Dollars and Percentages)

	1987	1990	1995	2000	2001	2002	2003
Value (in billions of US$)	92.2	121.6	221.4	348.1	337.2	330.2	364.5
Composition of exports (%)							
Primary products	50.9	49.1	30.8	27.5	26.4	27.9	30.2
Manufactures	48.1	49.8	67.2	70.9	72.0	70.4	67.9
Natural resources based	22.4	22.0	22.6	17.2	17.3	15.5	16.4
Low technology	9.0	9.6	12.1	11.8	11.9	12.1	11.3
Medium technology	14.5	15.6	23.8	25.3	25.9	26.6	25.4
High technology	2.2	2.6	8.7	16.6	16.9	16.1	14.8
Other transactions	1.0	1.2	1.7	1.5	1.6	1.7	1.9
Total	100.0	100.0	100.0	100.0	100.0	100.0	100.0

Source: ECLAC. Division of International Trade and Integration. *Latin America and the Caribbean in the World Economy 2005–6*, Table II.1A. ECLAC

their share increase by 166.4 percent during the 1985–2000 period, South America's share fell by 16.9 percent.

Furthermore, the difficulties in maintaining a share of manufactured exports is also reflected in the data contained in the Competitive Industrial Performance Index, which is regularly produced by the United Nations Industrial Development Organization. The latest available data for Latin America shows that between 1980 and 2000, only Mexico was able to move up the ranking of countries from thirty-first to twenty-sixth place; all the other countries in the region, including the former industrial powerhouses of Brazil and Argentina, slid downward. Brazil fell from twenty-fourth to thirty-first place, and Argentina fell from thirty-third to thirty-seventh place. Chile's case is most dramatic, falling from fiftieth to sixty-fourth place, scoring below El Salvador, Guatemala, Zimbabwe, Senegal, and Saudi Arabia in terms of industrial development indicators (UNIDO 2004).

Given these trends, it is easy to understand why a development discourse promising to secure the high road to globalization would be favorably received. Neostructuralist discourse restores the role of agency in shaping a country's ultimate location in the international division of labor: It is no

TABLE 4

Latin America and the Caribbean: International competitiveness in world imports, 1985–2000

	1985	1990	1995	2000	CHANGE 1985–2000
MEXICO AND THE CARIBBEAN BASIN					
Overall Market Shares	2.39	1.96	2.40	3.35	40.2
1. Natural resources	5.01	3.56	3.28	3.54	-29.3
2. Manufactures based on					
natural resources	2.09	1.82	1.86	2.10	–
3. Manufactures not based					
on natural resources	1.34	1.55	2.33	3.57	166.4
Low technology	1.25	1.53	2.48	3.92	213.6
Medium technology	1.27	1.64	2.51	3.68	189.8
High technology	1.66	1.40	1.91	3.19	92.2
4. Others	2.06	2.01	2.37	3.27	58.7
SOUTH AMERICA					
Overall Market Shares	3.40	2.76	2.76	2.62	-22.9
1. Natural resources	6.82	7.16	8.33	8.50	24.6
2. Manufactures based on					
natural resources	5.55	4.66	4.93	4.93	-11.2
3. Manufactures not based					
on natural resources	1.24	1.14	1.12	1.03	-16.9
Low technology	1.96	1.75	1.66	1.43	-27.6
Medium technology	1.20	1.21	1.34	1.27	5.8
High technology	0.47	0.36	0.29	0.45	-4.3
4. Others	2.10	1.15	1.35	1.56	-25.47

Source: Michael Mortimore. Oxford 2003 Presentation, "Foreign Direct Investment, Income Inequality, and Poverty: Experiences and Policy Implications," p. 21

longer fate or the "commodity lottery" that condemns Latin American countries to be the providers of natural resources. In the last analysis, neostructuralists assert the type of policies chosen and quality of leadership constitute the defining variables; countries have some say in shaping their future. However in weaving this very appealing narrative, Latin American neostructuralists marginalize key power relations that are deeply embedded in the current dynamics of the world economy and expansion of each country's export sector.

Off Ramping onto the High Road

Neostructuralism postulates both the necessity and feasibility for Latin American countries to switch from the low road onto the high road of globalization. Drawing from the experience of the Asian Tigers, neostructuralism asserts that such passage entails transforming each country's insertion in the world economy from competing via cheap labor and currency devaluations in the least dynamic segments of the world market (mostly natural resources with low levels of processing) toward an export profile in which exported goods preferably compete internationally, thanks to increased productivity and greater value added. Such a transition is critical for sustaining the neostructuralist promise that a relatively painless, yet alternative way exists for overcoming the shortcomings of the EO model of accumulation imposed by neoliberal reforms. Indeed, the integrity of the international competitiveness–social cohesion–political stability hypothesis rests on the feasibility of moving from the low road to the productivity-led high road to globalization. Yet, upon closer inspection, this notion reveals that in its most optimistic formulation during the early 1990s, important conditions crucial for such passage were effectively excluded from consideration.

To switch from a resource-intensive or labor-intensive export profile to one based on competing via value-added and technological change, more than just the right policy mix is required. As the much-touted historical experience of the Asian Tigers shows, specific structural conditions, a certain set of class and power relations reflected in historically specific arrangements made such a conversion possible (see Figure 10). Three important factors enabling such a changeover were (1) a state with a level of autonomy that enabled it to discipline both capital and labor and play the role of a "developmentalist" state; (2) international capital interested in investing and developing value-added sectors as part of their globally integrated production systems or their strategies to gain regional market niches; and (3) a domestic entrepreneurial class willing to assume risks, invest productively, and innovate (Amsden, 1989, 2004; Bello and Rosenfeld 1992; Evans 1995; Burke and Hart-Landsberg 2000; Kay 2002). Yet in exalting the benefits of systemic competitiveness and the example of the Asian Tigers, these three factors are mostly ignored by Latin American neostructuralists. Off-ramping on to the

Neostructuralist Claim	Latin American countries can off-ramp from the "low" to the "high road" to globalization by adopting the right set of policies
Omissions/ Crevices	1. Socio-economic and class structure-anchored requirements for transition to the high-road are understudied or altogether ignored:
	State with the capacity to discipline both capital and labor
	Transnational corporations interested in investing in the "high-tech" sectors
	Domestic capitalist class willing to invest productively and innovate
	2. Holds a liberal view of the State and of its functions in the present historical juncture
	3. Ignores old and new forms of production, appropriation and distribution of surplus under conditions of transnationalized capitalism
	Extraction and transfer of surplus abroad through profit remittances
	New forms of "unequal exchange: present in internationally integrated production systems and in the subcontracting and outsourcing arrangements that increasingly characterize "global value chains"
	4. Foreign-owned manufactured export-based growth is no panacea
	Rising sectoral balance of trade deficits within export sectors due to high degree of imported components and low backward and forward linkages
	Insignificant technology transfers as technology and know-how remain concentrated within TNCs structures
	Vulnerability of export sector workers (wages, insecurity, capital mobility, declining output–employment elasticity)
	Exaggerates Schumpeterian traits of Latin American bourgeoisie, ignoring its increasingly transnational and financial–parasitic character
	Even if successful, "high road" leads to control of key economic sectors by foreign capital

Figure 10. Foundational myth 1: the "high road" to globalization.

high road to globalization requires changes in production systems, investments, savings, and consumption patterns; it requires dynamic linkages between the export and nonexport sectors of the economy, the existence of a sufficiently deep domestic market, the fostering of productive clusters that will lead to innovation, and a diversification in the export profile of the economy (Gwynne 2004). Yet each of these variables along with the role of the state, transnational capital, and local conglomerates remains insufficiently explored for Latin America. Likewise the key role played by a number of preconditions rooted in the existing class structure and distribution of power brought about by the process of land reform carried out in Asia, for example, also remain understudied. Thus, off-ramping onto the high road is proposed as the most important plank of the neostructuralist program without a thorough analysis of existing power relations embedded in contemporary Latin America state, the class structure, and the dynamics of class formation. Equally ignored is the degree to which the actually existing process of transnationalization diverges from the sanitized version presented by ECLAC.

Important issues are either completely ignored or inadequately addressed in Latin American neostructuralism's notion of the high road. As Figure 10 suggests, questions critical for the internal consistency of this idea, such as the role of the state and the emergence of new forms of production, appropriation, and distribution of economic surplus under the present historical conditions of transnationalized capitalism, are not attended to. Complex issues, such as new modes of unequal exchange, denationalization, and control over technological know-how deeply embedded in the internationally integrated production systems, are also ignored. Finally, manufactured export-led growth is presented as the solution to Latin America's problems without examining some of the serious complications that this type of growth already exhibits in Mexico and Asia. Problems such as the rising sectoral balance of trade deficits within manufacturing export sectors due to high degree of imported components, low backward and forward linkages, limited or nonexistent technology transfers as technology and know-how remain concentrated within TNCs structures, and pollution all remain adequately addressed. Additionally, the vulnerability of export sector workers due to low wages and sweatshop conditions, capital mobility, and declining output/employment elasticity, crucial variables for the success of this type of development strategy, are also ignored due to the systematic exclusion of power from Latin American neostructuralism's mode of theorization. Never raised is the issue that, even if successful, the high road to globalization leads to greater control of a country's key economic sectors by foreign capital and a handful of large conglomerates.

Open Regionalism

A second foundational idea put forth by Latin American neostructuralism is its support for "open regionalism." According to ECLAC open regionalism refers "to a new process that results from reconciling . . . two phenomena . . . the interdependence that stems from special, preferential agreements, and that which basically arises from the market signals that are produced by trade liberalization in general" (ECLAC 1994, par 20). In other words, through open regionalism, neostructuralists and ECLAC claim that an underlying compatibility exists between regional trading arrangements and the global trading system and global economic rules sanctioned by the World Trade Organization (WTO): "A complementary objective is to make integration a building block of a more open, transparent international economy, instead of turning it into an obstacle to such an economy, thus curbing the options available to the Latin American and Caribbean countries. This means that integration agreements should tend to eliminate the barriers applicable to most trade in goods and services among the signatories, in line with their trade liberalization policies towards third parties, while at the same time making it easier for new members to accede to the agreements" (ECLAC 1994, par 22).

Support for open regionalism echoes demands by transnational corporations that economic globalization "should be governed by stable, transparent rules, so that reciprocal integration agreements can serve as unequivocal guarantees against all possible risks or uncertainties about access to the expanded market" (ECLAC 1994, par 28). ECLAC's posture elides any analysis of who controls the most dynamic export sectors of Latin America, who reaps the benefits of export expansion, and who gets to decide where the realized profits in those sectors are to be invested. Despite the 1998 Asian financial crisis, the negative results of the North American Free Trade Agreement (NAFTA) for Mexico, the rising popular opposition throughout the continent to WTO and NAFTA-based trade agreements, and the refusal by developed countries to eliminate subsidies to their own exports, ECLAC still promoted this approach a decade later, though with tempered enthusiasm: "Steady growth in international trade, the strengthening of multilateral rules under the auspices of the World Trade Organization (WTO) and open regionalism along the lines proposed by ECLAC are all helping to integrate developing countries better into the world economy. But these favorable processes are countered by the failure of developed countries to open their economies fully and by the demand that developing countries should comply with international regulations in a number of trade-related areas" (ECLAC 2004b, 40).

This continued support for "open regionalism" and WTO-based rules as they currently exist reveals important inconsistencies in neostructuralist discourse (see Figure 11). First and most importantly, "open regionalism" undermines the possibility for applying an activist industrial, technology, and trade policy, which is a basic prerequisite for attaining the high road to globalization. By supporting the WTO-based framework of global economic rules, open regionalism severely constrains the possibilities for counting with policy instruments that can impinge on structural dynamics favoring off-ramping onto the high road to globalization. Instead of challenging WTO rules, the power of transnational capital, and the demands of G-7 countries, neostructuralists have held fast to the concept of open regionalism and, for over a decade, have engaged in conceptual and discursive contortions, in vain attempts to paper over its contradictions.

As Latin American governments have been discovering, integration into the global economy imposes the acceptance of "new international trade disciplines," which "are clearly biased against their future growth prospects. . . . Many practices that were common in the past are simply no longer possible" (Katz 2001, 114). Among those policies no longer possible and removed by WTO rules from the policy tool chest are: export subsidies (forbidden, actionable, and nonactionable), quotas or other physical restrictions on imports, and local content requirements. Trade-Related Investment Measures (TRIMs) enforce investor rights to equal treatment and prohibit establishing any conditions, and Trade Related Aspects of Intellectual Property Rights (TRIPs) protect corporate property rights on knowledge–generation activities and innovation. NAFTA's chapter 11, the basis for FTAA and CAFTA—all of them enthusiastically endorsed by ECLAC—clearly stipulates that governments have extremely limited possibilities of imposing economic or environmental conditions on foreign investment. Much of the recent production by ECLAC is geared to argue that, in the new context, a "new type" of industrial policy is possible (Peres 2006). However, one fundamental characteristic of these policies is that, unlike those implemented in Latin America under the import-substitution industrialization (ISI) model of previous decades, or even those applied by countries like South Korea or Taiwan, they cannot

Neostructuralist Claim	Through open regionalism Latin America gains the benefits and ensures compatibility between regional trading arrangements and the global trading system sanctioned by the World Trade Organization (WTO).
Omissions/Crevices	1. Ignores how WTO-based rules and financialization undermine and constrain an activist industrialist, technology, and trade policy
	2. Complacent view of regional integration that ignores role of transnational capital and domestic conglomerates
	3. Issues of corporate governance and concentration, centralization of control over assets, and decision-making over social use of the economic surplus
	4. Economic and political control by transnationalized capitalist class
	5. Challenges to WTO and NAFTA-based models of integration such as the Alternativa Bolivariana para America Latina y el Caribe (ALBA) that aim to address poverty and inequality by challenging transnational capital are ignored.
	6. Corporate-led integration leads to dispossession and commodification of ever growing aspects of social life, not modernity.

Figure 11. Foundational myth 2: open regionalism.

discipline transnational capital or regulate investment but rather can seek only to facilitate its expansion.

A second flank opened by ECLAC's support of "open regionalism" is that it actively contributes to the intensification of the financialization of Latin American economies. As financial markets and financial elites become more dominant in the operation of the economy and its institutions, important distortion-inducing structures and dynamics have been unleashed. As I discuss with greater detail in the next chapter, these dynamics can undermine the possibility of reaching and remaining on the high road and, therefore, of achieving growth with equity. The 1998 Asian financial crisis, and its aftermath, once again demonstrated that volatility and contagion are brewing in internationally integrated financial markets and that qualitative changes in the structure of transnational capitalism have been under way that make it essential to analyze power relations under the present historical conditions.

ECLAC's embrace of "open regionalism" and its implicit assumption that no conflict exists between WTO and NAFTA-based models of free-trade agreements, on the one hand, and the development needs of Latin American societies, on the other, have left it endorsing an analytical framework incapable of adequately explaining, much less lucidly intervening, in one of the most important debates unfolding after 2000: the nature and character of regional integration. The launching by Venezuela, Cuba, and Bolivia of the *Alternativa Bolivariana para América Latina y el Caribe* (Bolivarian Alternative for Latin America and the Caribbean [ALBA]), recently endorsed by Ecuador and Nicaragua and which directly opposes the U.S. model of Free Trade Area of the Americas (FTAA), is forcing a debate that challenges one of Latin American neostructuralism's basic assumption, that is, no conflict exists between satisfying the requirements of transnational capital and reducing poverty and inequality in the region. ECLAC's implicit support for corporate-led globalization and regional integration models that prioritize the interests of transnational capital over the integrations of peoples has preempted neostructuralism from addressing how the current path of globalization leads to dispossession and commoditization of ever growing aspects of social life.

Dreams of Growth with Equity

Harnessing the powerful forces of globalization to simultaneously achieve productive modernization, greater equity, and social cohesion constitutes one of Latin American neostructuralism's most powerful claims (see Leiva 2006). The majority of the center–left coalitions scoring electoral triumphs in Chile, Argentina, Brazil, and Uruguay have incorporated this notion as one of the major planks of their electoral platforms. "Renovated" progressive and social democratic intellectuals serving as political and economic advisors to such coalitions have integrated it as a major component in their work. Thus, from the perspective of both the political economy of development and from the evolution of contemporary political discourse, the claim that growth with equity can be achieved within the current trajectory of globalization merits careful consideration and analysis.

The conviction that export growth and social equity can be made compatible to a great extent rests upon the next two foundational myths constitutive of the neostructuralist paradigm. The first of these is that, like train cars at a station, distribution can be decoupled from capital accumulation; the second is that a clear-cut dichotomy exists between "spurious" and "genuine" routes to international competitiveness and profits. Both notions are necessary to uphold the idea that growth with equity is possible under the conditions of the current EO regime of accumulation. Yet, as I discuss later in this chapter, Latin American neostructuralism engages in glaring "acts of omission" with important consequences for the viability of "growth with equity" under the present conditions. By casting aside the production, distribution, and appropriation of economic surplus as an important analytical entry point and marginalizing power relations, particularly those between labor and capital in the production process and in the sphere of social reproduction, Latin American neostructuralism significantly weakens its capacity to explain the increasing precariousness (temporary, part-time, socially unprotected, non-union) and informalization of labor–capital relations as exports and output rise.

Perhaps Latin American neostructuralism's most hope-laden claim is that growth and equity can be simultaneously attained under the current conditions of globalization. For productivity-led exports and social integration to mutually begin reinforcing one another, however, policy makers must trigger certain dynamics that cannot and will not emerge from the operation of market forces alone; institutions, politics, and culture must return to economic development thinking. Only then can adequate public policies be fashioned to take advantage of all that synergy patiently awaiting liberation. Accordingly, neostructuralists design policies to improve coordination among economic actors; eliminate market failures through dialogue and social accords; reduce transaction costs; and invest in human capital and training, all of which aim toward facilitating increases in productivity essential, in turn, for improving wages and working conditions.

Such policies—it is hoped—will help exporting firms discover that, in the medium and long-run, it is more profitable to base their international competitiveness upon productivity increases rather than upon easier, yet ultimately short-lived, cost reduction strategies, such as wage compression and exchange rate devaluation. At the same time, firms must keep up with global competition via continuous technological innovation, adaptation, and incorporation of quality control into the production process itself. To accomplish this, employers must raise wages and replace authoritarian labor–capital relations with more cooperation. Greater worker involvement and improved labor–capital relations, in turn, will fuel additional productivity increases, inducing the long-awaited virtuous circle: a better international insertion of the Latin American economies and a rising volume of exports sustain both rising profit rates for capitalists and improved real wages for workers. Herein lies the nub of the mutually reinforcing relationship between productive transformation (the shift toward productivity-led export growth) and greater social equity (rising wages and living standards) that globalization can engender for Latin America according to neostructuralists.

In the wake of sluggish growth rates and high levels of poverty and inequality brought about by neoliberal policies, the neostructuralist promise of coupling economic growth with equity acquired tremendous political appeal for political leaders. Despite recent positive gross domestic product (GDP) and export growth rates, in 2005 close to 41 percent of Latin America's population or approximately 213 million people still lived under the poverty line, urban unemployment remained above 10 percent, and the percentage of the labor force employed in the informal sector and the workforce lacking social security coverage continued climbing (see Table 5). Although during the 1990s and first half of the present decade, countries like Chile, Brazil, and

---

TABLE 5

Latin America: Basic indicators, selected years

YEAR	GDP %	URBAN UNEMPLOYMENT %	REAL WAGES (INDEX 1990=100)	POPULATION UNDER POVERTY LINE %	INFORMAL SECTOR	CONTRIBUTE TO SOCIAL SECURITY
1990	-0.6*	8.0	100.0	48.3	42.8	66.6
1995	1.1	9.1	111.4	45.7[a]	46.1	65.2
2000	4.0	10.5	118.8	42.5	46.9	65.7
2002	-0.8	11.7	121.0	44.0	46.5	63.7
2003	2.0	11.5	114.9	44.3[b]	47.4	63.6
2004	5.9	10.9	–	41.7[b]	49.2[d]	–
2005	4.5[c]	9.4[d]	–	40.6[b]	48.5[d]	–

Source: Compiled by author on the basis of ECLAC and ILO statistics
a Corresponds to 1994 data
b ECLAC, *Social Panorama 2005*
c ECLAC, *Survey of the Economies of Latin America and the Caribbean 2006*, Table A-1
d Organizacion Internacional del Trabajo, *Panorama Laboral 2006* (Lima: Naciones Unidas, 2007)

TABLE 6

Latin America and selected countries: Poverty and indigence 1990–2005

COUNTRY	YEAR	BELOW POVERTY LINE		BELOW INDIGENCE LINE	
		PERCENTAGE OF INDIVIDUALS	(MILLIONS)	PERCENTAGE OF INDIVIDUALS	(MILLIONS)
Latin America[a]	1990	48.3	200	22.5	93
	1994	45.7	–	20.8	–
	1997	43.5	204	19.0	89
	1999	43.8	–	18.5	–
	2000	42.5	207	18.1	88
	2001	43.2	214	18.5	92
	2002	44.0	221	19.4	97
	2003	44.3[b]	226[b]	19.2[b]	98[b]
	2004	41.7[b]	216[b]	17.4[b]	90[b]
	2005	40.6[b]	213[b]	16.8[b]	88[b]
Bolivia	1997	62.1		37.2	
	1999	60.6		36.4	
	2002	62.4		37.1	
Brazil	1990	48.0		23.4	
	1993	45.3		20.2	
	1996	35.8		13.9	
	1999	37.5		12.9	
	2001	37.5		13.2	
Chile	1990	38.6		12.9	
	1994	27.5		7.6	
	1996	23.2		5.7	
	1998	21.7		5.6	
	2000	20.6		5.7	
	2003	18.8		4.7	
México	1989	47.7		18.7	
	1994	45.1		16.8	
	1996	52.9		22.0	
	1998	46.9		18.5	
	2000	41.1		15.2	
	2002	39.4		12.6	

Continued on next page

TABLE 6 (CONTINUED)

Latin America and selected countries: Poverty and indigence 1990–2005 (continued)

COUNTRY	YEAR	BELOW POVERTY LINE		BELOW INDIGENCE LINE	
		PERCENTAGE OF INDIVIDUALS	(MILLIONS)	PERCENTAGE OF INDIVIDUALS	(MILLIONS)
Uruguay*	1990	17.9		3.4	
	1994	9.7		1.9	
	1997	9.5		1.7	
	1999	9.4		1.8	
	2002	15.4		2.5	
Venezuela	1990	39.8		14.4	
	1994	48.7		19.2	
	1997	48.0		20.5	
	1999	49.4		21.7	
	2002	48.6		22.2	

Source: CEPAL *Panorama Económico y Social 2004*.
*Data for Uruguay only for urban areas.

Mexico were able to reduce the statistically defined poverty level, the rate of poverty reduction slowed, and little certainty existed that such advances would not be reversed in the future (see Table 6). More significantly, despite positive growth rates, the trends toward greater income inequality and social polarization remained firmly entrenched in the region, so that the benefits of the current economic model accrued mostly to the richest decile of the population.

Unlinking Distribution from Accumulation

By promising growth with equity within the parameters of the current EO regime of accumulation, Latin American neostructuralism suggests that accumulation and distribution can be unlinked and that more effective and enlightened policies is all that is required. Such a maneuver goes against both classical political economy and decades of critical Latin American economic thinking in its structuralist and dependency variants, both of which emphasized the close connection between accumulation and distribution. In promising "growth with equity" without the need for structurally transforming the status quo, and by analytically decoupling capital accumulation from distribution, Latin American neostructuralism dispenses with a historically grounded analysis of the role that power relations play in contemporary Latin American capitalism (see Figure 12).

Despite Latin American neostructuralism's silences, capital accumulation and distribution are inextricable intertwined through structural and dynamic links in both directions. Refusal to analytically explore these links while focusing exclusively on ameliorative policies constitutes a gross error in neostructuralist theorizing, leaving a major flank of its "growth with equity" foundational myth vulnerable.

Despite neostructuralist acts of omission, capital accumulation and distribution have always been connected under capitalism and in economic

Neostructuralist Claim	"Growth with equity" is attainable within the parameters of the current export-oriented regime of accumulation through more enlightened policies Corollary: Present context allows for deployment of effective public policies to increase equity and social cohesion
Omissions/Crevices	1. Accumulation and distribution are inextricably linked, even more so under the current export-oriented regime of accumulation. 2. Key variables—the investment decision and control over the social surplus are in the hands of an even smaller minority that in the past, a handful of transnational firms and financial institutions. 3. The exports-labor flexibility–labor control-poverty-inequality nexus understudied. Exports require greater control over labor costs and expansion of flexible labor. Workers do not consume what they produce. Income from profits and interests accrue to an even smaller, transnationalized minority. 4. Export growth is not generating employment. 5. Transnationalization of capital and financialization concentrate income at a rate that cannot be counterbalanced by status quo friendly public policies.

Figure 12. Foundational myth 3: accumulation and distribution delinked.

studies carried out during the 1930–70 period of ISI or "inward-oriented" model of development. This interconnection is even stronger at present. If we start from the distribution side and consider the existing personal distribution of income, decisions about consumption and savings made within households will impact aggregate demand and economic growth rates. If we now consider the functional distribution of income as it is divided into profits, interests, wages, and rent, we can visualize one of the major traits of contemporary capitalism in operation: the volume of corporate profits and the decision by capitalists in general are the principal source of investment. The existing incentive structure will influence both the magnitude and manner in which profits are generated as well as how they are to be used.

At the same time, other conduits also connect accumulation and distribution. The degree of legitimacy and social unrest, the type of governmental intervention shaping existing incentive structures, the volume of economic surplus destined for infrastructure, social services, and upgrading labor skills constitute some of the variables that will impact the investment decision.

For these and other reasons, structuralists like Raúl Prebisch and Celso Furtado, dedicated a large portion of their intellectual energies and professional endeavors to understanding the links tying accumulation and distribution together in Latin American economies, that is, the factors determining the size and use of a country's economic surplus.

What then struck structuralists like Prebisch, Furtado, Aldo Ferrer, Aníbal Pinto, Nicholas Kaldor, and Pedro Vuskovic was the extent to which, in Latin America, existing power relations shaped and determined decisions about the size and use of the economic surplus. Their work and that of dependency theorists emphasized the limited growth of the internal market as a result of low wage levels and a highly concentrated income distribution. Low investment rates were a result of the appropriation of part of the surplus by foreign capital and its transfer abroad and due to luxury consumption by local elites' intent on imitating the consumption and cultural patterns the metropolis. For structuralism, unraveling the connection between accumulation and distribution was at the heart of understanding the root causes and the solution to Latin America's underdevelopment.

Export-oriented Accumulation and Distribution

Contrary to the current neglect by Latin American neostructuralists, accumulation and distribution are more codependent than ever before under the present EO regime, exposing the ideologically driven nature of their oversight. This heightened connection between accumulation and distribution under the present historical circumstances has increased on account of two main reasons.

First, higher concentration of ownership over productive assets means that it is primarily the spending behavior of an even smaller minority that determines the level of saving and investment in the current Latin American economy. In this sense, the market has replaced the state as the prime decision maker regarding how social surplus is to be used and investment materialized. Neoliberal policies of privatization, deregulation, and liberalization have intensified the processes of transnationalization and financialization of the economy, so that ownership and control of assets are more concentrated than any time during recent history. This accelerating process of concentration led the United Nations Conference on Trade and Development (UNCTAD), for example, to develop its Investment Concentration Ratio (ICOR) index in order to measure the share of private investment in GDP as a percentage of the share of the richest quintile in total income or consumption (UNCTAD 1997). Though only a general approximation, UNCTAD's efforts contrast sharply with ECLAC's neostructuralism, which has ignored this issue. UNCTAD at least seeks to capture how the investment decision in many Third World countries is tied to the spending behavior of a small minority. Other studies sought to explain how higher concentration in ownership has led to greater rise in the level of indebtedness and financialization of the economy. The extreme case of concentration of the investment decision is best represented by Chile, where highly concentrated and transnationalized private pension management companies, or *Administradoras de Fondos de Pensiones* (AFPs), control the bulk of the country's investment decision. One analyst has pointed out that *only three* of these AFPs wield enough power to decide where 50 percent of social surplus is invested (Arrau 2003). In February of 2005, for example, the equivalent to $61 billion were controlled by six of the AFPs operating in Chile, all of which in turn were controlled by transnational capital (*Banco Bilbao Viscaya Argentaria* [BBVA], Banco Santander, Citibank, Bank of New York, SunLife, ING). Thus, the investment decision—one of the key conduits linking accumulation and distribution—is based on maximizing profits and expansion strategies of these transnational conglomerates, further distancing the possibility that a country's economic surplus will be used with criteria of social efficiency and societal interest.

The second channel through which accumulation and distribution become even more inextricably enmeshed under the current EO regime of accumulation is through the exports–poverty–inequality nexus, also insufficiently analyzed by Latin American neostructuralism. In the past, structuralists and dependency analysts critiqued the ISI model for its inherent tendency to concentrate income in the higher income sectors of society, creating a bottleneck that not only constrained the size of the internal market but also distorted internal aggregate demand toward consumer durables and luxury goods bought by the upper quintile in the income distribution ladder. This tendency toward income concentration, choking of the internal market, biasing internal aggregate demand, and consumption patterns to serve the interests of the dominant classes justified the adoption of income redistributive measures defended by national–democratic development alternatives supported, for example, by Brazilian president Joao Goulart in the early sixties and Chile's Salvador Allende in the early seventies. During the 1960s, these tendencies, along with the increased control of productive sectors by foreign capital, stratified and split the capitalist class as different fractions supported two very different and opposing strategies for overcoming the crisis of the previous ISI model. One fraction wavered toward supporting national developmentalist and income redistribution measures defended by progressive coalitions. The other supported a program of liberalization, deregulation, and privatization that tended to further concentrate income and expand luxury consumption.

Jumping forward to the present, the process of neoliberal restructuring established, as we saw in chapter 3, a different regime of accumulation that mimics and turbo-charges the income-concentrating tendencies of the past with an important structural difference, however, that binds accumulation and distribution even more tightly. Under the current EO regime of accumulation, the distribution of income becomes more concentrated on the top decile than before at the same time that, for most Latin American countries, the economy's most dynamic sector is no longer the internal market but the export sector. Decisions about investment, production, and realization of surplus now are based on the changing competitive pressures of globalized markets and the expansion strategies of transnational corporations and financial institutions that dominate them. As a result, what we have in Latin America is not only a transition from a wage-led to a profit-led regime of accumulation but additionally a shift toward investments in external and not domestic markets. Though structuralists and post-Keynesian economists (among others) have sought to understand the changing relationship between accumulation and distribution under the new context, Latin American neostructuralists have been visibly absent from such endeavor.[1]

As a result of these structural constraints, we observe how, despite the recuperation of GDP growth rates, export dynamism, and the return of fickle foreign direct investments (FDIs) flows, the personal and functional distribution of income continues becoming more polarized and labor's share declines.

Going against the grain of the structuralist tradition that underscored the indissoluble relationship between the structure of accumulation and that of distribution, Latin American neostructuralists embrace globalization and the EO model hewed out by neoliberalism, implicitly claiming that accumulation and distribution can be decoupled from one another. Such a maneuver allows them to assert that "growth with equity" is possible within the parameters of the current EO economic model and globalization processes. While they neglect such connection, neostructuralism claims that compatibility between EO accumulation and equity requires active promotion of "new social pacts" that foster political stability and are sustained by "fiscal covenants" clearly delimiting the parameters for government spending. In the neostructuralist view, "growth with equity" does not require profound transformations in the pattern of accumulation or in those power relations constitutive of the global economy's present structure. These are excluded as possible, not only on account of past traumas and foreswearing a repetition of the "Greek social tragedy" of previous decades but also—and here is the key point—because of the deep conviction by Latin American neostructuralist that, given the nature of the technical–productive paradigm engendered by globalization, they enjoy ample room to deploy effective policies to promote greater equity and inclusion within the exiting patterns of capital accumulation and international economic relations. Such an assertion is based more on wishful thinking than careful empirical study of Latin America and Caribbean reality. It disregards classical approaches to the political economy of capitalism and Latin America's history as the region with the most unequal income distribution in the world; it is also challenged by the performance of neostructuralist-inspired policies and results obtained in Chile during the 1990–2007 period, as we will see with greater detail in chapter 9.

The key question seems to be then, what is the margin for maneuver for activist social policies within the parameters imposed by the current process of corporate-led globalization and the dynamics of Latin America's increasingly transnationalized capitalism? Latin American neostructuralists wager that, by relying on noneconomic means (social accords, new alliances between the state and civil society, capturing and tapping into the social capital of the poor, extolling the quality of policy making and profit-enhancing policies geared at symbolically protecting social cohesion) structural economic constraints can be overcome. I argue that, even freed from the willingly accepted International Monetary Fund (IMF)-imposed Structural Balance Rule, deployment of all of these noneconomic mechanisms, even under the most favorable political conditions, constitute no match for the tendencies toward dispossession, exclusion, and concentration of wealth deeply embedded in the dynamics and reproduction of the current EO regime of accumulation. Chile offers a good example to test this hypothesis. Symbolic politics have proved no match for the exploitative and centralizing logic of twenty-first-century EO capitalism. Neostructuralists' reliance on the political and cultural realm underestimates key structural transformations and dynamics that constitute the very soul of the current regime of accumulation such as (1) the extent to which politics becomes subordinate to the task of insulating markets and transnational investors from popular demands; (2) the subordination of social reproduction to the logic of internationalizing capital; (3) the imperative of labor control and the socially devastating effects of the international competitiveness through the labor flexibility, poverty, and inequality nexus; (4) the reduced scope for social policy in societies where commoditization and financialization have become intensified; and (5) income concentrating tendencies that cannot be stemmed by seemingly well-meaning but timid policy interventions. In sum, through the hyperbolizing of "growth with equity" discourse, by postulating that accumulation and distribution can be unlinked—a prerequisite to present a pragmatic view—neostructuralists have given up on rigorously examining the characteristics of the new pattern of accumulation in the region and the challenges that persistent poverty and inequality place on development. More specifically, they have failed so far to provide convincing explanations for some of the most important and worrisome trends that characterize current Latin American development. As income and profits increasingly accrue to an ever smaller and transnationalized minority and export growth fails to generate a sufficient volume of jobs (and much less of the quality promised), profits are increasingly destined to expand financial investments, thereby further lowering the level of productive investment in the local economy.

Spurious vs. Genuine Competitiveness: A Fallacy

Another pillar upholding the neostructuralist dream of "growth with equity" under the present conditions of globalization is the notion that a clear division exists between spurious versus genuine forms of competitiveness. Neostructuralists argue that, depending on the quality of leadership and incentive structure, firms and national economies can choose which of these two divergent paths they will follow. Despite the appeal of such formulation, the extent to which actually existing labor–capital relations are characterized by this neat and clear-cut dichotomy is highly debatable. When this fourth foundational myth of Latin American neostructuralism is explored, one finds that significant acts of omission are committed precisely around the defining relationship in capitalist society, namely that between wage labor and capital (see Figure 13). Fatal incoherencies result from excising power and power relations from this key realm of social analysis and point to the faulty core of Latin American's neostructuralism's political economy. For this reason, the inconsistencies surrounding this key element in neostructuralist discourse and political action require attention.

At an abstract level, a clear and distinct dichotomy between "spurious" and "genuine" competitiveness can be indeed constructed, but there is strong evidence that in the real world of capitalist production such conveniently stark separation does not exist. In fact, when one examines how power is exercised in a historically concrete labor process, one finds that a clear-cut separation between coercion and consent belies the complexity of production relations. When actual strategies deployed by firms are studied, their quest for international competitiveness (i.e., profits) cannot be decomposed neatly into "cost reduction–spurious" versus "productivity enhancing–genuine" components (Leiva 1998). That is, cost-reduction can be accomplished via innovation either in the organization and flow of production or by adopting new technology throughout the enterprise or within particular bottleneck sections. Increases in productivity can also be achieved by intensifying the pace of work or the labor intensity of production processes. Latin American neostructuralists' dualistic conceptualization of production into a clearly defined and mutually exclusive spurious–genuine dichotomy, though extremely useful in discursive terms, is analytically unsatisfactory because it ignores the contradictory social and technical character of production, the labor process, and the valorization of capital itself.

Neostructuralist Claim	A clear-cut dichotomy exists between two productive– competitive strategies at the firm as well as at the national level: "spurious": based on compression of labor cost and exchange rate devaluations "genuine": based on productivity increases and techno- logical innovation
Omissions/Crevices	1. Production not conceived as both a *social* and *technical* relationship
	2. Idealized conception of the labor process under condi- tions of globalization: problems of surplus extraction and labor control become even more important
	3. Technologically deterministic view of productivity increases
	4. Labor productivity can also be increased by intensifying pace of work, the extensive use of labor, reorganization of production, not just technological innovation
	5. Capital is always finding ways of combining "productivity- led" (genuine) with "cost-cutting" (spurious) strategies in ever more creative ways
	6. Workplace/Reproduction of Labor nexus: "genuine" competitiveness at the workplace, can coexist with "spurious" competitiveness" in the realm of the reproduction of labor (i.e., living conditions of certain export-sector workers)

Figure 13. Foundational myth 4: spurious vs. genuine competitiveness.

If we conceive production as a sociotechnical process, involving both technical relations between inputs and social relations (control, coordina- tion, monitoring, supervision, effort), we can better envision the limitations of the neostructuralist formulation (see Figure 14). In our simple schema, for a given level of technology, output will be not only a function of certain technical variables (amount of capital equipment and labor inputs) but also a function of social relations including the level of effort expended or extracted from workers and the existing levels of coordination, cooperation, and worker participation, for example. On the basis of this schema, we can see that there are *not two* but *three* different paths toward increasing productivity. At first

Production Function	$Y = a\,F(K, eL, x)$	Y = output K = capital equipment L = Labor a = Level of technology e = Level of effort expended by workers x = social relations of production (coordination, degree of labor management cooperation, worker participation, teamwork, etc.)
Socio-Technical Character of Production	**Social Relations** Labor Extraction, Coordination	**Technical Relations** Combination of inputs
	$\overline{a}$ (Technology remains constant)	
	e x	K L
Path to "Spurious" Competitiveness	↑ Y by ↑ e (wages fall, authoritarian labor-capital relations)	a, K remain constant
Idealized Path to "Genuine" Competitiveness	↑ Y by ↑ x (Changes in organization of production and introduction of team work)	↑ Y by ↑ K/L ratio thru ↑ K (Technical change strategy)
Paths in "Actually Existing" Capitalism	↑ Y by ↑ e thru changing x ("Lean production" and "management by stress")	↑ Y by ↑ K/L ratio thru ↓ L (Strategy of intensifying use of labor, outsourcing, without increased investment in capital and equipment)

Figure 14. Paths to competitiveness and the sociotechnical nature of production.

glance, productivity can be increased *spuriously* by increasing the intensity of work, which combined with wage and labor cost suppression will lead to rises in output and profit rate. At the other idealized extreme, productivity can be also increased through a second path that relies on innovation in the organization of production or through more cooperative forms of social relations. If greater coordination and cooperation are combined with technical change (increasing the relationship between capital and labor), then productivity increases will follow the *genuine* path defended by neostructuralists. However, neostructuralists overlook a third possibility, which is actually what is observable at the point of production in many firms. At the same time that management calls on workers to become more "engaged" in production, employers increase the capital–labor ratio by maintaining or increasing production levels without engaging in technological innovation by employing a smaller number of workers. After Chile's 1999 economic recession, this third path to increasing productivity reached such magnitude that even then-president Ricardo Lagos complained in 2003 that, "We now have levels of output similar or greater than those existing before the crisis, yet we are not capable of generating the jobs that we had then. That is very clear. The establishment had 100 jobs, it reduced them to 80, now it has 90 and it discovers that with those 90 it can produce what before it was producing with 100. That is where we are at now" (Lagos 2003, 41; my translation). To further add to the frustration of leaders that have embraced neostructuralist foundational myths, the actually existing dynamic of capitalism today is proving that labor productivity can also be increased by intensifying pace of work, the extensive use of labor, and reorganization of production, *without* investing in capital and equipment or engaging in technological innovation.

At the level of the individual enterprise, actually existing strategies deployed by capitalist firms take on very complex combinations of coercion and consent, circumscribed technological innovation with nineteenth-century work arrangements such as reliance on home working and contingent workforces in a variety of changing configurations defying neostructuralist dichotomous and dualistic thinking. By combining the intensification of the labor process (making workers work faster), changing organization of production, selective and partial technical innovation to ensure labor control and overcome bottlenecks in certain sections or parts of the production process, capitalists are waging a multidimensional and very real life-or-death battle to ensure profits and their own survival. Eliminating power relations from the analysis of the key node of capitalist society, the relationship between labor and capital, can only be done by sacrificing Latin American neostructuralism's internal coherence.

It is said that humans are the only animal that will stumble twice on the same stone. If this piece of *campesino* wisdom were true, then we could understand why ECLAC's economic-thinking, both in its structuralist variant of the 1950s and in the current neostructuralist version, repeatedly trips on the same analytical stone: the process of production. If in the past, its center-periphery framework could be faulted for its emphasis on circulation and not production, at present, the neostructuralist notion of a virtuous circle linked to globalization and productive transformation can be faulted for ignoring that production is both *a social as well as a technical process*. In the 1950s, when they were committed to a national-development project supported by a multiclass coalition of capitalist industrialists and unionized urban workers, this omission by structuralists could be understandable. Focusing on the contradictions at the workplace would have threatened such project at a time when the pattern of accumulation was being driven by the internal market and an institutionally sanctioned compromise between labor and capital.[2] In the case of Latin American neostructuralists, however, intent as they are on building a multiclass consensus supportive of the export drive and transnationalized production for export, their neglect of the sociotechnical nature of the capitalist production process, in which labor extraction and labor control constitute essential ingredients for successfully competing in world markets, is extremely problematic. Particularly as capital is continually finding new and more creative ways of combining "productivity-led" (genuine) with "cost-cutting" (spurious) strategies in Latin America and throughout its internationally integrated production and distribution networks.

The neostructuralist notion of a two-pronged strategy to achieve international competitiveness—one *spurious* attained at the expense of workers' wages and living standards and another *genuine* based on technical change—needs to be reframed therefore in light of the labor-process approach and the current realities of work organizations and labor practices.

Consensus, Cooperation, and International Competitiveness

Latin American neostructuralism's fifth and final foundational myth is that, if the state and the political system promotes consensus, cooperation, and new forms of "participatory governance" in the economic and noneconomic realms of society, such interventions will boost systemic competitiveness, export growth, and social equity. Although the politics of Latin American neostructuralism will be discussed in greater detail in chapters 7 and 8, it is important to remark here on the role neostructuralism attributes to political leadership for allowing the synergy between political democracy and economic growth to flourish. Neostructuralism sees multiple benefits arising from strengthening the complementary role of nonmarket and noneconomic forms of social coordination. Not only can this lead to an increased economic efficiency by reducing transaction costs, but it can also strengthen social cohesion and political legitimacy. All of this will ultimately favor winning the race toward international competitiveness, a race in which, when compared to Asian countries, Latin American economies have been lackluster and losing participants.

This apparently innovative emphasis on the interconnectedness among economics, politics, and culture is seriously flawed, however, due to the many acts of omission committed in its construction (see Figure 15). As in the past, the state is conceived by ECLAC along liberal lines as the depository of social rationality and agent of the common good, without considering its class character or how its functions in the reproduction of the system of domination have been transformed by neoliberal restructuring. No contradictions between its role in securing conditions for reproducing EO capital accumulation, on the one hand, and popular sovereignty and political democracy, on the other, are considered. The promotion of participatory governance through labor accords, the tapping of social–capital, and other forms of state–civil society alliances are seen as unilaterally strengthening democracy without entertaining the possibility that the existence of formal procedures could be part of consolidating new hegemonic regimes that do not necessarily strengthen the democratic character of society or the economy. The possibility that neostructuralist "society-creating" social policies, could very well lead to the destruction of the more or less autonomous social and political power of the poor and of other social sectors is ignored. These more complex issues, the engendering new forms of neoliberal governmentality and production of new self-regulating citizens for capital, or questions dealing with how power is exercised in contemporary societies are not addressed.

Though appealing and politically successful, each one of the five foundational myths discussed in this chapter is the product of important acts of exclusion and omission. These omissions undermine the coherence and

Neostructuralist Claim	Promoting consensus, participatory governance, new forms of state-civil society alliances, and incorporating social capital in the design of public policies can ensure both growth and equity.
Omissions/Crevices	1. Neostructuralism's liberal conception of the State as the depository of social rationality ignores both the class character of the state as well as the fundamental role that it plays in securing conditions for reproducing capital accumulation.
	2. The promotion of participatory governance through labor accords, a social-capital approach, and other forms of state–civil society alliances, leads to new hegemonic regimes that do not necessarily strengthen the democratic character of society or the economy.
	3. "Society-creating" neo-marginality poor alleviation social policies aimed at civilizing the poor as consumer of services and self-regulating citizens.

Figure 15. Foundational myth 5: concerted action and participatory governance.

consistency of Latin American neostructuralism. They limit its ability to play a transformative role of the status quo created by corporate-led globalization and increasingly funnel neostructuralism into a pragmatic stance of servicing private transnational capital. Despite the celebration of neostructuralism's conceptual and policy innovation, its flawed mode of theorization and consistent marginsalization of power relations from economic analysis and public policy design force it, time and time again, to stumble against the recalcitrant realities and dynamics of Latin American capitalist society; realities and dynamics that, despite their corrosive effects on economic growth, equity, social cohesion, and democracy, Latin American neostructuralism continually erases from view thanks to a political economy sanitized of power and power relations.

6

Effacing the Deep Structure of Contemporary Latin American Capitalism

Latin American neostructuralism's capacity to incisively explore the most salient transformations experienced by Latin American capitalism over the last decade is severely hampered by its omission of power and power relations. By discarding a systemic approach and jettisoning the notion of economic surplus, Latin American neostructuralism exhibits a startling laggardness when studying three current unfolding and accelerating processes in the region: the transnationalization of capital, the increasing financialization of the economy, and the growing informalization (or precarization) of labor–capital relations. This is not to say that facets of these processes have not been examined or measured by the highly qualified staff at the Economic Commission for Latin America and the Caribbean (ECLAC) headquarters and regional offices. On the contrary, ECLAC yearly produces an impressive amount of high-quality cross-country data and insightful reports on different aspects of the social, political, and institutional development in Latin America and the Caribbean. The argument I develop in this chapter is that the intellectual retreat enacted during the transition from structuralism to neostructuralism severely weakens Latin American neostructuralism's ability to give such transformations a coherent explanation, to envision their interconnectedness, and to fully realize that these are not mere side effects to be countered only through "innovative policies" but rather that these constitute the fundamental structures of currently existing Latin American capitalism. In other words, by effacing power from its political economy, Latin American neostructuralism disregards the "deep structure" of contemporary Latin American capitalism with tragic analytical and political consequences. A review of its institutional publications and the concerns of its senior analysts over the 1990–2007 period shows that these three dynamics have not been brought to the forefront of neostructuralism's research agenda and policy recommendation. This is particularly troubling because transnationalization, financialization, informalization, and precarization of labor capital relations mutually reinforce one another, deepening and expanding their effects on the economy, polity, and society. As we will see, each one of these processes casts doubt on Latin American neostructuralism's optimistic vision about the "high-road" to globalization, the feasibility of "productive transformation with social equity," and even the maintenance of social cohesion within acceptable levels without major structural reforms. More importantly, these three understudied trends puncture neostructuralism's development strategy and question the appropriateness of policies designed to further the region's transnationalization while ministering to the victims of the dispossession and exclusion that it engenders.

Transnational Capitalism and Surplus Extraction

While *Productive Development in an Open Economy*, published in 2004, can be seen as neostructuralism's belated acknowledgment that asymmetric relations indeed do characterize globalization, begetting "losers" and social polarization, this updated version of neostructuralism still naturalizes the transnationalization of capital and the expansion of transnational corporations. By rejecting economic surplus as an essential analytical entry point, Latin American neostructuralists are bereft of a lens through which these historically specific transnational forms of capital accumulation can be clearly understood. The accelerated process of transnationalization is explained as resulting either from the allegedly objective laws of technological transformation[1] or from the impact of transaction costs on business organization: "Depending on whether transaction costs can be reduced by most within the company or out in the market, this [location of the production] frontier will shift toward greater company size or preponderance of market transactions (outsourcing)" (ECLAC 2004, 29–30). I am not questioning here transnational capital's demonstrated capacity to reorganize production or push technological change. The point rather is that, for those coming from the center-periphery tradition and the system-wide perspective established by Raúl Prebisch, Celso Furtado and other ECLAC pioneers, this should not be the whole story. By marginalizing power relations from analysis, Latin American neostructuralism fails to adequately grapple with the scope, nature, and consequences of the increasing transnationalization of Latin America's productive structure, circuits of accumulation, class structures, and of the state itself.[2]

As presently configured, Latin American neostructuralism considers transnational corporations (TNCs) and transnational capital as the main protagonists in propelling the Latin American development process forward, given their alleged contributions to technology transfer and the revitalization of Latin American economies and societies. ECLAC's enthusiastic embrace ignores three important issues: (1) the magnitude reached by the transfer of surplus in the form of remitted profits and interest payments abroad; (2) the limitations that current transnationalization imposes upon countries for moving onto the "high road to globalization"; and (3) the new forms of surplus extraction and transfer embedded in transnationalized production and distribution value chains. A brief examination of each of these aspects illustrates the grim consequences resulting from the effacement of power from the political economy of development.

Profits, Interest Payments, and the Net Transfer of Surplus

Surplus continues to be extracted in significant amounts from Latin America and Caribbean countries as the internationalization of their economies intensifies. If during the 1982–90 period, known as the "lost decade," $221.5 billion dollars were the net transfer of resources from Latin America to center countries (an average of $24.6 billion a year), during the much shorter 1999–2004 period, Latin American has transferred a net amount of $157.9 billion abroad, or an average of $51.1 billion a year during the 2002–4 period (ECLAC 2004). In 2004 alone, the region transferred abroad $77.8 billion, the equivalent of 15.1 percent of the value of the total goods and services exported that year (see Table 7). Countries that have experienced intense transnationalization, like Chile, or those where privatization of formerly public assets has been relatively recent, like Brazil, display a rapid growth in net transfers. The volume of net resources transfered abroad climbed from $1.831 billion in 2002 to $9.689 billion in 2004 in Chile and from $10.252 to $31.612 billion in Brazil over the same period (see Table 8).

Without delving here into issues about foreign direct investment (FDI)—encompassing equity capital, undistributed profits, and loans from parent companies to affiliates—current data suggest that the problems raised by Theotonio dos Santos and other dependency theorists almost four decades ago continue to haunt Latin American economies today. Ignoring them will not make them go away.[3]

TABLE 7

Latin America and the Caribbean: Net Capital Inflows and Resource Transfers 1980–2004 (in billions of US dollars and percentage[b])

YEAR	TOTAL NET CAPITAL INFLOWS (1)	NET PAYMENTS OF PROFITS AND INTEREST (2)	RESOURCE TRANSFERS[a] (3)=(1)-(2)	RESOURCE TRANSFERS AS A PERCENTAGE OF EXPORTS OF GOODS AND SERVICES
1980	30.9	18.9	12.0	11.3
1981	40.1	29.1	11.1	9.6
1982	20.5	38.9	-18.4	-17.5
1983	7.9	34.5	-26.7	-25.3
1984	13.0	37.5	-24.5	-20.8
1985	3.9	35.5	-31.6	-28.1
1986	9.4	32.7	-23.3	-23.4
1987	12.4	31.0	-18.6	-16.4
1988	3.0	34.6	-31.6	-24.2
1989	10.2	39.0	-28.8	-19.7
1990	16.1	34.2	-18.1	-11.2
1991	35.1	31.4	3.7	2.3
1992	56.1	30.1	26.1	14.7
1993	66.4	34.5	32.0	16.5
1994	47.0	36.1	11.0	4.9
1995	61.0	40.8	20.2	7.6
1996	64.8	42.7	22.0	7.5
1997	80.2	47.7	32.6	9.9
1998	79.1	51.3	27.8	8.5
1999	48.6	50.4	-1.8	-0.5
2000	53.6	53.6	0.0	0.0
2001	51.8	54.7	-2.9	-0.7
2002	10.3	51.2	-41.0	-10.4
2003	21.4	55.8	-34.4	-8.1
2004[b]	-12.5	65.3	-77.8	-15.1

Source: ECLAC, *Statistical Yearbook*

a Net resource transfers are equal to net capital inflows (including non-autonomous capital) less the balance the income (net payments of profits and interest).

b Preliminary estimates

TABLE 8

Latin America and selected countries: Net resource transfers[a][b] 1991–2004 (in millions of U.S. dollars)

YEAR	LATIN AMERICA	ARGENTINA	BRAZIL	CHILE	MÉXICO	URUGUAY
1991	4210	-1573	-8570	-780	14777	-161
1992	26548	6402	584	1421	16406	8
1993	31470	9416	-1714	1070	17911	230
1994	10999	8147	-723	2005	-994	294
1995	20322	467	19951	-624	-1464	203
1996	22044	5195	19397	1684	-9169	185
1997	32559	9309	5863	4362	6073	486
1998	27837	10559	7222	-162	5371	793
1999	-1807	5678	-1227	-3079	2604	254
2000	2	1064	4078	-1621	6194	672
2001	-2894	-15947	6777	-2022	11498	702
2002	-40981	-20640	-10252	-1831	8786	-2602
2003	-34384	-11785	-14072	-3052	5709	964
2004[c]	-77826	-8346	-31612	-9689	-2932	-131

Source: ECLAC 2004, *Statistical Yearbook*, Statistical Annex, Table A-10

a   Net resource transfers are equal to net capital inflows (including non-autonomous capital) less the balance the income (net payments of profits and interest). Total net capital inflows correspond to the capital and financial accounts, plus errors and omissions, and the use of IMF credit and loans and exceptional financing. Negative figures indicate net outward resource transfers.

b   Negative figures indicate an outward transfers of resources.

c   Preliminary estimates.

Taxonomy of Transnational Capital's Strategy for the Region

These dismal results—increasing transfer of surplus abroad and declining positions of Latin America in the world manufacturing hierarchy—are, in part, the product of decisions and competitive strategies adopted by transnational corporations and transnational capital. The penetration of foreign multinationals into the major economies of Latin America rapidly increased in the 1990s. Over that decade, FDI exploded, rising from $14.2 billion a year during 1990 to 1992, to about $70 billion a year from 1997 to 1998, and peaking at $108 billion in 1999 (Mortimore 2000, CEPAL 2003a). In the wake of the 1998 Asian financial crisis, FDI declined to only $36.4 billion in 2003

(CEPAL 2005a). For 2005, net FDI flows in Latin America and the Caribbean were estimated to have reached around $47 billion (about 2 percent of the region's gross domestic product [GDP]), however, only 35 percent was estimated to be new investments, while the remaining $30.6 billion were destined for mergers and acquisitions (CEPAL 2005a).

FDI flows have played a major role in restructuring Latin American economies along with having important macroeconomic effects. FDI in the 1990s jumped from the equivalent of 1 percent to over 4 percent of the GDP. Between 1980 and 1997, for example, as a percentage of total investment in the region (what economists call gross fixed capital formation), FDI increased by a factor of more than four to 18.6 percent in 1997 (Mortimore 2000). The major reason behind escalating FDI flows during those years lies in the corporate strategies pursued by TNCs in Latin America. During the 1990s, transnational corporations deployed clearly differentiated strategies in different parts of Latin America and the Caribbean. Three discrete strategies initially identified:

1. *Search for efficiency* for their internationally integrated production systems by taking advantage of low labor costs in the assembly of products for reexport to third markets, as in the case of automobiles (Mexico), electronics (Mexico and Central America), and apparel (Mexico, Central America and Caribbean)
2. *Control of raw materials*, fundamentally in the oil and gas sectors (Argentina, Bolivia, Brazil, Colombia, Peru, Trinidad and Tobago, and Venezuela) and minerals (Chile, Peru, and Argentina)
3. *Access to national and regional markets (market-seeking)* in manufacturing and services, such as the cases of the auto industry (Argentina and Brazil), agro-industry (Argentina, Brazil, and Mexico), chemicals (Brazil), and financial services (Argentina, Brazil, Chile, Colombia, Mexico, Peru, and Venezuela), as well as in telecommunications, electricity, distribution of natural gas, and retail commerce in a host of different countries (CEPAL 2003a, Mortimore 2000)

In the pursuit of these strategies, TNCs have seized control over key economic sectors, becoming the dominant economic players to an extent never seen before in the region. TNCs control a rapidly growing share of the region's economic transactions; TNCs and their subsidiaries accounted for

43.7 percent of sales in the region from 1998 to 1999 compared to only 27.4 percent from 1990–92 (Carlson 2002, 22). A significant portion of FDI flowing into Latin America during the 1990s, however, did not create new productive capacity. For 1999 and 2000, for example, an estimated 50 percent of all FDI flows were to finance mergers, acquisitions, and participation in the privatization of already existing assets (Moguillansky 2002). By the end of the 1990s, foreign firms controlled 48 percent of sales for the largest five hundred firms, 62.7 percent of sales for the largest one hundred manufacturing firms, and 43.2 percent of sales for the two hundred largest exporting firms (see Table 9). At the same time, within the span of one decade, foreign banks came to control on average more than 60 percent of all banking assets in the largest Latin American countries, increasing their control from 1 percent to

TABLE 9

Latin America: Participation in key economic activities by type of enterprise (percentage)

	1990–92	1994–96	1998–99
Sales of 500 Largest Firms			
Foreign owned	27.4	32.1	43.7
Private domestic	39.4	41.0	37.2
State enterprises	33.2	26.9	19.1
TOTAL	*100.0*	*100.0*	*100.0*
Sales of Largest 100 Manufacturing Firms			
Foreign owned	53.2	59.3	62.7
Private domestic	42.6	38.6	37.3
State enterprises	4.2	2.1	1.2
TOTAL	*100.0*	*100.0*	*100.0*
Exports of 200 Largest Export Firms			
Foreign owned	–	29.2	43.2
Private domestic	–	35.9	32.7
State enterprises	–	34.9	24.1
TOTAL	–	*100.0*	*100.0*

Source: Table 7, Mortimore and Peres (2001) "Corporate Competitiveness in Latin America and the Caribbean," CEPAL Review, 47 (August).

90 percent of assets in Mexico between 1994 and 2001 and from 6 percent to 49 percent in Brazil between 1990 and 2001 (See Table 10).

Latin American neostructuralism's response to these trends has been to propose a strategy that shifts the focus from the *volume* to the *quality* of FDI under the slogan: better FDI = better benefits (Mortimore 2004). Rather than a blanket opening of the economy and elimination of controls, Michael Mortimore, head of ECLAC's Division on Foreign Investment, advocates better designed investment promotion policies. These new policies should aim to (1) identify, contact, and facilitate the entry of transnational corporations most closely aligned with national priorities and (2) analyze and benchmark the impact of FDI–TNC operations with regard to fiscal technology transfer and assimilation, training of human resources, production linkages, and local enterprise development. Unfortunately, a better understanding of TNC strategies can only go so far if it does not also address some fundamental issues that define the real and not the rhetorical path to the high road: the concrete capacity of the state to discipline foreign capital in the context of the WTO-based regime of global rules and to influence the interaction between transnational capital in reproducing a particular social structure and specific class dynamics. Without considering these options, ECLAC's proposed shift of emphasis can only lead to greater subordination and subservience to transnational capital and to a further intensification of the deeply skewed dynamics already in place.

TABLE 10

Latin America: Foreign control of bank assets (percentage)

	1990	1994	1999	2000	2001
Argentina	10	18	49	49	61
Brazil	6	8	17	23	49
Chile	19	16	54	54	62
Colombia	8	6	18	26	34
Mexico	0	1	19	24	90
Uruguay	4	7	33	40	61
Venezuela	1	1	42	42	59

Source: Comisión Económica para América Latina (2003). *La Inversión Extranjera en América Latina y el Caribe, 2002.* Santiago: Naciones Unidas. Table 3, p.19.

More recently, ECLAC admits that the inflow of FDI to Mexico and other Central American countries has yielded contradictory results as transnational corporations pursue their strategy of setting up export platforms. While these flows "have improved the international competitiveness of the subregion, measured as the share in world imports, [they] still [have] not produced the anticipated results in terms of international integration, especially from the perspective of the transfer and assimilation of technology, productive linkages, human resource training, and local entrepreneurial development" (ECLAC 2005; IED 2004, 17–18; my translation). In the case of South America, ECLAC's report on *Foreign Direct Investment in Latin America and the Caribbean 2005* depicts a rosy picture that disconnects the "gains" from the "shortcomings" of FDI flows. FDI has flowed in that region basically as multinationals (particularly those based in Europe) have sought to invest in the service sector and in natural resources. ECLAC asserts that "even though these flows *have increased systemic competitiveness* of these economies by improving their infrastructure and export support service activities, the international competitiveness of these countries continues to be low (ECLAC 2005, 18; my translation, emphasis added).

In the specific case of MERCOSUR, where Brazil and Argentina could be considered good candidates for emulating the industrial export growth of East Asian countries, the "market-seeking" strategies seem to predominate in the recent FDI boom. The trade performance of TNC affiliates operating there have led to a sort of "asymmetric integration": they produce for the internal market and, to some extent, for the regional ones, while importing large amounts of inputs and final goods from developed countries. A large part of the trade flows by these affiliates is intrafirm, that is, it flows between parent and subsidiaries of the same transnational corporation. Thus, even if TNC affiliates showed productivity gains in the 1990s, these gains were not fully reflected in a significant increase in exports and even less in extraregional exports by host countries. Hence, the boom in foreign direct investment has not contributed to improve MERCOSUR countries' participation in the world economy. As some studies show,

> MERCOSUR's TNC affiliates produce for the internal market and their exports are generally low. . . . [W]e must highlight the fact that trade liberalization has facilitated TNC affiliates to increment their imports both by replacing local suppliers for foreign ones as well as for complementing their local production with imported goods. . . .

Thus, even if affiliates have obtained productivity gains through specialization and restructuring (partly at the expense of reducing their linkages with the host economies), these gains have not yet been reflected in a significant increase in TNC affiliates exports, and even less in an increase in their exports destined towards the markets of developed countries. (Chudnovsky and Lopez 2004, 650)

Therefore, despite a significant increase in FDI inflow to the region, the beneficial effects are extremely limited because such flows have mainly contributed to increasing foreign control of already existing assets and to expanding TNC operations without comparable increases in exports or productive investment. Moreover, the dynamic influence of transnational capital's expansion in the region remains questionable because investment in research and development (R&D) for Latin American countries scores well below what would be required to follow the path of the Asian Tigers. Whereas in the United States, Finland, or South Korea, investment in research and development is close to 3 percent of the GDP, in Latin American countries it is below half of 1 percent. For Argentina, research and development expenditures as a percent of GDP has remained at 0.42 percent between 1996 and 2001, while in Chile it has declined from 0.58 to 0.54 percent over the same period (ECLAC 2005, table 6.1).

These issues, briefly itemized earlier, suggest the need to revisit concerns raised both by structuralism's founders and dependency theorists, reexamining the processes by which transnational corporations, banks, and international financial speculators transfer surplus abroad, strengthen monopolist and oligopolistic structures, deepen the region's technological dependence, and transform social structures. As long as the fantasy of a predetermined harmony of interests between transnational capital and Latin American development is upheld, Latin American neostructuralism will not be able to give these issues the necessary research and political attention they deserve.

Clusters, Global Commodity, Value Chains, and New Forms of Unequal Exchange

Neostructuralism's intellectual retreat handicaps it to vigorously address "old issues"—the contradictory effects of FDI flows, the increasing import intensiveness of transnational investment and production, the feeble linkages between exports and the domestic economy. It also renders it unprepared for critically evaluating *new forms of surplus extraction and unequal exchange* embedded in the more recent forms of organization emerging in the world economy. Thus, by promoting incorporation into global commodity and value chains, fostering export and service clusters, encouraging international subcontracting of production and services, and offering a more intense coupling of small and microenterprises to the activities of an export sector overwhelmingly dominated by transnational capital and domestic conglomerates, neostructuralism is unwittingly supporting new forms of surplus appropriation and unequal exchange.

Attention to these issues is particularly relevant given ECLAC's ardent support for open regionalism and free trade agreements, such as the North American Free Trade Agreement (NAFTA) and the Central American Free Trade Agreement (CAFTA), which contribute to expand internationally integrated systems of production and distribution for both buyer- and producer-driven commodity chains. Yet global commodities and value chains, clusters, and off-shoring take advantage of already existing spatially patterned inequalities, seizing and deepening them to maximize profits and fuel the self-valorization of capital. Therefore, it becomes imperative for Latin American and Caribbean countries to be able to assess just who captures productivity increases and how surplus is extracted and distributed along these chains.[4] Understanding how power is exercised in these expanding production and distribution networks is essential. By combining the notion of unequal exchange with the global commodity chain framework, some radical political economists once again have started to study the distributive consequences and expanding globalized manufacturing tied to affluent consumer markets linked through global commodity chains. So far, these questions have found no place on Latin American neostructuralism's research agenda. Today, differences in power no longer reside in the nature of the product (primary vs. manufactured) or the different characteristics of factor and labor markets in the center and the periphery ("sticky wages"), but rather they reside on the relative market power enjoyed by retailers and brand-name producers derived, in turn, from branding and similar forms of monopolistic competition that shape consumer preferences and competitive sourcing (Heinz 2003). Even if subcontractors and production workers face highly competitive conditions, in the long run, "they will be unable to capture the direct benefits of technological improvements or productivity enhancements in terms of higher standards of living, either in terms of increased profits or higher wages. The distribution of productivity gains will depend on the optimal competitive behavior of the large multinationals that possess some degree of monopoly power. Depending on the nature of the specific consumer market, the gains from low-cost production will be distributed between affluent consumers on the one hand and brand-name multinationals on the other" (Heinz 2003, 17).

It thus seems that under the new characteristics of a transformed global economy, the relocation of production "yields more than incremental advantages to the transnational companies; it entails conspicuous imbalances in the partition of the final value-added of the commodities in favor of transnational companies and other institutions in the developed countries (in "the North," i.e., the center of the world system), relative to the producers of the commodities located in developing countries ("the South" i.e., the periphery of the system)" (Somel 2004, 2). For these reasons, one author working with the Global Commodity Chain approach, first developed by Gary Gereffi, indicates that,

> asking how commodity chains reproduce and reinforce inequality
> in the global economy can be read as the obverse but apposite question of the one that orients current value chain research: how can
> developing countries leverage participation in these chains to benefit
> various constituencies, including firms, workers, and communities.
> Regardless of which way we ask the question, . . . the second generation of commodity chains research should expand the scope
> of analysis to include the various factors external to the chain—
> including the regulatory, institutional, and systemic contexts in
> which they operate—affecting the organization of these chains as well
> as the developmental outcomes associated with them. (Bair 2003, 28)

These authors suggest that Latin American neostructuralism's enthusiastic support for globalization has led it to neglect paying attention to new forms under which the development of the global capitalist economy continues to trap Latin American countries and direct producers in the underdeveloped pole, even as Latin America engages in the transition from natural resources to manufactured exports. Intense competition among southern producers— along with the market power of transnational corporations, their control over technology, financial resources, marketing skills, and access to northern markets—creates conditions for unequal terms of trade as transnational capital is in an ever more powerful position to control both purchase and sale prices of commodities.[5]

In its "early" optimistic version of "Productive Transformation with Social Equity," Latin American neostructuralism believed that a shift to manufactured exports would generate society-wide benefits and virtuous circles. In its "middle" stage, after tempering its initial optimism, it has refocused its efforts toward "productive change" and productive upgrading in open economies. This purportedly more enlightened policy encourages clustering, international subcontracting, and coupling small enterprises to the global commodity–value chains in the hopes that the benefits of value-added competitiveness will trickle down and irradiate to the entire economy. However, the structural and dynamic tendencies of global commodity–value chains suggest that power relations still forcefully shape who benefits from these arrangements. Hence, if the analysis of economists like Heinz and Somel is correct, then it is not farfetched to say that Latin American neostructuralists might be complicit in feeding the new global "satanic mills" *despite and on account of their more enlightened policies*, because they have effaced power from the analysis of international economic relations. Even when the sugar and cotton plantations of the past are replaced by global auto parts and apparel commodity chains, new and old forms of unequal exchange and appropriation of surplus from an increasingly super-exploited labor force still characterize Latin America's insertion within the world capitalist economy. These unequal and inequality producing relationships are also present in the international off-shoring and outsourcing of services, essential components of the emerging global value chains that countries like Chile aspire to join in their quest for the still elusive "high road" to globalization.

Financialization and Accumulation

Latin American neostructuralism's greatest blind spot is its incapacity to analyze financialization as one of the major transformations of the past decade. Though Latin American neostructuralists have thoroughly studied the impact of market failures created by financial liberalization and credit (Ocampo) and the macroeconomic instability created by international capital flows (Ffrench-Davis and Griffith-Jones), their emphasis has been on short-term policy management, not on understanding the deep structure and dynamics of the region's economy. The far-reaching consequences of financialization accompanying the development of capitalism in the region has remained below ECLAC's analytic radar.

Definition of Financialization

Financialization is a pattern of accumulation in which profits accrue primarily through financial channels (Arrighi 1994; Krippner 2005). It refers to "the increasing importance of financial markets, financial motives, financial institutions, and financial elites in the operations of the economy and its governing institutions, both at the national and international levels" (Epstein 2002, 3). The dominant trend in the advanced capitalist countries and in Latin America has been for domestic and transnational conglomerates to transfer a greater share of resources toward financial assets instead of productive investment. Financialization deserves greater attention for a number of reasons. It is one of the dominant transformations currently under way in the world economy radically transforming the logic of action of enterprises and the state. Persistent problems dogging Latin American economies—low rates of gross capital formation, economic growth without job creation, rising income concentration, informalization of labor-capital relations—are inextricably connected to financialization processes. In brief, financialization is recasting power relations, altering logics of action, and influencing contemporary patterns of economic growth, investment, and policy design. Through its far-reaching impact on the economy, enterprises, and the state, financialization is redrawing the parameters for achieving greater equity and political democracy in the region, yet it remains a process that Latin American neostructuralism has "not dared speak its name."

Consequences of Financialization

While the consequences of financialization have received increasing attention for the Organisation for Economic Co-operation and Development (OECD) countries (Power, Strong, and Epstein 2004; Epstein and Jayadev 2005; Stockhammer 2005; Krippner 2005), it has not yet become a core concern of critical political economist studying Latin America with only a few exceptions (Salama 2004). The existing literature suggests four major areas where financialization has impact and its effects on Latin American need further study: (1) weak growth rates due to a decline in productive investments; (2) precarization of labor as mergers and acquisition and downsizing intensify in a never-ending race to prop up shareholder value; (3) a shift in the structure and dynamics of class relations; and (4) a reduced margin for public policy. Let us briefly examine each of these to understand how financialization impinges upon neostructuralist claims about globalization and undermines its utopian vision.

Weak growth rates as surplus flows to speculative, not productive invest-ment. As the logic of profits in Latin American economies become subjugated to what Pierre Salama calls finance-dominated growth regimes, the rentier behavior among the transnationalized conglomerates that dominate the region's economy increases and productive investment falls. The rate of gross capital formation suffers as increasing portions of the economic surplus are destined to take advantage of speculative opportunities (Salama 2004).

Precarious and flexible employment. Financialization also transforms labor–capital relations through direct and indirect effects, increasing labor flexibility and precarious employment. A shift from a situation where corporate finance was based on the retention and reinvestment of revenues toward equity finance, combined with the rise of global financial actors, such as pension funds and neoliberal policies on capital mobility, has resulted in a heightened emphasis on "shareholder value" and short-term rates of return (Lazonick and O'Sullivan 2000). With financialization, the rate of profitability demanded by investors tends to increase, and institutions are transformed to meet this demand or lose out to competition from other firms. With financial liberalization and deepening capital markets, financialization alters the structure and motives of "industrial firms" as they increase their rentier motivation and dependence on share price appreciations.

One of the ways through which management props up a firm's value in local and international stock markets is by downsizing, outsourcing, and reducing labor costs. Privatization and mergers and acquisitions tend to increase labor flexibility. The boom of speculator capital in the 1980s in the United States and the boom of privatization and financial liberalization of the 1990s increased labor flexibility to boost share prices.

Financialization fosters labor flexibility and job insecurity in the modern, globalized firms, linked to national and international stock markets and in which downsizing and leaner workforces are demanded by shareholders composed by mutual funds, insurance companies, and pension funds. Less globalized and integrated, domestic firms, both medium and small, see their industrial profits fall as a result, among other things, of high interest rates set to discourage the outflow of international capital. These firms are also forced by financialization to defend their profits through strategies that rely on furthering labor flexibility and the informalization of labor capital relations (Lara 2002).

Shifts in the structure and dynamics of class relations. As the economy becomes increasingly dominated by global finance and short-term investment flows, financialization also changes the correlation of forces and dynamics of society. Financialization creates instability and generates difficulties in stabilizing the new regime of accumulation (Boyer 2000). The balancing of production and consumption, an always present challenge for a capitalist economy, becomes much more difficult under the conditions of the current global economy, restricting "the use of Fordist strategies that expand social wages to balance production and consumption" (Smart and Lee 2003, 153).

One of the most important consequences of financialization is that it encourages the concentration of wealth and income in an ever smaller and more powerful minority. The concentration of income severely distorts the incentive structure and signals sent by the economy in two important realms: the *generation* of profits and the *use* of profits. Thus, it comes to pass that "it is the spending behavior of a minority that determines savings and accumulation" (UNCTAD 1997, 158). Whereas under an import substitution industrialization (ISI) regime of accumulation, a rich minority exercised its distortion on the economy mainly through consumption, today an even smaller minority imposes its rules on how economic surplus is going to be invested. The example of Chile, Latin America's most globalized society, is illustrative. The rentier share of income from 1996 to 2003, that is, that share of GDP generated through financial motives, represented an average of around 22.2 percent of the GDP.[6] The rentier share of income—the sum of the profits of the financial sector, interest income of nonfinancial corporations, and household interest income as a percent of nongovernment GDP, bordered close to 25 percent during 1999 and 2000, in the midst of the post–1998 Asian recession, falling to around 18 percent by 2003. Whereas in 1996, the interest income of nonfinancial corporations represented only 25.9 percent of the total, by 2003 this proportion had risen to over 35 percent (see Table 11). When compared to other countries, Chilean rentiers occupy the upper echelons in an international ranking of countries: below the United States (35.4 percent), Mexico (32.7 percent), and the United Kingdom (24.5 percent) but above Germany (17 percent), South Korea (15 percent), and Spain (14.2 percent) (Epstein and Jayadev 2005).

The rentiers' share of GDP (23 percent in Chile; 33 percent for Mexico) reveals only one aspect of the problem. Data about corporate governance structures and the high degree of ownership concentration and control are another important aspect to consider. Studies about corporate governance in

TABLE 11

Chile: Rentier share of income 1996–2003 (in current pesos and percentage)

	1996	1997	1998	1999	2000	2001	2002	2003
Total Rentier								
Income*	6,463,613	6,677,254	7,723,371	7,953,558	8,653,885	8,353,680	8,332,420	7,798,321
Financial Sector	3,775,464	3,446,257	3,505,639	3,897,928	4,210,369	4,023,159	3,943,278	3,739,931
Interest Income								
Non Financial								
Corporations	1,679,592	2,009,130	2,807,528	2,716,359	3,113,339	3,033,433	3,193,097	2,767,260
Household								
Interest Income	1,008,557	1,221,867	1,410,204	1,339,271	1,330,177	1,297,088	1,196,045	1,291,130
GDP minus								
Government	27,811,234	30,862,160	32,337,751	32,534,714	35,519,458	38,065,986	40,397,909	44,417,012
Rentiers' Share								
of GDP (%)	23.2	21.6	23.9	24.4	24.4	21.9	20.6	17.6

Source: Author's calculations on the basis of Banco Central, *Cuentas Nacionales 1996-2003*.
*Following Power, Epstein and Abrena's methodology in "Trends in Rentier Incomes in OECD Countries: Estimates, Data and Methods," paper by the Political Economy Research Institute (PERI), Amherst, MA.

Latin America reveal that the single largest stockholder controls, on average, over 50 percent of corporate assets: 61 percent in Argentina, 51 percent in Brazil, 55 percent in Chile, and 52 percent in Mexico (see Table 12). The top three shareholders, on average, own over 80 percent of assets, and through preferred stock arrangements, and designated directors by the top controllers, these figures probably underestimate the level of concentration (Leffort 2000).

Reduced margin for public policy. Through a densely layered set of power relations, financialization significantly compresses the margins within which countries can design public policy. The international mobility of capital and liberalization of financial markets enhances the ability of institutional investors and speculators to blackmail governments into submission, forcing them to adopt policies convenient to their narrow interests. Shifts in government financing from reliance on the Central Bank to the private sector, through the issue of tax-free government bonds, increase the leverage that financial capital has over policy makers. From the point of view of macroeconomic policy

TABLE 12

Shareholder ownership concentration in Latin America

COUNTRY	SAMPLE SIZE	PERCENTAGE OWNED BY LARGEST SHAREHOLDER	PERCENTAGE OWNED BY LARGEST 3 SHAREHOLDERS	PERCENTAGE OWNED BY LARGEST 5 SHAREHOLDERS
Argentina**	15	61	82	90
Brazil*	459	51	65	67
Chile*	260	55 ·	74	80
Colombia**	74	44	65	73
Mexico**	27	52	73	81
Peru*	175	57	78	82

Source: Leffort, Fernando, "Corporate Governance in Latin America" Lefort F., Walker E. (2000 a), Corporate Governance: Challenges for Latin America. *Revista ABANTE*, Vol 2, No 2, octubre.

making, globalization forces upon governments an ironclad policy trilemma: the impossibility of simultaneously maintaining free capital flows, control over the exchange rate, and an active monetary policy through management of the interest rate (Blecker 1999; Mascarilla i Miró 2005).

Additionally, the International Monetary Fund's (IMF) recent support for a structural balance rule (SBR) creates an additional fetter further reducing the margins for public policy. In the case of Chile, the SBR was introduced in March 2000 with the stated objective of ensuring a fiscal surplus of 1 percent of the GDP in the medium-run. The explicit objectives of such policy were twofold: reduce the procyclical nature of fiscal policy and "improve the credibility of fiscal policy," which was an important goal in the face of the election of Socialist Ricardo Lagos. The adoption of the SBR was warmly welcomed by transnational capital and international financial institutions, seeing in its adoption one more step toward clinching the subordination of fiscal policy to the maintenance of profit friendly environment. Along with the existence of an "independent" Central Bank and the adoption of inflation targeting framework governing monetary policy, the SBR has to be seen as one more safeguard discouraging "populist" temptations.[7]

The case of Chile, to be examined in greater detail later in chapter 9, illustrates the way in which adoption of the SBR effectively constrains fiscal expenditure. One of these is the creation of a consultative body with ample representation of right-wing economists linked to right-wing political parties of the *Union Demócrata Independiente* (Independent Democratic Union [UDI]) and Renovación Nacional, as well as to the directorates of the local and transnational conglomerates, which acts as the panel that regularly meets to determine the economy's mid- and long-term trends and estimate two key variables that enter into the calculation of the SBR: potential GDP and the long-run reference price of copper, Chile's main export (Marcel, Tokman, Valdés, and Benavides 2001). These estimated values are then used to establish the government's "structural income," an amount that is stripped of cyclical variations in tax revenues and copper prices. Fiscal expenditure is then set to achieve a surplus of 1 percent in relation to structural income (IADB 2004, 285).

Underlying these political maneuvers, however, is the intense financialization of the Chilean economy and the requirements to ensure high rates of return for the domestic and internationally based transnational financiers and speculators that increasingly dominate its main sectors. In 2004, IMF directors "praised Chile's commitment to a prudent fiscal policy, reinforced by adherence to a structural balance rule, which calls for a surplus of 1 percent of GDP in the central government's fiscal accounts. They commended the authorities . . . for restraining overall spending, despite higher revenues from the surge in copper prices. They supported the decision to use surpluses accrued in the Copper Stabilization Fund to selectively prepay government debt" (IMF 2004, 2).

What the "autonomous" Central Bank, IT framework, and the SBR reveal is the level of subordination of monetary and fiscal policy to the requirements of rentiers and financial speculators. Exceedingly low inflation rates and constraints on proactive policies in the midst of high unemployment rates and sluggish growth can only be explained because those policies favor the interests of rentiers (Epstein 2005). In sum, financialization not only contributes to the concentration of income and lower productive investment but also severely constrains monetary and fiscal policy. Such results stem from the destabilizing macroeconomic effects of international capital flows–studied by ECLAC—and from the ignored transformations in power relations brought about by the financialization of Latin American economies, and in the very nature of contemporary capitalism.

The Precarization and Informalization of Labor–Capital Relations

Just as transnationalization and financialization of Latin American economies evidence both the limits of neostructuralist analysis and discourse, the informalization of labor–capital relations embedded in expanding export-oriented (EO) accumulation remains a major conceptual and policy stumbling block for Latin American neostructuralism.[8] Over the last decade, capitalist restructuring and export-led growth has brought structural changes in the relationship between output growth and employment creation and has intensified tendencies toward the precarization, terciarization, informalization, and feminization of the labor force. The magnitude and new conditions under which these trends unfold undermine the very foundations of the conceptual framework deployed by Latin American neostructuralism.

Data from Latin America and Chile attest to the failure of labor reforms in reducing unemployment, inequality, and poverty. The International Labour Organization's (ILO) regional office for Latin America and the Caribbean with headquarters in Lima publishes the *Labour Overview* annually, informing on the condition of workers and the evolution of labor markets in the region. Along with the Inter-American Development Bank's (IDB) 2004 report *Good Jobs Wanted: Labor Markets in Latin America*, they offer more than enough information to draw a composite picture of the major macro trends over the last decade and a half that continue mystifying neoliberal and neostructuralist economists alike.

1. *Rising unemployment despite growing economies.* Even with a recuperation of GDP growth rates during the 1990s, unemployment in the region has tended to increase. The fact that GDP and export growth rates have recovered in comparison to the 1980s and the 1998–2002 slowdown has not yielded an equivalent capacity to create jobs in sufficient numbers or reduce unemployment levels. Researchers affiliated with the IDB found that the rise in unemployment over the 1990s, "is not driven by a higher proportion of women, adults or urban workers in the labor force, nor can it be attributed to an increasing demand for skilled workers" (Duryea 2003, 2). The current pattern of EO growth has proved incapable

of generating jobs in sufficient volume. During the 2000–2004 period, Latin American economies grew at an annual average of 2.8 percent, yet the average annual unemployment rate was 11.8 percent, which is higher than the 9.6 percent for the 1995–99 years when the economy also grew at the rate of 2.6 percent per year (ECLAC 2004; ILO 2004).

2. *Growing informality*. Instead of declining, the informal sector grew significantly during the 1990–2003 period from 42.8 percent of urban employment in 1990 to 47.4 percent in 2003. At the same time, the majority of job creation took place in the informal sector: six out of ten jobs created in the 1990–2003 period were in the informal sector, while employment in large private establishments fell from 42.9 to 39.5 percent (ILO 2004). The unexpected persistence and expansion of the informal sector has led World Bank economists to sugarcoat rather than reexamine their basic assumptions regarding informality. Michael Maloney, Lead Economist in the World Bank's Office of the Chief Economist (LCRCE) of the Latin America and Caribbean region has proposed that "we should think of the informal sector as the unregulated, developing country analogue of the *voluntary entrepreneurial small firm sector* found in advanced countries" (Maloney 2004, 1159). At the same time that the size of the so-called informal sector has increased, the percentage of the labor forced employed in the goods producing sectors of the economy has consistently declined, even in countries posting above average growth rates. For Latin America, nonagricultural employment in the goods producing sector fell from 28.8 percent in 1990 to 25 percent in 2003. Data for Chile show that employment in the goods producing sector fell from 31.3 percent of the labor force in 1994 to 27.6 percent in 2003 (see Table 13).

3. *Falling Wages*. ILO data on the real wage index shows that real wages rose at an average yearly rate of 3 percent during the 1990–94 period and 0.7 percent during the 1995–99 period and began to decline at –1.2 percent during the 2000–2003 period. Measured in purchasing power parity (PPP)-adjusted U.S. dollars, other studies suggest that average wages "remained constant or declined throughout the decade both in the Mexico and Central America region and in the Andean region . . . wages in dollars increased in the Southern Cone, in particular in Chile and Brazil, relative to

TABLE 13

Latin America and the Caribbean: Nonagricultural employment by economic activity 1990–2003

COUNTRY/YEAR	TOTAL	GOODS PRODUCING SECTOR[b]	MANUFACTURING, MINING, WAGER GAS AND ELECTRICITY	CONSTRUCTION	SERVICES[c]
Latin America					
1990	100.0	28.8	21.7	7.1	71.2
2002	100.0	26.1	19.6	6.5	74.1
2003	100.0	25.0	18.9	6.1	75.1
Argentina					
1991	100.0	26.4	18.2	8.2	72.1
2000	100.0	23.9	16.8	7.2	76.1
2002	100.0	22.2	15.5	6.6	77.8
2003	100.0	22.0	14.5	7.5	78.0
Brazil					
1990	100.0	28.6	20.9	7.7	71.0
1995	100.0	25.0	16.7	8.3	75.0
2002	100.0	27.0 ·	18.0	9.0	73.3
2003	100.0	25.9	17.8	8.1	74.4
Chile					
1994	100.0	31.3	20.9	10.4	67.6
1996	100.0	28.0	17.7	10.3	72.0
2000	100.0	28.1	18.8	9.4	71.9
2003	100.0	27.6	17.8	9.8	72.4
México					
1990	100.0	30.0	25.0	5.0	69.9
1995	100.0	20.9	20.1	0.8	79.1
2000	100.0	30.0	29.3	0.7	70.0
2002	100.0	27.8	27.3	0.6	72.2
2003	100.0	26.6	26.0	0.6	73.4
Uruguay					
1991	100.0	31.3	24.2	7.1	68.7
1995	100.0	26.3	19.0	7.3	73.7
2001	100.0	25.5	16.8	8.7	74.5
2003	100.0	22.7	15.5	7.2	77.3

Source: Organización Internacional del Trabajo (OIT), *Panorama Laboral 2005* (Lima: Oficina Regional de la OIT, 2006), Compiled from Table 7.A

their values in the early 1990s despite the sharp increase in unemployment registered in this group of countries. Nonetheless, wages
did decline somewhat toward the end of the decade in Brazil and
Chile" (Duryea, Jaramillo, and Pagés 2003, 20).

4. *Increasing wage polarization.* Neoliberals predicted that wage inequality between skilled and unskilled workers would be reduced
as demand for the relatively more abundant unskilled workers
increased and the barriers that prevented unskilled workers from
entering into the formal sector were removed through labor market deregulation. Data collected by the IADB's 2004 study shows
the opposite trend: wage differentials increased substantially in
most countries (see IDB 2004, table 82).[9]

5. *Growing precariousness of jobs.* One dominant and unexpected
trend is the growing instability and precariousness of employment as measured by the high rates of turnover, the growth of
precarious employment, and of jobs that do not enable workers to
climb above the arbitrarily defined official poverty lines, much less
adequately reproduce their labor power. In a study of twelve Latin
American countries, the IDB found that job turnover ranges from
16 to 35 percent. In the case of Brazil, for instance, "a change of 1.1
percent in the unemployment rate hides an impressive amount of
activity in the labor market; gross flows indicate that each year one
out of three jobs is either created or destroyed, meaning total job
turnover is 31 percent" (IDB 2004, 6). Data from the ILO's *2004
Labor Overview* provide another indicator for growing insecurity
workers face: the proportion of workers contributing to a social
security has declined from 66.6 percent in 1990 to 63.6 percent in
2003, and these figures (as the case of Chile illustrates) significantly
overestimate the percentage of the labor force having effective
social security coverage.[10]

6. *Persistently high number of working poor:* At the same time, the
number of workers earning poverty wages remains extremely high
in the region. Using as a measure the number of workers employed
in jobs earning one PPP-adjusted U.S. dollar per hour or less, IDB
researchers find that the "percentage of workers earning 'poverty
wages' ranges from under 40 percent in Chile, Panama, Costa Rica,
Mexico and Uruguay to over 70 percent in El Salvador, Bolivia,
Nicaragua and Honduras" (Duryea, Jaramillo, and Pagés 2003,

22). They finally acknowledged what was obvious to critics in the region for many years: entry into the labor market does not ensure exit from poverty, given the nature of the region's flexible labor markets (see Leiva and Agacino 1994; P. Escobar 2003, 70–78).

7. *Feminization of the labor force.* Each one of the previously mentioned trends is itself a gendered process. ILO specialists like Laís Abramo stress the triple gender segmentation endured by Latin American women workers because they tend (1) to concentrate in the bottom level links of productive chains, where technological, productivity, working conditions, and job stability are more precarious; (2) to concentrate within firms and production processes, with the lowest levels of technology and where work is less skilled and more routinized; and (3) to be excluded from training, work enrichment, and participation mechanisms fostered by management (Abramo 2003). In the face of these trends, Latin American neostructuralists' acceptance that the role of public policy intervention is to be a handmaiden to EO growth, because such a strategy will be able to address the issues of social exclusion and inequality in the region requires vigorous questioning. Its flawed mode of theorization and its marginalization of power relations leads it to understudy (and underestimate) two contemporary tendencies: (1) the relationship between EO accumulation and labor flexibility and (2) the powerfully corrosive effect of the labor flexibility–poverty–inequality nexus on neostructuralism's dream of growth with equity.

A critical political economy approach would not paper over these contradictions but would explore them guided with five alternative propositions that challenges the waning neoliberal perspective and the ascending neostructuralist view by locating the study of power relations between labor and capital at the center of analysis (see Leiva 2006). A more incisive examination of the current processes of informalization of labor capital relations would be oriented by the following insights:

- Given the nature of labor power, labor control is a central, unavoidable, and defining component constituting the very base of the structure and functioning of the capitalist economy.

- Labor control exercised by capital has a dual dimension encompassing both the point of production (workplace) and the sphere of reproduction of labor (household and the community).
- The forms under which labor control is exercised changes historically given the rise, predominance, and decline of different forms of production.[11]
- The capitalist labor process represents the unity of the valorization of capital and the socio-technical organization of production.
- Labor control and the labor process itself are gendered processes (Humphrey 1987; Salzinger 2003).

The importance of these propositions is that unlike the neostructuralist vision, the realm of production is understood as *both a technical and a social process* where capital must exercise its control and domination over labor within specific conditions of valorization and class struggle (Humphrey 1980). The organization of industry and the labor process is not reduced to some immanent requirement of technical change but is seen rather as the outcome of (1) the need to control and organize labor through diverse monitoring systems; (2) the fact that this requirement is exercised in the context of increased capitalist competition; and (3) the fact that the accumulation of capital takes place under certain specific social and political conditions, and the precise form assumed by labor control depends on these conditions (Humphrey 1980). These constitute part and parcel of the competitive strategies being deployed by capital in the region and include: the extension of the workday; the lowering of the value of labor power; the intensification of the labor process and some more recent forms utilized in flexible accumulation strategies that have become generalized in the era of capitalist globalization. In general, these strategies seek to further transfer the costs of production and reproduction onto workers and their families through a wide gamut of ever more creative processes of informalization of labor–capital relations carried out by capitalists and abetted by the new institutional arrangements seeking to increase international competitiveness be it via the "spurious" or "genuine" paths.

The informalization of labor–capital relations that has intensified in the past decade cannot be fully explained by only alluding to sluggish economic growth rates or the inherent "structural heterogeneity" of Latin American societies. Informalization and precarization of labor–capital relations are the expression of far-reaching redrawing of class, gender, race, and ethnic power relations in society so as to enable the reorganization and relaunching of a new process of valorization of capital. The strategies observed in Latin America during the past decade and a half combine some old and new efforts toward achieving this goal. Lowering the value of labor power, intensifying the pace of work, lengthening of the working day, and transferring the costs of production and reproduction away from capitalist and the state onto the shoulders of workers, their families, and mostly women, all form part of the wide menu of firm-based employer initiatives, legalized by the labor reform process and intensified by export-led growth and corporate-led globalization. None of these can be adequately examined by the utopian vision defended by Latin American neostructuralism.

7

The Politics of Neostructuralism and Capital Accumulation

Without social cohesion, a country is conflict-ridden. A conflict-ridden country cannot be competitive. To be able to compete internationally, it is necessary to have social cohesion.

—Ricardo Lagos, *El Merurio Online* 2003

The neostructuralist paradigm assigns political leadership, concerted action, and participatory governance key roles in forging systemic competitiveness at every level of society. In contrast to neoliberals who envision only the market as the defining space for their modernizing project, neostructuralists have a much keener understanding of the role institutions, politics, culture, and subjectivity play in economic development and management of globalizing processes. Therefore it is in the realm of politics more than the strictly economic where neostructuralist conceptualizations seem to be currently having their greatest impact. This chapter examines the contradictory outcomes of the conceptual turn toward reconnecting politics and economics enacted by neostructuralists under the present historical circumstances. Perhaps it is here where we find the most politically and ideologically potent of Latin American neostructuralism's core foundational ideas, namely that concerted action, effective leadership, and promotion of participatory governance can best ensure the adaptability of society to the requirements of international competitiveness while deepening equity and social cohesion. It is here where neostructuralism fully assumes its role as providing a grand narrative for Latin America's path toward modernity in the twenty-first century. This grand vision promotes the active, though carefully circumscribed, agency by a broad spectrum of social actors ranging from state managers, capitalist exporters, unionized workers, party leaderships, nongovernmental organizations (NGOs), and community leaders. Participation and concerted action are seen as the most effective means for marshaling the forces of cooperation in a society thrust into the raging fires of competition, constantly fanned by globalization. Leadership provided by a restructured state, according to Latin American neostructuralism, is essential for orchestrating and guiding the cultural transformations required; such state intervention constitutes the linchpin guaranteeing that the virtuous international competitiveness–social cohesion–political stability circle can prosper.

A Contradictory Restoration of Institutions and Politics

The incorporation of a nonmarket and nontechnocratic lexicon is widely celebrated as the triumph of a more holistic, alternative approach to development, signaling a resounding defeat of economic fundamentalism. This chapter inscribes Latin American neostructuralist discourse within a broader historical context in order to examine how its political interventions interact with the new matrix of social power, decisively contributing to the establishment of a new mode of regulation, an indispensable component for consolidating and legitimizing the existing export-oriented (EO) regime of accumulation. More specifically, this chapter traces how the politics of neostructuralism are oriented toward constructing that "ensemble of socially embedded, socially regularized and strategically selective institutions, organizations, social forces and actions organized around (or at least involved in) the expanded reproduction of capital as a social relation" (Jessop 2002, 5).

To present such analysis, this chapter examines the logic behind the politics of neostructuralism and how by promoting consensus and new forms of participatory governance, laudable goals in themselves, it actively supports the quest for international competitiveness as the overarching societal goal. First, the notions of orthodox and heterodox paradoxes are presented, remarking on the conceptual flounderings faced both by neoliberalism and neostructuralism when assessing changing state–society interactions over the last decades. Second, by revisiting the French Regulation School (FRS) and its concepts of regime of accumulation and mode of regulation discussed in chapter 3, I explore how neostructuralist "participatory" public policies sustain capitalist profits and the accumulation process. The neostructuralist approach is oriented by a notion succinctly summed up by Chile's former president, Ricardo Lagos: Without social cohesion a country is conflict-ridden. A conflict-ridden country can not be competitive. To be able to compete internationally, it is necessary to have social cohesion" (*El Mercurio Online*, August 17, 2003; my translation).[1]

State and Society: From the "Orthodox" to the "Heterodox" Paradox

In addition to short-circuiting its own foundational myths and evidencing analytical myopia regarding the transformations experienced by Latin American capitalism, the contradictions embedded in Latin American neostructuralism's mode of theorization also find expression in a third ambit, that of politics through what I call the "heterodox paradox." Such a notion best captures both the historical role and the political impact that Latin American neostructuralist ideas and policies are having on the reorganization of state–society relations in the region. The term "heterodox paradox" encapsulates a unique political outcome: in the quest of international competitiveness, Latin American neostructuralism's carefully crafted policies aimed at consensus building, expanding participatory governance, and fostering a new type of civil society–state alliances deepen the subordination of the public sphere and society's noneconomic realm to the logic of private transnational capital.

Such an outcome, so distant from the progressive intentions of Latin American neostructuralists (and heterodox economists) should not be that surprising. Time and time again, history has punctured the emancipative pretensions of a wide gamut of economic and development discourses and progressive political projects.[2] What we need to discern is how neostructuralism's unwillingness to explicitly consider the interaction of the state with the many facets of class power leads to outcomes that I denote as the heterodox paradox.

As we have seen earlier, neoliberalism and laissez-faire dogmatism gave rise to the "orthodox paradox," a process whereby "economic policy reforms aimed at expanding the role of markets *appear to strengthen the power of the core of the state*, the executive branch and to enhance its control over key economic policy variables which affect the outcome of key economic activity" (Bates and Krueger 1993, 463; my emphasis). The notion of the "orthodox paradox" became the elegant term to represent that outcome witnessed during much of the 1980s in Latin America, which surprised mainstream thinkers. Free market economic discourse and policies of liberalization, deregulation, and privatization gave rise first to dictatorial regimes, the systematic commission of summary executions, forced disappearances, and other crimes against humanity perpetrated by state terrorism and massive government bailouts of private capitalists later.

In the same fashion, by excising power from the analysis of both the economy and politics, Latin American neostructuralism deploys a set of public policies that, while aimed at improving the quality of "democratic governance," ultimately contribute to consolidating the domination of transnational capital over all aspects of social life in the region, legitimizing the export-oriented regime of accumulation initially structured by neoliberalism.

Neostructuralism's Public Policy Palette

The conceptual underpinnings behind the politics of Latin American neostructuralism are an amalgamation of different intellectual trends, ranging from the mea culpa for their structuralist past, a technologically deterministic view of current transformations in the world economy (flexible specialization, third industrial revolution, arrival of "information," and "knowledge" society), new institutionalist economics, neo-Schumpeterian evolutionary models, post–modernism, and, more recently, the political theorizations about citizenship, social policy, and risk management spawned by the Third Way and post-neoliberal European social democracy.[3] Elements from all of these currents, along with a critical assessment of Latin America's recent political history of authoritarianism and negotiated transitions, have found their way into the intellectual stew, providing the conceptual rationale for the politics of Latin American neostructuralism. The late Norbert Lechner, a political scientist associated with the Facultad Latinoamericana de Ciencias Sociales (FLACSO, Latin American Faculty of the Social Sciencs), the Economic Commission for Latin America and the Caribbean (ECLAC), and the United Nations Development Program (UNDP) in Chile, was one of the first to pose a question to which the politics of Latin American neostructuralism attempts to provide the answer: "What is the structural context in which the question of the democratic governance of Latin American society is currently posed?" (Lechner 1997, 7). His work suggested that perhaps Latin American leaders should step back and ask themselves to identify all those mechanisms through which a society ensures a certain degree of basic coordination among the different processes and actors (both individual and collective) that constitute it. For him, this approach required nothing less than "a very far-reaching reconstruction of all our theories. Basically, it is a question of *forming a whole new conception of social coordination under the new conditions*" (Lechner 1997, 7; emphasis added). Such reframing led to a revalorization of the political role of the state and politics. These not only had to foster extra-market forms of social coordination capable of improving a country's international competitiveness, but in doing so, they also had to consciously seek to produce social cohesion in the face of uncertainty and fragmentation produced by modernity and globalization.[4]

Influenced by Chile's own economic and political experience from 1990 to 2007, Latin American neostructuralism has conceptualized and reconceptualized the competitiveness–social cohesion–political stability nexus, developing over the years a sophisticated discourse and expertise to design policies aimed at transforming such a vision into a reality. The most important components of the public policies formulated by Latin American neostructuralism include the promotion of different modalities of: (1) consensus-building; (2) participatory governance; (3) public–private sector partnerships; (4) taking advantage of and nurturing social capital; and (5) the construction of new forms of citizenship relying on state-civil society alliances (see Figure 16). Although these are not uniquely ECLAC creations, the merit of Latin American neostructuralism lies in using these to formulate a seemingly coherent framework for strengthening the political and ideological role of the state and establish guidelines through which to politically direct its contribution to the long-term stabilization of the export-oriented regime of accumulation.

Consensus and Concerted Action

Consensus and concerted action rather than coercion are the preferred means for managing social conflicts and for capturing and unifying social energies behind the push for competitiveness. Successful implementation of "changing productive structures with social equity" and producing social cohesion in the era of globalization demands the "structuration of a national project that will foster that the main actors in the development process (entrepreneurs, workers, intellectuals, political and social leaders) privilege a logic of cooperation over one of confrontation" (Villarzú 2002; my translation). Through the promotion of national accords among political and social actors behind this national societal project (*proyecto país*), labor accords, fiscal covenants, and advisory panels, Latin American neostructuralism attempts to exercise leadership over society and manage the major conflicts that stand in the path of a favorable investment environment and the export drive.

Extra-economic policy initiatives	1. Consensus-building 2. Stimulating cooperation 3. Promotion of public-private sector partnerships 4. Nurturing and tapping social capital 5. New forms of state-civil society alliances 6. Construction of "new citizenship" and participatory governance
Critique from the perspective of political economy	Innovative" social policy: Re-edits the old marginality approach: the state through its "society-creating" actions must "civilize" the poor and discontented, so they participate through new market and non-market mechanisms. The Heterodox Paradox: Public policies may facilitate the subordination of the non-economic sphere and of colonization of public space to the logic of transnational capital.

Figure 16. Neostructuralism's extra-economic policy palette.

Participation

Although seen uncritically as an expression of the "third wave" of democratization (Brautigan 2004), the expanding rhetoric on "participation" has complex, and often overlooked, international origins. Within international development agencies, three different sources have fueled the expansion of the "politics of participation" over the last quarter century: (1) an imperial logic of counter-insurgency; (2) a technocratic logic of international development institutions; and (3) the managerial and globalizing logic of the "Third Way." In their own particular manner, each of these has percolated into the neostructuralist discourse. A brief detour reviewing each one of these feeder streams is necessary to underscore that in the present historical context, participation has a profoundly contested character. Because a wide set of different actors—ranging from multinational mining conglomerates spewing mercury and cyanide into the groundwater needed by indigenous agricultural communities, politicos intent on ensuring that investment projects by multinational conglomerates go forward unchallenged, to marginalized local communities aiming to gain voice in national policy making—will

wield the rhetoric of participation to achieve different objectives, it is important to carefully analyze the context and purposes for which the notion of
participation is today being used.

"Participation" in the imperial and counterinsurgency logic. In the case
of Latin America, emphasis on participation began to emerge in the mid-
1980s in the context of the U.S. counterinsurgency and low-intensity conflicts in Central America, particularly in El Salvador. "Decentralization" and
"participation" became important complements to military force in the U.S.
counter-insurgency effort. In 1986, for example, the United States Agency
for International Development (USAID) fostered the reform of El Salvador's
Municipal Code to promote "decentralization." In 1987, it launched the *Municipalidades en Acción* (MEA) Program: "To promote popular support for
the government and increased community involvement, USAID linked the
disbursement of MEA funds for municipal-level infrastructure improvements to local resident participation in the identification of projects at open
town meetings, called *cabildos abiertos.* While the existing municipal code of
1986 formally required mayors to hold *cabildos* four times a year, the potential of receiving MEA funds provided mayors with a real financial incentive
to convene *cabildos*" (USAID, 1997). USAID evaluated the 1987–94 MEA
program as successful because "the MEA became a vehicle for strengthening
local democracy, enabling local governments to become more active, providing municipalities with the responsibility for reconstructing war-damaged
infrastructure, and addressing some of the fundamental grievances which
fueled insurgency—a lack of voice in local affairs and a lack of basic services"
(USAID 1997, 2).

The initial counter-insurgency logic of winning "hearts and minds" became generalized beyond the scope of USAID itself. After 1993, the promotion of "participation" evolved from its counter-insurgency dimension toward becoming an important component in efforts to "bring participation
into USAID's support for policy reforms,"[5] *neoliberal* policy reforms, that is.

From the initial experience of municipal decentralization run by USAID
in El Salvador, promoting the "participation of civil society" evolved further
to become incorporated in project guidelines or handbooks of the World
Bank, the Inter-American Development Bank (IDB) and the Organization of
American States (OAS). This seemed the logical next step as these institutions
sought to shore up support for the neoliberal reform program in the region
and for governance structures that could facilitate economic liberalization.[6]

"Participation" in the Technocratic Logic of the International Development Institutions. According to the IDB, "the more attuned that state and civil society actions are to the myriad of ways in which poor households confront their poverty, the more effective poverty reduction programs and policies are likely to be" (Lustig and Deutsch 1998, 3). Starting in the mid-1990s, most international development organization set up specialized teams to introduce the concept of "participation" in their programmatic activities. The World Bank, IDB, and OAS adopted guidelines to ensure the "participation of civil society" in project implementation.[7] Embracing the "politics of participation" came to be seen as crucial for increasing the efficiency and effectiveness of these institutions' loans and policies. According to the IDB's Participation Resource Book, "Participation empowers and mobilizes people as actors and overseers of their own development; it is one of the ends of development as well as one of the means. It can help create and maintain stable democracies and good governance as well as economic growth. . . . When poor and marginalized people participate in development projects, they acquire skills and *develop attitudes* which may facilitate their integration into the wider society. From the Bank's viewpoint, *participation also improves the financial and developmental sustainability of projects, thereby enhancing portfolio performance"* (IDB 2008; emphasis added).

"Participation" in the Logic of the "Third Way." In his influential book *The Third Way*, Anthony Giddens offered a new policy framework for politically responding to changes in the global order. In his view, the "Third Way" refers "to a framework of thinking and policy-making that seeks to adapt social democracy to a world which has changed fundamentally over the past two or three decades. It is a third way in the sense that it attempts to transcend both old style social democracy and neoliberalism" (Giddens, 1998, 26). According to Giddens, with the end of collectivism and the undermining of tradition and custom brought on by modernity and globalizing markets, social cohesion can no longer be guaranteed by the top-down action of the state or the appeal to tradition: "We have to make our lives in a more active way than was true of previous generations, and we need to more actively accept responsibility for the consequences of what we do and the lifestyles we adopt" (Giddens 1998, 37). The state is obliged therefore to construct a new relationship with civil society. According to Giddens, "the overall aim of the third way politics should be to help citizens plot their way through the major revolutions of our time: globalization, transformations in personal life and relationship to nature" (Giddens 1998, 64). In the new context of

globalization, the legitimacy of the state depends on its capacity to contribute to "risk management." The Third Way conceives participation as critical for ensuring legitimacy of institutions and, above all, as the expression of individualized social agency in which individuals accept responsibility for their choices in a context in which social life becomes increasingly subordinated to the whims and myopia of global market forces.

The three logics succinctly reviewed have had a powerful impact in Latin America, influencing both ECLAC and government planners. The experience of USAID in El Salvador and the "counterinsurgency" logic, for example, influenced the Municipal Reform decreed by General Augusto Pinochet and framed subsequent debates and legislation on municipal decentralization. It imprinted within military and civilian-regime officials an acute awareness about the crucial role that municipalities played in channeling discontent, ensuring social control, and generating electoral support. The technocratic logic of "improving portfolio performance" sought to raise the efficiency of poverty alleviation programs, reduce transaction costs, and tap into the survival strategies of the poor themselves to reduce fiscal and employer expenditures on social services. Finally, the logic of the Third Way is at the core of the *Nuevo Trato* or New Covenant (analyzed in chapter 8) offered by President Lagos and the Concertación III government; it is also behind the new generation of "risk-abatement" social policies that have recently gained popularity among international development institutions and within ECLAC (cf. Tokman 2003; Sojo 2003) and lies at the heart of ECLAC's 2007 document *Social Cohesion: Inclusion and a Sense of Belonging in Latin America and the Caribbean*. In its latest versions, the "politics of participation" have been designed, in part, to preempt disenchantment and discontent with globalization, averting therefore the spread of "neocommunitarian" movements that refuse to accept the cosmopolitan elite's notion of progress and orient the state's political interventions so that the population willingly come to accept that all aspects of social life become subordinate to the forces of commodification and the logic of capitalist competition.

Public–Private Sector Partnerships

Neostructuralism's explicit acknowledgement that private entrepreneurs (and private investment) is the key actor in the development process lies at the base of its support of public–private sector partnerships at every level of society, including the export-drive, the process of technical innovation, and, more recently (after 2004), funding measures to ensure social cohesion. Promoting this type of partnership ensures that the whole gamut of command and network-based forms of social coordination are brought to bear to support and complement market and profit-driven forms of coordination. The negotiation of free trade agreements such as the North American Free Trade Agreement (NAFTA), the Central American Free Trade Agreement (CAFTA), and the Mercado Común del Sur (MERCOSUR, Common Market of the South) has offered a key opportunity for promoting such partnerships as close and ongoing relationships between government ministries and different business associations flourish to define national policy and negotiating stances.

Social Capital

Social capital has become the latest conceptual fad to be embraced by the development establishment (recall "informal sector" and "microfinance") attributing to it all sorts of explanatory and healing powers by those unwilling to look for answers by looking directly at the face of Latin American capitalism itself and its structural and dynamic uses and misuses of the economic surplus. Like the World Bank (Woolcock and Narayan 2000), neostructuralist planners have dedicated much time to studying the concept and reflect on its importance for policy design (Atria et al. 2003; Arriagada 2005). Though social capital remains a highly contested and debated concept (Fine 2002), the building of trust and attention to sociability has been actively incorporated in the design of social policy by neostructuralism and Latin American governments. Extensive use of the concept reinforces neostructuralism's self-image that, through its more holistic approach, it is possible to design public policies that effectively take advantage of all a society's resources. As the ECLAC staff member in charge of this policy has stated, "The model of social capital that we have elaborated with some ECLAC colleagues can be summed up as follows: Social capital is the content of certain social relations and institutions characterized by behaviors of reciprocity, cooperation, feedback and attitudes of trust" (Durston 2005, 48; my translation).[8]

Following a line of reasoning similar to other international development agencies, Latin American neostructuralism has honed its conception of social capital along two different and interrelated dimensions: (1) as an economic asset that can be tapped to support the accumulation process and (2) as a field that opens promising new forms of political intervention. Dagmar Raczynski and Claudia Serrano, long-time Chilean experts on social policy and ECLAC consultants, emphasize that the economic dimension of social capital can only be tapped effectively *once its socio-emotional dimension is clearly understood*: "Social capital is realized and manifests itself through social relations, but what gives it specificity is the notion of capital in an economic sense; that is, that it a resource that can be activated to generate greater wealth" (Raczynski and Serrano 2005, 100; my translation). Valuing the economic potential that social capital has must also be accompanied by fully grasping its unique character, which requires, in turn, "keeping in mind that such a resource is not only material and tangible, but that it *also has important socio-emotional content*, for example, self-esteem, self-awareness and the exercise of influence, autonomy, power and control." Other productive resources, natural resources, physical capital, financial capital, human capital, they point out are the property of an individual. Social capital, however, "is deposited on social relations which form the basis of social capital, they assume a given framework of trust and reciprocity, and lead to acting together: cooperation to achieve shared goals and objectives" (Raczynski and Serrano 2005, 100; my translation, emphasis added). It is these relations of trust and reciprocity that state intervention must be able to skillfully tap into in order to produce the desired policy objectives: greater international competitiveness and social cohesion. Neostructuralism's superiority to dogmatic neoliberalism is thus revealed: *its ability to identify the socio-emotional dimension and the building of trust as the self-conscious objects of state policy in order to ensure greater international competitiveness*.

New Forms of Citizenship and State–Civil Society Alliances

Under the "post–Washington Consensus," economists and other social planners have come to challenge the market-dogmatism of neoliberalism but not the pillars of the export EO economic model imposed on the region over the past decades. In their view, "participation" is closely tied to "good governance" because, among other benefits, it improves the process of "revealing preferences" and raises allocative efficiency in the provision of public goods. According to ECLAC/ and Instituto Latinoamericano de Planificación Económica y Social (ILPES) specialists on decentralization and state reform:

> Citizen participation in the process of the provision of public and collective goods is not only a fundamental social and political

objective but also a prerequisite for reducing inefficiencies. Whether citizens participate, however, depends on their perceiving that the benefit of participating is higher than the cost; if they are given the opportunity to participate in decisions that affect their current and future income, this can be a strong incentive for them to do so. In order to achieve this condition, political decentralization must be more than the mere transfer of power from one center to others; indeed, it must be based on a reform aimed at *encouraging citizen involvement in (public and collective) cooperative solutions*, with the limit on such involvement being the point at which efficiency gains are equal to the economic cost of participation. (Finot 2002, 137; emphasis added)

Neostructuralism superimposes upon a thinking still imbued with cost–benefit calculations, an emphasis on the emerging postmodern forms of citizenship currently being produced by globalization. In the new context, the state and political leadership must discover how to leverage these new forms so as to produce both legitimation of existing institutions and maintaining social cohesion. As the resident social theorist at ECLAC headquarters, Martin Hopenhayn explains that such an effort must be based on the understanding that at present,

citizens's actions do not converge on a single focal point (the State, the political system, or the nation, as its territorial expression) but are scattered over a multitude of fields of action, spaces for the negotiation of conflicts, territorial areas and interlocutors. The citizen ceases to be a mere depositary of rights promoted by the State of Law or the State as society, and instead becomes an individual who, insofar as his rights permit, seeks participation in areas of empowerment which are defined according to his capacity for action and also his instrumental appraisal of which area is most favorable for the demand he is trying to make. And as the role of individual consumption (both material and symbolic) grows in importance in the life of society, the sense of belonging *shifts from the Nation-State to a wide variety of fields in the production of such a sense and the interaction of individuals*. The republican idea of citizenship reappears, but not so much in the field of political participation as in a great variety of forms of association or communication at the citizen's social level which do not necessarily converge on the public or State spheres. (Hopenhayn 2001, 116–17; emphasis added)

Neostructuralist discourse argues, then, that because globalization has re-cast the notion of citizenship becoming now more focused on individuality, difference, and cultural identity based on gender, race, ethnicity, and so on, a new realm of intervention for producing a sense of belonging opens up, dur-ing the current historical period in which all that is solid seems to be melting into thin air. Additionally, the alleged existence of a "new technico-economic paradigm"—the information revolution—creates the material basis for new forms of social coordination that emphasize networks over and in addi-tion to those of command and market.[9] Hopenhayn, with a gaze focused on Chile, where bourgeois hegemony was successfully constructed, posits that "citizens are leaving the streets and meeting-points and concentrating on the individual processing of information in front of their television sets or computer monitors" (Hopenhayn 2001, 118). This is not how teachers in Oaxaca or the residents of Cochabamba or El Alto or Chile's indigenous construct citizenship. Based on this highly questionable reading of the new context, Latin American neostructuralism goes forth in the design of public policies, fusing economics and politics in a discourse about Latin America's path to modernity, where the overarching objectives are increasing interna-tional competitiveness, safeguarding social cohesion, and ensuring political stability.[10] These lofty goals are to be accomplished by consciously relying on the political system to promote consensus-building initiatives, participatory forms of governance, public–private partnerships, state–civil society alli-ances, and new forms of social coordination that take advantage and nurture existing social capital. To be successful, such policies much ensure greater harmony among the market, command and network forms of social coordi-nation, at the same time that greater emphasis is placed on operating at the socio-emotional or symbolic levels to create new forms of citizenship.

Capital Accumulation and the Politics of Neostructuralism

Mainstream development economists, not just neostructuralists, have in-creasingly turned to examine how institutions contribute to economic devel-opment. In "Concepts for Analyzing and Designing Institutions," a Techni-cal Appendix to *Beyond the Washington Consensus: Institutions Matter*, for example, World Bank lead economists Shahid Burki and Guillermo Perry offer a useful catalogue of six areas where attention to institutions has been considered important: (1) asymmetrical information and principal-agent problems; (2) feedback devices; (3) property rights, contracts, and enforcement mechanisms; (4) transaction costs; (5) provision of public and collective goods; and (6) predictability and credibility for economic development (Burki and Perry 1998). Latin American neostructuralists, on the other hand, while incorporating such a framework, go a bit further, stressing the importance of democratic institutions and participatory governance in managing economic outcomes. Beyond the debate between enlightened orthodox mainstream and neostructuralist economists, a number of other actors such as state planners, political leaders, and corporate managers, have also embraced the politics of participation for much more concrete reasons: at this juncture of the restructuring process—when the dirty work of the first two stages of capitalist restructuring, stabilization and structural reforms, have been for the most part already carried out—mechanisms for participatory governance can *create more favorable conditions for the accumulation of capital.* Thus a space of confluence opens up, where the banners of participation and citizenship raised by neostructuralism and the center-left, and the current requirements for the valorization of capital, commingle and become mutually supportive.

But just how do deploying "participatory governance" and the gamut of public policy initiatives contained in the neostructuralist public policy palette contribute to raise capitalist profits, the main driving force in the capitalist economy? For the case of Latin America, a tentative inventory can be offered. "Participation," as conceived by neostructuralists, contributes to increase profits and assuage contradictions that arise from the accumulation process itself through a number of channels. Among the most important of these, we can identify the following: (1) increasing worker acquiescence and productivity; (2) reducing the burden on capitalists for assuming the costs of reproduction of the labor force; (3) subsidizing capital by coupling the survival strategies of the informal proletariat and informal firms with the cost-cutting strategies of export and domestic-market oriented firms; (4) promoting relations cooperation and trust that facilitate the constitution of clusters, subcontracting relations, and incorporation of firms into global value chains; and (5) influencing the expectations of investors by creating a stable political and social environment and planning horizon. An analysis of the forms that the politics of neostructuralism is directly contributing to the accumulation of capital reveals that there are many different ways in which this unfolds (see Figure 17).

Systemic Competitiveness, Productivity, and Profits. As we saw, the core neostructuralist concept of systemic competitiveness calls upon the State to generate a consensus and concerted action behind the export drive and to

Raising the profit rate and assuaging contradictions stemming from capital accumulation itself through:	Subordinate nonmarket-based forms of coordination to capitalist profitability and capital accumulation:
1. Productivity—Worker consent	• Participatory wages • Tripartite agreements • Pro-active labor flexibility • Elicit worker engagement in constant reorganization and monitoring of production processes
2. Subsidize capital by coupling survival strategies to cost-cutting plans of private firms	• Social policy that makes the poor protagonists in the poverty-reduction policies • State–civil society alliances and municipality-based poverty alleviation policies
3. Facilitate formation of clusters, subcontracting, and incorporation into global value chains	• Enhance relations of cooperation and trust • Promote network forms of social coordination, in addition to command and market based coordination
4. Reduce costs of reproduction	• Subcontracting of social programs to the NGO sector • Social policy based on Competitive Social Funds • Legitimization and better regulation of privatized social security, health, and education services • Fiscal covenants and structural balance rules preventing neo-populism
5. Create long-term expectations that facilitate the investment decision	• Reduce conflict • Build consensus • Fiscal covenant

Figure 17. Capital accumulation and the politics of neostructuralism.

actively improve the interface between society's different sub-systems (education, infrastructure, public administration, etc.) with private exporters' efforts to penetrate international markets. "Systemic competitiveness" also had important consequences for labor as it had to promote worker involvement in production. Success in changing Latin America's export profile toward manufactured goods with greater value-added, would be achieved to the extent that worker consent and active worker involvement in the struggle for competitiveness is forthcoming. Moving toward differentiated and better quality products calls for replacing vertical and hierarchical labor relations with more horizontal and flexible ones, "characterized by an intensive exchange of information, so that the initiative, creativity and responsibility of the labor force can be taken advantage of" (CEPAL 1992a, 23; my translation).

A political economy approach such as the Regulation or the "Social Structures of Accumulation"[11] schools envision production as having a social and technical character. Consequently, productivity growth will be affected by the nature of social relations of production and the degrees of conflict or cooperation existing at the workplace. For a long time, it has been observed that, under certain conditions in advanced capitalist countries, cooperative labor–management relations improve the rates of technical and organizational innovations, which in turn raise labor productivity (Buchele and Christiansen 1999). Greater participation can have an impact at the level of the individual worker by helping solve the labor extraction problem, while at the collective level it improves the quality of coordination in the production process. As some have argued, capitalist production, the transformation of inputs into a final output via wage labor, has to be understood as a two step process: (1) the transformation of labor time into effort (the question of labor intensity) and (2) the effectiveness of labor effort (Buchele and Christiansen 1999). It is clear that how much the effort that workers exert will affect productivity; at the same time if "workers' efforts are not appropriately organized and coordinated, they may exert increased efforts without increasing value added (the quantity and quality of output)" (Buchele and Christiansen 1999, 91).

Nevertheless, the parameters for participation at the workplace have to be clearly delineated. While greater worker involvement will increase productivity, it might also generate negative consequences. If workers lack job security, increases in output per hour may lead to layoffs and rising wages: "workers can only be expected to contribute to productivity growth to the extent that their jobs are secure and they can count on sharing its rewards. Furthermore, they are only able to contribute to the extent that they have a say about how work is organized and carried out" (Buchele and Christiansen 1999, 88).

Through multiple initiatives, such as the encouragement of a "new" type of labor movement supportive of systemic competitiveness and not class conflict, the adoption of variable wages, proactive labor flexibility, promoting labor accords, and its discourse of growth with equity, Latin American neostructuralism is able to navigate, for a while at least, the conflictive waters of promising both higher profits and greater labor empowerment. Political and ideological interventions via the state apparatus and the political party system ensure that unions and workers acquire the required modern attitude: that they participate but do not threaten the prerogatives of capital. Political intervention by Latin American neostructuralism at the workplace through the promotion of consensus, concerted action, and worker involvement is aimed at increasing productivity, profits, as well as constructing workers with a winning attitude. This is one of the outcomes of neostructuralism's politics, because, "at the foundation of the capitalist mode of production is the production of subjectivity in both senses of the genitive: the constitution of subjectivity, of a particular subjective comportment, and in turn the productive power of subjectivity, its capacity to produce wealth" (Read 2003, 153).

"Participation," Capturing the Social Energy of Poor, Coupling it to Export Strategies. The technocratic logic of "improving portfolio performance" has sought to subsume the poor's survival strategies to capital's valorization strategy by appropriating the social energy of the poor. Maintaining international competitiveness requires a cheap and flexible labor force that fully shoulders the daily and generational costs of the reproduction of labor. "Participatory" social policy discourses encourage both the self-provisioning of services, as well as the NGO-assisted expansion of "micro-entrepreneurs" and home-based production activities. Both can be relied upon to increase the competitive edge of exports and to lower costs for domestically oriented enterprises. Increasing international competitiveness and the efficiency of social expenditure is at the core of neostructuralist concern. This technocratic logic of increasing efficiency by replacing universal social rights (health, education, etc.) with the poor's "entrepreneurial spirit" has informed the design of Concertación social policy in Chile, and via its discovery of "social capital" has increasingly become a component of neostructuralist public policy in the entire region.

Participation, Coordination, Clusters, and Externalization. In order to couple small and medium firms to the dynamic high-speed sector of Latin American economies already incorporated into global markets, neostructuralists have increasingly focused on public policies geared to enhance relations of cooperation and trust among these enterprises so that they can become attractive enough to be part of EO clusters, subcontracting networks, and be incorporated into global value chains through which transnational capital organizes its internationally integrated systems of production and distribution of goods and services. Market forces alone will not create conditions for such participation and, through neostructuralist public policies, a win–win situation is offered. Transnational corporations (TNCs) can find favorable local conditions to organize their outsourcing and cost-cutting strategies, while local firms can find a way of getting a foot into globalized networks and initiate a process of productive and technological upgrading.

Costs of Reproduction of Labor. According to the FRS, one of the defining characteristics of a regime of accumulation is the distribution of surplus between accumulation and consumption. Neostructuralist policies maintain the profitability of EO regime of accumulation by reproducing structural conditions that reduce the costs of reproduction of labor and liberate capital and the state from having to share these costs with workers and their families. Through social programs subcontracted to the NGO sector and poverty alleviation policies that rely on competitive social funds, the state significantly reduces its direct responsibility. At the same time, through the political legitimization and better regulation of privatized social security, health, and education, the relation between public and privatized social services is eased, ensuring that an important portion of social spending helps expand the commodification of social services, supports the profit rate of private social service providers who have "cherry picked" the most profitable customers, those wealthier and healthier than average. Through the adoption of fiscal covenants and mechanisms, such as the Structural Balance Rule (SBR) or inflation targeting (IT), structural guarantees are given to transnational capital that popular pressures to cover the costs of reproduction of labor will be effectively contained. Fiscal spending will be restrained even when there are abundant surpluses, so proactive policies do not lead to inflationary pressures or exchange rate fluctuations that threaten the profits of exporters and financial speculators.

Expectations. Capitalist profits can only be realized at the end of the accumulation process when the money advanced in hiring workers, purchasing raw materials, and expanded through the surplus value generated in production can be realized. In order to invest, capitalists must be able to "make reasonably determinate calculations of their expected rate of return" (Gordon 1980, 12). The requirements to make these calculations include, among others: (1) the availability of raw materials at stable prices; (2) the effective organization and control of the labor process; (3) an appropriate structure of final demand; and (4) an appropriate system of money and credit that can help capitalists finance the three stages of the capitalist accumulation: the purchase of the means of production and labor power, the production process, and the realization process (Kotz 1994a).

In addition to these five broad areas where the promotion of carefully choreographed and delimited forms of participation directly contributes to sustain the profit rate, Latin American neostructuralism also fosters a gamut of other initiatives—at the workplace and the local level. These indirectly contribute to the accumulation process by laying foundations for those institutions, norms, and behaviors that will ensure the management of conflicts and reproduction of the social system. By establishing institutional and concerted means for channeling conflict and forging consensus, the politics of neostructuralism facilitate the creation of a stable horizon for expectations, demanded by national and transnational productive as well as speculative investors who have seized control of Latin American economies.

The material consequences of the "politics of participation" is that they contribute to resolving contradictions that arise from the valorization of capital itself through the promotion of policies, behaviors, and expectations in key sites and moments of the accumulation process. As analysts of the Chilean experience have indicated, "the forging of a basic consensus on the economic model in Chile, has been an important stabilizing factor to boost investment and national savings" (Solimano 1999, 123). This consensus must be produced not only at the "commanding heights" of the economy; it must also be generated in the different microsites where the valorization of capital takes place: the workplaces, households, and communities where workers and their families, through their paid and unpaid labor, facilitate the self-expansion of capital. Neostructuralism's historical role then cannot be fully grasped by only examining how the "politics of neostructuralism" contribute to smooth out those contradictions arising from the accumulation process itself. As we shall see in chapter 8, it is essential to explore how these also decisively contribute to institution-building and the cultural conditioning of the population, forging not only new institutional arrangements but also those subjectivities vital for constructing a new system of regulation.

8

Erecting a New Mode of Regulation

By conceptually linking recent transformations in Latin American economies with the need for institutional arrangements to promote a new citizenship in the era of globalization, Latin American neostructuralism makes a decisive contribution to the post-neoliberal politics of development. Through a broad spectrum of public policies, which in the wake of dogmatic neoliberalism appear as innovative, Latin American neostructuralism fosters the construction of new social arrangements and institutional mechanisms. With its heightened attention to the "extra-economic," Latin American neostructuralism designs and erects a new set of mediations for managing contradictions engendered by export-oriented (EO) accumulation of capital, thereby ensuring that social cohesion remains within parameters compatible with the overall reproduction of the system. These include, and are not restricted to, policies and institutional arrangements geared to promote (1) the expansion of the new forms of nonmarket social coordination; (2) the creation of new expectations and subjectivities, the "new citizens" capable of constructing meaning, a sense of belonging, and allegiances to existing institutions; (3) the cooptation, domestication, or destruction of autonomous social organizations resisting and challenging the state and its policies; (4) the development of a new bureaucratic complex within the state apparatus capable of deploying social policies at the submunicipal scale and establishing new forms of social control in finely targeted microsocial and spatial territories and the socio-emotional dimension; and (5) new state–civil society alliances that enable the enduring colonization of the public sphere and noneconomic realm by the logic of transnational capital and of the EO regime of accumulation (see Figure 18). These specific types of mediations were absent in the political practice of dogmatic neoliberalism and were not prevalent under the bygone import-substitution industrialization (ISI) regime of accumulation. As we review these, it is useful to recall the discussion of French Regulation School (FRS) in chapter 3, particularly the notion that a regime of accumulation also

requires the existence of a set of interiorized norms, habits, laws, and networks ensuring that individual behaviors will be compatible and supportive
of the reproduction of the system as a whole. This set of mediations it calls
the "mode of regulation." Along with the production of the corresponding
forms of subjectivity, these new institutional arrangements are central to
stabilize and manage the conflicts arising from the new patterns of capitalist
accumulation.

Let us briefly examine each one of these five mechanisms to illustrate
how Latin American neostructuralist discourse interacts with existing social
power, establishes foundations for the mode of regulation in EO accumulation economies and does so under the rhetoric of participatory governance,
democracy enhancing public policies, and construction of a new sense of
belonging. To further illustrate how the politics of neostructuralism are deployed in the region toward achieving these goals, in addition to discussing
the previously mentioned set of public policies, I also examine the politics of
Nuevo Trato, or New Covenant, offered by Chile's Third Concertación government led by Ricardo Lagos (2000–2005), heavily influenced by Economic
Commission for Latin America and the Caribbean (ECLAC) and neostructuralist thinking. Such analysis provides the basis for discussing the contradictions of neostructuralist politics and its attempts to overcome the inherent contradictions of Latin American capitalism with a conceptual apparatus
that systematically marginalizes power from analysis. I close with a fuller
discussion about the historical role of Latin American neostructuralism than
what has been offered in previous chapters.

Expanding Forms of Social Coordination

Neostructuralism is acutely aware that those traditional forms of political
representation that prevailed under the ISI developmentalist state from the
1940s to the 1970s have exhausted themselves and, similarly, that neoliberalism's sole reliance on market-based coordination has also reached its limits.
As Norbert Lechner suggests, "there can be no social coordination unless
individuals are guided by some kind of 'common good'. . . . The *symbolic dimensions of coordination* is therefore extremely important. In contrast, the
market offers neither a collective idea of the existing order nor a forward-
looking horizon. In other words, coordination through the market does not
include two typical dimensions of political coordination: representation
and leadership" (Lechner 1997, 11; emphasis added). Based on such line of

Contribution to Erecting a "Mode of Regulation"	Colonize the Public Sphere and the Non-economic Realm
1. Expand forms of social coordination	Promote networks to supplement state and market based mechanisms Foster forms of cooperation, trust, reciprocity, and associativity Social Funds under joint state and civil society management Promote state, corporate, and civil society-based entrepreneurial philanthropy to share burden of promoting social cohesion
2. Orient State action in the construction of globalization's new "market citizens"	Promote the distribution of symbolic goods (participation, sense of belonging, common vision, etc.) Design policies aimed at the socio-emotional dimension to reorganizes the practices and experiences of vast groups of individuals and collectivities (Schild 2000) Foster policies in which citizens are conceived as empowered clients of services, "who as individuals are viewed as capable of enhancing their lives through judicious, responsible choices as consumers of services and other goods" (Schild 2000: 276).
3. Destroy autonomous social organizations, creating channels for coopted and institutionalized participation	Micro-enterprise training programs Social policy increasingly based on Competitive Social Funds (Fondos Concursables) Decentralization/Municipalization undermines de-facto organization and leadership role of women Nuevo Trato geared only to "non-materialistic" organizations that do not see the state as the recipient of social demands
4. Expand the State apparatus: State–Civil Society–NGO Complex	State–Civil Society Alliances in the design, funding, implementation and evaluation of social policies Competitive Social Funds (Fondos Concursables) Extension Workers/Promotores linked to State and Planning Ministry that penetrate the social territories of the poor Change of Legislation to facilitate NGO development and private philanthropy

Figure 18. Erecting a new mode of regulation.

thinking, neostructuralism's contribution is precisely that it provides a new interpretative framework for the emergent social relations, which, in order to be sustainable over time, require redefining the role of the state and of politics. Redefining politics and the role of the state is essential so that an active inter-penetration of market, state, and network-based forms of coordination can be encouraged at a time when the quest for international competitiveness has been defined as the supreme societal objective. In the process, new conceptions of citizenship, identity, and subjectivity are to be fashioned. Understanding how market, command, and network forms of coordination can be best brought to bear upon the production of social cohesion has become one of the central concerns for the politics of neostructuralism. Accepting existing limitations (the "realities on the ground"), neostructuralists seek to expand the "degrees of freedom" for public policies through more creative and better ways of coupling market, state, and network-based forms of social coordination and enhancing this mutual support through purposeful leadership from the political system. As neostructuralism becomes increasingly aware that globalization imposes constraints on national level macro policies, it also realizes that it faces new political challenges. The nature of these were voiced during a visit to ECLAC headquarters by President Lagos: "how to generate additional spaces for social cohesion without having these conspire against more private investment, and as a result, against more employment? And . . . how to support such cohesion through the establishment of an alliance between the State and the private sector upon a different basis than what has traditionally existed, *so that public entities are no longer the only ones exclusively burdened with financing social cohesion?*" (Lagos 2003, 47; my translation, emphasis added).

Guide State Action to Create "New Citizens"

ECLAC's social theorist, Martin Hopenhayn, officer in charge of the Social Division at ECLAC headquarters, has identified where the new frontiers for such public policy lie. Afer all, in open and globalized economies, any public policy that burdens transnational investors can lead to their stampede and rapid exit from the offending country. Therefore the leading edge in novel forms for citizenship construction is to be found through an important paradigm shift, since, it is not just a question, within the bounds of modern democracy, of returning once again to the question of the *redistribution of material resources, but rather of bringing up the question of the distribution of symbolic resources*, such as participation, access to information, and presence in the exchange of messages (communication). Closer links must be promoted among the organizations that express the demands of those groups least integrated in to the benefits of modernization. This requires that the political system above all and after it the State social sector, should promote *actions to strengthen the network of social movements which have the capacity to discern* both the immediate and long-term demands of those groups and to help exert pressure in favour of those demands on the relevant decision-making bodies, *within a framework of political viability and the further consolidation of democracy*. (Hopenhayn 2001, 120; emphasis added)

Thus, since in the era of globalization the main goal of state policy has been redefined as consisting in the distribution of symbolic rather than of material resources, then the state must selectively encourage only certain types of social movements: those deemed capable of discerning what is and what is not "viable." In other words, as we shall see in this chapter, for the case of Chile, the state must seek an alliance with those movements that, though engaged in demand-making, do so in modalities that do not question the hegemony of transnational capital. In this sense, like it did in the 1960s through "popular promotion" programs, the Latin American state must once again undertake a "civilizing" mission, this time however, oriented toward creating the "new market citizens" required by the modernity being hewed out by globalizing capital (Schild 2000). This task demands active state intervention through different "society-creating" initiatives that increasingly rely on nongovernmental organizations (NGOs) willing to enter into state–civil society alliances. The purpose of such policies is to reorganize the practices, experience, and perceptions of those sectors of society "who as individuals are viewed as capable of enhancing their lives through judicious, responsible choices as consumers of services and other goods" (Schild 2000, 276). In this civilizing and society-building task, the political system plays a decisive role by self-consciously and purposely *choosing to operate at the socioemotional and personal psychological level*; it must provide the horizon or reference framework within which it is now up to each person to become a "participant" in an individualized, and no longer collective, process of identity construction and a sense of belonging. In order to be successful, state efforts must support the formation of community social capital, empower weak social actors (workers, indigenous peoples, women, youth), and most importantly, forge an emotional link between the community and state agent deployed in the new microspatial scales of state intervention (Durston 1999). Only in this manner, will it be possible to fully deploy in all of its power the socio-emotional nexus between the agents of the state and client population to produce mainly at the symbolic level, a sense of belonging in an increasingly polarized society.

Domestication of Autonomous Social Organizations

Producing these new type of citizens for the "new times" requires that leadership from the political system must also shape a new mindset and a new political culture, capable of guiding actions by social organizations along what have been defined by policy makers as politically viable orientations and practices. Traditional organizations such as unions, urban squatters, rural indigenous communities, and community-based organizations that still see the state and capital as the main adversary and target of their demands have to be reeducated and reoriented.[1] Alliances between the state and those civil society organizations that do not limit the scope of their actions to pressuring the state have to be encouraged. This type of pedagogic political and cultural intervention—envisioned as a responsibility of the entire political system (government, political parties, legislatures, etc.) and specialized ministries (ministry of planning, social organizations directorate, etc.)—must be carefully designed and executed. As Hopenhayn clarifies,

> in order to promote linkages among organizations representing marginalized groups it may be useful to do the following: spread information and communication technology to the grassroots level; redefine cultural policies in line with the organizational culture of that level; strengthen State initiatives aimed at mobilizing the social and cultural capital of the masses in order to optimize the effect of social aid on different types of programmes; and support the linking role of the "external agents," whether these be NGOs, municipalities or social programmes, in order to *link up the rationales of the socio-cultural movements with the tendencies of society as a whole*, thus

reducing the degrees of segregation and fragmentation. (Hopenhayn 2001, 125; emphasis added).

However, for this to happen, the state must actively differentiate between those traditional organizations that continue envisioning the state as their interlocutor or adversary and those new type of organizations that see their demand-making as geared toward civil society. This vast political intervention program is justified because the new political culture must go beyond mere formal procedures; it must transform political action into activities that contribute to socially internalize norms of reciprocity and mutual recognition between different actors. As Hopenhayn emphasizes, "such a pact should serve as a dual fulcrum: first, as a mechanism for linking a new political culture with the different socio-cultural actors, with their demands and expectations, and second, as a mechanism for strengthening a new political culture of reciprocity which extends to the whole of society" (Hopenhayn 2001, 125). From these words, it is evident that reductionist views, which limit Latin American neostructuralism to just the realm of economic development, seriously underestimate its political and cultural ambitions and impact.

Reorganize the State Apparatus: The Municipal-NGOs-Local Leaders Complex

By emphasizing the civilizing role of the state, neostructuralist politics recasts 1960s "marginality theory" and fosters the creation of new-complex of state, municipal, NGOs, local, and party leaders, an apparatus that can more effectively intervene with public policies specifically targeting the socio-emotional level so as to re-educate targetted sectors in the new political values and behaviors.

From 2000 onward, different neostructuralist analysts linked to ECLAC's Social Division and UNDP's Chile office, have explored the challenges presented by this new context. It is worthwhile to follow their reasoning to discern the new forms of public intervention endorsed and how these conceptions and practices engender policies that ultimately forge a new mode of regulation.

The jumping-off point for this new generation of public policies is the notion that poverty is not rooted in the structural characteristics of Latin American capitalism or globalizing processes but rather on the individual traits and psychic state of those who endure it. Consequently, the state must deploy effective forms of political intervention, targeting different strata of the urban and rural poor who, due to their own shortcomings and historical conditioning, are unable to effectively "participate" in the new context. This new edition of 1960s Latin American marginality theory, then advanced by Roger Vekemans and DESAL, justifies novel forms of state intervention. As Dagmar Raczynski and Claudia Serrano, consultants to ECLAC's Social Affairs Division and key players in the design of Concertación social policy assert,

> confirmation exists that poverty is not only a matter of material wants; at the heart of many situations of poverty one finds the "animic state" resulting from life experiences which one must eliminate; overcoming it requires a change in the relationships between people and social groups. Diverse variables such as memory and dignity, trust and the ability to engage in actions, having an opinion and being able to express these, to have expectations, constitute some of the elements that enable an individual or a group to visualize alternatives for action, that originate from oneself, as well as develop a capacity for self-direction in life instead of remaining an object at the mercy the positive and negative life events. (Raczynski and Serrano 2005, 106; my translation)[2]

Through social programs such as *Chile Solidario*, carefully monitored and supported by ECLAC, neostructuralist-inspired policies directed at alleviating poverty using this approach have resulted in the creation of a new apparatus and cadre of state agents, prepared and trained to intervene directly at the individual's socio-emotional level, ultimately seen as the main factor behind destitution and abject poverty. Such "innovative" programs have as specific objectives to (1) provide psychological support to families in extreme poverty so that they can develop their own potential to transform themselves so that they can become "autonomous subjects"; (2) bring indigent families in touch with social services and benefits available through territorial (municipality-based) networks; and (3) create the minimum conditions so that the more vulnerable family members (women, children, the elderly) have the ability to improve their lives. An awareness of gender, spatiality, the relationship between culture, identity, and empowerment, and the socio-emotional basis of personal and behavioral change, provided by neostructuralist analysts, is placed at the service of state-policy and the construction of capitalist hegemony. Through state agents [*monitores*] that typically oversee about thirty families, carry out home visits, and get to intimately know the local environment, a new social service delivery system is constructed, organized to supply social assistance through individually and family tailored interventions. In this manner, social policy is given a more precise system of socially and spatially based targeting, but the poor receive the full-range of available assistance services (protection bonuses and traditional cash transfers), including psychosocial support specifically designed for them (Raczynski and Serrrano 2005, 115).

Enhancing the more traditional social targeting of the past, with more finely tuned territorial and socio-emotional targeting, ECLAC planners have accumulated a wealth of experience on the richly textured interactions that exist among the different levels of policy interventions and why these require both formal and informal interfacing between the state, the electoral system, community organization, business elites, and municipal level actors. Based on such experience, ECLAC functionaries have understood how leadership by the state can be made more persuasive if it also unfolds through nonformal channels. To be effective, these new type of interventions depend not only on the political vision and will of state agencies but also rely heavily upon cultivating a set of local leaders who can become the essential nexus or brokers between state agencies, NGOs, and the local community. The progressive aura of such policies is essential for successfully cultivating local leaders.

In this sense, ECLAC analysts have fully understood that those traditional forms of political intervention afforded by the disappeared welfare state or corporatist, clientelistic or populist regimes that accompanied the ISI regime of old are no longer possible. Under the now prevailing EO accumulation and globalized economies, new arenas for political management, political leadership, and the construction of hegemony have become available and must be seized. To the "passive paternalist" clientelism of old that combined "authoritarian, technocratic, and party-related" aspects, John Durston of ECLAC's Social Division argues in favor of the benefits and opportunities offered by new "semi-clientelism," the enlightened form of deploying social policy in the new historical context of globalization and export-oriented regimes: "Semiclientelism, on the other hand, is an alliance of subaltern communities and organizations with reform minded sectors existing within, on the one hand, the state apparatus, and political parties, on the other. It is based in an agreement to bring about change towards greater degrees of control by the clientele. It emerges when windows of opportunity exist in which the presence of many favorable factors come together: grassroots movements, democratic elections and the influence of progressive politicians" (Durston 2005, 53; my translation).

By understanding the dynamics of semi-clientelism, government functionaries can find a key that, according to Durston, opens up the possibility for producing a rapid transition in the socio-political system, existing within a specific municipal territory toward greater degrees of democracy and more effective forms for overcoming of poverty. While economic liberalization can bring about economic restructuring, the politico-cultural restructuring of society will require these new forms of state intervention. Semi-clientelism enables the disruption of the previous institutions supportive of what Durston calls "passive clientelism," because in constrast, it favors and promotes the elaboration of proposals and the capacity for negotiation on the part of the "clients." Thus, "clientelism is more than an exchange of favors for votes. As a constellation of personal relations—with *affective and diffused reciprocity components*—that operates as if it were an extension of mutual support networks, *it fits fully within the theoretical framework of social capital* previously discussed, as a vertical, asymmetric form of individual social capital"(Durston 2005, 54; my translation and emphasis).

On the basis of this brief review, it is clear that Latin American neostructuralists advocate new forms of political intervention that are designed to bring about a more effective system of mediation and management of conflicts. Deployed in localized social territories, wielding the discourse of participation and social capital, these interventions rely on weaving networks of trust and symbolic reciprocity, linking state agents, municipal representatives, progressive politicians and community leaders, all essential components for the delivery of social policies and the management of social conflicts in the macro and microspaces of state intervention. In conjunction with political decentralization, municipalization, and a civilizing mission aimed at tapping into and enhancing the social capital of the poor, this new type of political intervention purposely targets the socio-emotional dimension of individuals, families, and local communities. At the same time that the progressive horn insistently toots "Equity!" "Participation!" "Active social actors!" it carefully circumscribes these laudable aspirations within channels designed to never reach the point of questioning the appropriation and distribution of the economic surplus by a transnationalized capitalist class. Such "progressive" interventions build capitalist hegemony over and within those social, geographic, and subjective territories where dogmatic neoliberal state policy, and even military repression, found access forbidden. Resistance is to be replaced by acquiescence, and dirigisme by the command of the state or the heartless logic of the market can now be boosted by the celebration of self-regulating citizens and the action of the more diffuse and effective techniques of the self.

Lagos, Concertacion III, and the Politics of the "Nuevo Trato"

A revealing example of how the politics of Latin American neostructuralism operate to support capital accumulation and to erect a new mode of regulation is provided by the administration of Ricardo Lagos in Chile (2000–2005).[3] The role of prominent neostructuralists and ECLAC staff members such as Osvaldo Rosales, Eugenio Lahera, and Ernesto Ottone as strategic advisors to the Concertación III government, not to mention the extensive crossover among social policy experts affiliated with different political parties or party-affiliated think tanks, underscore how the intimate relationship between ECLAC and the Concertación administration has shaped the Chilean center–left's political discourse and design of public policy. Most observers have noted that a distinct transformation of the Concertación's discourse on participatory governance took place when President Lagos was elected in late 1999. Whereas under Aylwin (1990–93), the politics of participation were deployed to meet the challenge of governability and under Frei (1994–99) they sought to sanctify the market, under Lagos, participation carefully orchestrated from the state and the political system was reconceptualized to tackle an even more demanding challenge: producing legitimacy under conditions of globalization (Leiva 2005a). The Concertación IV administration, led by Michelle Bachelet, initially promised to build a "citizens' democracy" in Chile as a way of addressing the crisis of democracy in Latin America identified by the United Nation's Development Program influential study on the shortcomings and challenges faced by democracy in the region (UNDP 2004).

The Concertación III government headed by Ricardo Lagos promised Chileans a "New Deal" or "New Covenant" (*Nuevo Trato*), reasoning that, "in order to Grow with Equity, we need to grant greater power to the citizenry, so that it can more actively participate in decisions that pertain to their neighborhood, their community, their region, with a style of government closer to people and policies more committed to an equitable distribution of resources" (Concertación de Partidos por la Democracia, 1999, 48; my translation).

Though seemingly reflecting Concertacion III's greater political commitment to deepening Chilean democracy, such a shift was also based on
less lofty and more instrumental concerns. Toward the end of the 1990s,
Chile's governing coalition and international development agencies arrived
at a shared diagnosis, noting, "despite the efforts of these past years to resolve the main problems of the citizenry, recent research indicates a growing distancing between existing institutions and individuals" (MSGG 2001,
1; my translation, emphasis added).[4] As we shall see, what distinguished the
current Concertación III policy shift on participation was the performance
of a double movement. On the one hand, it acknowledged the growing gap
between individuals and institutions, and on the other hand, it theorized
such distancing as rooted outside Chile, locating its origins in the "epochal
change" brought by the process of globalization sweeping the planet: "Even
though the causes for such phenomenon [the distancing between institutions and individuals] are *explicable within a global process that encompasses
not only our country*, the current government has the conviction and the will
to bridge such gap" (MSGG, 2001, 1; my translation, emphasis added).

Following up on these campaign promises, on December 7, 2000, President Lagos signed a Presidential Directive (*Instructivo Presidencial*) laying
out the government's plan to ensure participation in public policies at all levels of the executive power. On May 2, 2001, President Lagos announced the
Commitment for Strengthening Civil Society (*Compromiso para el Fortalecimiento de la Sociedad Civil*), pledging the government to pass new legislation,
provide training, and new funding mechanisms for strengthening of civil society. Many of the concrete proposals contained in the *Compromiso* were the
outcome of the *Consejo de Fortalecimiento de la Participación Ciudadana*, a
consultative body made up of selected NGOs, political think tanks, private
volunteer organizations and business foundations.[5] These initiatives enjoyed
political backing from Chile's largest NGOs and with the technical and financial support of the Inter-American Development Bank (IDB). Indeed,
Chile became the first country where the Inter-American Bank endorsed a
$15 million CH-0165 project or "Program to Strengthen Alliances Between
Civil Society and the State" (Yamada 2001). This program was specifically
designed to "provide support for generating favorable conditions so that the
citizenry participate more actively in the design and implementation of actions aimed toward the common good" (IDB, 2001b, 7; my translation). The
2001 IDB Country Paper justifies such a novel project because "in order to
foster greater interaction between the State and its citizens, work must be

done to identify the factors that now limit that interaction and on political institutions for channeling and resolving demands sometimes of a conflict-ing nature, that arise from a more highly organized society" (IDB 2001a, 20; emphasis added).

The new politics of participation or "*Nuevo Trato*" (New Covenant) un-furled by the Lagos administration was produced by a broad array of ideo-logical and politico-economic factors. On an intellectual level, in addition to the theorizations carried out at ECLAC, its formulation can also be partly explained by the sway held by Europe's "Third Way" over Ricardo Lagos's close advisors (Martínez 2000; Cáceres and Jeri 2000; Ottone 2000). The for-mulation of the *Nuevo Trato* was also informed by surveys carried out by the United Nations Development Program (UNDP) in preparation for the 1998 and 2000 *Chile Human Development Reports*. Both publications explored the marked "asynchronicity" between Chilean "modernity" and "subjectivity," evidenced by an increasing sense of personal insecurity and mistrust detect-ed in the midst of a booming economy (Progama de Naciones Unidas para el Desarrollo, 1998, 2000). Additionally, the *Nuevo Trato* discourse also gained prominence, because it established a common ground between two *Concert-ación* factions that were increasingly divided between the self-complacent (*auto-complacientes*), such as José Joaquín Brunner, Eugenio Tironi, Enrique Correa, and Alejandro Foxley, and the self-flagellating (*auto-flagelantes*), such as Carlos Ominami, Camilo Escalona, and others. It accomplished this feat by displacing the state–market debates of the 1990s toward a new axis: discussions on "civic values," trust, associativity, and the strengthening "so-cial capital" needed in twenty-first-century Chile. On a political level, then, the *Nuevo Trato* emerged as the last best attempt at countering declining support for Chile's economic and political institutions. Within such a con-text, Marcelo Martínez, chief in 2001 of the Secretaría General de Gobierno's (SEGEGOB) Division for Social Organizations' Research Unit and one of the main proponents of *Nuevo Trato* (Martínez 1999a, 1999b, 2000, 2001), argued that, "given the epochal change under way, *the only means available for sav-ing the legitimacy of the State would be an alliance with a strong civil society*, conceived as the articulation of actors capable of building horizontal and relatively stable networks of trust and cooperation"(Martínez 2001).

Globalization, Uncertainty, Risk, and the Limits of Market Self-regulation

In the view of *Concertación* policy planners, which given the symbiotic rela-tionship with ECLAC discussed in chapter 4 closely follows neostructuralism, globalization has brought about an "epochal change" in the structure of society and on culture, a change characterized by the disappearance of the welfare state and an explosion in the plurality of identities (Martínez 1999a, 1999b). The SEGEGOB team asserted that *uncertainty* has been ingrained in every interstice of society, consequently "states, enterprises, social movements and above all subjects, appear to be incapable of constructing certainties on the basis of any development program. Globalization and plurality are experienced as expressions of uncertainty" (Martínez 1999b, 8; my translation). In the view of Martínez, expanding markets and consumption does not automatically translate into greater civic consciousness; increased consumerism has not played a "civilizing" role in Chile: "Despite the evidence about globalization of markets, information and technology, we continue being distrustful, State-oriented, intolerant and prejudiced" (Martínez 1999b, 30–31; my translation). For the closest advisors of President Lagos, "enough data is available to question the thesis of a cultural revolution, at least with respect to civic values that would spring forth from modernity linked to the market.[6] In effect, even though there is greater access to consumer goods, that has not meant greater civility" (Martinez 1999b, 30; my translation). The problem faced by Chile and the *Concertación* is that old structures have fallen but old values remain. It is precisely this void and asynchronicity between economic change and cultural laggardness that neostructuralism's civilizing mission aims to fill and solve.

What worried analysts was that such widespread and deep sentiments of insecurity produced paradoxically by Chile's modernity could potentially turn into an explosive mixture, generating two types of responses that would further undermine the legitimacy of the state. Given the malaise produced by globalization, a first type of response could lead to retreating to the personal sphere, a product of disenchantment with society, politics, and political institutions. The second alternative, the one that raised the greatest concern within Concertación III policy makers, was the constitution of "neocommunitarian" movements that could "become highly organized, visible and hostile," operating at the margins of society. According to Martínez, "We are referring to religious sects, millennium groups, youth belonging to the hardcore soccer fan clubs 'barras bravas,' to proto-anarchist groups whose members coordinate using the Internet" (1999b, 37). Such potential for disruption and for puncturing the facade of consensus had already been displayed in the 1998 Seattle protests and increasingly by the indigenous peoples social movements in Bolivia and Ecuador and, up until then, only in very embryonic fashion in Chile.

"Nuevo Trato": Teaching Skills for Living Globalized and Modern Lives

To prevent the emergence of such potentially problematic responses to the uncertainties and risks created by globalization, Jorge Navarrete, head of the *División de Organizaciones Sociales* (DOS, Social Organizations Division), stated that individuals "need a reference line, an explanatory and argumentative horizon, a *proyecto país*" (Navarrete 2001, 4). The Lagos government's politics of participation, the *Nuevo Trato*, sought to provide precisely such a horizon by fostering an "ethos of trust." By enhancing the capacity to cooperate and to establish "long lasting relations of trust," Navarrete argued, it becomes possible for individuals "to acquire the skills enabling them to . . . live modern life" (Navarrete 2001, 4). To achieve such an objective, the state's "politics of participation" has to draw on society's "social capital," namely that "set of social relations based on trust and cooperation that enable people to plan common actions for achieving socially valued objectives" (Navarrete, 2001, 4). In the context of globalization, therefore, *political intervention by the state* becomes crucial in the "battle to manage the so-called uncertainties and created risks attributable to the cultural process of present day modernization." (Navarrete 2001, 5).

Such a diagnosis leads to a significant shift in the conceptualization of politics, social policy, and the very notion of "participation" itself. As Marcelo Martínez, chief of the Research Unit of the *División de Organizaciones Sociales*, emphasizes, "This is why both the proposals of this international body [the UNDP] as well as the policies of the Chilean government, what has been called *Nuevo Trato* (i.e., New Deal or New Covenant), is a proposition that seeks to strengthen civil society, social capital, care for and deepen the different forms of sociability, promote relations of trust and cooperation; in sum, to strengthen social bonds among individuals" (Martínez, 2000, 16; my translation). That is, the cutting edge of neostructuralist and center–left thinking in Latin America today proposes that the state must actively intervene through society-creating initiatives that strengthen relations of cooperation, trust, and reciprocity but with the purpose of strengthening the legitimacy of existing institutions.

"Materialist" and "Postmaterialist" Social Organizations

Establishing this *Nuevo Trato* is a daunting task in Chile and Latin America. According to its proponents, three key prerequisites that exist in Western Europe are missing in the Chilean case: already constituted social actors, a level of reflexivity and awareness of risks, and "the ability to establish links that can constitute a relatively solid and active network of trust and cooperation" (Martinez 2000, 43). The "politics of participation" promoted by the *Nuevo Trato* seeks to address all three of these shortcomings. The $15 million IDB project is an important first step in this direction. Based on the diagnostics performed by the UNDP, the *División de Organizaciones Sociales* designed concrete steps toward making the *Nuevo Trato* feasible. Through a careful analysis of more than eighty thousand social organizations existing in Chile, the DOS defined a profile of the type of actors best suited for taking part in this New Convenant and identified those organizations best excluded from such an endeavor.

Based on the UNDP's National Map of Associativity and their own qualitative research, DOS sociologists adopted a taxonomy that categorized the 83,386 organizations of forty-five different types existing in Chile into either "materialist" or "postmaterialist" categories. Such classification hinged on whether a social organization constantly invoked the state or whether—according to DOS researchers—they cultivated civic values and promoted a logic of action in which the state was not the central target. "Materialist" organizations were deemed all those linked "to social gains having to do with welfare and security, that is, with traditional responsibilities of the Modern State, while 'postmaterialist' organizations encompass those that beyond the concerns of political modernity, and that deal with the conquest of new freedoms, greater autonomy, the beautification of the environment, as well as quality of life issues" (Caceres and Jeri 2000, 38). Applying such criteria, DOS researchers found that 80.3 percent of these organizations were of the materialist sort, while only the remaining 19.7 percent are classified as postmaterialist (see Figure 19). The crucial point of this classification is that "only postmaterialist organizations will be considered for the New Covenant."[7] Allegedly only post–materialist organizations are willing to sign such a pact, by virtue of "their conviction that by fostering those values rooted in their own freedoms and rights, they can do much to change their own lives and influence the currently existing model of development" (Martínez 2000, 22; my translation).

Hence the new "politics of participation" developed by Chile's Concertación III government seeks to promote relations of trust and cooperation and to strengthen social bonds *among individuals*. It targets, however, a limited number of social organizations and leaders: those that have *expunged from their practice actions that pose material demands from the state* and,

Materialist Organizations = *Orient Action toward the State*	Postmaterialist = *Do Not Orient Demands toward the State*
Materialist (*Traditional*) 67%	Postmaterialist (*Traditional*) 7.3%
Cooperativas (*Cooperatives*) Organizaciones de salud (*Health groups*) Centros de madres (*Mothers' centers*) Juntas de vecinos (*Neighborhood associations*) Clubes deportivos (*Sports clubs*) Centros de padres y apoderados (*School parent groups*) Sindicatos (*Labor unions*) Asociaciones gremiales (*Labor associations*) Comunidad de aguas (*Water rights associations*) Bomberos (*Volunteer firefighteers*) Agrupacion empresarios (*Trade associations*) Organización estudiantil (*Students*) Comités de agua poFigure (*PoFigure water committees*)	Grupo Scout (*Boy Scout groups*) Clubes (*Social clubs*) Asociaciones indígenas (*Indigenous associations*) Centro cultural (*Cultural centers*) Colegios profesionales (*Professional associations*)
Materialist (*Emerging*) 13.3%	Postmaterialist (*Emerging*) 12.4%
Comités de allegados (*Homeless committees*) Comités de pavimentación (*Pavinig committees*) Taller laboral (*Unemployment coops*) Organización agrícola (*Agricultural organizations*) Comité de seguridad ciudadana (*Public safety*) Comité habitacional (*Housing committees*)	Club de adultos mayores (*Seniors clubs*) Grupos artísticos (*Artistic groups*) Corporaciones (*Corporations*) Organizaciones de mujeres (*Women's organizations*) Organizaciones ecológicas (*Environmental organizations*) Organizaciones de consumidores (*Consumer organizations*) *Continued on next page*

Figure 19. Classification of social organization according to Concertación's Nuevo Trato Policy. Source: Cáceres y Jeri (2000, 7).

Materialist Organizations = *Orient Action toward the State*	Postmaterialist = *Do Not Orient Demands toward the State*
Materialist (*Emerging*) 13.3%	Postmaterialist (*Emerging*) 12.4%
	ONGs (*NGOs*) Coordinadoras de desarrollo local (*Local development associations*) Fundaciones (*Foundations*) Comités de adelanto (*Community development organizations*)
Total Materialist 80.3 %	Total Postmaterialist 19.7%

Figure 19. (Continued) Classification of social organization according to Concertación's Nuevo Trato Policy. Source: Cáceres y Jeri (2000, 7).

N=83,386 social organizations identified by the Chile Office of the United Nations Develop Program's (UNDP), *Mapa Nacional de Asociatividad* (1999).
Traditional: Organizations that have existed for more than fifteen years
Emerging: Organizations created during the last fifteen years.

conversely, that accept the existing regime of accumulation and abide by the new mechanisms of mediation. Excluded from the New Covenant is the bulk of social organizations, precisely those "materialist" organizations (unions, cooperatives, urban dwellers) that through their collective action and class-politics shaped Chile at the macro and the micro-social levels; it excludes those sectors and organizations that before the 1973 military coup and during the military dictatorship, worked to construct a democratic society and a culture of solidarity and equality.

The new "politics of participation," following ECLAC's rationale for novel public policies, has been designed to produce legitimacy of political institutions and the state under conditions of globalization. It seeks to do so by symbolically—not materially—reducing individual uncertainty. Thus, under Lagos and following neostructuralist orientations, the "politics of participation" have been rhetorically and practically displaced to the psycho-cultural and socio-emotional level of trust, cooperation, sociability, and lifestyle choices in the quest of international competitiveness.

Contradictions of Neostructuralist Politics

Despite its sophisticated character, the politics of neostructuralism presents important shortcomings. Some of these are evident from the experience of Chile's Concertación III government. Taking note of these allows us to assess some of the likely tensions that neostructuralism will also face as these type of public policies are implemented in other countries.

Strengthen "Civil Society" or the Profits Rate

While rhetorically emphasizing the principles of democracy, transparency, and accountability, neostructuralism does not promote the exercise of participation in key sites of the economy, such as the point of production, property relations, or the sphere of reproduction. The nature of Chile's EO model, in which profits are tied to the export of natural resources with low levels of processing produced by cheap and unprotected labor, like in other Latin American countries, places structural limitations to the sites and scope of participation. Citizen participation is banned from all sites—workplaces, markets, corporations, the private pension companies that manage the savings of Chilean workers, and institutions like the Central Bank—where the exercise of such principles could threaten the inviolability of the rights of international productive and financial capital, the concentration of power by local conglomerates, and the preservation of a labor legislation that guarantees an ample supply of cheap, malleable male and female labor along with protects the prerogatives of employers over labor.

In order to raise the efficacy of public policies, neostructuralism promotes participation in carefully delimited areas. As Oscar Muñoz points out, "it is fundamental that the poor, workers, and those excluded from regions, municipalities, and localities, begin to participate in a more *systematized and institutionalized* manner. Nobody is thinking ... of something like popular assemblies, in which the assembly designs policies. What I am talking about is that there has to be a dialogue between authorities and citizenry, between employers and workers, among local authorities, like mayors, and social organizations that can make a valuable contribution" (Muñoz 2003, 106). It becomes important to scrutinize the type of participation promoted by neostructuralism to understand its restrictive and exclusionary character. Is participation being promoted to genuinely strengthen the democratic nature of society? Or is it a "hegemonic participation" that contributes to gain the active consent of subordinate classes to reproduce and defend the status quo (Greaves 2004)? It seems likely that, though neostructuralist intent is one of ensuring governability, the definitive answer to which character participation will take is to remain highly contested. Whether in Latin America, participation leads toward a strengthening of capitalist hegemony or whether it genuinely supports the development of the capacity of popular sectors to assert their rights and challenge the power of capital, remains still to be defined. So far, Latin American neostructuralism aims to decisively support the former.

Destroying the Social Fabric through "Participation:"

The most salient inconsistency is to be found at the level of policy outcomes: in its evolving formulations the "politics of participation" have contributed to destroy, not strengthen, the social fabric of Chilean society, particularly in popular sectors. Under Aylwin and Frei, massive governmental programs sought to transform community-based organizations (communal soup kitchens, *talleres* or training workshops, health groups, etc.) into micro-enterprises. Drawn out internationally funded micro-enterprise training programs sought to eradicate traditional values of solidarity, democracy, and collective identity from the consciousness of the membership, replacing them with individualism, competition, hierarchy, and profit-driven rationality that is the mark of the successful entrepreneur. The outcome was the destruction and cooptation of the majority of these community organizations (Petras and Leiva 1994; Leiva 1995; Schild 2000; Paley 2001).

Toward the mid-1990s, the "politics of participation" revolved around governmental competitive funds (*Fondos Concursables*) tailored for servicing distinct and separate target populations (indigenous people, youth, neighborhood associations, disabled, cultural workers, etc.). The idea was that leaders from each of these organizations or sectors, in competition with each other, would present a funding proposal to carry out the particular community improvement project (paving streets, building a soccer field, establishing a rehab center, etc.). By 1996, fifty-five different competitive funds set up by the state and the *Fondo de las Americas*[8] operated in Chile. This new mechanism for allocating state funds—pioneered in Chile under the Fondo de Solidaridad e Inversión Social (FOSIS)—required again extensive training programs, so that community leaders could become intermediaries, creators and managers, of the "participatory projects" deemed presentable for funding. However, instead of strengthening the local social fabric, the competitive funds have had, in many instances, the opposite effect. The director of CORDILLERA, a well-respected Santiago NGO that has pioneered work on issues of municipal democratization, local government, and local development, considers that "participatory policies rain down on people," but policies like the *Fondos Concursables* "have led to the destruction of sociability" in many communities.[9] First, the competitive funds promote a task, project, and efficiency-oriented mentality. "People work in the Participatory Pavements. The celebration inaugurating the finished work comes, and that's the end of social participation. Everybody then goes home."[10]

Whether state-supported postmaterialist organizations linked through a new network created by the municipality–NGO–local leaders complex can provide an effective circular defense of the capitalist state and class power, preempting the emergence of autonomous and combative social movements, remains to be seen, though in Chile the fragility of neostructuralist politics in this regard is already becoming evident. Without a real and not merely symbolic redistribution of resources, the long-neglected demands of social majorities cannot be adequately addressed.

Individual User–Consumer Satisfaction or Popular Sovereignty

Neostructuralist politics and public policies oriented toward promoting participation rhetorically emphasize the importance of "civil society" and "citizen involvement." Upon closer examination it becomes evident, however, that the politics of participation hollows out traditional liberal democracy: participation and accountability are exulted *only in the limited realm of selected public policies and programs* at the same time that the political identity of citizens is recast as consumers or as individualistic users of limited social services or self-reliant decision makers about lifestyle choices, as has been attempted in Chile. Consequently, neostructuralist politics contributes to delink "participation" from broader, foundational, collective concepts of "popular sovereignty" and "citizenship." In Chile, the prolonged existence of "designated" and "lifelong" senators and persistence of a binomial political system under the permanent tutelage of the military, a 1980 constitution under the guardianship of a National Security Council and Constitutional Tribunal that trumps popular sovereignty, the use of repressive legislation from the Augusto Pinochet era to persecute and repress indigenous demands for control over material and cultural resources make Chile, at best, a "procedural democracy" quite limited by international standards. The Concertación's seventeen-year-long endorsement of the 1980 constitution and of the resulting "low intensity" democracy cannot be ignored as a key variable explaining the erosion in the legitimacy of political institutions. In the December 2001 elections, for example, 40 percent of all Chileans with the right to vote expressed their discontent with the political system, either by not registering in the electoral rolls, casting a blank vote, or annulling their vote.

In sum, the politics of participation embraced by Latin American neostructuralism, Chile's Concertación, and increasingly by international development agencies should be understood in the context of consolidating and legitimizing neoliberal restructuring, inoculating against "reform fatigue" and addressing the loss of legitimacy of political institutions inherent to the new EO and internationally integrated pattern of accumulation. In such a context, they constitute part of a hegemonic project legitimizing neoliberal restructuring rather than of strengthening a genuine democracy, where the region's popular sectors have an effective voice and decision making over key variables of socio-economic life. The novel type of public policies endorsed by neostructuralism, operate at the socio-emotional level to create a new set of expectations, behaviors, and identities within the tightly constrained parameters of an EO regime in which the benefits accrue to an ever smaller minority. This remains one of the fundamental internal tensions of the neostructuralist politico-economic project.

Conclusion: The Role of Latin American Neostructuralism

The politics of Latin American neostructuralism displays important achievements along with significant contradictions. These need to be registered and tracked more closely. Such monitoring will help us elucidate the future trajectory of Latin American neostructuralism as it enters after 2007 into the "late period" of its development.

Among its achievements we need to acknowledge the following. First, it has been able to garner widespread intellectual and political support. Electoral victories by political coalitions led by the center–left in Chile, Brazil, and Uruguay whose political discourse draws extensively from Latin American neostructuralism, attest to its capacity to forge a discourse that, independently of its shortcomings, resonates with the times, offers a vision and a narrative for the future and a credible set of action-oriented beliefs through which social change, democracy, and modernity can be linked to capitalist globalization with the promise of beneficial outcomes for everyone. Second, it has managed to restore the centrality of politics and cultural issues to economic development, albeit in a manner in which these become subordinate to the quest for international competitiveness and the requirements of transnational capital. Nonetheless, Latin American neostructuralism's ability to shape how politics and cultural issues are incorporated into the design of public policies is a tribute to its ability to integrate elements from different intellectual traditions and put these to the service of managing and regulating capitalist globalization. Finally and most important for the future, Latin American neostructuralism has been able to create a cadre of intellectuals, mid-level state managers, and practitioners who are reproducing and contributing to the further refinement of the neostructuralist paradigm and its foundational myths. Schooled at ECLAC training centers like the *Instituto Latinoamericano de Planificación Económica y Social* (ILPES) in Santiago and the *Instituto de Pesquisa Económica Aplicada* (IPEA) in Brasilia, reinforced through the organization of training courses on state reform, on how to design of "integrated" public policies, on the imperative of international competitiveness, ECLAC ensures that a younger generation of intellectuals, state functionaries, and political leaders, weld their consciousness and career success to defending the neostructuralist historical project of globalization with a human face. Such achievements guarantee that, in the near future, Latin American neostructuralism will remain a vital and important participant in the region's political landscape and debates in the social sciences.

Already prefigured by Chile's Concertación, the politics of Latin American neostructuralism will continue transforming the erstwhile critics of neoliberalism into the celebrants and safe-keepers of the EO regime of accumulation. As it was specified during the fourth Concertación government led by president Michelle Bachelet, in the future, the driving force behind political interventions will be to fashion even more effective public policies that create a favorable environment for private investment as well as provide only symbolic security to individual citizen consumers. The politics of neostructuralism will have to face a challenge Alejandro Foxley, Bachelet's Minister of Foreign Relations, identifies as "the possibility of consolidating the trend towards globalization and avoiding, from a political point of view, a type of backlash, a reversal towards much more autarkic forms of growth" (Foxley 2003, 25; my translation).

The contradictory nature of the politics of Latin American neostructuralism will play itself out in the concrete experience of different countries where this paradigm is influencing politico-economic discourse and public policy formulation. After seventeen years of a neostructuralist-inspired Concertación coalition, the case of Chile already foretells some of these nodal points around which such contradictions will emerge: (1) a strengthening of an autonomous civil society versus an institutionalized and hegemonic form of participation that subordinate civil society and the socio-emotional component of social relationships to the requirements of globalization and the capitalist profit rate; (2) the expansion of autonomous social movements capable of building on their every day sociability and historical memory to defend their rights and challenge capital and the state or the destruction of their social fabric, grassroots dynamics, and leaderships through state-designed and NGO-enforced social programs and civil society–state alliances; and (3) struggles over whether the objectives of strengthening social solidarity should be to increase the power of the dispossessed and exploited or to provide an individualized and symbolic more than material sense of security so that citizens do not rebel against a daily existence made more precarious by the expansion of capitalism.

Ultimately, the question is what purposes are being served by increasing coordination among the state, markets, and existing networks. Is it to raise profits and the self-expansion of capital, or is it to increase the satisfaction of human needs and human dignity? The grand narrative provided by Latin American neostructuralism about the region's path to twenty-first-century modernity sacrifices everything in its altar to international competitiveness. The political future of Latin American neostructuralism will be ultimately defined by the shape and outcome of conflicts between the promotion of systemic competitiveness and popular resistance to the further commodification of social life and the attending processes of dispossession that are accompanying it.

The foregoing analysis strongly suggests that Latin American neostructuralism's historical role has to be examined with a much broader lens than just the traditional economic development perspective. Neostructuralism's utilization of a broad palette of policy initiatives—concerted action, covenants, social capital, civic-state alliances, private-public partnerships, promotion of social cohesion—reflective of its attention to institutions, political leadership, and culture—do not automatically grant it carte blanche to claim an inherently progressive character. As I have shown, a more nuanced and altogether different assessment of its historical impact can be reached. When compared against laissez-faire dogmatism and the "one size fits all" neoliberal policies attributed to the Washington Consensus, indeed Latin American neo-structuralism appears as a more enlightened approach. However, in light of capitalist restructuring in the region and the glaring restructuring of power relations in favor of transnational capital conveniently ignored, the assessment of Latin American neostructuralism and center–left political forces is not so unequivocal. Due to deeply imprinted commitments to furthering international competitiveness and intervening in the institutional, political, and cultural realms so as to better use moral suasion and political leadership to achieve it, Latin American neostructuralism can be seen as playing a unique role in the consolidation, legitimization, and regulation of capitalist restructuring in the region. Instead of an "alternative" to neoliberalism, it should be seen as playing a complimentary role, making decisive contributions toward the construction of capitalist hegemony by enabling the subordination of the extra-economic realm to capitalist profitability and abetting the expanded colonization of the public sphere by the rationality of transnational capital. Thus, instead of seeing them as opposing paradigms, neoliberalism and neo-structuralism should be seen as part of a tag team.

Once explored in all of their multifaceted complexity, Latin American neostructuralism and the new ECLAC, at least in their present form, have to be stripped of their progressive halo. A new covenant or new deal that continues placing global capitalist competition as the preestablished foundation for "progressive" politics cannot but fail in fully interpreting the demands of the vast majority of the people of the Americas. For this reason, it will also fail in guaranteeing enduring social cohesion. Herein lies the Achilles heel of the politics of neostructuralism and its fateful inability to escape the heterodox paradox. As we shall see in chapter 9, a "progressive" political economy that does not address questions of power and the role of transnational capital can well end actively contributing to strengthen capitalist hegemony in the region, as seventeen years of Chile's Concertación so dramatically illustrate.

9

Chile's Evanescent High Road and Dashed Dreams of Equity

In June 2006, thousands of Chilean high school students went on strike and, during a three-week period, occupied school-buildings in the country's major cities. Showing a high level of organization and combativeness, the *pingüinos* (penguins), as secondary students are affectionately known, caught Chilean political observers by surprise as many convinced themselves that direct and collective forms of action decided in mass assemblies had become obsolete under Chile's post-neoliberal modernity.[1] The mobilized students denounced the deficient and classist nature of Chile's public education, a system admired throughout Latin America before the military coup, but undermined by the voucher and private provider system created by General Augusto Pinochet's last legal decree, the *Ley Orgánica Constitucional de la Enseñanza* (LOCE). More than just the failure of Chile's public educational system, these massive student protests also illustrate the shortcomings of both Chile's Concertación governments and Latin American neostructuralism itself: the "high road to globalization" and "growth with equity" are nowhere to be found after more than a decade and a half of pragmatic incremental policies.

This chapter contrasts Chile's portrait as the region's "success story" with the often ignored more "toxic" results of recent economic growth. One such outcome is that the uncontested and under-theorized power of transnational capital has forced Chilean neostructuralists to successively reformulate their notion of the high-road to globalization, compressing it beyond the point where it has become an unrecognizable shadow of its former self. A tortuous road has led Chilean policy makers who, in the late 1980s and early 1990s, declared the importance of achieving a "second-phase" of the export-orientation (EO) model to their current stance: trashing all aspirations of changing the country's profile toward manufactured exports, marketing Chile after 2005 instead as a dependable springboard (*país plataforma*) for transnational capital intent on expanding its financial, telecommunications, and service activities to neighboring countries. Such a trajectory reveals that neo-structuralist concepts and policies deployed over the past eighteen years are incapable of shaping Chile's insertion in the world economy so as to deliver the virtuous circle promised by the Economic Commission for Latin America and the Caribbean (ECLAC). Celebrating Chile's role as a springboard for transnational investors also has important implications for the country's social structure and quality of democratic life. Even if successful, such a choice severely fetters the possibilities for "growth with equity." Two mechanisms used by the "Asian Tigers" to reach the high road to global-ization—the provision of a high-quality educational system based on merit and the state's capacity to steer investment toward strategic export sectors—lie outside the realm of current policy objectives as Chilean youth forcefully reminded the country's complacent political class. As we shall see in this chapter, the constraints to such policy initiatives are to be found precisely in Chile's character as one of the most transnationalized and financialized economies of the region. Like no other country in the Americas, the Chilean case illustrates that the existence of "right" policies, "quality of leadership," and high propensity for compromise are not enough to reach the high road. Rhetorical flourishes and a heightened ability for conceptualizing and enact-ing symbolic politics, all extensively displayed in by Chile's *concertacionista* political class and ECLAC headquarters, cannot be a substitute for policies that remove internal and external obstacles to development, through real material changes in a society's power relations.

Chile a Model: But of What?

In the debates about economic ideas, both neoliberals and neostructur-alists have claimed Chile as a model proving the superiority of their own analytical and policy frameworks. As we saw in chapter 3, Chile was the first Latin American country to successfully complete the basic three-stage restructuring process prescribed by the World Bank. After a thirteen-year economic boom driven by exports (1985–98) and a recession and slowdown (1999–2002) in the wake of the Asian financial crisis, the Chilean economy has shown a capacity to recuperate high growth rates of 6.2 percent in 2004 and an estimated 6.3 percent in 2005 (CEPAL 2006).

High growth rates in gross domestic product (GDP), exports, and foreign direct investment (FDI), along with higher than average (for Latin America) productivity growth and fixed capital investment rates lend credence to the

Chilean success narrative (see Table 14). In addition to high levels of consensus among business and political elites, the existence of pro-capital legislation and institutions have transformed Chile into an investor's dream. The Davos-based World Economic Forum, for example, lists Chile as the top Latin American country in terms of its global competitiveness index (GCI) ranking it in twenty-third place, above Malaysia, Luxembourg, Ireland, and Israel (World Economic Forum 2006, xiv).[2] On the basis of its human development index (HDI), the UNDP's *2005 Human Development Report* ranks Chile in thirty-seventh place, second in Latin America only to Argentina (thirty-fourth). At the same time, the center–left coalition in power since 1990 can also display significant reductions in official poverty rates from 38.6 percent in 1990 to 20.6 percent in 2000 and 18.8 percent in 2003.[3] Based on these and other published indicators, Chile indeed seems to be an all-around success story.

Fracture Lines in Chile's Growth with Equity

Beneath this first layer of apparent success in which both the desires of transnational capital and the objectives of human development appear to have

TABLE 14

Chile: Economic and labor market indicators, selected years

YEAR	GDP %	URBAN UNEMPLOYMENT %	REAL WAGES MANUFACTURING SECTOR (INDEX 1990 = 100)	INFORMAL SECTOR %	CONTRIBUTE TO SOCIAL SECURITY %
1990	–	7.4	100	37.9	79.0
1995	10.8	6.6	128.5	38.8	67.0
2000	4.5	9.2	144.2	38.0	62.8
2001	3.4	9.1	144.8	–	–
2002	2.2	9.0	146.8	–	–
2003	3.9	8.5	148.1	–	67.5
2004	6.2	8.8	150.0	35.8	–
2005	6.3	8.0	152.0	–	–

Source: CEPAL 2006 *Estudio Económico de América Latina y el Caribe*
Data from Statistical Annex of Organización Internacional del Trabajo, Panorama Laboral 2005 and 2006.

been compatibly matched, lies another too often neglected but equally important aspect of present Chilean reality: being one of the country's with the highest level of inequality in Latin America (DeFerranti, Ferreira, Perry, and Walton 2004). In fact, according to World Bank and UNDP data, Chile is among the dozen of most unequal countries in the world, ranking alongside South Africa (see Table 15). Its highly unequal distribution of income

TABLE 15

Countries with the most unequal income distribution in the world

RANKING (WORST)	COUNTRY	GINI COEFFICIENT
1	Namibia	70.7
2	Lesotho	63.2
3	Botswana	63.0
4	Sierra Leone	62.9
5	Central African Republic	61.3
6	Swaziland	60.9
7	Guatemala	59.9
8	Brazil	59.3
9	Paraguay	57.8
10	South Africa	57.8
11	Colombia	57.6
12	Chile	57.1
13	Zimbabwe	56.8
14	Panama	56.4
15	Honduras	55.0
16	Mexico	54.6
17	Cape Verde	53.2
18	Zambia	52.6
19	Argentina	52.2
20	Papua New Guinea	50.9
21	Nigeria	50.6
22	Mali	50.5
23	Niger	50.5
24	Malawi	50.4

Source: Compiled on the basis of Table 15, *Human Development Report 2005*

combines a high concentration of wealth among the elite as the richest decile concentrates most of the income, while differences between the poorer and middle sectors are much less marked (Torche 2005). Equally not captured by most indicators is the fact that Chile's working class is one of the most super-exploited in the hemisphere. Initially structured by neoliberalism and state terrorism under Pinochet (1973–89), such a situation has been maintained by the center–left, neostructuralist-inspired, civilian coalition in office from 1990 to the present. Flexible labor markets—the cornerstone of the economic model's success—have steadily increased the level of precarious employment, heightening the lack of protection and vulnerability for a growing number of male and female workers. At the same time, the environmental costs of natural resource-intensive export growth and weak regulatory institutions, such as loss of biodiversity, extinction of species, reduction of biomass, widespread pollution, contamination of land and water, acid rain, and monopolization of water resources by transnational mining, constitute a burden that disproportionately falls on the shoulders of Chile's poor, have also been ignored (Larraín, Palacios, and Paz-Aedo 2003; Aedo and Larraín 2004). A closer look at the issues of poverty, inequality, and labor flexibility reveals that it is presumptuous to declare Chile a success story to be emulated by others.

The Transient Nature of Poverty Reduction

Undoubtedly, one of the most celebrated accomplishments of the Concertación is the significant reduction of poverty from 4.97 to 2.9 million (see Table 16). This impressive decrease was accomplished mainly due to drastic reductions in unemployment levels of the 1980s and rising real incomes. However, as significant as they are, and beyond questions about methodology, such numbers hide two crucial aspects: (1) employment has not meant durable exit from poverty given the rise of a vast segment of "working poor" (Leiva and Agacino 1994) and (2) the extraordinarily high levels of mobility out and into the ranks of those officially classified as poor over the past decade.

The peculiar nature of Chile's social mobility has been evidenced by panel studies carried out by Chile's Planning Ministry (MIDEPLAN), which compared a representative sample of those classified under the poverty line in 1996 and looked at them again in 2001, revealing startling trends. What the MIDEPLAN study shows is that "76.1 percent of the households who in 2001

TABLE 16

Chile: Evolution of poor individuals as a percentage of the total population 1987–2003

YEAR	INDIGENT POOR NUMBER OF INDIVIDUALS*	PERCENTAGE	NONINDIGENT POOR NUMBER OF INDIVIDUALS	PERCENTAGE	TOTAL POOR NUMBER OF INDIVIDUALS	PERCENTAGE
1987		17.4				45.1
1990	1,659.3	12.9	3,306.3	25.7	4,965.6	38.6
1992	1,169.3	8.8	3,162.4	23.8	4,331.7	32.6
1994	1,036.2	7.6	2,743.8	19.9	3,780.0	27.5
1996	813.8	5.8	2,474.5	17.4	3,288.3	23.2
1998	820.0	5.6	2,340.1	16.1	3,160.1	21.7
2000	849.2	5.7	2,231.9	14.9	3,081.1	20.6
2003	728.0	4.7	2,179.6	14.1	2,907.7	18.8

Source: MIDEPLAN, Encuestas CASEN 1990, 1992, 1994, 1996, 1998, *Indicadores de Pobreza*
* Excludes live-in domestics and their family. Indigent poor defined as earning less than 1 basic basket
NonIndigent Poor defined as earning more but less than the equivalent of two basic baskets
** Category of Poor includes "Indigent Poor".
*** Preliminary figures

were below the line of absolute poverty [indigence], in 1996 were above it" (MIDEPLAN 2002, 8; my translation). Likewise, 50.3 percent of those households who in 2001 were below the poverty line, in 1996, only five years earlier, had received an income that classified as them as non-poor (see Table 17).

When the 1996–2001 MIDEPLAN panel data are processed according to income deciles, the extreme vulnerability of the Chilean population to fall into poverty is further underlined. High vulnerability to sinking below the poverty line and high mobility in the middle range of income distribution led some experts to state that, "Poverty declined from 22 percent to 18 percent between 1996 and 2001, but more than 34 percent of the population was in poverty at some point and 46 percent of those poor in 2001 had been non-poor in 1996" (Contreras, Cooper, Herman, and Neilson 2005, 10; my translation.). This highlights that the available data on poverty reduction are only a photograph in time and do not fully capture the real dynamics of poverty in Chile. In a very short period of time, these classifications can vary significantly. In fact, the 2002 MIDEPLAN panel study shows that between 1996

TABLE 17

Chile: Origin of poverty categories in 2001. Evolution of households according to situation of poverty 1996–2001

| | YEAR 2001 | | | |
YEAR 1996	INDIGENT POOR	POOR	NON POOR	TOTAL
Indigent Poor	23.9	13.8	2.2	4.8
Nonindigent Poor	29.1	35.8	11.3	15.5
Non-poor	47.0	50.3	86.5	79.8
Total	100.0	100.0	100.0	100.0

Source: MIDEPLAN (2002) *Dinámica de la pobreza*, 8.

and 2001, "while a total of 220,623 households had climbed out of indigence and poverty, a total of 181,799 had fallen below into a situation of poverty or indigence" (MIDEPLAN 2002, 10; my translation).

Such renewed emphasis on the high levels of mobility and vulnerability provides a more balanced view of the limited nature of current official statistics. Some have called for the need to recalculate the official poverty line, raising it from two to three and a half times a minimum food basket used in official calculations. If the official poverty line is raised from a monthly income of around Ch$43,500 (approximately US$65) to $115,000 (US$184) as some authors suggest, the percentage of the population living in poverty would rise to over 70 percent of Chile's population.[4]

Persistent Inequality

If we now focus on inequality, it turns out that "Chilean case is extreme if one compares it to industrialized and even other Latin American countries. What is unique about Chile, is that it combines a very high concentration of income among the elite, with high levels of mobility among other income deciles, in which social mobility reproduces the pattern of inequality" (Torche 2005, 2–3; my translation). Income inequality has characterized Chilean society for decades, but longitudinal time series only available for Santiago show that it has become increasingly more acute after the military coup of 1973. Whereas income inequality as measured by the Gini coefficient was at its lowest during the 1970–73 period under Salvador Allende (0.467), inequality increased reaching 0.553 for the 1999–2001 period (Larrañaga 2001). What national level data show is that more than fifteen years of Concertación governments and neostructuralist-inspired policies have not been able to reduce income inequality; on the contrary, such inequality has increased. The share of the richest 10 percent of the population in national income increased to 47 percent in 2000, and all of the measurements of inequality presented by a World Bank study—Gini Coefficient, the 10:1 decile and 90:10 ratios, among others, show income inequality rising between 1990 and 2000. In 1990, for example, the richest 10 percent perceived an income that was 36.2 times that of the poorest 10 percent; by 2000 that ratio had grown to 40.6 times (see Table 18).

Though a matrix displaying movement across income deciles between 1996 and 2001 shows high levels of social mobility in the mid-range of income

TABLE 18

Chile: Distribution of household per capita income and income inequality (share of deciles, income ratios and Gini Coefficient)

INCOME DECILES	1990	1996	2000
1	1.3	1.2	1.2
2	2.3	2.2	2.2
3	3.0	3.0	2.9
4	3.8	3.8	3.7
5	4.8	4.7	4.7
6	6.0	5.9	5.8
7	7.6	7.6	7.4
8	10.1	10.3	10.0
9	15.4	15.7	15.2
10	45.8	45.5	47.0
Measurements of Inequality			
10/1	36.2	36.4	40.6
90/10	11.1	11.5	11.4
95/80	2.9	2.7	2.9
GINI	55.9	56.1	57.1

Source: Table A.2, De Ferranti, et al. *Inequality in Latin America: Breaking with History?* (Washington DC: World Bank Latin American and Caribbean Studies, 2004), 287; Gini Coefficient from Table A.3

deciles, social and intergenerational mobility reproduce the patterns of acute inequality. Chile exhibits, for example, extremely low levels of intergenerational income mobility. Using a method that calculates the income elasticity of the children with regards to the income of the parent, recent research has shown that the "intergenerational persistence of income inequality is by far greater than that reported for developed countries, including countries like the United States and England, which are pointed to as those having highest indices of persistence among developed countries (Nuñez and Risco 2005, 7; my translation). Chile occupies the bottom rankings and "Chile is unequal because its elite concentrates a disproportionately high share of national income. This contrasts with what happens with the middle and lower classes, where the distribution of income is more equal" (Torche 2005, 9; my translation). As Florencia Torche points out, if the richest decile is excluded, Chile becomes the most equal country in Latin America, even ranking higher than the United States. This suggests that inequality's roots lie in the fact that the richest 10 percent appropriates an inordinately high proportion of the economic surplus, a line of thinking that Latin American neostructuralism has been reticent to explore: "At a theoretical level, the study of the Chilean case highlights the shortcomings of a perspective that links inequality and mobility by only focusing on micro mechanisms, such as individual resources and incentives endowments. Results from research suggest that such theories should be preceded by a macrolevel understanding of the pattern as well as the topography of inequality and social mobility in each country so that the distance between classes, in terms of assets associated to each one of them can be precisely determined" (Torche 2005, 20). Failure to examine structural factors linked to class power, class structure, and class formation have had dramatic consequences for the design of effective policies.

The Underside of the Chilean Model

Three factors must be considered to explain the persistence and deepening inequality accompanying macroeconomic success in Chile: (1) policies that have failed to target and redirect the use of social surplus; (2) an export model whose profitability depends on deepening labor flexibility and the precariousness of workers; and (3) the narrowed parameters for policy permitted by the source of capitalist profits under the current transnationalized and financialized export-oriented economy. As long as Latin American neostructuralism ignores these factors and marginalizes power relations from analysis, government policies seeking the high road to globalization and greater equity will continue floundering, as the Chilean case shows.

Existing patterns of inequality have been exacerbated by government policies. The unwillingness to tax transnational capital or the profits of the *grupos económicos* (economic conglomerates) or question Pinochet's 1980 Constitution led the Concertación to opt for funding its social policies by raising value-added taxes (VAT), a highly regressive measure in terms of income distribution. Even a government agency like MIDEPLAN, concludes that, "before taxes, the highest income quintile received 56.2 per cent of total income, while the poorest quintile received only 4.2 percent. Nonetheless, after taxes, income distribution is slightly more unequal. . . . On average, the five poorest deciles paid 15.3 percent of their income as taxes, against only 13.0 percent paid by the richest five deciles." (MIDEPLAN 2000, 38). The report goes on to state that the second poorest decile is the group that pays the highest proportion of their income as taxes (16.0 percent), while the richest decile only pays 11.8 percent of its income in taxes, the lowest share of all income groups.[5] As a result of the Concertación's tax policy, the Gini coefficient went from 0.4883 to 0.4961, and the ratio between the top and bottom quintile increased from 13.41 to 14.12 after taxes (MIDEPLAN 2000, see Table III.1).

A Meandering Quest for the High Road

A vivid example of the evanescent nature of the high road to globalization is offered by Chile's experience during the 1990–2005 period. Over those years, the rhetoric about the high road dramatically regressed, evolving from a future to be shaped by the interests of all of Chilean society (the "second phase of the export model") to servicing the whims of transnational capital. The compression of the high road by Chilean neostructuralists illustrates the faulty assumptions upon which such a strategy was originally conceived.

The Second Export Phase: The Case for Manufactured Exports

Abundant literature exists making the case that increasing nontraditional and manufactured exports represents a critical feature for a country's dynamic economic development (Lord 1992). The benefits of manufactured and nontraditional exports have been extolled for different reasons: "In addition to enhancing overall economic growth by increasing the financing capacity for needed imported inputs, nontraditional export growth (NTEG) can also lead to productivity-induced growth as a result of competitive pressures on the international market and economies of scale" (Paus, 1989, 173).

In Chile, during the second half of the 1980s, the advantages of manufactured exports were applauded by referring to its obverse: the limitations inherent to natural resource-led export growth.[6] Numerous reasons were given about the flaws of exclusively basing export expansion on natural resources. International prices for manufactured exports were historically more stable than the highly erratic and downwardly moving prices of natural resource exports. Consequently, a country that failed to export manufactured goods would be much more vulnerable to international shocks, exchange rate fluctuations, and low productivity growth. One manifestation of the "curse of natural exports" was "Dutch disease." Price increases of natural resource exports would generate a rise in the availability of foreign exchange, depressing the domestic price of tradable goods, creating negative incentives for their production (Meller 1996). Manufactured exports were seen as bearers of technological innovation through different spillover effects, economies of scale, and learning processes. The emergence of a manufactured goods exports sector was deemed crucial for modernizing a country's productive structure therefore.

In addition to these general considerations, by the early 1990s, certain trends in the Chilean economy also led observers to emphasize the need for changing the country's export profile. The very success of the EO model, along with rising foreign direct and portfolio investments, flooded the Chilean economy with U.S. dollars, appreciating of the peso. At the same time that the exchange rate was falling, increases in real wages fueled concern that pecuniary incentives (low wages and a high real exchange rate) were about to exhaust their potential to sustain increases in competitiveness. Caught between the pincers of a falling exchange rate and rising real wages, many saw the appearance of forces that could choke off the competitiveness of exports. Calls for a second-export phase of manufactured and more value-added content in Chile's exports forcefully emerged (Ominami and Madrid, 1990). "No other road is left, but a strategy of technological modernization and increases in productivity" (Muñoz 1992, 5). The need to move to a "second phase" of the EO model became a pressing concern to the neostructuralist-influenced economic team that after 1990 replaced Pinochet's neoliberal "Chicago boys."[7]

Prominent neostructuralists, like Carlos Ominami who would go on to become President Aylwin's first Minister of Economics, forcefully wielded the neostructuralist argument that would appear in ECLAC's *Changing Productive Structures with Social Equity* and applied it to the Chilean case. By specializing in natural resource-based exports with low levels of processing, despite impressive export growth after 1985, he argued that Chile had failed to make significant advances in the more dynamic sectors of the world market; the technological content of exports remained abysmally low and had not improved over the 1980s.[8] These outcomes fueled discussions on the future evolution of Chile's EO model and necessity of a "second export phase." However as the mid-1990s approached, such debates about how to move the country toward this second phase were completely abandoned.

Second Phase Redefined: The Benefits of Processed Natural Resources (PNR)

After 1993, the "second phase" of the EO model was completely relabeled. Originally, this phase corresponded to the expansion of manufactured exports that would allow for the development of endogenous technical innovation, competitiveness based on quality and design, increases in productivity, and the profusion of forward and backward linkages. However, this initial vision that such exports would be either labor or capital intensive manufactured consumer goods, openly clashed with the decisions by Chile's powerful conglomerates or *grupos económicos*. As this gap became more evident, the nature of the second phase of Chile's EO model began to be openly questioned by economists close to the Concertación government. The writings of Patricio Meller and Alvaro Díaz provide insight into how the "second-export phase" of the EO model was reformulated and transformed into a celebration of the very profitable natural resource processing activities already under way. Both argued that processing natural resources would have beneficial effects thanks to their alleged capacity to promote technological innovation and modernize labor–management relations, since output did not depend on the intensity of work. Neostructuralism's original promise of "productive transformation with equity" would still remain valid for the case of Chile, even though it was processing natural resources and not exporting manufactured consumer goods. In fact, Díaz and Meller argued that the years of wandering through the neo-liberal desert were over and, without realizing it, Chilean society had already stumbled onto the Promised Land of the "second-export phase." Patricio Meller in particular, a leading member of the *Corporación de Estudios para Latinoamérica* (Corporation of Latin American Studies [CIEPLAN]) and one of Chile's most prestigious economists, challenged the prevailing common wisdom about the mythical second export phase: "Why should exports of US$100 million of blue-jeans be preferable to the export of US$100 million of grapes?" (Meller 1996, 9). By calling into question the supposed "curse" befalling countries endowed with natural resources, Meller dared to consider that a strategy of processing of natural resources (PNR) was, in fact, equivalent to the long-awaited second phase of the EO model. The shift from exporting raw natural resources to the processing of those natural resources (i.e., the move from tomato to tomato paste) was a logical step given Chile's comparative advantages: technological (proximity to inputs), environmental (social acceptance of pollution levels associated with natural resource exports), and transport costs (processing reduces volume and weight). The foreseeable disadvantages of making such a transition would be the high levels of capital investment required and the fact that such processing would be relatively capital intensive and, therefore, provide for a reduced share of labor costs in total costs of production. As a viable strategy, the processing of natural resources was additionally criticized for its limited potential for direct and indirect job creation. Furthermore, moving into processed natural resources would make it difficult to sell such products given developed countries generalized practice of resorting to a sliding tariff scale, making it more difficult for products with higher levels of processing to gain entry (Meller 1996). Weighing all the advantages and disadvantages of the PNR strategy for the case of Chile, Meller concludes that one of the crucial criticisms leveled against the PNR strategy does not hold. Based on a study at the 4-Digit International Standard Industrial Classification (ISIC) level of industrial groups exporting more that US$10 million in 1994, Meller concluded that PNR and other manufactured products (OMP) are both labor intensive and would provide many of the benefits accorded to nonnatural resource related manufacturing. Therefore, Chile's incorporation of greater value added to natural resources constitutes a viable alternative for reaching the second export phase.[9] To overcome the obstacles facing the expansion of such a strategy, entry into the North American Free Trade Agreement (NAFTA), or at the very least the signing of a bilateral free-trade agreement with the United States and Canada, was highly advisable.

If Patricio Meller expressed some reservations, another economist linked to the Concertación government, Alvaro Díaz, became the enthusiastic prophet of the second export phase, proclaiming "Chile already entered into the first stage of the Second phase in its export development" (Díaz 1995, 70). Díaz based such a claim on the coexistence of five trends, which he considered already firmly consolidated: technological modernization of primary natural resource exports; the expansion of industrially processed natural resources; the presence of manufactured exports not linked to natural resources; the export of non-financial services; and the rising volume of foreign direct investment by Chilean corporations in neighboring countries. All of these indicated higher levels in the production of commodities (fishmeal, cellulose, refined paper, copper, etc.) for world markets, which provided proof of the dynamic modernization already experienced by Chile's EO model.

During this period, other analysts argued on solid empirical grounding that export diversification had not led to a diversification of the productive structure (Agacino 1995; Geller 1993). Against the notion of productive modernization, Agacino contended that what happened was that natural resource processing activities were gaining a greater weight in the overall performance of the industrial sector. The five manufacturing branches that in the 1990–92 period were responsible for over 62.5 percent of all manufactured exports—canning of fruits and vegetables (3113), processing of seafood (3114–15), wood (331), and paper and printing (341)—represented 20 percent of the value added and 22.4 percent of the labor force of the entire manufacturing sector. This was a significant increase from the 1983–85 period, when these five branches represented only 14.2 percent and 9.8 percent respectively of the value added and employment in the entire manufacturing sector (Agacino 1995, 10). Instead of contributing to diversify the industrial sector, the outcome—at least for the period examined—was greater specialization in the productive structure of the manufacturing sector in activities linked to natural resources, sectors where competitiveness was based on Ricardian rents and not on genuine forms of competitiveness. Though Chile had entered into a new phase of its EO model, this was a far cry from the "second export phase" as envisioned by its original proponents, where international export, social integration, and political stability would naturally reinforce one another.

Short Lived Fantasy: "High-tech Maquila"

The quest for the second phase of the EO model would continue, partly because, despite the talk of a Golden Age on the part of Concertación affiliated economists, the processing of natural resources increasingly displayed important shortcomings. It became ever more evident that such a strategy prevented modernity from flowing to the rest of the economy: ownership was concentrated in the hands of few dominant conglomerates and labor conditions and labor–capital relations left much to be desired.

The next station in the quest was the idea that Chile could become a member of the global high-tech sector and a direct and not merely symbolic participant in the information economy. Alvaro Díaz had become undersecretary of the economy and was later appointed czar of information technology. With great fanfare, Chile opened an office in Silicon Valley and, through tours and presentations, attempted to market itself as an attractive location for both computer chip manufacturing and software development. Talk about becoming a high-tech *maquila* (factory) and about the prospective benefits grew like a bubble. However, such talk lasted only as long as it took Intel Corporation to make up its mind, deciding to choose finally Costa Rica as the site of its Latin America manufacturing operations. The Chilean government's office in Silicon Valley, like the dream of becoming a high-tech regional center, was abandoned.

The itinerary followed by Chilean government planners of originally envisioning Chile's future linked to manufactured exports, then as a successful country with an economy built around processed natural resources and briefly as high-tech maquila, illustrates the extent to which the imagined high road was being shaped, not by the state's activist industrial trade and technology policy or by a domestic entrepreneurial class willing to assume the risks involved in innovation. On the contrary, the future of Chile's EO model was being molded by the decisions of transnational capital. This is how under President Lagos, Chile's neostructuralists finally discovered that the country's path to the high road lay in embracing its destiny of transforming itself into a *país plataforma*. All previous talk about emulating the Nordic Model, the Celtic example, or the Dutch Experience boiled down to newly defined aspiration: becoming, if not the Singapore, at the very least, the Miami of South America.

País Plataforma: A Springboard for Transnational Capital

On January 8, 2003, President Lagos, flanked by the Minister of Economics and representatives from the government's Foreign Investment Committee and Corporación de Fomento de la Producción (CORFO), the state development corporation, met with five hundred business executives to launch an international media campaign called *Chile, País Plataforma* (Chile the Springboard Country). The purpose of the campaign was to publicize Chile's advantages as a business operations platform for transnational corporations interested in expanding to neighboring countries. With this announcement, the second phase of the EO model, originally raised by neostructuralists in 1990, was finally buried without ceremony.[10] Governmental endorsement of Chile as a *país plataforma* reflects important realignments in the correlation of forces, as a new political project for subordinating the state and society to the requirements of transnational capital emerged. That this happened under President Lagos, closely advised by high-level functionaries of ECLAC headquarters (Ottone, Lahera, and Rosales), while he claimed the socialist mantle of Salvador Allende, is one of those cruel but not infrequent ironies of history.

A crucial component of this strategy was the *Agenda Pro Crecimiento*, which sanctioned the co-government between the Lagos Concertación III administration, the country's powerful business associations, and the over-represented right-wing political parties in a congress still not elected through fully democratic procedures. The "Pro-Economic Growth Agenda" was the full-scale acceptance on the part of the Lagos government of the business class's own policy program for addressing the lasting effects of the Asian financial crisis. It included eight major policy areas: regulatory changes to favor greater competitiveness, technological policy, tax structure, capital market, efficiency of public expenditure, labor legislation, simplification of procedures, and export development.

An additional component accompanying this pro-business policy package was a heightened sensitivity to the emerging requirements of transnational capital. As the Government's Foreign Investment Committee recognized, "in recent years, a new trend has emerged in foreign investment in Chile. Prospective investors are no longer looking only at the country's natural resources or the potential of its domestic market; instead, they are also weighing its advantages as a springboard into other markets around Latin America and, indeed, in other countries around the world" (Foreign Investment Committee 2005). Addressing foreign investors directly, President Lagos stated, "I think that "Chile *país plataforma* is an initiative in accordance with the new realities that we face as a nation. . . . What we are now looking for is to also convince you that Chile is also an adequate platform so that from here you can go to other places with investments. To take advantage of other markets is the reason why we have expanded the bridge that Chile has extended to the rest of the world" (ASEXMA 2003; my translation). The purpose of the campaign was to disseminate Chile's advantages as a base of operations for high-tech and service firms interested in establishing their regional operations in Chile:

> Chile has long been attractive to first-time investors in Latin America, who are reassured by its political and economic stability and by its straightforward business environment. But, increasingly, investors are taking this learning-curve approach a step further and using Chile not only to find their feet in Latin America, but also as a base from which to supply other markets. Examples abound, from the mining companies such as BHP Billiton, Placer Dome and Anglo-American in the north—which export copper to world markets—to Canada's Methanex in the extreme south, which produces methanol and sells it throughout the world. Growers and manufacturers—in sectors that range from the food industry to salmon farming and from ship building to computer assembly—now supply overseas markets from Chile, taking advantage of the country's increasing network of trade agreements. (Foreign Investment Committee 2005)

By October 2005, almost sixty leading multinational companies had already selected Chile as the location for their call centers, information technology support centers, back and front office operations, shared services centers, and regional headquarters, as well as using it as a platform from which to export to markets around the region and, indeed, other parts of the world. According to executives from these companies, Chile's first-rate infrastructure, frequent air services, world-class telecommunications services, and its excellent quality of life were key factors in the decision to use it as their springboard into other markets.

In its standard presentation, Chile's *Comité de Inversiones Extranjeras* (CIE, Foreign Investment Committee) emphasizes the trend toward the growth of service off-shoring in the coming years and identifies specific areas in which Chile was wooing foreign investors: (1) Business Processing Outsourcing (BPOs) consisting of call centers, front and back office operations, billing, data processing, human resource management, services, and sales and (2) value-added services such as telemedicine, management, drafting and technical drawings, marketing, legal services, engineering and construction, software design, postproduction of advertising, film dubbing, academic consulting, and others. The objective of the government was to transform Chile into a site to be seriously considered by transnational corporations and their global strategies aimed at creating shared service centers (SSCs). As then director of the Foreign Investment Committee and former Minister of Mining under President Bachelet, Karen Poniachik explained, through the *Chile, País Plataforma*, "a reasonable but demanding goal, is to generate 10,000 jobs in the next three and half years" (Poniachik 2005b).

Thus in Chile, where neostructuralists for more than a decade and a half have had inordinate influence shaping public policies, they have performed a full 180-degree turn. In 1990, while still under the optimistic influence of early neostructuralism, the notion of systemic competitiveness sought to forge a national consensus behind the "export drive." In 2005, after the high road showed its evanescent character, the task of consensus-building was now redirected toward transforming Chilean society into an attractive platform for off-shoring and outsourcing the service activities of transnational corporations. As the Consejo de Inversiones Extranjeras (CIE) states, "Having the ideal legal framework is useless, if we do not know how to use it with creativity, imagination, and entrepreneurial drive. That is what will set us apart from the rest of countries that compete for the market in offshoring." Adding, "That is a task that corresponds to all of us together: government, academic centers, students, entrepreneurs and workers" (Poniachik 2005a).

In a country with high degrees of functional illiteracy, where fourth- and eighth-graders consistently score below international standards,[11] and only 8 percent of students go to private schools, Sergio Bitar, a prominent neostructuralist and Minister of Education under President Lagos, set a key objective of transformation of Chile into a bilingual, English-speaking country within a decade. Interviewed by *The New York Times*, Minister Bitar explained, "We have some of the most advanced commercial accords in the world, but that is not enough. . . . We know our lives are linked more than ever to an international presence, and if you can't speak English, you can't sell and you can't learn" (Rohter 2004, 4). The government program known as "English Opens Doors" has set a goal for all Chilean elementary and high school students to be able to pass a standardized listening and reading test a decade from now. As the *New York Times* explains, "the more ambitious long-term goal is to make all 15 million of Chile's people fluent in English within a generation. 'It took the Swedes 40 years" to get to that point,' said Mr. Bitar, adding that he sees the Nordic countries and Southeast Asian nations like Malaysia as models for Chile. 'It's going to take us decades too, but we're on the right track'" (Rohter 2004, 4). Nonetheless, it took hundreds of thousands of high school students taking to the streets to jolt Bitar and others into realizing that perhaps nondiscriminatory basic access to quality education and not bilingualism is what most interests the new generation.

When President Lagos and the third *Concertación* government were elected in 2000, the inaccessibility of the high road to globalization, as initially conceived, was overwhelmingly apparent. After seventeen years of neo-structuralist-inspired policies, Chile's "dynamic entry" into the world economy was reduced to remaining an EO economy of natural resources with low levels of processing onto which was grafted the conversion of the rest of Chile into a *país plataforma* for transnational capital. All the talk about the information economy seems to have been reduced to creating the infrastructure, institutions, and disciplined labor force to staff transnational capital's call centers and subcontracted low-paying service centers.

As the consensus among elites, the political class of both the right and center–left coalesces more strongly behind this vision for the future, the malaise among Chileans, already detected by some studies, continues growing. According to the 2002 UNDP Survey, *Informe de Desarrollo Humano en Chile*, almost 75 percent of Chileans have negative feelings about the present economic system, and 52 percent feel like "losers" in the economic transformations unleashed by globalization (PNUD 2002). The growing sense of insecurity among an ever-widening group of Chileans, given the flexible nature of jobs, class discriminatory education, health, social security, legal services, and credit-fueled consumption, cannot be staved off for too much longer through the mostly symbolic incorporation into modernity offered by transforming Chile into a *país plataforma*, the new Miami in the Southern Cone. If Chileans could no longer claim to be "the English of South America," at least they could now look forward to becoming English-speakers of South America, and all of it to better compete with Barbados, Belize, and India in becoming another outsourcing and off-shoring sweatshop site for transnational capital.

Dashed Dreams of Growth with Equity

Numerous indicators suggest that despite planners' pretensions, Chile's EO economic growth has not generated quality employment and that, to the contrary, it has tended to transform existing jobs into precarious ones. Data for Chile strongly indicates that, during the 1990s and first half of the present decade, economic growth expanded the number of unstable jobs, additionally characterized with low levels of benefits and remuneration. The result has been a short-circuiting of the "virtuous circle" promised by neostructural-ists. Promises to transform Chile into a springboard country do not bode well for improving wages, working conditions, or the staggering inequality experienced by the majority of Chileans. Though momentarily abated by the post–2005 rise in the price of copper, cellulose, salmon, and other exports, the trend toward the increasing precariousness of labor persists as a defining trait of Chilean contemporary capitalism.

A Growing Proportion of Workers with Short-term or without Labor Contracts

One indicator of the quality of employment is whether or not a worker has a labor contract. Social security, health, vacation, and other benefits are di-rectly associated with the existence of a written contract between a worker and an employer and with the *type* of contract (permanent vs. temporary).[12] Using a broader definition of "precarious employment"—that which is "un-stable, can be interrupted at any time, is not for a single, identifiable employ-er, does not necessarily take place in the establishment of the employer, has low or no access to social security and is performed with scant protection for the physical and psychological integrity of workers"(Echeverría 1996, 5)—we can gauge the significant role of such jobs in the Chilean economy. Based on the 1994 Encuesta CASEN, Chile's Dirección del Trabajo concluded that 33 percent of all salaried workers and 56.6 percent of all unskilled workers suf-fered precarious employment (Espinosa 1997, 10). According to Dirección del Trabajo statistics, in 1996, the percentage of workers with precarious jobs represented a significant portion of export sector workers: 55 percent of agri-cultural workers; 52.1 percent of workers in forestry; 50.7 percent of workers in lumber extraction; and 36 percent of workers in fishing sector, precisely the more dynamic sectors constituting the main pillars of Chile's EO model.

Chile's flexible labor market and labor legislation continue to provide business firms and employers with an incentive structure that encourages transferring the costs of social reproduction and the risks of production onto workers and their families. The institutional matrix underpinning Chile's flexible labor markets has been an important factor in stimulating the adop-tion of productive strategies based on cost-reduction and cost-externalization through hiring of fixed-term, short-term workers, and the use of subcontract-ing (Echeverría and Lopez 2004) instead of technological innovation and

investment in capital and equipment. At best, data for Chile shows that employers have combined spurious neoliberal strategies with very limited neostructuralist genuine forms of competitiveness. No indications exist that—at
the level of the firm—the clear dichotomy posited by neostructuralists leads
to a transition from the "savage" authoritarian neoliberal phase to a more
"consensual" neostructuralist phase. Processes of greater economic globalization, further economic concentration, and financialization have all intensified over the past decade, increasing the volatility, precariousness, and uncertainty faced by Chilean male and female workers.

Recent studies carried out by the Research Department of Chile's Labor
Bureau, the regulatory agency of the Ministry of Labor, portray that the traits
already present during the mid-1990s acquired frightening levels. In the wake
of the 1998–99 recession, labor legislation implemented by the Lagos administration further enhanced capital's ability to promote labor flexibility. Using
an innovative approach of carrying out longitudinal studies of employment
trajectories rather than just examining the cross-sectional data offered by
periodic employment and household surveys, the head of the Bureau's Research Department, Helia Henríquez, and her collaborators have produced
a valuable set of quantitative and qualitative data depicting the volatility and
insecurity faced by Chilean workers (Henríquez and Uribe-Echevarría 2004;
Acuña and Perez 2005). By following employment trajectories during an
eighteen-month period in 1998–2000 through a special processing of the National Employment Survey (ENE), they provide a picture of the magnitude
and gendered nature of high turnover rates, structural volatility, and uncertainty experienced by the majority of Chilean workers.[13] If from the data,
those who never reported themselves as part of the labor force during this
period are not considered and the remainder is classified according to shifts
in their employment status (employed, unemployed, not in the labor force
[inactive]) and their class of workers (waged, salaried, or self-employed), a
more accurate picture of the insecurity and volatility emerges (see Table 19).
They find that 78 percent of the labor force switched their classification at
least once in terms of one or both of the variables studied (employment status
and class of worker). Only 42 percent of the labor force remained employed
throughout the eighteen-month period, reflecting the high level of instability
present in the labor market. Fifty-seven percent of those in the labor force
remained as waged and salaried workers and 16 percent possessed only self-
employed jobs. A considerable segment representing more than a quarter
of the labor force moved back and forth between the categories of waged

dependent and autonomous self-employed workers. A relatively small portion (31.8 percent) of the workers remained employed throughout the period and did not change their occupational category.

The precariousness and instability experienced by the majority of workers in the 1990–2005 period illustrates the emerging patterns in a country that has been "successful" in completing a wrenching process of capitalist restructuring. Chile's neostructuralist-inspired policy makers failed in achieving three promised goals: (1) the creation of quality productive jobs and the basis for an expanding process of social integration; (2) the promotion of "growth with equity" so as to significantly improve income distribution; and (3) the establishment of the microeconomic foundations within each

TABLE 19

Instability and volatility of Chilean workers: Patterns of trajectory*

TYPES OF TRAJECTORY ACCORDING TO TYPE OF DEPENDENCE AD PERMANENCE OF EMPLOYMENT	POPULATION HOLDING A JOB AT LEAST ONCE	
	FREQUENCY	PERCENTAGE
ONLY SALARIED JOBS		
Always employed	1,100,490	24.6
From employed to inactive	751,744	16.8
From employed to unemployed	714,457	15.9
Total	2,566,691	57.3
SALARIED *AND* SELF-EMPLOYED JOBS		
Always Employed	541,333	12.1
From employed to inactive	274,694	6.1
From employed to unemployed	363,878	8.1
Total	1,179,905	26.3
ONLY SELF-EMPLOYED JOBS		
Always Employed	324,221	7.2
From employed to inactive	317,132	7.1
From employed to unemployed	91,968	2.1
Total	733,321	16.4
TOTAL	4,479,917	100.0

Source: Table 15, Henríquez and Urbina-Echeverría (2004) "Trayectorias laborales: la certeza de la incertidumbre." *Cuadernos de Investigación*. Santiago: Dirección del Trabajo, 53 (Based on a special processing of the Encuesta Nacional de Empleo, 18 months).
* Classification according to salaried condition and job permanence as a percentage of the population employed at least once.

productive establishment for a self-propelling process of equity and *con-certación social*. Despite some positive trends in the 1990–2005 period—a decline in poverty, rising real wages though at decreasing rates and below the rate at which productivity increased—there is another reality of precariousness, volatility, and turnover rates that has been less captured by existing indicators. As a result of the profound realignment of class power relations condensed in the new political and labor institutions, workers' increase in real wages over the past decades was "financed" by workers themselves (see Table 20). The fact that increases in labor productivity have outstripped increases in real wages, means that such increases are mostly captured by employers, further concentrating benefits in a small minority and transforming "growth with equity," even in "successful" countries like Chile, into nothing more than a chimera.

TABLE 20

Chile: Evolution of productivity and real wages, 1990–2005 (Base 1989=100)

YEAR	PRODUCTIVITY	REAL WAGES	RATIO REAL WAGES/PRODUCTIVITY
1989	100.00	100.00	100.00
1990	101.42	101.85	100.42
1991	107.51	106.84	99.38
1992	116.68	111.65	95.69
1993	119.54	115.77	96.85
1994	125.54	123.25	98.18
1995	139.53	129.20	92.60
1996	148.04	134.53	90.87
1997	154.99	137.36	88.63
1998	157.25	141.42	89.93
1999	159.56	144.86	90.79
2000	165.02	146.86	89.00
2001	170.14	149.24	87.72
2002	172.03	152.26	88.51
2003	173.10	153.68	88.78
2004	177.86	156.48	87.98
2005	172.25	159.79	92.77

Source: Centro Nacional de Desarrollo Alternativo (CENDA), "Chile: Indicadores Economico Sociales," Julio 2005.

The Bonanza of Copper Prices and the Constraints on Fiscal Spending

Nothing better represents the ephemeral nature of Chile's success story than what happens during boom years. Rising copper prices resulted in a government surplus of $13 billion by the end of 2006 and could climb to an estimated $20 billion by the end of 2007. However, instead of being able to use these extraordinary resources to address the pressing problems of Chilean development, signifcant constraints emerging from existing power relations have led the Chilean government to invest these resources abroad. By the end of June 2006, two thirds of the government's increased revenue, an estimated $4.5 billion, had been invested outside of the country, four-fifths of these in U.S.-dollar denominated financial assets.[14] Can the Chilean government increase fiscal spending, even though it is enjoying one of the largest fiscal booms in its history?[15] It is not only the International Monetary Fund's (IMF) endorsed Structural Balance Rule (SBR) that limits government expenditure but also the fact that, if invested in the national economy, the bonanza of dollars could bring about an appreciation of the Chilean peso and inflationary pressures that would cut into the profits of exporters and financial investors. To assure business elites that this will not be the case, the Bachelet government has proposed legislation guaranteeing that such a surplus will be spent over a protracted period of time and that the profits of Chilean and foreign transnationalized elites will not be affected.[16]

Bachelet's Finance Minister, Andrés Velasco, riled many by stating that Chilean government spending would not rise over two digits, making such a categorical statement even before the two committees established under the IMF-approved SBR had not yet had a chance to meet and recalculate the medium term price of copper used to define the government budget and estimate potential GDP. As Alexis Guardia, a prominent Concertación economist summarizes,

> we could conclude the following. In the 16 years of Concertación
> governments, prudence and fiscal responsibility have prevailed. In
> the beginning it started with a reform to the tax code that enabled
> us to address the social debt of the military regime and permanently
> maintained a fiscal savings, before the structural balance rule was
> established. The latter seems to have been established, not to prevent a
> populist temptation, but for launching the economy in a deep process

of financial globalization. In doing so, the goal of equity and a notion of development has been sacrificed, thus opening the gates for conservative ideas in macroeconomic management. (Guardia 2006)

Potholes, Car-jackings, and Mirages on the High Road

In the case of Chile, the high road to globalization so far has shown itself to be more a mirage than a tangible reality. The insufficiently examined processes of transnationalization and financialization have cursed it with potholes and "car-jackings," preventing the economy and society from ever reaching the lofty destination promised by Latin American neostructuralism. The fundamental reason for these failures is neostructuralism's incapacity for resuscitating, if not Raúl Prebisch's original analysis, at least his spirit of intellectual courage. Such spirit is much needed today in order to scrutinize those new forms through which transnational capital and domestic conglomerates control the economic surplus and exercise control over the political system. The power of the state, its leadership role, and the collective action of the population cannot be marshaled to better facilitate capitalist competition but should be assembled to regulate and limit transnational capital's destructive role; it should be used to discipline capital so that it serves the needs of society, not the other way around, to discipline society, communities, individuals, and subjectitivies to serve capital.

Neglecting power relations has had far-reaching consequences that are starkly illustrated by the case of Chile. First, such omission compelled major reaccomodations in neostructuralist discourse, forcing it, after 1998, to belatedly acknowledge that important asymmetries characterize the international economy. While some might justify these shifts as part of neostructuralism necessary learning process, such a view conveniently glosses over the fact that these changes stem from a comprehensive intellectual and methodological retreat. Initially, such a retreat was unconvincingly justified as resulting from recent transformations in the world economy. When neostructuralists had the opportunity to shape public policies and implement their vision, like they have had in Chile, the result was a parody of its original claims.

Second, and from the perspective of critical political economy, such changes reveal the utopian strains embedded in neostructuralism's conceptual apparatus and the deeply flawed nature of its assumptions. Chile, the vaunted showcase for post-neoliberal policies and the benefits of EO regimes, shows disappointing results. The net outcome is that, like the grin of the Cheshire cat in Alice in Wonderland, the high road to globalization and growth with equity evanesce, leaving behind only the satisfied smile of those few at the very top who have materially benefited from this act of inter-temporal seduction. At least Chile's *pingüinos* seem to have figured this out.

10

Neostructuralism and the Latin American Left

This chapter extends the critical analysis of Latin American neostructuralism by exploring its relationship with the Latin American Left and the ongoing efforts to construct alternatives to the present neoliberal order. In this chapter, I review the Economic Commission for Latin America and the Caribbean's (ECLAC) latest formulations so as to gauge whether Latin American neostructuralism is successfully prolonging its shelf-life both as an economic development discourse and as a narrative about Latin America's path to modernity. By contrasting Latin American neostructuralism's strategy of "globalization with a human face" with two other proposals for a post-neoliberalism future that have appeared in the region, namely Venezuela's "twenty-first-century socialism" and Bolivia's pursuit of "Andean-Amazonic capitalism," we can also assess the extent to which neostructuralism's discursive innovations, enacted during the 2002–7 period, contribute to overcome its numerous shortcomings and contradictions analyzed in previous chapters.

Conceptual Renewal and the Left in Latin America

With large reddish-orange letters running across its cover, the May 20, 2006, issue of *The Economist* alerted that "The Battle for Latin America's Soul" was at hand. According to its editors, such confrontation was not between the continent's poor, numbering more than 40 percent of the population, rising against the small transnationalized capitalist class immiserating them; rather the region's spiritual and material salvation hinged on the outcome of the clash between "liberal democrats—of left and right—and authoritarian populists."[1] To further clarify matters, the weekly avowed: "broadly speaking, one camp is made up of moderate social democrats, of the sort in office in Chile, Uruguay and Brazil. The other camp is the radical populists, led by Mr. Chávez, who appears to have gained a disciple in Evo Morales, Bolivia's new president."

Only months earlier, in early 2005, Teodoro Petkoff, an ardent opponent of Venezuelan president Hugo Chávez, published *Dos Izquierdas en América Latina* (*Latin America's Two Lefts*), offering similar misleading characterization. According to Petkoff, the Left in Latin America divided into what he called *la izquierda borbónica* (Royal House of Bourbon Left) and *la izquierda moderna* (modern Left). Petkoff compared the "unreconstructed left" to the doomed royal line of the Bourbons: one that "does not learn or forget" and best represented by "throwbacks" like Fidel Castro and Hugo Chávez. His updated list of who's who in this doomed and cognitively challenged Left would presumably also include Bolivia's Evo Morales and Ecuador's Rafael Correa. Like the leaders of Cuba and Venezuela, they fail the test of having fully learned the lesson that, in the path to modernity, U.S. imperial interests and the power of transnational capital should not be challenged, even if, with the exception of Cuba, these challenges have been mostly rhetorical. Nonetheless this "backward–modern" characterization is repeatedly invoked by other Latin American analysts, such as Jorge Castañeda and Alvaro Vargas Llosa[2] The implication of such analysis is clear: this is a Left destined to failure and historical irrelevance. Or as Jorge Castañeda pontificates, its lack of statesmanship and vision is reflected in that "rhetoric is more important than substance, and the fact of power is more important than its responsible exercise. The despair of poor constituencies is a tool rather than a challenge, and taunting the United States trumps promoting their countries' real interests in the world. The difference is obvious: Chávez is not Castro; he is Perón with oil. Morales is not an indigenous Che; he is a skillful and irresponsible populist" (Castañeda 2006, 38).

In sharp contrast, the allegedly "good," "vegetarian," "modern" Left has successfully attuned its conceptual apparatus to contemporary historical realities and modes of thinking. Represented by Chile's Ricardo Lagos and Michelle Bachelet, Brazil's Luis Inácio (Lula) da Silva, Uruguay's Tabaré Vázquez, and of course Petkoff and Castañeda themselves, this "modern" Latin American left claims to have found the formula for marrying capitalist globalization with social equity. Formulating a twenty-first-century political discourse that allegedly taps into the lived experience of individuals and the constitution of modern day subjectivities through consumption and reliance on the Internet, this pragmatic, cosmopolitan, and modern Left presumably has the winds of history behind it as it blazes a path toward progressive modernity and eagerly promotes free trade agreements with the United States. Since this self-proclaimed "modern" Left shares many of Latin American neostructuralism's politico-economic perspectives, it is not far-fetched to assert that, just like Fajnzylber's optimism regarding neostructuralism—"Here is the solution to all our problems"—Petkoff's confidence on the "modern left" is also misplaced.

The simplistic dichotomy of a good and bad Left, though analytically flawed, has proved useful at least in one respect: it has allowed center-left regimes to gain the tolerance, if not active political support from the U.S. administration, transnational capital, and local conglomerates. It is a dichotomy crafted to educate these powerful actors so they can better "separate the sensible from the irresponsible and to support the former and contain the latter," as Castañeda recommends. At the same time, it is seriously inconsistent, because it misrepresents complex historical processes of social mobilization and popular resistance in Venezuela, Bolivia, and Ecuador under the catch-all term of "authoritarian populism,[3] while simultaneously enrobing the neostructuralist-inspired governments of Chile, Brazil, and Uruguay with the undeserved, or at the very least, questionable mantle of success.[4]

Deeply aware that a definitive judgement is premature, this chapter explores the role of Latin American neostructuralism vis-à-vis the Latin American Left through two complimentary methods.[5] First, it assesses ECLAC's latest formulations and innovations. Do the latest neostructuralist conceptions address and resolve their own methodological and theoretical problems? Second, it evaluates the nature of Latin American neostructuralism's contribution to the quest for alternatives to the transnationalized export-oriented (EO) regime of accumulation in the region. Does neostructuralism offer any glimmer of hope that, after almost two decades of existence and given recent political shifts in the continent, it is moving toward a politico-economic program seeking to transform existing power relations? The preliminary comparison offered in this chapter shows Latin American neostructuralism becoming even more entrenched as a "status-quo defending" neodevelopmentalist strategy.[6] Venezuela and Bolivia's experiments, on the other hand, retain a strong "status-quo transformative" character and, depending on how they resolve their own contradictions over the coming years, the processes unfolding in both countries could lead to significant reforms of the present order. In other words, by purposely seeking to transform existing power relations in the economy and society, even if gradually and within carefully circumscribed sectors, Venezuela and Bolivia's social actors and government leaders, not ECLAC's current paradigm, might prove to be more effective in clearing the way to a more democratic and fulfilling Latin American twenty-first-century modernity.

ECLAC's Latest Conceptual Innovations

When the conceptual innovations introduced by ECLAC over the 2002–7 period are reviewed, one cannot avoid the sense that Latin American neostructuralism has finally painted itself into a corner.[7] Stubbornly clinging to problem-ridden notions analyzed in chapter 1, it continues upholding its commitment to equity and social cohesion, while it remains unwilling to address the root causes of social polarization. As a result, increasing intellectual and organizational resources have been allocated toward performing the demanding, yet ultimately ill-fated task of prolonging Latin American neostructuralism's coherence and relevance. In recent years, such efforts have yielded new types of social policies and refurbished analytical categories aimed at papering over the gap between its rhetoric on growth with equity and the reality of persistent exploitation of workers and dispossession of communities.

Neostructuralism's recent discursive innovations demand an even more precarious white-knuckled balancing act. Policies to enhance equity must be designed without being perceived as threatening to the profit rate of domestic conglomerates and transnational capital; they cannot restrict capital mobility, flexible labor markets, or upset stable expectations for investors. The banner of equity must be prominently displayed and flutter high, becoming part of a governing coalition's political discourse so as to sustain legitimacy and electoral support. Yet all this must be accomplished without somehow encouraging emancipatory aspirations on the part of the dispossessed or impoverished middle classes in the most unequal region in the world—truly a labor of Herculean proportions, one at which neostructuralism has been successful so far, if at the cost of renewed acts of omission that touch on the self-delusional.

Since 1990, but especially after 2002, ECLAC has sought to thread the needle of "growth with equity" in an increasingly restrictive global environment through more creative policies. This newly conceived framework rests basically upon three components: (1) the primacy of economic growth and the preservation of a favorable climate for private investment; (2) the promotion of a system of individualized risk management serviced by the financial industry (individual unemployment insurance schemes for example); and

(3) the fostering of society-creating and society-disciplining fiscal and political covenants. Understanding the logic behind each one of these elements is crucial for grasping how in recent years the abandonment of neostructuralism's original dream of "productive transformation with social equity" leads to the hyperbolization of discourse and a greater reliance on the symbolic and subjective dimensions of politics to manage and reproduce the current status quo.

With the publication of *Productive Change in Open Economies* in 2004, neostructuralists acknowledged that equity would not easily flow from productivity-led export growth as originally thought. A more focused set of differentiated policies was necessary as neostructuralism shifted emphasis toward society-creating and social cohesion-enhancing policy interventions. Not surprisingly, the more policies target enhancing social cohesion, the more Latin American neostructuralism exacerbates its descriptive rather than analytical prowess. Let us examine these salient components of neostructuralism's conceptual innovations enacted during the 2002–7 period to illustrate how status-quo defensive traits have gained predominance in current neostructuralist thinking.

Retreading Structural Heterogeneity: The Three-speed Model

With the publication of *Productive Development in Open Economies* in 2004, Latin American neostructuralism attempted to fill the gaping holes in its analytical apparatus, finally discarding the exuberant optimism supporting "productive transformation with social equity" that prevailed during much of the 1990s. This shift took the form of dusting off and updating the old structuralist notion of "structural heterogeneity" via a new characterization of Latin America as a "three-speed" economy. With this three-speed model" in hand, Latin American neostructuralism sought to better capture the unique diversity of Latin America's productive structure. Using a classification based on the size and legal status of enterprises, it identified three sectors: (1) informal enterprises, "that because of their structure and capacity, are of lower productivity and operate in an environment that offers them little opportunity for development and learning" (ECLAC 2004, 21); (2) formal small and medium enterprises that face difficulties "accessing resources (particularly financial) and gaining access to certain markets; and (3) large national and foreign enterprises with "productivity that often rivals businesses operating on the global scale but with few links to the rest of the economy and, in some cases, with poor capacity for innovation" (ECLAC 2004, 21). Except for sharing a common space bounded by the nation-state, nothing structurally or dynamically connects these three sectors, not the underlying process of capitalist accumulation or its unfolding on a world scale. All pretense of rooting the existence, structure, and reproduction of these three sectors in the overarching logic of capitalist accumulation on a world scale have been discarded.

Based on this overtly descriptive three-speed model hollowed of any real explanatory, analytical, or empirical value, *Productive Development* designs policies for inclusion, modernization, and "densification" (incorporation of more knowledge and a more articulated web of productive, technological, entrepreneurial, and labor relations).[8] While some see this classification as "opening up a clear-eyed view of the area where policies are necessary,"[9] the only "clear-eyed" aspect in this formulation, as we shall see, is the explicit acknowledgement that neostructuralist public policies will not meddle with the dynamics of the fastest of Latin America's purported three-sector economy, namely the one controlled by transnational capital and domestic conglomerates.

The Undisputable Centrality of Economic Growth and Flexible Labor Markets

At the same time that ECLAC was revising its initially optimistic vision, other United Nations agencies, like the United Nations Development Program (UNDP), were also looking for more insightful approaches, organizing a series of regional seminars on social policy. At a UNDP Regional Workshop, "Social Protection in an Insecure Era: A South-South Exchange on Alternative Social Policies" held in Santiago during May of 2002, the ILO's Guy Standing presented a starkly critical vision of the relationship between globalization and equity, questioning the assumptions which for more than a decade had been at the root of Latin American neostructuralism. Globalization, according to Standing, was leading to greater social and political instability because the "three systems that embed the economy in society—the regulatory system, the social protection system, and the redistributive system —were incompatible with the underlying economic and technological system" (Report 2002, 8). In the words of Standing, globalization had not only "decimated some countries' export sectors, enfeebled the state, but ... also resulted in more unequal social income and greater social vulnerability." He called for transforming the twenty-first century into the historical turning point when fundamental economic rights such as the right to equal basic security were enshrined as part of universally accepted human rights. In measured and diplomatic language, the workshop's final report noted that, "Mr. Standing's keynote speech was immediately and sharply countered by Ms. Barbara Stallings, Director of the Economic Development Division of the UN Economic Commission for Latin America and the Caribbean, ECLAC" (Report 2002, 11). Criticizing Standing's perspective, Stallings stressed that in Latin America, "it all starts with jobs, that is, with economic growth, and consequently, social policy should not impair economic growth, and need not to, if intelligent and appropriate fund mobilization and allocation strategies are employed" (11).

The debate illustrates a wider conservative conceptual shift in how neostructuralists conceive the relationship between economic and social policy. At the same time that the nexus between accumulation and distribution was conveniently dissolved, the more immediate short term conditioning relationships of social policy were brought to the forefront: social policy must support and be subordinate to economic growth, i.e., capitalist profits. Another prominent neostructuralist, Victor Tokman, sums it up this way:

> The fact that employment is being created overwhelmingly by the private sector introduces conditioning factors regarding public policies, because to a great extent the solution depends on *creating an appropriate environment and climate so that businessmen invest.* This requires stability, not only of prices so that there is no inflation, but also *of entire societies and rules of the game that are also stable.* This is very difficult to achieve, when different social groups perceive that they are being treated unjustly, do not receive something back for their efforts. Therefore, there is a growing interaction between social and economic policies, as they are not matters that can be treated separately. (Tokman 2003, 34–35; my translation, emphasis added)

The pragmatic postures of Stallings and Tokman establish a new hierarchy of priorities and policy mandates that must be defended at all costs, if social and economic policies are to effectively support the neostructuralist vision.[10]

What room has neostructuralism found after 2004 for the design of equity-enhancing policies within this self-imposed decision matrix? The answer to this question is that in its middle stage, neostructuralism has shifted its emphasis away from "equity" and repayment of the "social debt" toward "risk management" and social covenants that promote social cohesion. The ordering of social policy designed by ECLAC after 2000 and filtered to policymakers of center–left governments is very clear: (1) economic growth is primary; (2) flexible labor markets are to be defended; (3) social spending is constrained by fiscal responsibility; (4) adaptability of the population to the demands of the new system must be produced through the political system; (5) social and public financing of social protection should be fully supportive of market forces, not interfere or constrain them; and (6) the ownership structure of assets is not to be spoken as a possible policy option. All of these orientations, characterizing the "modern–cosmopolitan" or "good Left" are not part of the rhetoric or practice of reformers in Venezuela and Bolivia.

Segmented Transnationalization, Heterogeneity, and Equity

In "Elusive Equity in Latin American Development: A Structural Vision, A Multi Dimensional Approach," a document originally presented to the IV Meeting of Former Presidents of Latin America celebrated in June of 2005, José Luis Machinea, then Executive Secretary of ECLAC, and Martin Hopenhayn, from ECLAC's Social Division, identify the "Strategic Lines of Action for a Pro-Equity Agenda" conceived according to the previously mentioned guidelines and ECLAC's new three-speed model. This document is of interest because the authors identify specific key policies "whose effects can be more encompassing over society, such as policies toward the productive sector, employment, education, and conditional transfers" (Machinea and Hopenhayn 2005, 35). The root explanation for persistent inequality is structural heterogeneity, which tended to intensify during the 1990s, not on account of transnationalization per se but as a result of "segmented transnationalization" defined as the "segmented incorporation of the productive sector into the information and knowledge economy" (Machinea and Hopenhayn 2005, 8). In other words, unequal and differentiated development is not the product of capitalist globalization but rather of *not enough* capitalist globalization.

The notion of "segmented transnationalization" enables Latin American neostructuralism to attempt to resolve some of its many internal inconsistencies arising from its failure to ask what happens to the economic surplus. Accordingly, a tautological explanation is proffered on the basis of an analytical and historical potpourri concocted from disconnected elements. According to Machinea and Hopenhayn, a differentiated incorporation into the information and knowledge economy results in "segmented productive sectors in terms of the knowledge required to compete in the new scenario, access to financing, and linking practices with external markets." This process intensifies the structural heterogeneity of Latin American economies, "turning even more dramatic the social exclusion in the new modernizing phase" (Machinea and Hopenhayn 2005, 8).

ECLAC and Latin American neostructuralism now have a model that supposedly explains why the outcomes promised in 1990 failed to materialize:

> Just as ECLAC has recently affirmed, it is possible to identify three broad groups of firms, differentiated by their levels of productivity, degree of formality and size. The first is composed of large firms integrated into the global economy with productive standards located on the technological frontier, but with scant linkages with the local economy, and limited job creation. The second, includes medium and small size enterprises of the formal sector that confront barriers to entry to some productive factors (mainly financing and technology) and with low levels of articulation, both within itself as well as with the other two groups. The last grouping is that of the informal economy, composed of micro and small enterprises, with the lowest level of productivity, lower incomes, reduced access to funding and broad markets, precarious levels of social protection and very limited incorporation of knowledge and technical progress. In this manner, the development of Latin America's productive sector confronts a three speed economy that reinforces the secular structural heterogeneity, exacerbating income and wage gaps. (Machinea and Hopenhayn 2005, 8)

Beyond specific policies (microcredit, training, management skills) for the lowest speed informal sector, ECLAC recommends horizontal policies (simplification of procedures, tax reduction, regularization of land titles) aimed at transferring as many micro and small enterprises from the informal to the formal sector. For the "medium speed" layer, ECLAC suggests targeting firms of the formal sector with a combination of horizontal (better access to information, credit, technology, and marketing) and selective policies. The aim is to encourage the formation of producers' associations and to strengthen the network of exchanges linking large with the small and medium-size enterprises acting as suppliers or clients. In sum, this set of policies aims to strengthen territorially based productive clusters of firms and their linkages to global value chains. A complex web of small, medium, and large firms linked, for example, to wood-assemble your own furniture for export, food processing, paper, packaging, and printing complexes supporting the export drive are to be encouraged.

A major omission, however, is that, despite the assurances that the "strategic lines of action" being outlined are those that will have the greatest impact, not a word is said about the "high speed" rung of the economy. Such absence is not an oversight. Rather, it indicates two de-facto acknowledgements by Latin American neostructuralism one political, the other analytical. Politically, ECLAC is announcing that its "Strategic Lines of Action for a Pro-Equity Agenda" will not consider touching that third fast speed sector composed by large transnational enterprises where income is being concentrated at the fastest rate, namely that top 2 or 3 percent of the population constituted by an increasingly transnationalized capitalist class. From an analytical point of view, such policy design reveals that Prebisch's key question in economic development, namely how is the economic surplus being captured, distributed, and used by enterprises owned by the domestic conglomerates, transnational corporations, and banks making up the "high speed" sector?, has not even been imagined, much less raised as a possible component of ECLAC's "forward-looking" new policies. All of these innovations are reflected in ECLAC's 2007 publication *Social Cohesion: Inclusion and a Sense of Belonging in Latin America and the Caribbean* prepared for the November 2007 Ibero-American Summit of Heads of State and Government. This document seeks to relink economics, politics, and culture by showing that, "in terms of economic rationality, societies with higher levels of social cohesion provide a better institutional framework for economic growth that constitutes an attractive factor for investment by offering an environment of confidence and clear rules" (ECLAC 2007).

Alternatives: Post-neoliberal Futures for the Americas

From the 1980s, when no alternatives to neoliberalism seemed possible, to the present, much has changed. Since then, and particularly after 2000, at least four alternatives to neoliberalism appeared in Latin America, each one of them with different emphasis, credibility, and degrees of social support. The first and most elaborate of these has been Latin American neostructuralism, with its "globalization with a human face" strategy and ability to influence center–left governments in Chile, Brazil, and Uruguay, which I have characterized as a "status-quo defending" neo-developmentalist strategy. Its "progressive" emphasis on politics, institutions, and culture allow it to legitimize and regulate the EO regime of accumulation established by neoliberalism. More recently, we have also witnessed in Venezuela and Bolivia the emergence of two other theoretically informed and politically vibrant alternative strategies, which in turn can be described as "status-quo transforming neodevelopmentalist" strategies, each with its own particular character. This cumbersome label captures the core nature of both experiments: a genuine attempt at reshaping existing power structures through a gradual reform process that promotes a mixed economy and strengthened state role that channels economic surplus and steers the development process to serve the less powerful. It is this self-aware and explicit goal of transforming the status quo by redirecting society's economic surplus that most clearly differentiates these two experiences from Latin American neostructuralism.

Despite this defining difference—a focus on the surplus in Venezuela and Bolivia and its silencing in the case of neostructuralism—one finds similar concepts and neodevelopmentalist rhetoric in ECLAC, Venezuela, and Bolivia, such as the use of "endogenous development," the importance of enhancing the role of civil society, equity, and private–public sector alliances. These similarities can be deceiving, however. Whereas Latin American neostructuralism deploys such a neodevelopmentalist discourse and policies to facilitate the logic of capitalist competition, subordinating everything, including social policy, to the logic international competitiveness and to servicing the needs of transnational capital, Venezuela's "twenty-first-century socialism" and Bolivia's "Andean-Amazonic capitalism" do not. In terms of their stated objectives and given the nature of the political and social forces sustaining them, Venezuela and Bolivia have only superficial resemblances to the "authoritarian populism" of previous decades. There exists a fourth, latent alternative that could be denoted as "social movement-based socialism." So far it is politically undeveloped in the region and has not yet shown itself capable of becoming more than just the aspiration of small political groupings, movements, and radical intellectuals. Latin American neostructuralism, twenty-first-century socialism, and Andean-Amazonic capitalism, on the other hand, have become national-level and increasingly regionally based alternatives to the present order, with enough mettle and historical possibility to inspire millions of people and rattle transnational elites and cosmopolitan intellectuals. For these reasons, Venezuela and Bolivia's recent experience are the alternatives deemed here deserving closer examination.

Venezuela's Twenty-first-century Socialism

During a January 30, 2005, speech at the Fifth World Social Forum, President Hugo Chávez announced his support for the creation of a "twenty-first-century socialism" for Venezuela.[11] More than a year later, in another speech, he said, "We have taken up the commitment to lead the Bolivarian Revolution towards socialism and build a path towards socialism, a 21st century socialism that is based on solidarity, brotherhood, love, liberty and equality."[12] Venezuela's twenty-first-century socialism is unique in many ways. It aims to construct socialism while keeping a democratic representative political system along with a constitutionally sanctioned defense of private property. Under Chile's Popular Unity government (1970–73) led by Salvador Allende, Latin America first attempted a peaceful road to socialism, which ended being brutally crushed by the military and the United States. In Venezuela, however, conditions seem to be very different than those faced by Allende. President Chávez's supporters enjoy a consistent electoral and parliamentary majority on the heels of the crisis of the old political system, significant backing from the Armed Forces, and the availability of oil export revenues, all of which partially explain the unique nature of what is unfolding in Simón Bolivar's birthplace.

Heinz Dieterich, a close observer of the Bolivarian Revolution, suggests that it is the simultaneity of four historical "macrodynamics" that explain the singularity of the process unfolding in Venezuela: (1) it is an anti-imperialist revolution; (2) it is a democratic–bourgeois revolution; (3) it is a neoliberal counterrevolution; and (4) it has set itself the goal of arriving at a twenty-first-century socialist society (Dieterich 2005). He equates the Venezuelan process to "democratic bourgeois revolution," because it seeks to achieve two historical objectives traditionally attributed to such revolutions: the construction of a state-based on the rule of law; and the development of the productive forces. While achieved in Europe, both dynamics have been historically undermined and opposed by landowning elites and by national and international monopolies in Latin America. Crucial to fulfilling these objectives is the notion of "endogenous development," which depends on having a "market economy guided and given impetus by a corporatist state in the past, and a more democratic state at present" (Dieterich 2005). Dieterich defends such a neo-developmentalist strategy because: "At present in the Third World, this is the only possible path for achieving economic development by a popular project. It is the lesser evil in light of neoliberalism.

With a democratic developmentalism regional in scope, there is the possibility of escaping underdevelopment. With neoliberalism, the final destiny is to become like Africa. A Third Way does not exist. There are no objective conditions for socialism at present. They must be developed in accordance with democratic developmentalism. This is what Hugo Chávez is trying to do and he is on the correct road" (Dieterich 2005; my translation).

Dieterich, a key contributor to the theoretical foundations of Venezuela's twenty-first-century socialism, defines it as a "New Historical Project for the Majorities of the Global Society." More specifically, through this sui generis Bolivarian Revolution, Venezuela aims to replace the institutional framework upholding the old status-quo, substituting the current market economy with a democratically planned value-based economy; substituting the current classist state with the administration of public affairs at the service of the majorities; and superseding plutocratic democracy with a direct democracy (Dieterich 2002; 2005). Nonetheless, forms of ownership of economic property have not been fully clarified. Of the three types of property existing under capitalism—the stock corporation of variable capital characteristic of large corporations, family-owned enterprises, and cooperatives—only cooperatives are seen as nonvertical and democratic forms of organization.[13] Rather than attempting to seize control of the first two by expropriating factories, the strategy so far seems to encourage the formation and expansion of such cooperatives. The number of cooperatives has increased by a hundredfold over a seven year period, going from only eight hundred in 1998, to over 100 thousand in 2005, employing over 1.5 million Venezuelans or 10 percent of the country's adult population (Wilpert 2006). At the same time, President Chávez has promised to create forms of co-ownership and co-management between workers and the state in public enterprises.[14]

If for Lenin, socialism in 1922 could be defined by the formula "Soviet power plus electrification," Dieterich suggests that Venezuela's twenty-first-century socialism can be defined by the following six tasks: (1) Construction of an efficient State based on the rule of law; (2) Development of the productive forces; (3) Construction of popular power; (4) Advancement of the theory of developmentalist and socialist transformation; (5) construction of a Latin America wide "Regional Power Block"; and (6) development of the vanguard and of middle level cadre (Dieterich 2005).

Venezuela's twenty-first century socialism expands nonmarket forms of trade and distribution that emphasize "cooperation, complementarity, and solidarity over competition" (Wilbert 2006) within a capitalist economy, without aiming to end private ownership of the means of production, the profit motive, or capitalist competition. Citizen participation is encouraged through local planning councils, social programs, and citizen audits (*contraloría social*), not to safeguard the transnationalized EO model and give legitimacy to the institutions created by neoliberal restructuring but to weaken the power of capitalist interests and capitalist competition. All in all, these initiatives and policies, "are more social democratic than socialist" (Wilpert 2006), yet they mark a significant shift not only from "savage" neoliberalism but also from timid Latin American neostructuralism as presently constituted.

Bolivia's "Andean Amazonic Capitalism"

The election of Evo Morales in Bolivia in December 2005 was an important victory for Bolivia's social movements. Product of more than five years of grassroots mobilization, Bolivians elected not only the first indigenous president in the region but also endorsed a campaign program promising the nationalization of oil and gas, the convening of a constituent assembly to refound the nation, and the creation of a new economic model in the service of the country's vast majorities and not local and transnational elites. As vice-president Alvaro García Linera has indicated, the new social and political forces in government seek to build what he has provisionally denominated Andean Amazonic capitalism: "By this I mean the construction of a robust State that regulates the expansion of the industrial economy, extracts its surplus and transfers it to the community level so as to strengthen forms of self-organization and petty commodity development of an Andean and Amazonic character" (Garcia Linera 2006a). Instead of twenty-first century socialism, Bolivia's García Linera specifies, "We are not against the free-market. We are in favor of a socialist model with a Bolivian capitalism, where the profits from oil and gas are transferred to other economic sectors, like the rural sector, where our people are still working with the Egyptian plow brought over by the Spanish" (Ibarz 2005; my translation).

Bolivia's formulation for an alternative to the present order is based, then, on strengthening the capacity of the state to capture via the tax system part of the nation's economic surplus and redirect it toward micro and small producers in rural areas and cities. Again, this strategy significantly differs from Latin American neostructuralism's fatuous platitudes about "virtuous circles," which consistently ignore the question of how a transnational capitalist class captures the economic surplus. In contrast to ECLAC, García Linera justifies such a stance with his own version of a "three-sector" model:

It is a question of building a strong state, which can coordinate in a balanced way the three "economic-productive" platforms that coexist in Bolivia: the community-based, the family-based and the "modern industrial." It is a question of transferring a part of the surplus of the nationalised hydrocarbons [oil and gas] in order to encourage the setting up of forms of self-organisation, of self-management and of commercial development that is really Andean and Amazonian. Up to now, these traditional sectors have not been able to develop because the "modern-industrial" sector has cornered the surplus. Our idea is that these traditional sectors should have an economic support, should have access to raw materials and markets, which could then generate prosperity within these artisan and family-based processes. Bolivia will still be capitalist in 50 or 100 years. (Stefoni 2005)

Following these orientations and attempting to deliver on his campaign promises, President Evo Morales nationalized hydrocarbons, a smelting plant and is attempting to renationalize the privatized telecommunications company (ENTEL). Through such measures, the state has increased its control from 6 percent of the gross domestic product (GDP) to 18 percent in 2007, and this participation is expected to rise to 30 percent of the country's productive structure. The goal is to transform the processing of oil and gas into the backbone of the country's industrialization. Thus, García Linera sums up the positive results of such policies highlighting the changed destination of oil and gas revenues: "Three out of four dollars produced by the oil and gas sector ended going outside of the country; today, only one dollar leaves, and the rest remains in Bolivia. . . . The Bolivian state has started to regain its presense in oil and as, in mining, telecommunications, and other industrial sectors, to become the only locomotive in this homeland, to generate wealth, and equitably distribute it" (Bolpress 2007). All of this as part of an overall belief that "it is possible to create a type of economic modernity linked to global markets, current technological development trends, and entrepreneurial sectors" (Garcia Linera 2006a).

This approach has received numerous criticisms from within and from outside Bolivia. One author has complained, those who today occupy the Presidential Palace are not Stalinists nor MNR populists, but a variegated mass of indigenists and middle-class postcapitalist leftists. How are they going to build the mythic working class if what that they defend is "Andean and Amazonic capitalism," which is neither developmentalism nor 1950s industrialism, but its exact opposite? From whence will the phalanx of conscious workers emerge? From the microenterprises of El Alto? From the mining cooperatives in Llallagua? (Rodriguez Ostria 2006)

Beyond the surprise caused by the displacement of traditional actors, Bolivia's strategy, like Venezuela's Bolivarian Revolution, poses a number of legitimate questions that require theoretical attention and which relaunch debates from the 1960s and 1970s about the essential features of Latin American capitalism, the nature of the capitalist class, and consequently, about strategies for social transformation. Thus, Atilio Borón pointedly asks: "How realistic is it today, in a world of transnational markets and globalization of productive, marketing and financial processes, to bet on the possibility of national capitalist development?" (Borón 2007). Doesn't such a development strategy require the existence of a national bourgeoisie? Yet, the existence of a national bourgeoisie in the periphery, even in the largest countries like Brazil, Mexico, and even Argentina, has been further undermined over the past decades (Chibber 2005). The Bolivian and Venezuelan processes have also been critiqued because they are not revolutionary enough, and though they might increase state influence over the economy, they do not explicitly aim to the revolutionary transformation of property or social relations of production (Petras 2006; 2007).

In terms of actual revolutionary reforms, both Venezuela and Bolivia have made only modest transformations. In Venezuela, where 75 percent of the land is in the hands of 5 percent of the owners, President Chávez announced that only those farms over five thousand hectares whose owners could not certify ownership would be expropriated (Heller 2005). Along with limited expropriation of abandoned or ill-run factories where some levels of worker participation have been instituted, the Venezuelan government has focused on expanding state management, creating new state-owned enterprises in key sectors, such as petrochemicals, telecommunications, and air travel (Wilpert 2006). Whether Venezuela's experiment of twenty-first-century socialism succumbs to its external obstacles—U.S.-directed imperialist intervention—or its own internal shortcomings (patronage, personalism, etc.) remains an open question. What cannot be disputed is that it represents a sincere effort to address the problems of Venezuelan society by democratizing power relations and such an effort cannot be ignored by labeling it as "populism."

In the case of Bolivia, the nationalization of oil and gas has been undermined by "Annex F" to the decree nationalizing the country's oil and gas. Multinationals agreed to a contract where they became service providers and the state oil company, *Yacimientos Petrolíferos Fiscales Bolivianos* (YPFB), became the proprietor and assumed possession and control over these resources. Such annex, however, transforms the contracts for operation with the oil companies into contracts for shared production, so that the private oil companies can carry out exploration and exploitation activities on their own in the name of YPFB (Soliz Rada 2007). In Bolivia, it remains to be seen not only whether the state can redirect part of the economic surplus but also what portion of the surplus from the national oil and gas sector the government will be able to actually control.

The gradual reform approach explicitly chosen by Venezuela and Bolivia does not preclude the enormous challenges and dilemmas that such strategy for transforming the status-quo still must confront. Can Venezuela and Bolivia blaze new forms of public control over the economy different from those of the past? (Borón 2007). How long can Venezuela and Bolivia hold in check the contradiction between a neodevelopmentalist strategy seeking to support the development of capitalism and choosing to move toward socialism (Katz 2006)? These important issues remain unresolved. Their resolution will depend not on the teleological operation of some preordained abstract truths but on the creative intervention of social and political actors and these choices will inevitably be shaped by the internal and external correlation of forces.

Though not oriented toward eliminating capitalist competition as some would expect, the newly emerging alternatives actively and methodically seek to constrain it within certain boundaries so that society and equity may thrive. Whether such a reform strategy can yield the desired results remains an open question that will ultimately be answered by the actions of the social forces involved. Reforms can have a progressive and radical character if they stem the colonization of the public sphere and stop the commodification of every aspect of social life by the logic of transnational capital. Policies that ensure that the state captures and uses the economic surplus for social well-being and not for subsidizing capital, speculation or lining the pockets of elected officials and state functionaries; that articulate export and nonexport sectors of the economy, acknowledge and support the different forms of caring and noncommodified labor performed mostly by women, and democratize every aspect of social life, including workplaces, communities, and households, fostering the active participation of everyone, can have a progressive character. Aimed at increasing the dignity of human life, such policies have as common elements: the understanding that the expansive drive of capitalism, the commodification of social life, and the logic of competition need to be constrained by radically realigning the correlation of forces existing in society today.

Latin American Neostructuralism at the Crossroads

It is evident that there are major differences between twenty-first-century socialism, Andean-Amazonic capitalism, and Latin American neostructuralism, even though they might share some of the same neodevelopmentalist rhetoric. Whereas ECLAC has firmly opted for preserving the status-quo, Hugo Chávez and Evo Morales are leading processes aimed at transforming existing power structures. The questionable dichotomy of a "right Left" and a "wrong Left" cannot serve as cover up for the ironic twist enacted by contemporary Latin America: the genuine followers of *Raúl Prebisch* and Celso Furtado, the true heirs of structuralism and ECLAC's original transformative zeal are not to be found at the Santiago headquarters of the new ECLAC. Prebisch is alive and well, not only in Asia (as Alice Amsden proclaims) but also in Venezuela and Bolivia's efforts to relaunch a reform-oriented and anti-imperialist development project, one that locates the logic and interests of the impoverished majorities and not those of transnational capital in political and cultural command.

The exploration undertaken in this chapter allows us now to tentatively answer some questions about Latin American neostructuralism's role vis-à-vis the Latin American Left. First, Latin American neostructuralism's role in the current progressive and leftward trend experienced since 2000 has been to raise the banner of the "high road" to globalization, giving ideological sustenance to the supposedly, "modern, pragmatic, forward looking" Left, which transnational elites not only have found palatable but also worthy of support. In a vain attempt to overcome its internal inconsistencies and present itself as a viable progressive alternative for the region, ECLAC has heavily engaged in symbolic politics without tackling the core issues of the Latin American development process.

In sharp contrast to Latin American neostructuralism, Venezuela and Bolivia show that the insights and lessons drawn by social movements, political leaders, and intellectuals over approximately two decades of resistance to neoliberal policies are nurturing innovative thinking and policies that have little to do with nostalgia or melancholy for a bygone era. On the contrary, both in Venezuela and Bolivia, policy makers are looking forward and shaping the future by transforming structures, power relations, and hierarchies that have reproduced the old order for too long.

It is in a renewed radical political economy perspective, instead of neostructuralism's unsupported assumptions and over-ideologized claims, where contemporary innovative and forward-looking thinking is to be found. With their sanitized version of the present, neostructuralists have apparently banished from their lexicon the idea that societal transformation involves altering power relations. If this is so, then it is not at all surprising that, with a keen strategic sense, *The Economist* correctly pins on the neostructuralist-inspired center–left its hopes for a favorable outcome in the current "battle for Latin America's soul."

11

The Future of Latin American Neostructuralism

Previous chapters have sought to reverse "the imposing tapestry" with which Latin American neostructuralism presents itself to the world so as to better understand its strengths and weaknesses. This last chapter draws these threads together to discern the future direction of neostructuralism and Latin American political economy.

A central conclusion emerges: the winds billowing the sails of Latin American neostructuralism and propelling it toward discursive predominance among development planners originate more from historical opportunity and timing than from the internal coherence of the neostructuralist paradigm itself. The historical opportunity seized by Latin American neostructuralism was created by the blatant limitations of neoliberalism in managing the region's process of capitalist restructuring. Wielding a market-centric and dogmatic approach, neoliberal economic ideas orchestrated the destruction of the old import-substitution industrialization (ISI) regime of accumulation and, through liberalization, privatization, and deregulation policies, helped establish the foundations for the current export-oriented (EO) regime of accumulation. Neoliberals proved themselves incapable of finishing the historical task, however. In every country of Latin America, they failed in providing legitimacy, consolidating and establishing an institutional framework capable of regulating the new order. Caught between the pincers of rising popular discontent and handicapped by reductionist thinking (not to mention the blood on their hands from supporting military regimes, particularly in the Southern Cone), neoliberal ideas and managers could not ensure the long-term profitability for the new regime of accumulation they helped engender. Toward the end of the 1990s and first half of the decade of the twenty-first century, social unrest and citizen mobilizations against neoliberal policies, fostered the leftist turn in most of the countries in the region.

Bolstered by the resources of ECLAC and with the Chilean experience vividly in their minds, Latin American neostructuralists in 1990 launched a more "holistic" vision that challenged the market-centric and reductionist neoliberal approach to economic thinking and which acknowledged the role of institutions, culture, political leadership, equity, democracy, and agency in economic development. Drawing from a variety of intellectual influences and under the leadership of Fernando Fajnzylber, they forged a new development discourse that sought to tap nonmarket-based forms of coordination at the firm and national level for the twinned goals of promoting economic growth and political stability. This paradigmatic turn was presented as both progressive and pragmatic, an indispensable shift for more efficiently managing the race for international competitiveness. Initially expectations were high that neostructuralism and its strategy of productive transformation with equity were to be, as Fajnzylber once remarked upon arriving in Rio, "the solution to all of our problems" (Bresser-Pereira 1992, 6; my translation).

Neostructuralism's Double Movement

During its ascent, Latin American neostructuralism thus performs a double movement, the basis both of its widespread appeal and its numerous internal contradictions. On the one hand, it successfully challenged the market-centric approach of neoliberalism, reestablishing the value of institutions, consensus-building, and political leadership. Middle classes, organized labor, and intellectuals who had been excluded by the technocratic discourse and exclusionary political project of neoliberals welcomed the relief heralded by this more holistic and integrated mode of conceiving development and more encompassing approach to policy formulation. They suddenly found the space for inscribing their own aspirations within the more inclusive project of "changing productive structures with social equity" proposed by neostructuralists for the current era of globalization. This ability to develop a discourse that blends deeply felt aspirations of economic growth, equity, democracy, and solidarity with globalization and modernity has been an admirable achievement by Latin American neostructuralists and the new Economic Commission for Latin America and the Caribbean (ECLAC). Thus, this new approach provided the intellectual foundations for the "progressive modernity" and "growth with equity" development strategies promised by many of the center–left governments elected in Latin America after 1990, and especially after 2000.

To accomplish such a feat, Latin American neostructuralists felt compelled to discard all traces and twitches of the transformative ambitions stemming from their structuralist past. Traumatized by the "Greek tragedy of social change" and inspired by a newly found admiration for transnational capital, they jettisoned structuralism's most significant contribution to Latin American thought, namely that of critically framing the problems of Latin American economies and societies within the overall development of a single capitalist system on a world scale. As a result they excised power relations from economic analysis, specifically those linked with the production, appropriation, and circulation of economic surplus. They thereby expunged from their newly minted political economy, the explanatory role of conflict-driven dynamics rooted in capitalist accumulation and replaced it with a sanitized vision of economic relations in which competition and cooperation, capitalist profit and wage labor, transnational capital and human development could not only coexist but also be mutually supportive.[1] Consequently, the shift from neoliberalism to Latin American neostructuralism can be interpreted as a transition from dogmatic to utopian promoters of capitalism.

Despite repeated claims to the contrary, this new paradigm represents a drastic rupture with the method of Raúl Prebisch, Celso Furtado, and other ECLAC pioneers. Though defended as a realistic "adaptation" to new historical circumstances, neostructuralists enact a major intellectual retreat from the best traditions of Latin American critical thinking. Certainly the crisis of the old ISI inwardly oriented model of development required new policies and a new development project; it did not necessitate the whole scale scuttling of the methodological foundations of the structuralist approach, despite its many shortcomings. Such a retreat has more to do with the fear and suffering created by state terrorism and the power gained by transnational capital in the region. Prebisch and Furtado's "historico-structural" approach was buried by neostructuralists without ceremony or regrets. Yet, a political economy approach that focuses on the production, appropriation, and distribution of economic surplus under the conditions of transnationalized capitalism is more relevant today than ever before.

Despite a pragmatism born of impotence rather than historical wisdom, Latin American neostructuralism has deployed an attractive politico-economic development discourse that promises to overcome the profound problems brought about by neoliberalism and corporate-led globalization. Furthermore, it promises to do so without reliving or reviving the major disruptions and traumas of the past by merely reorienting economic and public policies. Latin American neostructuralists are firm believers and proponents of change, but it is a change in social relations that does not affect property rights, the fundamental rules of the market, existing class power, or capitalist profitability. It is a cultural and behavioral change to better comply with and adapt to the overarching logic of capitalist competition, international competitiveness, and valorization of capital unfolding on a global scale.

As a result, Latin American neostructuralism is profoundly flawed. Despite enunciating all the expected bon mots about equity, democracy, and participation, it is an economic discourse stripped of any analysis of the old and new power relations embedded in the production, appropriation, and distribution of economic surplus under transnationalized capitalism. Despite its discursive prowess and firm grasp of the value of symbolic politics, neostructuralism has quickly become analytically sterile. Instead of offering tools for better understanding and redirecting powerful economic forces, Latin American neostructuralism plays the historical role of contributing to emplace new and more effective forms of stabilizing, legitimizing, and regulating the status quo, as both Chile's Concertación and Brazil's Lula administration demonstrate. By embracing neostructuralist conceptions of systemic competitiveness, proactive labor flexibility, concerted action, participatory politics, and virtuous circles, a "new breed" of economists, policy makers, and intellectuals associated with Latin America's center–left has gained access to the halls of power but at the price of mortgaging their capacity to examine the profound dynamics of contemporary Latin American capitalism entailing the further commodification, dispossession, superexploitation and subsumption of labor under capital.

If the analysis presented in these pages is on the right track, what implications do the strengths and weakness of Latin American neostructuralism portend for the future of Latin American economic and political development? In what follows, I offer some insights into how to build on Latin American neostructuralism's strengths and transcend its fatal weaknesses.

Development Theory and Economic Restructuring

From the point of view of the history of economic ideas and how these interact with class power, the ascendancy of neoliberalism and neostructuralism present us with three cruel ironies. First, neoliberalism and neostructuralism gain predominance and engage in vast processes of societal transformation at a time when intellectual interest in issues of power and class were probably at its lowest point within development economics. Yet, over the past three decades, Latin America has experienced the most profound realignment of class power and restructuring of social classes and social relations in seven decades. From the mid-1970s onward, class, gender, race, and ethnic power relations and other hierarchies of power constitutive of Latin American societies have been profoundly reconfigured. A second irony is that neoliberalism, the paladin of "getting the state out," actually strengthened the coercive role of the state, a result dubbed the "orthodox paradox." The state fell off the radar screen precisely when it wielded its most coercive and destructive power. The third irony has Latin American neostructuralism as the protagonist. Because it subsumes its concern for social equity, concerted action, and participation to the exultation of the international market as the prime force behind modernity and because it places international competitiveness as the touchstone of all social and political rationality, neostructuralism disarms Latin American society of its recourse to collective action, weakening its capacity to defend itself from the destructive and disintegrative effects of capitalist competition.

These ironies can be understood by evaluating the historical role of each of these schools of thought. To understand the role of neostructuralism in the post-neoliberalism era in Chile and Latin America, it is useful to recall the historical context in which the original liberal theorists defended their ideas: "The ideology of the market was constructed as part of a multifaceted attack on the working class. Its proponents set themselves on a crusade to destroy the moral economy of the poor, to undermine their claim to a right of subsistence . . . the ideology of the market has been concerned centrally with the creation and maintenance of a market in human labour-power. To that end, all fetters on that market—from common lands, to perquisites, to the old poor law, were defined as violations of economic liberty which would also have to be destroyed" (McNally 1993, 218).

Just as liberals in the nineteenth century attacked the "moral economy of the poor," neoliberals destroyed ISI institutions that provided workers and other social sectors with certain levels of autonomy from the dictates of the market.[2] Additionally, by promoting different forms of labor flexibility, neoliberals have not only reduced the autonomy of workers from the labor market but also expanded the power of capital at the point of production.

CEPAL neostructuralist, blinded by the mirage of modernity, have constructed a richly textured discourse on "systemic competitiveness" and "productive transformation with equity," later changed to "productive develop-ment in open economies" and the production of "social cohesion and a sense of belonging" that uncritically places insertion in the international market as the prime healing force for Latin American and Caribbean economies. The arguments presented in the previous chapters challenge several assump-tions upon which neostructuralist conceptions are founded. First, the idea that increases in productive efficiency brought about by international com-petitiveness would translate into the expansion of quality productive jobs is not borne out by the Chilean experience or that of other countries. A second limitation is the notion of a dichotomy between "genuine" and "spurious" forms of competitiveness and between "passive" and "proactive" forms of labor flexibility. The productive strategies followed by manufacturing firms in Chile and elsewhere indicate that such clear demarcation only exists in theory but not in the day to day operation of "actually existing capitalism."

Neostructuralist utopian discourse on international competitiveness comes up against the concrete conditions under which the valorization of capital takes place. What the case of Chile indicates is that under an EO regime of accumulation, the fundamental contradiction between capital and labor are intensified, as competitiveness in international markets requires a greater ability on the part of capital to control labor. In their own historically specific ways, neoliberalism and neostructuralism acting through the state attempt to facilitate this hegemony for capital at different societal levels.

If the basis of export competitiveness lies in a complex socio-historical pro-cess by which already unequal class and gender relations are further changed in the favor of capital, then the whole idea of a "high road" to globalization needs to be more carefully examined. If even in the case of manufactured exports, the attainment of export competitiveness involves the radical re-alignment of class and gender power relations, then the thesis of export-led accumulation as the bearer of increased social equity and political legitima-cy needs to be thoroughly reconsidered. The most troubling aspect of the analysis presented in the previous chapters lies in what I call the heterodox paradox. Neostructuralism's holistic approach actively enables the coloniza-tion of the public sphere and the subordination of nonmarket and noneco-nomic dimensions of social life to the requirements of transnational capital. Latin American neostructuralism forges policies that actively promote such colonization, while attempting to preserve social cohesion by offering the velvet handshake between the state and civil society actors as crucial for producing the new citizens and subjectivities required by the new regime of capitalist accumulation.

Shelf Life of Neostructuralism

Analytical incisiveness and internal coherence, though admirable qualities, have never been the crucial ingredients for the rise to predominance of a school of thought or development paradigm. Time and time again, we have seen how a set of action-oriented beliefs emerges, because it captures the Zeitgeist and is able to represent this "spirit of the time" in a manner that is finely attuned with the interests of relevant social actors and the unresolved problems of society of the time. This explains why, despite analytical short-comings, inconsistencies, and contradictions, Latin American neostructuralism enjoys and will continue to enjoy a longer than expected shelf-life. At present, it is the only paradigm that offers a viable route for both ensuring capitalist profitability and creating the institutions, policies, mindset, and behaviors that can legitimize and regulate the transnationalized regime of accumulation that has emerged in Latin America and the Caribbean. At the present, it is the only extant discourse that offers a social imaginary of modernity with solidarity in the context of today's global capitalism.

As Terry Eagleton suggests, when referring to discourses in general, Latin American neostructuralism needs to be "deconstructed" in terms of its inter-action with social power and social interests, not just in terms of the coherence (or lack thereof) of its own enunciations. By historicizing its role we can evaluate the legacy of Latin American neostructuralism with a metric that transcends the petty realm of debates about its internal consistency, macroeconomic performance, coherence of its speech acts or the great expectations it has evoked from many heterodox thinkers.

Paradoxically, Latin American neostructuralism's impressive discursive performance over the past eighteen years is anchored precisely on the erasure of power and conflict and in raising the banner of a viable, nonantagonistic path to globalization. This is where the limitations of the new ECLAC, Latin America's new center–left, and Latin American neostructuralism come together and are revealed. Latin American neostructuralism is powerless to eliminate conflicts, since these are an upshot of capitalist relations of production and exchange in general and, in more historically specific terms, such conflicts are deeply embedded and sharpened under the EO regime of accumulation initially hewn out by neoliberalism. Neostructuralist policies and discourse are, therefore, in a constant state of flux—that is, immersed in a never-ending but ultimately doomed quest to overcome the gaps between its signifying activity idealizing capitalism and the conflict-ridden nature of accumulation under the present historical conditions.

An overview of its trajectory over the 1990–2007 period suggests that efforts to overcome such crevasses lead Latin American neostructuralism down two separate but interconnected directions. On the one hand, it has been forced to acknowledge, belatedly, that indeed asymmetric power relations can and do emerge from globalization processes. Such a view was absent prior to 1998, during what I have called neostructuralism's "early" period in which it promoted "productive transformation with social equity." On the other hand, acceptance that asymmetrical relations do in fact characterize globalization have not led Latin American neostructuralism to revise its analysis of the current characteristics of capitalist accumulation. As a result, from 2004 to 2007, under the umbrella of "productive development in open economies," ECLAC produced many policy proposals aimed at the "medium" and "low" speed sectors of the economy and presented novel policy initiatives geared to enhance social cohesion, inclusion, and a sense of belonging; however, nothing was aimed at influencing how the dominant "high" speed sector that produces, distributes, and appropriates the bulk of surplus generated in the most dynamic branches of the economy, namely those controlled by transnational capital and a handful of local conglomerates. Such was not the road followed by the developmentalist states of the admired Asian Tigers, where robust export, industrial, and investment policies had the capacity to discipline transnational capital. ECLAC's recent hyperbolization of politics, which many celebrate as signs of heterodoxy's further progress against reductionism and economicism in development thinking, should be seen as more smoke and mirrors on the part of Latin American neostructuralism, a new Sisyphus-like effort to overcome the perpetual gaps between its rhetoric and reality.

Whither Latin American Neostructuralism?

Along with providing it with the formula for success, Latin American neostructuralism's "double movement" has trapped it into a dead end of its own, successfully challenging neoliberal economic ideas with a theoretical framework that renders it rhetorically potent but analytically powerless, at least so far, as challenging and transforming the constellation of power embedded in the current transnationalized regime of capital accumulation. Having gone through its "early stage" and reaching the end of its "middle stage," Latin American neostructuralists face a fork in the road ahead. Its future depends on which path it chooses from here onward: increasing subordination to the status quo or reconnecting with its heritage of critical thinking and going against the grain of mainstream thinking, not out of spite, but because Latin American reality requires it so.

Asserting that Latin American neostructuralism has come to a fork in the road is not a mere expository device. It is an acknowledgement that, from this point on, the future trajectory of Latin American neostructuralism will increasingly feel the gravitational pull of two emerging powerful forces. The first of these is the rising pressure from social and political movements that have recently attained national level political expression and positions within the state apparatus—in Venezuela with president Hugo Chávez, in Bolivia with president Evo Morales, and even in Ecuador with president Rafael Correa. The second of these is the mounting evidence of the failure of corporate-led globalization and the unraveling of U.S. hegemony over the international system. Both of these historical developments will increase the pressure on the new ECLAC and its staff to display the intellectual audacity, creativity, and verve associated with Prebisch and Furtado rather than the blander and unimaginative postures displayed so far by the new ECLAC and Latin America's domesticated center–left. Both of these trends may encourage Latin American neostructuralists to refocus their gaze on the unique historical popular grassroots revolts against neoliberalism and the EO regimes of accumulation currently unfolding in the region, and which are contributing to create greater political and intellectual spaces for alternatives. The new situation may encourage them to free themselves from the current subordination to intellectual and policy trends emerging from Washington, the International Monetary Fund (IMF)–World Bank–Wall Street complex, and professionalized, trained mainstream economists.

It seems probable that, in the coming years, Latin American neostructuralism will be tugged in opposite directions. On the one hand, egged on by rising social movements, popular discontent, and growing evidence of the shortcomings of its current policies, it may decide to move ahead by choosing the path forking off to the left. Through refashioning and resharpening its conceptual tools, renewing its own transformative will and confidence on the boundless creative potential of the popular sectors of Latin American society, it may move in the direction of more effective policies that call upon using all of the resources in society to discipline transnational productive and financial capital. For this path to be chosen, a number of yet unlikely events would have to transpire. First, a sufficiently important number of ECLAC analysts would have to come to the realization that Latin American neostructuralism as outlined in its most important documents, *Changing Production Patterns with Social Equity* (1990) and *Productive Development in Open Economies* (2004), is seriously flawed and must be thoroughly revised. Second, such a revision would entail conceptually relocating the production, appropriation, and distribution of the economic surplus in a transnationalized capitalist regime of accumulation as a critical (though not exclusively as the only) analytical entry point. Third, if the social surplus is to play a structurally and dynamically efficient role, then politics, institutions, and public policies would have to be reconceptualized not in the service of producing governability and governmentality designed to satisfy the whims of transnational capital but in the service of the democratic interests of the majority. For all of this to come to pass in the coming years, Latin American neostructuralism would have to experience a veritable Copernican revolution: International capitalist competitiveness must be subordinate and constrained by societal interests, not the other way around as currently held by ECLAC. Undoubtedly, this will not happen unless the radical or critical political economy currents, still dispersed and caught up in their own renewal, can forcefully emerge from their embryonic stage with an incisive and politically generative conceptual approach. Without a corresponding significant realignment in the social, political, cultural, and intellectual forces in the region and a spirited debate within ECLAC, the renewal of Latin American neostructuralism toward a more radical reformist direction seems an unlikely scenario.

On the other hand, faced with a crossroads, Latin American neostructuralism can choose the path veering off to the right, leading toward greater convergence and subordination to the existing hierarchies of power and the economic status quo. Evidence from the experience of Chile under the Concertación, and Brazil under Lula, as well as from a careful reading of ECLAC's recent literature, suggests this as the most likely course of events as Latin American neostructuralism enters into its "mature" stage. Lulled into ever greater degrees of complacency by access to the levers of power, approaching (if not passing) retirement age, driven by the electoral imperative of devising short-term policies to better manage the current regime of accumulation, and given its propensity to interact and listen more to the rising generation of younger liberal technocrats like those grouped in Chile's

Corporación Expansiva rather than indigenous and grassroots leaders,[3] Latin American neostructuralism most likely will choose the path of least resistance, that is, to continue occupying the leading edge in a politico-economic project centered on constructing new forms of regulation and social management for the region's new system of domination. After all, since the death of Prebisch and Furtado, nothing suggests that Latin American neostructuralism is interested or much less capable of theoretically or politically resisting the gravitational pull represented by the self-expansion of transnational capital. Choosing this probable path will further enfeeble ECLAC and Latin American neostructuralism as a source of creative thinking capable of bridging the growing social chasm in the region.

Nonetheless, acknowledgement that public policy should be geared toward creating a favorable investment climate for private capitalists has heightened awareness about the interconnectedness between economic, social, and cultural policy. After 2000, neostructuralists have become acutely aware that social policy must not only generate price stability but also produce stable societies and rules of the game. Social policies then are increasingly designed to operate on a symbolic dimension, aimed at erasing the notion that only a minority benefits from the present status quo and devised to create the perception that risks created by globalization can and should be responsibly self-managed. Such a message is essential to avoid what Alejandro Foxley calls a "backlash" against globalization. Despite Latin American neostructuralism's sophisticated discourse and intellectual influence, it may already be too late.

Strategic Transformations: Old and New Debates

The shortcomings of Latin American neostructuralism strongly suggest that we need to relaunch old and new debates about the nature of capitalist development in Latin America, about the methods of political economy in the era of globalization, and concerning the type of economic development that can ensure equity, justice, dignity, and happiness for the majority of Latin Americans at present and in the future. The debates and issues raised during the 1960s by structuralists and dependency theorists have not disappeared on account of the crisis of ISI, the neoliberal counterrevolution, neostructuralism's ascent, or the utopianism deeply embedded in the post–Washington Consensus. Old issues are still very much alive: What is the nature of the actually existing production, distribution, and appropriation of economic surplus in Latin America and what are its consequences? What is the role assigned to transnational capital and foreign direct investment (FDI) in the region? Have the past decades of export-led growth contributed to the emergence of a national capitalist class? Is a national development project today possible? How are the functions of the state being reoriented and recalibrated and to what extent are these compatible with genuine citizenship and democracy? At the same time, the dynamic and creatively destructive forces of capitalist accumulation have added on a host of new issues that require a more critical and renewed radical political economy. The structural transformations of transnationalization, financialization, and informalization of labor capital relations as the EO regime consolidates requires a new way of thinking about society and the economy. To raise these questions is to challenge the basic assumptions and foundational ideas of Latin American neostructuralism and the uncritical mindset lodged in the development strategy supported by the new ECLAC.

At this historical juncture, a solid foundation for a genuinely progressive political economy proactively defends society and the economy from the forces of capitalist competition, actively proclaims the necessity for arresting the processes of commodification of social life, and confronts and reverts the current dynamics of dispossession embedded in global capitalist expansion. Progressive and radical politics must conceive of new and more creative forms of public accumulation, not just the production of public goods. As we have established in the preceding chapters, the conceptual underpinnings of the new ECLAC and of Latin American neostructuralism do not offer such a platform.

Toward a Critical and Radical Political Economy

What are the political, economic, and socio-structural conditions necessary for Latin American countries, individually and in a united fashion, to have agency in defining their role in the international division of labor? Can such agency be ensured without major transformations in the internal correlation of class forces in society reflected, among others, in the nature of the state and in the prerogatives granted to transnational capital and the domestic conglomerates?

Given the inability of Latin American neostructuralism to address the contradictions inherent in Latin American capitalism, the future of Latin American development, just as that of the Latin American Left, does not lay in joining the a priori Euro-U.S. centric cosmopolitan consensus. The future is to be forged by renewing a critical political economy perspective that once again frames the study of Latin American economies and societies within the development of capitalism on a global and world historical scale and does not a priori exclude structural transformation but places them as a main point of theorization and praxis. If Latin American countries are to confront the challenges of the present, then it is necessary to renew a critical political economy perspective that, unlike ebbing neoliberalism and ascending neo-structuralism, is explicitly attentive to the role of power and power relations in the accumulation process and in the reproduction of society. An explicit awareness is equally required of how economic development discourse and formulation of economic policies contributes to either consolidate and or challenge the existing constellation of power in a particular community, country, or region. After more than three decades of wrenching processes of capitalist transformation in the Americas, a critical political economy is one that is acutely self-aware as to how its theorizing and policy formula-tion influences power in micro-sites of the household, the workplace, and the community.

Forging such an approach, and not in Latin American neostructuralism's idealized and sanitized version of an evanescing high road to globalization, is where the still unanswered intellectual and political challenges of post-neoliberal development lie in an ever more impatient wait.

Notes

Introduction

1. This chapter draws from two of my articles: "Latin American Neostructuralism: The Contradictions of ECLAC's 'Post-Neoliberal' Development Paradigm" to appear in *Review of International Political Economy*, and "Toward a Critique of Latin American Neostructuralism" to appear in the 2008 Winter issue of *Latin American Politics and Society*.

2. Though neostructuralism pioneered the formulation of an alternative development discourse, it later incorporated many of Giddens insights into how the role of the state and public policies had to be reconceptualized, as I argue in chapters 7 and 8.

3. For examples of alternatives programs, see *Hemispheric Social Alliance* (1999), *International Forum on Globalization* (2002), and *Bello* (2002). The signing by Bolivia in April 2006 of the Bolivarian Alternative for the Americas (ALBA) joining Venezuela and Cuba marks an important leap in the formulation of alternatives to U.S.-dominated proposals for regional integration.

4. A growing literature exists on the positivist pretensions of economics. A good example is Philip Mirowski's 1989 book *More Heat Than Light* and the 2001 volume, *Postmodernism, Economics and Knowledge*, edited by Steven Cullenberg, Jack Amariglio, and David Ruccio. Incisive critiques of postmodernism are offered by Terry Eagleton's *The Illusions of Postmodernism* and Lee B. Artz's 1997 article, "Social Power and the Inflation of Discourse," appearing in *Latin American Perspectives* 24, no. 1: 92–113.

5. Attempts to examine how economic shortcomings regarding self-awareness about how its "truth claims" are constructed have taken different paths. Within the United States, one important strand traces the intersection of knowledge, language, and rhetoric within economics: Arjo Klamer (1988) and Donald (now Deidre) McCloskey (1985; 1994). For a feminist perspective on the use of language in metaphors in mainstream economics, see Julie Nelson (1990) and Diane Strassman (1990), among others. Four key edited volumes containing the work of many of the authors that have taken part of this effort are *Economics as Discourse: An Analysis of the Language of Economists*; *Economics and Language*; *The New Economic Criticism: Studies*

at the Intersection of Literature and Economics; and *Postmodernism, Economics and Knowledge*. Development theory and development discourse has also been studied as rhetorical, discursive, and ideological formations. *Encountering Development: The Making of the Third World* and *Critical Development Theory: Contributions to a New Paradigm* are examples of poststructuralist and postmodernist approaches.

6. The rupture with the structuralist past is evident in four key dimensions: (1) internationalization of productive structures is now welcomed and no longer seen as contributing to the reproduction of international asymmetries; (2) foreign capital and multinational corporations are envisioned as a key positive force in economic development: (3) private capitalists and the market, not the state, are celebrated as the key actors in development; and (4) distribution is now conceived as autonomous from accumulation. This is discussed in greater detail in chapter 2.

7. Every discourse inevitably commits certain acts of omission and exclusion in the process of its formulation; what becomes relevant is identifying these, determining their impact upon that discourse's internal coherence, and more importantly, following Eagleton, the impact that such omissions have on social power.

8. Stallings and Peres (2000) identify three inconsistency syndromes—that is, policies that operate at cross-purposes—embedded in Latin America's neoliberal reform process. These revolve around (1) capital account liberalization and the short- and long-term effects of reversible capital inflows; (2) financial liberalization and monetary policy, which resulted in higher interest rates; and (3) reducing fiscal deficits at the same time that tax reform lowered fiscal revenues by lowering tax rates on corporations and individuals.

9. My analysis of Latin American neostructuralism aims to reveal how, in a historical context fraught with contradictions, this new paradigm attempts to (1) chart a new course for societal development; (2) maintain and recreate the unity of the bloc in power; and (3) dissolve the acts of oppositional forces that resist the direction and character of the transformations brought about by transnational capital on the region (Eagleton 1991). See chapter 3 for a fuller discussion.

10. The *Concertación de Partidos por la Democracia*, commonly known as the *Concertación*, is a coalition of center and left political parties that has governed Chile since March 11, 1990. Composed by the Christian Democratic, Socialist, Radical, and the Party for Democracy, it is one of the most successful political coalitions in Chilean history in terms of its longevity in office. It has elected four consecutive administrations: Patricio Aylwin (1990–93); Eduardo Frei Jr. (1994–99), Ricardo Lagos (2000–2005), and Michelle Bachelet (2006–10).

11. Exploring the links and mutual influence among neostructuralists from the "North" and "South" is an important part of the intellectual history not undertaken here. For a preliminary effort in this direction, see the paper by Diego Sanchez-Ancochea, "Anglo-Saxon Structuralism vs. Latin American Structuralism in Development Economics," delivered at the Conference of the Eastern Economic

NOTES TO CHAPTER 1 · 249

Association, New York, March 4–6, 2005. http://americas.sas.ac.uk/about/die
_structuralism.pdf.

1. Conceptual Innovation: Combining Growth, Equity, and Democracy

1. Fernando Fajnzylber died prematurely at the age of fifty-one at the end of 1991, without seeing the full results of his efforts.

2. In rigor, none of these concepts are original creations of Latin American neostructuralism. "Systemic Competitiveness" has been borrowed from Porter 1990. The view on the role of labor draws heavily from the "flexible specialization" literature (mainly but not only Piore and Sabel 1984), and the notion of "virtuous circles" is rather an old device in development economics, resurrected from the analysis of the East Asian experience.

3. In the 1980s, different analysts emphasized the "epochal change" transpiring in the organization of production under contemporary capitalism from vertical integration, rigidity, and monopoly to vertical disintegration, flexibility, and deconcentration. As a result of these transformations it was alleged that workers could materially and politically benefit from new flexible labor process and more horizontal organization of production. The profound contradictions characteristic of capitalism could be assuaged if not altogether eliminated through the "healing powers" of "flexible specialization" (Piore and Sabel 1984). Others saw empirical, methodological, and theoretical weaknesses in this approach, aimed at undermining the importance of class and class analysis (Burrows et al., 1992; Rainnie 1993).

4. After a careful study of the historical experience of the United States, Germany, and Japan, he concluded that "increased competitiveness is an inescapable necessity in a period of transition between two technological models and it is a decisive factor in the medium- and long-term changes in the relative position of countries in the international economy" (Fajnzylber 1988, 11).

5. This shift appears to have been successfully consummated by 1997, when the World Bank's *World Development Report* was dedicated to analyzing the supportive role of a market-friendly state. By the mid-1990s, neoliberals began to soften their position vis-à-vis the state. Whereas during the 1970s and 1980s they vehemently attacked the state's role, by the early 1990s they started to frame the discussion in a less dogmatic manner. "The central issue, then, is one of the state and the market, but it is not a question of intervention versus laissez faire—a popular dichotomy but a false one.... [I]t is rather a question of the proper division of responsibilities between the two and of efficiency in their respective functions" (Summers and Thomas 1993, 244).

6. In addition to mediocre growth rates, neostructuralist Ricardo Ffrench-Davis (2000) points out the following limitations of the Washington Consensus policies: low value-added exports; fiscal equilibrium that does not prioritize for productive

and social modernization; low levels of productive investment; and recurring disequilibria in the real macro economy that subjects workers and entrepreneurs to a roller coaster ride of highly volatile and unstable economic variables. Assessments of neoliberalism by North American scholars are not as damning. See, for example, Weyland 2004; Huber and Solt 2004; and Walton 2004.

7. For a defense, see Williamson 2002, and for a "complementary" critique see Birdsall and de la Torre 2001.

8. For a text of the Buenos Aires Consensus, see http://www.socialistinternational .org/6Meetings/SIMEETINGS/Council/BAires-Jun99/SICounBA-e.html.

2. Methodological Retreats

1. Both neoclassical endogenous growth theory and evolutionary models emphasize the role that technical progress plays in economic growth. For a discussion of their differences see Hounie, Pittaluga, Porcile, and Scatolin's (1999) "ECLAC and the New Growth Theories."

2. My thanks to Claudia Vilches and the other staff from the library at ECLAC headquarters in Santiago for their assistance in helping me locate these publications. As yellowed and mimeographed publications from the early 1960s were retrieved from storage, I could not suppress my excitement at rescuing from oblivion a crucial part of the history of Latin American critical thought. Before me was the evidence that, at the height of its influence, Latin American thought was neither copy or imitation, but heroic creation as José Carlos Mariátegui had once suggested.

3. Aníbal Pinto Santa Cruz held important posts at ECLAC. He was director of the Rio de Janeiro CEPAL/ILPES office (1960–65) and director of the Economic Development Division at ECLAC (1970–79), among other posts.

4. Ricardo Bielschowsky, a prominent ECLAC staff member considers it an exaggeration to say that the center-periphery paradigm is abandoned. In a personal communication (October 17, 2005), Bielschowsky, an economic historian with the Brasilia office of ECLAC who has written extensively on the history of ECLAC, pointed out: "ECLAC does not renounce to the center-periphery concept. See for example Ocampo's text in *CEPAL Review* on past and present asymmetries. Perhaps ECLAC is being more careful now than before in the terms (the tone) it employs, but in essence it does not renegue the center-periphery idea, nor many of the key concepts of the past that characterized Latin America as a periphery in opposition to the conditions existing in center countries; deterioration of the terms of trade; the inexistence of an automatic convergence between countries of different per capita income; dualism and structural heterogeneity; lack of sufficient diversity in the productive structure and an inadequate specialization in external trade; structural imbalance in the balance of payments; the need to design national development models, etc." (my

translation). Though there has not been an explicit rejection, the changes are more than just a more cautious tone. As I argue in this chapter and throughout the book, there is a de facto rejection of the methodology behind Prebisch's center-periphery paradigm.

5. In defense of agency, Evans points out: "In a world of constructed comparative advantage, social and political institutions—the state among them—shape international specialization. State involvement must be taken as one of the sociopolitical determinants of what niche a country ends up occupying in the international division of labor" (Evans 1995, 9–10).

6. At a time of increasing power of capital, politics and institutions are reformatted subordinated to the market's international competitiveness, "the economic problem is defined in terms of the allocation of scarce resources, and economic institutions are considered only for their allocative properties. In this way, the nature of capitalist institutions is defined in efficiency terms, as a comparison between allocative mechanisms" (Ankerloo and Palermo 2004, 217). Additionally, the development of productive innovation and national innovation systems, which is central to the neostructuralist proposal, also encourages a vision of institutions that is influenced by endogenous growth theory: "the technology market has flaws due to the fact that technical knowledge and information is a non-pure public good, and these flaws lead to under-investment in technological matters and justify direct State intervention through mesoeconomic or 'horizontal' policies" (Hounie et al. 1999, 24).

7. Bowles et al. define power as follows: "A has power over B if by imposing costs on B (or threatening to do so), A can cause B to act in a way that is to A's advantage" (2005, 55). Despite the methodologically individualistic framework through which power is conceived in economic relationships, this definition is still useful. Latin American critical thought—structuralism and dependency theory in its reformist and revolutionary variants—has opted for a more structural analysis: How is social surplus produced? Who controls it? How is it distributed? What are the consequences on the social structure given these historical patterns? Many of these questions were raised by Raúl Prebisch, Celso Furtado, Aníbal Pinto, and other founders of Latin American structuralism without becoming Marxists or, as Lustig says, without becoming concerned about exploitation.

8. Rosenthal in his contribution to the fiftieth anniversary ECLAC publication, describes the context as follows: "In part we drew from the tendencies that were already emerging: First, as a result of the resurgence of orthodoxy (remember that it was the time of Margaret Thatcher and Ronald Reagan); Second, as a reaction to the emerging phenomenon of economic internationalization; Third, as a response to the grave economic crisis that scourged the region starting in 1982; Fourth, because the obsession of the time was simply to survive which meant giving preponderance to short term economic policy as opposed to medium and longer term proposals; Lastly, because already from the 1960s onward, there were indications

that the import substitution strategy was reaching its end" (Rosenthal 2000, 77; my translation).

3. Historicizing Latin American Neostructuralism

1. Drawing on the European and U.S. experience, FitzGerald and Thorpe (2005) identify three "drivers" explaining shifts in economic thinking. These are (1) the influence of epistemic communities; (2) the extent of external pressure on the part of international forces; and (3) the role of internal political actors. In this chapter I offer a complementary approach that examines the interplay between changing economic discourses and the changing nature of capitalist restructuring and capital accumulation.

2. A former cabinet Minister of the Salvador Allende government, Orlando Letelier was assassinated by General Pinochet's secret police in Washington, D.C., on September 21, 1976, only a few weeks after this article appeared. As "next of kin" along with Edmundo del Solar, my grandmother's brother, I identified my uncle's remains at the District of Columbia city morgue that day.

3. Recall the initial caveats: when I speak of neoliberalism, I am referring to it as a set of ideas, not an "economic model" or a "mode of experiencing" contemporary capitalism.

4. The Inter-American Development Bank (1996) developed its own ex-post vision of the stages followed by Latin American countries.

5. For a while, the emergence of "political economy of reform" became a new field in development economics. With its ever more elaborate modeling of political-economic considerations, these enrich and do not challenge the core conceptualization of economic restructuring originally envisioned by World Bank analysts.

6. It is not a coincidence that during this period two of the World Bank's Chief Economists for Latin America and the Caribbean, Marcelo Selowsky and Sebastián Edwards, were Chilean. This allowed the Bank to weave the Chilean experience into the formulation of policies. Edwards and Selowsky have personal and academic contacts with neoliberal and ECLAC economists, right-wing think tanks, and members of Concertación economic teams.

7. Economic discourses such as Latin American neostructuralism can be seen as engaging in one of the following six crucial ideological tasks in the construction of meanings: (1) *unifying and lending coherence* to groups and classes that hold them, allowing them perhaps to impose a certain unity upon society as a whole; (2) providing *a set of action-oriented beliefs* that can be translated into a "practical state," thereby supplying their adherents with goals, motivations, and prescriptions; (3) *rationalizing* the provision of "plausible explanations and justifications for social behavior which might otherwise be the object of criticism" (Eagleton 1991, 58); (4) *legitimating*

the existing ruling social power, securing from its subjects at least tacit consent to its authority; (5) *universalizing* and presenting space and time-specific beliefs and values as interests of all humanity; and (6) a *naturalizing* role rendering the beliefs and values promoted by a particular ideology as self-evident, "identifying them with the "'common-sense'" of society, so that nobody could imagine how they might ever be different" (58).

8. A critical review of the FRS and the SSA is beyond the scope of this chapter. An insightful overview can be found in Jessop (1997).

9. This is analyzed in greater detailed in chapters 7 and 8.

10. The notion that the state's functions need to be reorganized, reoriented, and recalibrated is borrowed from Jessop (2002) and his very lucid analysis of the transformations in the functions of the capitalist state in developed countries.

4. Neostructuralism in Chile and Brazil

1. "Microenterprise training," social capital, participatory governance, state-civil society alliances, ethnodevelopment and "development with identity," and microfinance—all of the latest conceptual commodities have been implemented in Chile after 1990.

2. The Chilean daily, *La Nación*, reported on July 17, 2006, that Ricardo Ffrench-Davis was also elected president of the Christian Democratic Party's Socio-Economic Committee, illustrating the strong ECLAC government–political party linkages that allow neostructuralist ideas to circulate.

3. Chile became one of the first countries in the Americas that replicated the European Popular Front experience. In the early 1960s, the Alliance for Progress found in the Eduardo Frei administration and its Revolution in Liberty the opportunity to test the reforms with which U.S. imperial policy attempted to respond to the increasing attraction provided by the Cuban Revolution. On September 4, 1970, Chileans elected the first Marxist president that promised to solve the pressing problems of poverty and underdevelopment through the "peaceful road to socialism." Three years later, the violent overthrow of president Salvador Allende and the coming to power of the military junta headed by General Pinochet provided the first country in the world, years before Ronald Reagan and Margaret Thatcher, to systematically try the ideas of Milton Friedman and the economic policies that came to be known as neoliberalism. Following this long tradition of being a site of socio-economic and political experimentation, Chile, that "balcony hanging from the Andes over the Pacific," became the first country to witness the deployment of Latin American neostructuralism. In effect, the launching and evolution of Latin American neostructuralism is inextricably linked to the Chilean experience.

4. Ricardo Bielschowsky, Personal Communicaiton with author, September 29, 2005.

5. ECLAC staff at the Brasilia office have attempted to rescue the main lines of Celso Furtado's work and inject it into neostructuralist formulations. See for example Bielschowsky 2006.

6. Matías Vernengo, Personal Communication with author, October 10, 2005.

7. Ibid.

8. In the strongest terms possible, this latest manifesto expresses that "the current economic policy is coherent with the maintenance of the privileges by the richest strata of the population, by the financial sector and those oriented toward exports. Our proposal of economic policy is different. It is framed by a support for a Project of National Development, guided by guaranteeing the interests of those that depend on their labor and the immense majority of the Brazilian people." To that effect the manifesto proposes a ten-point program that clearly delinks economic policy from serving the interests of the financial sector.

5. Foundational Myths, Acts of Omission

1. For a structuralist analysis of the relationship that uses a two-gap model to explain capital accumulation in terms of the distribution of income between wages and profits and the propensity to reinvest profits and the amount of foreign exchange, see Sánchez-Ancona 2004. For a post-Keynesian approach see Lima 2003.

2. For this reason many of Latin America's Communist Parties during the 1940–60 period, stressed the antifeudal and antioligarchic character of the national–democratic revolution, upheld the national–democratic bourgeoisie as important allies, and sacrificed organizing wage workers in the countryside and smaller and medium size industries.

6. Effacing the Deep Structure of Contemporary Latin American Capitalism

1. From Fajnzylber onward, Latin American neostructuralists transformed the post–Fordist "technico-economic paradigm" and healing powers of "flexible specialization" into an explicative universal remedy. "The appearance of new technologies and the increasing rapidity with which the existing ones are changing have resulted in significant alteration to the way production is organized within companies, production sectors, and ultimately the world economy. This new way of organizing production can be typified with reference to six activities, all of which use information and communication technologies to bridge the gulf between the design and production phases" (ECLAC 2004, 29). Citing Oman (1994), ECLAC lists the following defining traits: (1) simultaneous engineering, which integrates the design

and manufacturing stages into a single process; (2) continuous innovation, achieved in some cases by means of quality circles; (3) teamwork, involving workers with multiple skills; (4) just-in-time and real-time stock production and management, enabling production to be adjusted more quickly to changes in demand; (5) incorporation of quality control into the actual production process, thereby avoiding the costs incurred when mistakes have to be corrected subsequently; and (6) the growing importance of supplier-user interaction in respect to innovation, design and production, which translates into global production and marketing networks and chains. While these might be characteristics of limited robotized production facilities in the developed countries, they are not the dominant traits of Latin America.

2. Compare ECLAC 1990 or 2004 with Robinson 2004 to get a sense of the conceptual gap.

3. Debates about the contribution of FDI to development need to be reopened. More than half of the total outflow of what is labeled "FDI" from the United States consists of foreign subsidiaries' retained earnings not remitted to the United States. Additionally, if China is excluded from the data, the share of mergers and acquisitions in cumulative FDI for 1992–97 turns out to be 72 percent, up from 22 percent during the 1988–91 years (Raghavan 1999). For a more recent discussion, see Petras 2005.

4. Gereffi, Humprey, and Sturgeon (2003) derive a theory of governance for global value chains by looking at variables, such as the complexity of transactions, the ability to codify transactions, and the capabilities in the supply-base. Based on this, they identify five types of global value chain governance—hierarchy, captive, relational, modular, and market—which range from high to low levels of explicit coordination and power asymmetry. Though relevant, such work is much more in the frame of institutionalist economics than of an unequal exchange perspective. For an interesting resource on Global Value Chain approach as developed by Gereffi and his colleagues, see the Web site for the Global Value Chain Initiative hosted by the Institute for Development Studies at Sussex, http://www.globalvaluechains.org/.

5. Somel (2004) and other authors point to a whole host of variables that reflect how the unequal distribution of power impacts variables along the commodity chain with negative effects for peripheral countries.

6. These are preliminary calculations that form part of an unfinished research project called "Measuring Financialization of the Chilean Economy," which aims to test a methodology for a comparative study of Latin American countries (see Leiva and Malinowitz 2007).

7. The inflation targeting (IT) framework was announced in September 1999 and fully implemented in 2001. With its adoption, "the objective of monetary policy is to maintain a continuous target at the midpoint of the 2–4 percent target band by looking ahead to inflation over the 'policy horizon' of 1–2 years" (IMF 2003, 12). Accordingly, the elements of IT in Chile include (1) a prespecified continuous inflation

target band; (2) a preannounced "policy horizon"; and (3) timely communication of the authorities' inflation forecast, the rational for their policy decisions, and the reasons for any temporary deviations from the inflation target (IMF 2003). For a critique of the IT approach, see Epstein 2005.

8. This section draws from Leiva 2006.

9. This table compares the hourly wages between workers in the ninth decile (D9) to those of the first decile (D1). For example the D9:D1 ratio in Argentina went from 6 in 1993 to 8.4 in 2001; for Mexico it went from 4.95 in 1990 to 6.96 in 2001. For Bolivia it went from 12.60 in 1990 to 39.07 in 2001.

10. The fact that a worker "contributes" or is affiliated to a social security system does not imply that he or she has effective coverage. Chile, the paragon of privatized social security provides a good example (See Leiva 2005b). "Given Chile's, highly deregulated and 'flexible' labor markets, most workers do not have stable employment or adequate wages. Though 7 million workers are affiliated to the AFP system, only about 3.5 million contribute regularly. . . . Even so, job instability means that more than 70 % of the labor force contributes less than 6 months of the year into the pension accounts, while 50% of the workforce does so less than 4 times a year. The average density of the system—the number of months workers contribute—is very low, averaging about 4.9 months in the year. The result is that only about 25% of affiliated individuals to the AFP system will be able to save enough—approximately US$23,350 over the span of their work life—to be entitled to a retirement above the minimum pension of about US$130 a month. Another 25% will not be able to save that amount but at least will have made the 240 monthly contributions required for the government subsidy to fill the gap required to reach the minimum pension" (Leiva 2005b, 10–11).

11. The historical evolution of labor control systems has been studied extensively. Two studies of its evolution in the U.S. economy are Edwards 1977 and Gunn 1994.

7. The Politics of Neostructuralism and Capital Accumulation

1. Former President Lagos finds in the notion that international competitiveness is inextricably linked to social cohesion the possibility of projecting his thinking beyond Chile. After leaving office in 2006, his vision is being supported by four different foundations led by close collaborators, *Fundación Democracia y Desarrollo* (Clara Budnick), *Fundación Proyect America* (José Antonio Viera-Gallo), *Fundación Chile 21* (Eugenio Lahera), and the School of Government of the Universidad Alberto Hurtado (Francisco Vidal). Not surprisingly the relationship between social cohesion and international competitiveness is also highlighted by ECLAC's latest publications (i.e., Ottone and Sojo 2007). See "Ricardo Lagos Escobar: El más poderoso de todos," *El Merurio*, August 6, 2006, page D-8.

2. Plenty of historical examples illustrate this. The Chinese revolution led by Mao and the Chinese Communist Party ended up facilitating the path to capitalist development; land reform in Chile under Frei (1964–70) and Allende (1970–73) created conditions for capitalist development and the expansion of agro-exports.

3. A good example of this amalgamation appears in ECLAC 2007.

4. It should be noted that the March 2006 thirty-first period of sessions of ECLAC in Montevideo Uruguay was dedicated to the topic of "Social Protection: Looking towards the Future." Likewise, the Ibero-American Summit of Heads of State and Government to be held in November 2007 in Chile will discuss ECLAC's document on social cohesion.

5. The *Participation Forum: Participation in Policy Reform* were a series of monthly noontime meetings held during the mid-1990s for USAID personnel to explore how to put into practice the administrator's mandate to "build opportunities for participation into the development processes in which we are involved" (USAID 1995, 1). Summaries were drafted and distributed to development planners beyond USAID.

6. On March 27, 2000, secretary of the treasury Lawrence Summers at the IDB's Annual Meeting in New Orleans explained that "For all of these reasons, international institutions that can help to promote more rapid and inclusive growth within countries—and a more stable flow of capital between them—may be the most effective, and cost-effective investment that we can make in forward defense of America's core interests. And among the IFIs the IDB continues to make a crucial contribution to these goals." Summers explained: "Right from the beginning, the Clinton Administration's approach to the Inter-American Development Bank has been framed by the recognition that Regional Development Banks are as important to the new world order as the regional security organizations were to the old one. Just as the regional security organizations were directed to the challenge of combating communism, so the Regional Development Banks are directed to the *central challenge of shared prosperity* and enlarging the circle of prospering democracies" (ibid.; emphasis added). According to Summers, the most "cost-effective way to defend the United States core interests" and meet its security assignment in the "new world order" is for the IDB to ensure that "40 percent of the total volume and 50 percent of the number of IDB operations are allocated to poverty reduction and social equity." Such expanding programs increasingly incorporated "civil society participation" as one of their core components.

7. Most of the Washington-based international development organizations launched campaigns to reeducate their staffs on the importance of incorporating "participation" into their projects. See, for example, World Bank 1996; IDB 1994; and OAS 1999. Reading of each of these manuals gives the impression that the proponents of the "politics of participation" faced huge obstacles converting the staff of these bureaucracies to the new thinking.

8. John Durston, with ECLAC's Social Division, is one of the leading analysts on the role of social capital and policies designed to subordinate the noneconomic realm to capital accumulation and state legitimization by tapping into relations of reciprocity and trust: "Reciprocity involves relational and not mercantile transactions. That is to say, it involves exchanges whose goal is to build and strengthen a social relation based on favors and gifts, in contrast with your typical market exchange of equivalent values, that is anonymous and instantaneous. Cooperation is, at the same time, that complimentary action oriented towards achieving shared objectives. Trust is defined here as the willingness to turn over to others, control over one's own resources" (Durston 2005, 48; my translation).

9. "The impact of the information revolution is transforming Fordist societies into information-based societies, production societies into societies based on knowledge and information and the world of work into a world of communication: in short, transforming discipline-based logics into network-based approaches. All this spreads unevenly among and within countries. However, we are living our different historical periods in a more and more synchronous manner, so that in Latin America too the exercise and concept of citizenship are affected by the 'information society'" (Hopenhayn 2001, 117).

10. Similar interpretations are put forth by Chilean social scientists, such as Eugenio Tironi, José Joaquín Brunner, and to a lesser extent Manuel Antonio Garretón, who argue that consumption and watching CNN have become the new forms of participation and collective action. Not only is this a U.S.–Eurocentric reading of current societal trends that generalize on the basis of what happens to the top 25 percent of the income pyramid and in the wealthy neighborhoods where they live. It is an approach totally incapable of explaining collective forms of action and participation widespread in Argentina, Bolivia, Brazil, and Mexico and among the conveniently ignored sectors of their own Chilean society. The June 2006 massive demonstrations and school takeovers by thousands of Chile's high school students and by subcontracted workers in the copper, lumber, and fishing export sector attests to the shortcomings and bias of their analysis. Like in other parts of the world conveniently ignored by this elitist vision, text messaging and cell phones were used to organize combative forms of anti-neoliberal and anti-capitalist collective action and protest.

11. According to Bowles and Weisskopf, the main differences between U.S.-based Social Structures of Accumulation (SSA) and the French Regulation School (FRS) are as follows: "First, the SSA model determines the level of aggregate demand (and hence the level of capitality utilization) through an endogenous fiscal and monetary response to varying degrees or labor market tightness. By contrast, the Regulationists have aggregate demand determined by the distribution of income, in the fashion of Nicholas Kaldor. Second, the primary focus of the SSA approach is long-term productivity growth, and this is determined through a model of social as well as economic influences on labor discipline, motivation, and effort; whereas the regulationists

approach favors a Verdoorn relationship of productivity growth to output growth" (1999, 10). Veerdoorn's law states that faster growth in output will increase growth in productivity due to increasing returns to scale.

8. Erecting a New Mode of Regulation

1. For a case study of how this policy is applied in indigenous communities, see Fernando I. Leiva and Michelle Smith, "Ethnodevelopment, Globalization and the State: Programa Orígenes and Aymara Communities in Northern Chile," paper presented at the June 6–8, 2008 Globalization Studies Association conference, "The Nation in the Global Era: Nationalism and Globalization in Conflict and Transition," Pace University, New York.

2. This formulation is eerily similar to that attributed to Roger Vekemans and the DESAL approach to marginality of the early 1960s that justified the launching of state-organized "popular promotion" in Chile and other Latin American countries to help overcome the "psycho-cultural" shortcomings of the rural and urban poor.

3. The ideas in this section were first presented in my paper "'Participation' and Social Control Under Chile's Concertación Governments: New Forms of Representation or an Emergent Global Strategy for Disciplining Social Actors?" Prepared for delivery at the 2001 Meeting of the Latin American Studies Association, Washington, D.C., September 6–8, and also in Leiva 2005.

4. The 2001 Third Survey on Chilean Youth determined that only 39 percent of those in the 18–29 age range had registered in the electoral rolls (*La Tercera*, September 2, 2001). This indicates that roughly only two out of every five 18–29-year-old is interested in exercising the "citizenship" offered by the political system based on Augusto Pinochet's 1980 Constitution. For a country with historically high rates of electoral participation, these figures caused concern and public debate.

5. Interview with Ana María Medioli, president of the Chilean National Association of NGOS, August 5, 2001, Santiago, Chile.

6. The notion of a "cultural revolution" created by widespread access to consumption was put forward by Eugenio Tironi in his book *La Irrupción de las Masas y el Malestar de las Elites* (Santiago, Grijalbo, 1999).

7. Author's interview with Marcelo Martínez, head of the Research Department, Social Organizations Division, Ministerio Secretaría General de Gobierno. August 10, 2001. Santiago, Chile.

8. The *Fondo de las Americas* was set up jointly by the U.S. and Chilean governments as part of the 1991 Bush Initiative for the Americas, the precursor of NAFTA and the FTAA.

9. Ana María de la Jara, Executive Director of the nongovernmental organization CORDILLERA, Interview with author, August 10, 2001, Santiago.

10. Interview with Ana María de la Jara.

9. Chile's Evanescent High Road and Dashed Dreams of Equity

1. Examples of this type of analysis can be found in Brunner (1996), Tironi (1999), and Garretón (2002).

2. The next Latin American country is Uruguay, ranked in 54th place. To construct the Global Competitiveness Index (GCI), the World Economic Forum "identifies "three pillars": the quality of the macroeconomic environment, the state of the country's public institutions, and, given the importance of technology and innovation, the level of its technological readiness. The GCI uses a combination of hard data—for example, university enrollment rates, inflation performance, the state of the public finances, the level of penetration of new technologies, such as mobile telephones and the Internet—and data drawn from the World Economic Forum's Executive Opinion Survey.

3. In 2003, the "poverty line" was defined by Chile's Ministerio de Planificación (MIDEPLAN, Social Planning Ministry) as the minimum per capita income needed to cover the cost of an individual minimum basket necessary to cover food and non food necessities. "Poor households" were those whose income do not allow it to satisfy the basic necessities of its members (Ch$43,712 or US$69.88) in urban and Ch$29,473 (US$47.12) in rural areas. The line of indigence is established by the income per capita necessary to cover the basic food basket. Homes below the line of indigence are those which, even when they destine all their income to food expenditures, are unable to cover the basic food requirements of its members. In November of 2003, the line of indigence stood at Ch$21,856 (US$34.94) in urban areas, and Ch$16.842 (US$26.93) in rural areas (MIDEPLAN 2003, 26). I have calculated the U.S. dollar equivalent using data from Chile's Banco Central. In November of 2003, the exchange rate was US$1 = Ch$625.47.

4. See Marcel Claude, "Determinación del Nuevo Umbral de la Pobreza para Chile" (Una Aproximación desde la Sustentabilidad), Fundación Terram, Mayo 2002.

5. As the MIDEPLAN study concludes, "In particular, the richest decile on average spends 2.5 percent of its income on income taxes, while 6.3 percent goes to VAT payments, and 3.0 percent to other taxes. On the other hand, the poorest decile, does not pay any income taxes, but allocates 11,0 percent of its income to VAT payments and 3.4 percent to other taxes, paying a total of 14.4 percent of its income on taxes" (MIDEPLAN 2000, 39; my translation).

6. This section draws from Meller 1996.

7. Oscar Muñoz sounds a national alarm when he says, "All this means that productivity is systemic, that is, that it dos not only depend upon what happens within firms or on the efficiency of markets. It requires inputs from the rest of the socio-economic system, such as specialized education, good information and transport systems, centers for technological diffusion, physical infrastructure, a modern and fast legal system, etcetera" (1992, 5; my translation).

8. During the 1980–1994 period, for example, Chile's exports to the key Organisation for Economic Co-operation and Development (OECD) market barely increased from 0.23 percent to an equally insignificant 0.26 percent. While its share of the market for raw materials increased from 0.26 to 0.75 percent, in the case of manufactures, its share decreased from 0.21 to 0.11 percent between 1980 and 1994 (OIT 1998, 247). Thus, Chile's export boom failed to gain a significant foothold in the most dynamic niches of the world market: OECD and manufactures. Even in the Latin American market, Chile's share declined from 1.61 percent in 1980 to 1.18 percent in 1994. A second shortcoming in Chile's export performance is reflected in ECLAC's Index of Technological Specialization (ITS), which shows how, from a dynamic perspective, a country's market share of exports with high technological content changes in relation to those with lower content (OIT 1998). Chile's ITS is the lowest in the Latin American region and has remained practically unchanged during the 1977–94 period. In 1994, for example, Mexico (1.63) and Brazil (0.22) were at the top the list followed by Argentina (0.09) and the Caribbean (0.09). Even Central America had a higher ITS (0.06) than that of Chile (0.01), who was at the bottom of the list behind Venezuela (0.02) and Peru (0.02) (OIT, 1998).

9. The other paths to the second phase of Chile's EO model considered by Meller are (1) the Hong Kong model where Chile becomes platform; (2) an exporter of export-linked services; (3) deepening export activities through a greater incidence of private banks; and (4) the internationalization of production and operations by Chilean conglomerates.

10. This announcement raises interesting issues about whether the degree of financialization and transnationalization of the Chilean economy is leaning toward something not seen before in Latin America: the transition, thanks to neostructuralist inspired policies, form an extractive EO model to a finance-led regime of accumulation. As it should be obvious, this issue lies beyond the scope of this chapter. See Leiva and Malinowitz (2007) for a preliminary examination.

11. According to international tests such as the 2003 Trends in International Mathematics and Social Science (TIMSS) applied to eight graders in math, Chile scored 387.5, which is less than the previous testing and well below the international average of 467 points. Chile only tops countries like the Philippines, Bostwana, Saudi Arabia, Ghana, and South Africa. Fifty-nine percent of Chilean students do not even score above the minimum necessary to score these type tests. In 1999, only 54 percent of students scored below such minimum. In Social Sciences, Chile scored 413 points, which is seven points less than in 1999, while the international average was 474. Chile only scored higher than Tunisia, Saudi Arabia, Morocco, Lebanon, Phillipines, Bostwana, Ghana, and South Africa. Círculo de Economistas para el Desarrollo 2006, 22.

12. This section draws from Leiva 2006.

13. Through longitudinal instead of cross-sectional data, Henríquez and Urbina-Echeverría: (1) confirm that Chilean women's labor market participation is

underestimated as much as 30 percent while it is 14 percent for men; (2) though both male and female workers experience high rates of volatility and turnover, these are deeply gendered affecting female workers more intensely; (3) the erasure of the dichotomy between dependent (waged or salaried) and autonomous (self-employment) employment, one of the pillars upon which labor protection and labor legislation has been constructed.

14. "Chile invierte 65 por ciento de los excedentes en el exterior," *El Diario*, August 2, 2006.

15. The $133 million allocated by the Bachelet government to education in the wake of the June 2006 student protests is the equivalent of what the three largest domestic conglomerates Matte, Luksic, and Angelini make as profit on a daily basis. By comparison, the Chilean Armed forces spend $2.8 billion on F-16 planes, Leopard 1 tanks, and submarines, that is more than twenty times the resources allocated for the education of Chilean students (Círculo de Economistas para el Desarrollo, 2006).

16. Legislation on "fiscal responsibility" stipulates that government surplus will be destined to a Social Security Reserve Fund (to be spent over the coming decade), an Economic and Social Stabilization Fund, and a Fund for Capitalizing the Central Bank. The first two could be constituted entirely by investments outside of Chile.

10. Neostructuralism and the Latin American Left

1. According to the liberal weekly, "to portray what is happening in the Americas as a battle between the United States and its Latin neighbours is mistaken. . . . It is between liberal democrats—of left and right—and authoritarian populists." "The Battle for Latin America's Soul," *The Economist*, May 20, 2006, p. 11).

2. See Castañeda (2006) and Vargas Llosa (2007) for examples of this analysis. Castañeda at times sounds more like a U.S. State Department official: "The rest of the world has begun to take note of this left-wing resurgence, with concern and often more than a little hysteria. But understanding the reasons behind these developments requires recognizing that there is not one Latin American left today; there are two. One is modern, open-minded, reformist, and internationalist, and it springs, paradoxically, from the hard-core left of the past. The other, born of the great tradition of Latin American populism, is nationalist, strident, and close-minded. The first is well aware of its past mistakes (as well as those of its erstwhile role models in Cuba and the Soviet Union) and has changed accordingly. The second, unfortunately, has not" (Castañeda 2006).

3. For a critique of these characterizations, see Borón (2007), García Linera (2006b), and Maxwell Cameron (2006).

4. For the case of Brazil, see, for example, Zibechi 2007. Zibechi explains, "During his first government, Lula transferred . . . about $4.5 billion to the poor through

the program Bolsa Familia. But he transferred 10 times more ($45 billion annually) to the debtors of the public debt. That is to say to financial capital. Large Brazilian banks were the most favored sector of his government, under which they made the largest profit in history. As a result, the financial sector was the main donor of the PT's electoral campaign. According to the data provided by the authorities, out of the $45 million dollars spent by the PT during the electoral campaign, at least $5 billion came from the financial sector. . . . Given this situation, how is Lula ever going to break with the elites that finance him?" See http://www.rebelion.org/noticia .php?id=44785&titular=brasil-no-va-a-la-izquierda-.

5. This should be seen as a preliminary approach to the subject.

6. Claudio Katz, an Argentine radical economist, explores the tension between "neodevelopmentalism" and "socialism" in current debates (Katz 2006). I have borrowed the former term from him, but the characterizations of "status-quo defending" and "status-quo transforming" are my own. He speaks of "social liberalism" to refer to the policies of Chile and Brazil, not realizing that their orientation is a Latin American creation emanating from ECLAC in the form of Latin American neostructuralism.

7. I am referring mainly to publications that have the ECLAC's institutional imprimatur, including ECLAC 2004; Machinea and Hopenhayn 2005; Solimano 2005; and Ottone and Sojo 2007.

8. Not to be left behind, the ILO with its neostructuralist inspired new emphasis on "decent work" for all, also launched its own version of the "three-speed model" composed of the (1) large formal enterprises, (2) micro-enterprises, and (3) residual informal sector.

9. Enrique Brú (2003). De la calidad del empleo al trabajo decente para todos. Politicas de empleo en Chile y America Latina: Seminario en honor de Victor Tokman. Santiago: Organización Internacional del Trabajo, 57–58; my translation.

10. Tokman, a prominent staff member of the International Labour Organization's (ILO) Latin American office, is an advisor to ECLAC and has played an active role in writing key chapters of ECLAC's *Productive Development in Open Economies* and in introducing the notion of "flexi-security" to serve the production of social cohesion in ECLAC's 2007 institutional publication, *Social Cohesion: Inclusion and Sense of Belonging in Latin America and the Caribbean.*

11. Javier Biardeau (2007) attempts to trace the intellectual roots of Venezuela's twenty-first-century socialism. He tracks its orientation to the work of Russian philosopher Alexander V. Buzgalin translated into Spanish by Pedro Sotolongo; the work of Heinz Dieterich; the Edinborough school and Paul Cockshott and Allin Cottrell (1993); Marta Harnecker (1999); Tomás Moulian (2000); critics of the Third Way; postmodern and postcolonial thinkers of resistance; and the World Social Forum.

12. Speech at the II Conference of Alternative Relations, Vienna, May 13, 2006 (http://www.gobiernoenlinea.ve) cited by Gregory Wilpert, "El significado."

13. For Heinz Dieterich, "An economy is socialist when, it operates on bases of value, carries out exchange of equivalents, and democratically plans the main economic parameters, at a macro economic level, the investment rate and the national budget for example, as well as the microeconomic level, particularly in relationship to the rate of surplus-value (the rate of surplus labor over variable capital), that is to say, the intensity of the exploitation of labor" (Dieterich 2005). He seems to attribute the failure of socialism in the USSR to the unavailability of input–output Leontieff matrices and the lack of computers.

14. President Chávez promised, "We are going to give a percentage of stocks to the workers so that they become co-owners along with the government of the assets and new firms that are being created. In this manner, we will soon be transforming the socio-economic model, capitalism, neoliberalism, toward a different model that of a social productive economy of co-management, workers self-management, where male and female workers will have a decisive and essential role in giving impetus to the new economy at the service of human beings, to distance ourselves from capitalism, and savage neoliberalism" (Reyes 2006, 96; my translation).

11. Th e Future of Latin American Neostructuralism

1. Though ECLAC's structuralism of the 1950s was not a class-centric approach, it at least incorporated power relations into its analysis, and the issue of the surplus and use of the surplus were central in development of its core-periphery analysis. As pointed out in previous chapters, though class struggle was absent from its framework, ECLAC's structuralism promoted a vast process of transformation through a national-popular project of industrialization, based on the internal market. Exhaustion of the ISI regime of accumulation, intensifying class struggle over the historical projects to overcome this crisis of profitability, not "mistaken economic policies," led to the displacement of structuralists by neoliberals based in the University of Chicago and the World Bank during the 1970s and 1980s. Traumatized by the events of the 1970s, a generation of policy makers bunkered down at ECLAC headquarters.

2. Edward Nell points out another role played by neoliberalism when he indicates that, "dismantling the state deprives popular movements of any means to enforce their will. Even if they succeed in putting legislation on the books, if budgets are cut and state agencies are gutted and demoralized, nothing will be done" (Nell 1984, 236).

3. It is symptomatic that the technocrats for the fourth Concertación government initially came not from ECLAC but from the Harvard University linked Corporación Expansiva, a think tank of younger, liberal, technocrats having experience either in U.S.-based international development institutions or as high-level managers in large national public and private enterprises. See http://www.expansiva.cl.pr.

References

Acuña, Eduardo, and Ernesto Pérez. 2005. "Trayectorias laborales: El tránsito entre el trabajo asalariado y el empleo independiente." *Cuadernos de Investigación No. 23*. Santiago: Dirección del Trabajo, Departamento de Estudios.

Aedo, María Paz, and Sara Larraín, eds. 2004. *Impactos ambientales en Chile: Desafíos para la sustentabilidad*. Santiago: LOM Ediciones.

Agacino, Rafael. 1995. "El sector industrial chileno: Los problemas del crecimiento y la distribución en un contexto de apertura comercial." *Documentos de Trabajo No. 108. Santiago: Programa de Estudios del Trabajo (PET)*.

Aglietta, Alain. 2000. *A Theory of Capitalist Regulation: The U.S. Experience*. London: Verso.

Alia2. 2004. "E Nada MudouManifesto dos Economistas," November 24, 2004. http://www.voltairenet.org/article122925.html#article122925.

Amsden, Alice. 1989. *Asia's Next Giant: South Korea and Late Industrialization*. New York: Oxford University Press.

———. 2004. "Import-substitution in High-tech Industries: Prebisch Lives in Asia!" *CEPAL Review* 82:77–91.

Arrau, Patricio. 2003. "Competencia en el mercado de fondo de pensiones." Presentation to the seminar "Desafíos de los sistemas de pensiones en América Latina [Challenges Faced by Latin America's Pension System], 11–12 November, Santiago. Santiago: Gerens S.A.

Arrighi, Giovanni. 1994. *The Long Twentieth Century: Money, Power and the Origins of Our Time*. London and New York: Verso.

Artz, Lee B. 1997. "Social Power and the Inflation of Discourse." *Latin American Perspectives* 24 (1): 92–113.

Asociación de Exportadores de Manufacturas (ASEXMA), "El presidente Lagos anunció la radicación de Nestlé en Chile." January 8, 2003. http://www.asexma.cl/contenido/fomento/reportajes/2704.html.

Bair, Jennifer. 2003. "From Commodity Chains to Value Chains and Back Again?" Paper presented at the Rethinking Marxism conference. Amherst, Mass., November 6–9, 2003.

Barrett, Patrick S. 2001. "Labour Policy, Labour-business Relations and the Transition to Democracy in Chile." *Journal of Latin American Studies* 33:561–97.

Barrón Pérez, María Antonieta. 2005. "Emigración internacional, ¿mecanismo de re-producción social?" *Comercio Exterior* 55 (12): 1043–49.

Bates, Robert, and Anne Krueger. 1993. *Political and Economic Interactions in Economic Policy Reform: Evidence from Eight Countries*. Oxford: Basil Blackwell.

Bello, Walden. 2002. *De-globalizaiton, Ideas for a New World Economy*. London: Zed Books.

Bello, Walden, and Stephanie Rosenfeld. 1992. *Dragons in Distress: Asia's Miracle Economies in Crisis*. San Francisco: Food First.

Bertholomieu, Claude, Christophe Ehrhart, and Leticia Hernández-Bielma. 2005. "El neoestructuralismo como renovación del paradigma estructuralista de la economía del desarrollo." *Problemas del Desarrollo* 36 (143): 9–32.

Bianchi, Andrés. 2000. "La CEPAL en los años setenta y ochenta." In *La CEPAL en los 50 años: notas de un seminario conmemorativo*. Santiago: Naciones Unidas.

Biardeau, Javier. 2007. "El nuevo socialismo del siglo XXI. Una nueva guía de referencia." *Aporrea*. http://www.aporrea.org/ideologia.a32781.html.

Bielschowski, Ricardo. 1989. "Formação econômica do Brasil: uma obra-prima do estruturalismo cepalino." *Revista de Economia Política* 9 (4): 38–55.

———. 1998. "Evolución de las ideas de la CEPAL." *Revista de la CEPAL* (Numero Extraordinario):21–45.

———, ed. 2000. *Cinqüenta anos de pensamento na CEPAL*. Rio de Janeiro: Conselho Federal de Economia—COFECON/Ed. Record.

———. 2006. "Vigencia de los aportes de Celso Furtado al estructuralismo." *Revista de la CEPAL* 88:7–15.

Birdsall, Nancy, and Augusto de la Torre. 2001. "Washington Contentious: Economic Policies for Social Equity in Latin America." Washington, D.C.: Carnegie Endowment for International Peace and Inter-American Dialogue.

Birdsall, Nancy, Carol Graham, and Richard H. Sabot, eds. 1998. *Beyond Tradeoffs: Market Reform and Equitable Growth in Latin America*. Washington, D.C.: Inter-American Development Bank and The Brookings Institution.

Bitar, Sergio. 1988. "Neoliberalismo versus neoestructuralismo en América Latina." *Revista de la CEPAL* 34:45–63.

Blecker, Robert. 1999. *Taming Global Finance: A Better Architecture for Growth and Equity*. Washington, D.C.: Economic Policy Institute.

Boeninger, Edgardo. 1982. *Concepto, Objetivos y Oportunidades de Participación*. Santiago: Centro de Estudios del Desarrollo.

Bolpress. 2007. "El Estado Será la Locomotora Económica en Los Próximos 50 Años;" *Visiones Alternativas*, April 21, 2007. http://www.bolpress.com/art.php?Cod =2007041602.

Bonelli, Regis. 2000. "Fusões e Aquisições no Mercosul." In *Texto para discussão*. Brasilia: Instituto de Pesquisa Econômica Aplicada (IPEA).

Borón, Atilio. 2007. "El mito del desarrollo capitalista nacional en la nueva coyuntura política de América Latina." *Rebelión*, February 18.

Bowles, Samuel, Richard Edwards, and Frank Roosevelt. 2005. *Understanding Capitalism: Competition, Command, and Change*. New York and Oxford: Oxford University Press.

Boyer, Robert. 2000. "Is a Finance-led Growth Regime a Viable Alternative to Fordism? A Preliminary Analysis." *Economy and Society* 29:111–45.

Braga, Márcio Bobik. 2001. *Integração Econômica Regional na América Latina: uma Interpretação das Contribuições da Cepal*. http://ideas.repec.org/p/anp/en2001/008.html.

Brazil. 2003. *Plano Plurianual 2004–2007: mensagem presidencial*. Brasilia: Ministry of Planning. Office of the Budget and Management.

Bresser-Pereira, Luiz. 1992. "Homenagem a Fernando Fajnzylber." *Revista de Economía Política* 12 (4): 5–6.

———. 2001. "Decisões Estratégicas e 'overlapping consensus' na América Latina." *Revista de Economía Política* 21 (4): 3–29.

Brú, Enrique, ed. 2003. *De la calidad del empleo al trabajo decente para todos*. In *Políticas de empleo en Chile y América Latina: Seminario en honor de Victor Tokman*, ed. OIT. Santiago: OIT.

Brunner, José Joaquín. 1996. *Participación y democracia: Viejos y nuevos dilemas*. Santiago: Ministerio Secretaría General de Gobierno. División de Organizaciones Sociales.

Burke, Paul, and Martin Hart-Landsberg. 2000. "Alternative Perspectives on Late Industrialization in East Asia: A Critical Survey." *Review of Radical Political Economics* 32 (2): 222–64.

Burki, Shahed Javid, and Guillermo E. Perry. 1998. *Beyond the Washington Consensus: Institutions Matter*. Washington, D.C.: The World Bank.

Burrows, Roger, Nigel Gilbert, and Anna Pollert. 1992. "Introduction: Fordism, Post-Fordism and Economic Flexibility." In *Fordism and Flexibility: Division and Change*, ed. N. Gilbert, Roger Burrows, and Anna Pollert. New York: St. Martin's.

Cáceres D., Viviana, and Tamara Jeri. 2000. "Participación y estado: Viejos y nuevos discursos para el 'Nuevo Trato.'" *Documento de discusión no. 1*. Santiago: Ministerio Secretaría General de Gobierno, División de Organizaciones Sociales.

Calderón, Fernando. 1995. "Governance, Competitiveness and Social Integration." *CEPAL Review* 57:45–56.

Callinicos, Alex. 2001. *Against the Third Way*. Cambridge, UK: Polity.

Cameron, John D. 2004. "The World Bank and New Institutional Economics: Contradictions and Implications for Development Policy in Latin America." *Latin American Perspectives* 31 (4): 97–103.

Cameron, Maxwell. 2006. "A False and Dangerous Dichotomy." *The Guardian*, June 21, 2006.

Cardoso, Fernando Henrique. 1994. "Plano Fernando Henrique Cardoso." *Revista de Economía Política* 14 (54 [2]): 114–31.

———. 2004. "Beyond Economics: Interactions between Politics and Economic Development." *CEPAL Review* 83:7–12.

Carling, Alan. 2002. "The Principal-agent Problem for Egalitarians: Bowles, Gintis and Their Critics." *Science & Society* 66 (3): 408–16.

Carlson, Beverly. 2002. "Job Losses, Multinationals and Globalization: The Anatomy of Disempowerment." *Serie desarrollo productivo no. 132*. Santiago: ECLAC.

Castañeda, Jorge. 1998. "After Neoliberalism: A New Path." In *Report to the Meeting of the Latin American and Caribbean Forum on Poverty, Inequality and Vulnerability, October 28–29, 1998 at Buenos Aires*, ed. Ariel Fiszbein and Robert L. Ayres. Washington, D.C.: The World Bank Institute.

———. 2006. "Latin America's Left Turn." *Foreign Affairs* (May–June) 85 (3): 28–43.

CEPAL. 1992. *Equidad y transformación productiva: Un enfoque integrado*. Santiago: Naciones Unidas.

———. 1994. *América latina y el caribe: Políticas para mejorar la inserción en la economía mundial*. Santiago: Naciones Unidas.

———. 2000. *La CEPAL en sus 50 años: notas de un seminario conmemorativo*. Santiago: Naciones Unidas.

———. 2001. *Capital social y reducción de la pobreza: en busca de un nuevo paradigma*. Santiago: Naciones Unidas.

———. 2003a. *La inversión extranjera en América Latina y el Caribe, 2002*. Santiago: Naciones Unidas.

———. 2003b. "Panorama Social de América Latina 2002–2003. Se estanca superación de la pobreza." *Notas de la CEPAL* (31): 1–10.

———. 2004a. *Capital social y pobreza 2001*. Documento preparado por la CEPAL http://www.redelaldia.org/IMG/pdf/Capital_Social_y_Pobreza.pdf.

———. 2004b. *Panorama social de América Latina 2004*. Vol. LC/L. 2220. Santiago: Naciones Unidas.

———. 2005a. *La inversión extranjera en América Latina y el Caribe, 2004*. Santiago: Naciones Unidas.

———. 2005b. *Panorama social de América Latina*. Santiago: Naciones Unidas.

———. 2006. *Estudio económico de América Latina y el Caribe*. Vol. LC/G. 2314–P/E. Santiago: CEPAL.

Chalmers, D., et al., eds. 1997. *The New Politics of Inequality in Latin America: Rethinking Participation and Representation*: Oxford University Press.

Chibber, Vivek. 2005. "Reviving the Developmentalist State? The Myth of the National Bourgeoisie." *Socialist Register* 2005: 226–46.

Círculo de economistas para el desarrollo de Chile. 2006. "Los primeros cien días de Bachelet (Un Balance Crítico de una Gestión Estancada)." http://www.cepadech.cl/contenidos/documentos/Balance_Bachelet.pdf.

Chudnovsky, Daniel, and Andrés López. 2004. "Transnational Corporations' Strategies and Foreign Trade Patterns in MERCOSUR Countries in the 1990s." *Cambridge Journal of Economics* 28 (5): 635–52.

Cincuenta años de pensamiento de la CEPAL: Textos seleccionados Vol I y II. 1998. Comisión Económica para América Latina y el Caribe (CEPAL). Santiago: CEPAL/ Fondo de Cultura Económica.

Colclough, Christopher. 1991. "Structuralism versus Neo-liberalism: An Introduction." In *States and Markets: Neoliberalism and the Development Policy Debate*, ed. C. Colclough and J. Manor. Oxford: Clarendon.

Concertación de Partidos por la Democracia. 1999. Programa Electoral. Santiago: Edición Arcoiris.

Contreras, Dante, Cooper Ryan, Jorge Herman, and Christopher Neilson. 2005. "Movilidad y Vulnerabilidad en Chile." *En Foco 56*. Santiago: Corporación Expansiva.

Cullenberg, Stephen, Jack Amariglio, and David Ruccio, eds. 2001. *Postmodernism, Economics and Knowledge*. London and New York: Routledge.

de Barros, José Roberto Mendonça, and Lídia Goldstein. 1997. "Avaliaçao do proceso de reestruturaçao industrial brasileiro." *Revista de Economía Política* 17 (2 [66]): 13–31.

de la Fuente Lora, Gerardo. 1994. "El pensamiento económico latinoamericano." *Problemas del Desarrollo* 25 (98): 55–120.

de Magalhães, Rogério Antonio Lagoeira. 2004. "Valor, essência e aparência e o conceito da mais-valia extraordinária." *Economia* 5 (1): 67–97.

De Martini, Isabel, and Enrique Mujica. 2005. "Rolf Luders: La Concertación ha administrado mejor el modelo que la derecha." *Revista Qué Pasa*, October 15, 2005.

DeFerranti, David, Francisco Ferreira, Franciso, Guillermo E. Perry, and Michael Walton. 2004. *Inequality in Latin America: Breaking with History?* (*World Bank Latin American and Caribbean Studies*). Washington, D.C.: World Bank.

Di Filippo, Armando. 1984. "Uso social del excedente, acumulación, distribución y empleo." *Revista de la CEPAL* (24): 117–35.

———. 1998. "La visión centro periferia hoy." *Revista de la CEPAL* Número Extraordinario: 175–86.

Díaz, Alvaro. 1995. "Chile en la segunda fase exportadora. Dilemas para una estrategia de desarrollo." *Estadística y Economía* (10): 67–85.

Dieterich, Heinz. 2002. *El socialismo del siglo XXI*. Madrid: Editorial Siglo XXI.

———. 2005. "La revolución bolivariana y el socialismo del siglo XXI." August 18. http://www.aporrea.org/ideologia/a16108.html.

dos Santos, Theotonio. 1970. "The structure of dependence." *American Economic Review* 60 (2): 231–36.

Durane, Cedric. 2005. "La inversión extranjera directa (IED) como fuente de ideas para el crecimiento de las economías en desarrollo." *Problemas del Desarrollo* 36 (140): 11–41.

Durston, John. 1999. "Building Community Social Capital." *CEPAL Review* 69: 103–18.

———. 2005. "Superación de la pobreza, capital social y clientelismos locales." In *Aprendiendo de la experiencia: El capital social en la superación de la pobreza*, ed. I. Arriagada. Santiago: CEPAL-Cooperación Italiana.

Duryea, Suzanne, Olga Jaramillo, and Carmen Pagés. 2003. "Latin American Labor Markets in the 1990s: Deciphering the Decade." *IDB Working Paper* #486. Washington, D.C.: Inter American Development Bank

Eagleton, Terry. 1986. *Against the Grain: Essays 1975–1986*. London: Verso.

———. 1991. *On Ideology: An Introduction*. London: Verso.

———. 1996. *The Illusions of Postmodernism*. Oxford: Blackwell Publishers.

Echeverría, Magdalena. 1996. "Mejores condiciones de trabajo: Un desafío actual." *Temas Laborales* I (2). Santiago: Departamento de Estudios, Dirección del Trabajo.

Echeverría, Magdalena, and Diego López. 2004. *Flexibilidad laboral en Chile: Las empresas y las personas*. Santiago: Departamento de Estudios, Dirección del Trabajo.

ECLAC. 1990. *Changing Production Patterns with Social Equity*. Santiago: United Nations.

———. 1992. *Social Equity and Changing Production Patterns: An Integrated Approach*. Santiago: United Nations.

———. 1994a. *Latin America and the Caribbean: Policies to Improve Linkages with the Global Economy*. Santiago: United Nations.

———. 1994b. *Open Regionalism in Latin America and the Caribbean. Economic Integration as a Contribution to Changing Productions Patterns with Social Equity*. Santiago: Naciones Unidas.

———. 2002. *Globalization and Development*. Santiago: United Nations.

———. 2004. *Productive Development in Open Economies*. Santiago: United Nations.

———. 2007. ECLAC Press Release, "New Publication from ECLAC: Social Cohesion: Inclusion and a Sense of Belonging in Latin America and the Caribbean," February 16, 2007. http://www.eclac.org.

Edwards, Richard. 1977. *Contested Terrain: The Transformation of the Workplace in the Twentieth Century*. New York: Basic Books.

El ladrillo: Bases de la Política Económica del Gobierno Militar Chileno. 2002. Ed. Centro de Estudios Públicos. Santiago: Centro de Estudios Públicos.

El Mercurio. 2006. "Ricardo Lagos Escobar: El más poderoso de todos," August 6, 2006, p. D-8.

El Mercurio On-Line. 2003. "Lagos: "No tengo fuerza política para reovocar la Amnistía." August 17, 2003.

Epstein, Gerald. 2002. "Financialization, Rentier Interests, and Central Bank Policy." Paper prepared for PERI Conference on "Financialization of the world economy," December 7–8, 2001. Amherst, Mass.: University of Massachusetts-Amherst.

———. 2005. Alternatives to Inflation Targeting Monetary Policy For Stable and Egalitarian Growth: A Brief Research Summary," Political Economy Research

Institute (PERI), University of Massachusetts, Amherst (June 2005). Paper presented at WIDER Jubilee Conference, 'WIDER Thinking Ahead: The Future of Development Economics', Helsinki, Finland, June 17–18, 2005. http://www.wider.unu.edu/conference/conference-2005-3/ conference-2005-3-papers/Epstein.pdf.

Epstein, Gerald, and Arjún Jayadev. 2005. "The Rise of Rentier Incomes in OECD Countries: Financialization, Central Bank Policy and Labor Solidarity." In *Financialization and the World Economy*, ed. G. Epstein. Cheltenham: Edward Elgar.

Erber, Fabio Stefano. 2002. "The Brazilian Development in the Nineties—Myths, Circles, and Structures. *Nova Economia* 12 (1): 11–37.

Escobar, Arturo. 1984. "Discourse and Power in Development: Michel Foucalt and the Relevance of His Work to the Third World." *Alternatives* 10 (3): 377–400.

———. 1995. *Encountering Development: The Making of the Third World*. Princeton, N.J.: Princeton University Press.

Escobar, Patricio. 2003. "The New Labor Market: The Effects of the Neoliberal Experiment in Chile." *Latin American Perspectives* 30 (5): 70–78.

Espinosa, Malva, 1997. "Sindicalismo en la empresa moderna: Ni ocaso, ni crisis terminal. análisis de encuesta de empleadores y trabajadores." *Cuadernos de Investigación No. 4*. Santiago: Dirección del Trabajo, Departamento de Estudios.

Evans, Peter. 1995. *Embedded Autonomy: States and Industrial Transformation*. Princeton, N.J.: Princeton University Press.

Fajnzylber, Fernando. 1983. *La industrialización trunca de América Latina*. México, D.F.: Editorial Nueva Imágen.

———. 1988. "International Competitiveness: Agreed Goal, Hard Task." *CEPAL Review* (36): 7–23.

———. 1989. "Industrialización en América Latina: de la "caja negra" al "casillero vacío." Comparación de patrones contemporáneos de industrialización." *Cuadernos de la CEPAL* 60.

———. 1991. "International Insertion and Institutional Renewal." *CEPAL Review* 44:137–66.

Falcoff, Mark. 2002. "Two Latin Americas." *Latin American Outlook, American Enterprise Institute Online*. November 1, 2002.

Ffrench-Davis, Ricardo. 1986. "Neoestructuralismo e inserción externa." Paper read at Mesa Redonda sobre Estilos de Desarrollo en América Latina y Desafíos del Futuro, 6–8 January 1986, at Santiago, Chile.

———. 1988. "Esbozo de un planteamiento neoestructuralista." *Revista de la CEPAL* 34:37–44.

———. 2000. *Reforming the Reforms in Latin America: Macroeconomics, Trade, Finance*. New York: St. Martin's.

———. 2002a. *Economic Reforms in Chile: From Dictatorship to Democracy*. Ann Arbor: The University of Michigan Press.

———. 2002b. "El impacto de las exportaciones sobre el crecimiento en Chile." *Revista de la CEPAL* 76:143–59.

Ffrench-Davis, Ricardo, and H. Tapia. 2001. "Three Varieties of Capital Surge Management in Chile." In *Financial Crisis in "Successful" Emerging Economies*, ed. R. Ffrench-Davis. Washington, D.C.: ECLAC-Brookings Institution.

Figueredo, Ferdinando de Oliveira. 1990. "As transformações do pós-guerra e o pensamento econômico da CEPAL." *Revista de Economía Política* 10 (4): 138–50.

Fine, Ben. 2002. "Economic Imperialism and the New Development Economics as Kuhnian Paradigm Shift." *World Development* 30 (12): 2057–70.

———. 2002. "They F**K You Up Those Social Capitalists." *Antipode* 34 (4): 796–99.

Fine, Ben, Costas Lapavitsas, and Jonathan Pincus, eds. 2001. *Development Policy in the Twenty-First Century: Beyond the Post-Washington Consensus*. London: Routledge.

Finot, Ivan. 2002. "Decentralization and Participation In Latin America: An Economic Perspective." *CEPAL Review* 78:133–43.

Fiori, José Luís. 1992. "Para repensar o papel do estado sem ser um neoliberal." *Revista de Economía Política* 12:76–89.

FitzGerald, Valpy, and Rosemary Thorpe, eds. 2005. *Economic Doctrines in Latin America: Origins, Embedding and Evolution*. New York: Palgrave Macmillan.

Folha de Sao Paulo (Folha on Line). 2003. "Economistas do PT querem "inversão total" na Fazenda." December 6.

Foreign Investment Committee. 2005. *A Springboard into New Markets*. December 13. http://www.cinver.cl/index/plantilla2.asp?id_seccion=4&id_subsecciones=95.

Foro de Sao Paulo. 2007. Declaración Final, XIII Encuentro del Foro de Sao Paulo. El Salvador.

Fortuna, Juan Carlos, and Suzanna Prates. 1989. "Informal Sector versus Informalized Labor Relations in Uruguay." In *The Informal Economy: Studies in Advanced and Less Developed Countries*, ed. A. Portes and L. A. Benton. Baltimore: The Johns Hopkins University Press.

Foxley, Alejandro. 2003. "Políticas de empleo en el marco de la globalización." In *Políticas de empleo en Chile y América Latina: Seminario en honor de Victor E. Tokman*, ed. OIT. Santiago: Organización Internacional del Trabajo.

Fromin, Luis. 2001. "La mano invisible de la Cepal en Chile." *Revista Qué Pasa*. July 10.

Gazeta de Alagoas. 2004. "Economistas do PT dizem que governo é pauperizador." November 16, 2004.

García Arias, Jorge. 2004. "Mundialización y sector público: mito y enseñanzas de la globalización financiera." *Comercio Exterior* 34 (11): 856–75.

García Linera, Alvaro. 2006a. "El capitalismo Andino-Amazonico." *Le Monde Diplomatique*, Chilean Edition, January. http://www.lemondediplomatique.cl/El-capitalismo-andino-amazonico.html.

———. 2006b. "El evismo: lo nacional popular en acción." *Revista Observatorio Social América Latina (OSAL)* VII (19): 25–32.

Garretón, Manuel A. 2002. "The Transformation of Collective Action in Latin America." *Revista de la CEPAL* 76:7–24.

Geller, Lucio. 1993. "Cambio tecnológico, trabajo y empleo: Industrial manufacturera del Gran Santiago 1988–1990." Santiago de Chile: PREALC/OIT-ACDI. Santiago: PREALC-OIT-ACDI.

Genoíno, José. 2004. "Um novo modelo de desenvolvimento." *O Estado de Sao Paulo*, April 24, 2004.

Gereffi, Gary, John Humphrey, and Timothy Sturgeon. 2005. "The Governance of Value Chains." *Review of International Political Economy* 12 (1): 78–104.

Gereffi, Gary, and Timothy J. Sturgeon. 2004. "Globalization, Employment, and Economic Development." A briefing paper, edited by Sloan Workshop Series in Industry Studies. Rockport, Massachusetts.

Giddens, Anthony. 1998. *The Third Way: The Renewal of Social Democracy.* Cambridge, Mass.: Polity.

Giovagnoli, Paula, Georgina Pizzolitto, and Julieta Trías. 2005. "Chile: Monitoring Socio-Economic Conditions in Argentina, Chile, Paraguay and Uruguay." La Plata: CEDLAS.

Giulani, Elisa, Carlo Pietrobelli, and Roberta Rabelloti. 2004. "Upgrading in Global Value Chains: Lessons from Latin America." *World Development* 33(4): 549–73.

González Martínez, Carlos. 1994. "Transformar el sistema. Prebisch: la idea de la regulación estatal del excedente económico." *Problemas del Desarrollo* 25 (98): 121–40.

Gordon, David. 1980. "Stages of Accumulation and Long Economic Cycles." In *Processes of the World System*, ed. T. Hopkins and I. Wallerstein. Beverly Hills, Calif.: Sage Publications.

Greaves, Edward F. 2004. "Municipality and Community in Chile: Building Imagined Civic Communities and Its Impact on the Political." *Politics and Society* 37 (2): 203–30.

Green, Duncan. 2003. *Silent Revolution: The Rise and Fall of Market Economics in Latin America.* New York: Monthly Review.

Guardia, Alexis B. 2006. "La tentación conservadora en la economía chilena." *El Mostrador*, August 3, 2006.

Gunn, Christopher. 1994. "Workers' Participation in Management: Capital's Flexible System of Control." *Review of Radical Political Economics* 26 (2): 119–26.

Gwynne, Robert. 2004. "Clusters and Commodity Chains: Firm Responses to Neoliberalism in Latin America." *Latin American Research Review* 39 (3): 243–55.

Gwynne, Robert, and Cristóbal Kay. 2004. *Latin America Transformed: Globalization and Modernity.* London: Hodder Arnold Publications.

Haggard, Stephan, and Robert H. Kauffman, eds. 1992. *The Politics of Economic Adjustment: International Constraints, Distributive Conflicts, and the State*. Princeton, N.J.: Princeton University Press.

Hall, Stuart. 1991. "Brave New World." *Socialist Review* 21 (1): 57–64.

Harnecker, Marta. 1999. "La izquierda en el umbral del siglo XXI." Mexico, D.F.: Siglo XXI Editores.

Heinz, James. 2003. "The New Face of Unequal Exchange: Low-wage Manufacturing, Commodity Chains, and Global Inequality." *Working Paper Series No. 59*. Amherst, MA: Political Economy Research Institute, University of Massachusetts.

Hemispheric Social Alliance. 2002. *Alternatives for the Americas*. Hemispheric Social Alliance. http://www.art-us.org/system/files/alternatives+dec+2002.pdf.

Henderson, Willie, Tony Dudley-Evans, and Roger Backhouse, ed. 1993. *Economics and Language*. New York and London: Routledge.

Henríquez, Helia, and Verónica Uribe-Echevarría. 2004. "Trayectorias laborales: la certeza de la incertidumbre." *Cuadernos de Investigación No. 18*. Santiago: Dirección del Trabajo.

Hernández Haffner, Jacqueline A. 2002. A CEPAL e a integração regional latino-americana. *Revista análisise económica* 20 (37): 107–27.

Hilton, Isabel. "Soros Comment," *The Guardian*, September 20, 2002. http://www.guardian.co.uk/comment/story/0,3604,795505,00.html.

Hodara, Joseph. 1977. "On the Article by Raúl Prebish 'A Critique of Peripheral Capitalism.'" *CEPAL Review* 4:187–91.

———. 1998. "Las confesiones de don Raúl: El capitalismo periférico." *Desarrollo Económico* 38 (150): 643–53.

Hoff, Karla, and Joseph E. Stiglitz. 2000. "Modern Economic Theory And Development." In *Frontiers of Development Economics: The Future in Perspective*, eds. G. Meier and J. Stiglitz. Oxford: Oxford University Press: 389–459.

Hopenhayn, Martín. 2001. "Old and New Forms of Citizenship." *ECLAC Review* 73:115–26.

Hounie, Adela, Lucia Pittaluga, Gabriel Porcile, and Fabrio Scatolin. 1999. "ECLAC and the New Growth Theories." *ECLAC Review* 68:7–33.

Huber, Evelyn, and Fred Solt. 2004. "Successes and Failures of Neoliberalism." *Latin American Research Review* 39 (3): 150–64.

Humphrey, John. 1980. "Labor Use and Labor Control in the Brazilian Automobile Industry." *Capital and Class* 12 (1980): 43–58.

———. 1987. *Gender and Work in the Third World: Sexual Divisions in Brazilian Industry*. London: Tavistock Publishers.

Ibarz, Joaquim, "Entrevista a Alvaro Garía Linera, el futuro vicepresidente de Evo Morales," *Clarin*. December 23, 2005. http://www.clarin.com/diario/2005/12/23/elmundo/i-04401.htm.

IDB. 1992. *Economic and Social Progress in Latin America. 1992 Report. Manufacturing Exports*. Washington, D.C.: Inter-American Development Bank and Johns Hopkins University Press.

———. 1994. *Resource Book on Participation*. Washington, D.C.: Inter American Development Bank.

———. 2001. *Competitiveness: The Business of Growth. Economic and Social Progress Report in Latin America. 2001 Report*. Washington, D.C.: Johns Hopkins University Press and Inter-American Development Bank.

———. 2004. *Good Jobs Wanted: Labor Markets in Latin America*. Washington, D.C.: Inter-American Development Bank and Johns Hopkins University Press. http://www.iadb.org//aboutus/vi/resource_book/table_of_contents.cfm.

ILO. 2004. *2004 Labour Overview*. Lima: ILO/Regional Office for Latin America and the Caribbean.

ILPES. 1962. "Prospecto del curso básico para el periodo 1962/63." In *INST/7 (Cap/1)*. Santiago de Chile: Instituto Latinoamericano de Planificación Económica y Social (ILPES).

IMF. 2003. Country report. Chile: Selected issues. Country report 03/312 Washington, D.C.: International Monetary Fund.

———. 2004. "IMF Concludes 2004 Article IV Consultation with Chile," IMF, Public Information Notice (PIN) No. 04/83, August 5, 2004. http://www.imf.org/external/np/sec/pn/2004/pn0483.htm

Instituto de Estudos para o Desenvolvimento Industrial. 1992. "Rumo ao modelo de competição vitorioso nos países desenvolvidos." *Revista de Economía Política* 12 (4): 138–52.

International Forum on Globalization. 2002. *Alternatives to Economic Globalization: A Better World Is Possible*. San Francisco: Berret-Koehler Publishers.

Jessop, Bob. 1997. "Twenty Years of the (Parisian) Regulation Approach: The Paradox of Success and Failure at Home and Abroad." *New Political Economy* 2 (7): 503–26.

———. 2002. *The Future of the Capitalist State*. Cambridge, Mass.: Polity.

Jones, Ronald, Henryk Kierzkowski, and Chen Lurong. 2005. "What Does Evidence Tell Us about Fragmentation and Outsourcing?" In *UNU-WIDER Jubilee Conference WIDER thinking ahead: The future of development economics*. Helsinki, Finland.

Katz, Claudio. 2006. "Socialismo o neodesarrollismo." *Rebelión*. December 1.

Katz, Jorge. 2001. *Structural Reforms, Productivity and Technological Change in Latin America*. Santiago: United Nations Economic Commission for Latin America.

Kay, Cristóbal. 1989. *Latin American Theories of Development and Underdevelopment*. London and New York: Routledge.

———. 2002. "Why East Asia Overtook Latin America: Agrarian Reform, Industrialisation and Development." *Third World Quarterly* 23 (6): 1073–1102.

Kay, Cristóbal, and Robert Gwynne. 2002. "Relevance of Structuralist and Dependency Theories in the Neoliberal Period: A Latin American Perspective." In *Critical Perspectives on Globalization and Neoliberalism in Developing Countries*, ed. R. L. Harris and M. J. Seid. Leiden. Boston, Koln: Brill Academic Publishers.

Keaney, Michael. 2005. "Social Democracy, Laissez-Faire, and the 'Third Way' of Capitalist Development." *Review of Radical Political Economics* 37 (3): 357–78.

Khan, Shahrukh Rafi, and Sajit Kazmi. 2003. "Revenue Distribution Across Value Chains: The Case of Home-based Sub-contracted Workers in Pakistan." *Working Paper No: 2003–04*. Salt Lake City: Department of Economics, University of Utah.

Klamer, Arjo. 1988. "Economics as Discourse." In *The Popperian Legacy in Economics*, ed. Neil de Marchi. Cambridge, UK: Cambridge University Press.

Kliksberg, Bernardo. 1999. "Social Capital and Culture: Master Keys to Development." *CEPAL Review* 69:83–102.

———. 2000. "Six Unconventional Theses about Participation." *International Review of Administrative Sciences* 66:161–74.

Korzeniewicz, Roberto P., and William C. Smith. 1999. *Growth, Poverty and Inequality in Latin America: Searching for the High Road*. http://www.columbia.edu/cu/ilais/smith&korzeniewicz.htm.

Kotz, David. 1994a. "Interpreting the Social Structure of Accumulation Theory." In *Social Structures of Accumulation: The Political Economy of Growth and Crisis*, ed. David Kotz, Terry McDonnough, and Michael Reich. Cambridge and New York: Cambridge University Press.

———. 1994b. "The Regulation Theory and the Social Structure of Accumulation." In *Social Structures of Accumulation: The Political Economy of Growth and Crisis*, ed. David Kotz, Terry McDonnough, and Michael Reich. Cambridge and New York: Cambridge University Press.

Krippner, Greta. 2005. "The Financialization of the American Economy." *Socio-Economic Review* (3): 173–228.

Kuntz Ficker, Sandra. 2005. "From Structuralism to the New Institutional Economics: The Impact of Theory on the Study of Foreign Trade in Latin America." *Latin American Research Review* 40 (3): 145–62.

Kuri Gaytán, Armando. 1995. "El cambio tecnológico en los análisis estructuralistas." *Revista de la CEPAL* (55): 183–90.

Laclau, Ernesto. 2006. "La deriva populista y la centroizquierda latinoamericana." *Nueva Sociedad* (205): 56–61.

Lagos, Ricardo E. 2003. "Cohesión social y mas empleo: El nuevo desafío." In *Políticas de empleo en Chile y América Latina: Seminario en honor de Victor Tokman*, ed. OIT. Santiago: Oficina Internacional del Trabajo.

Lagos, Ricardo A. 1994. "¿Qué se entiende por flexibilidad del mercado de trabajo?" *Revista de la CEPAL* (54): 81–95.

Lahera, Eugenio. 1988. "Technical Change and Productive Restructuring." *CEPAL Review* (36): 33–47.

Lahera, Eugenio, Ernesto Ottone, and Osvaldo Rosales. 1995. "Una síntesis de la propuesta de la CEPAL." *Revista de la CEPAL* (55): 7–25.

Lara Cortés, Claudio. 2002. "Auge de la financierización y estancamiento de la economía chilena." *Economía Crítica y Desarrollo* I (2): 55–85.

Larraín, Sara, Karim Palacios, and María Paz Aedo. 2003. *Por un Chile sustentable: Propuesta ciudadanas para el cambio.* Santiago: Chile Sustentable/LOM Ediciones.

Larrañaga, Osvaldo. 2001. "Distribución de ingresos en Chile, 1958–2001." *Documentos de Trabajo No. 178.* Santiago: Departamento de Economía, Universidad de Chile.

Lazonick, William, and Mary O'Sullivan. 2000. "Maximizing Shareholder Value: A New Ideology for Corporate Governance." *Economy and Society* 29 (1): 13–36.

Lechner, Norbert. 1997. "Three Forms of Social Coordination." *CEPAL Review* 61:7–17.

Leffort, Fernando. 2000. "Corporate Governance: Challenges for Latin America." *Revista ABANTE* 2 (2): 99–111.

Leiva, Fernando Ignacio. 1995. *Los límites de la actual estrategia de lucha contra la pobreza y los dilemas de las ONGs.* Serie de Documentos de Análisis No. 7, Taller de Reflexión. Santiago: PAS.

———. 1998. "Neoliberal and Neostructuralist Theories of Competitiveness and Flexible Labor: The Case of Chile's Manufactured Exports, 1973–96," Unpublished PhD Dissertation, Department of Economics, University of Massachusetts, Amherst, MA.

———. 2005a. "Chile's Privatized Social Security System: Behind the Free-Market Hype," *Network Connection,* May–June 2005. http://www.networklobby.org/connection/index.html.

———. 2005b. "From Pinochet's State Terrorism to the "Politics of Participation." In *Democracy in Chile: The Legacy of September 11, 1973,* ed. Silvia Nagy-Zekmi and Fernando I. Leiva. Brighton, UK: Sussex Academic Press.

———. 2006. "Neoliberal and Neostructuralist Perspectives on Labour Flexibility, Poverty and Inequality: A Critical Appraisal." *New Political Economy* 11 (3): 337–59.

Leiva, Fernando Ignacio, and Rafael Agacino. 1994. *Mercado de trabajo flexible, pobreza y desintegración social.* Santiago: OXFAM UK-Universidad ARCIS.

Leiva, Fernando Ignacio, and Stanley Malinowitz, 2007. "Financialization in the Americas: Evidence and Consequences." Paper presented at 2007 Congress of the Latin American Studies Association (LASA), September 5–8, 2007. Montréal, Canada.

Letelier, Orlando. 1976. "The Chicago Boys in Chile: Economic Freedom's Awful Toll." *The Nation.* August 28: 137–42.

Lichtensztejn, Samuel. 2001. "Pensamiento económico que influyó en el desarrollo latinoamericano en la segunda mitad del siglo XX." *Comercio Exterior* 51 (2): 91–99.

Lima, Gilberto Tadeu. 2003. "Acumulação de Capital, Distribuição de Renda e Inflação por Conflito em um Modelo Macrodinâmico Pós-Keynesiano." In *Liberalização Econômica e Desenvolvimento*, ed. Joao Carlos Ferraz, Marco Crocco and Luiz Antonio Elias. Rio de Janeiro: Editora Futura.

Lipietz, Alan. 1986. "New Tendencies in the International Division of Labor: Regimes of Accumulation and Modes of Regulation." In *Production, Work, Territory*, ed. A. Scott and M. Storper. Boston: Allen and Unwin.

Lira, Máximo. 1988. "Prebisch's Long March Towards the Criticism of 'Peripheral Capitalism' and His Theory of Social Transformation." *Concepts and Methods in Geography* 3:107–27.

Lord, Montague. 1992. "Latin America's Exports of Manufactured Goods." In *Economic and Social Progress in Latin America, 1992 Report*. Washington, D.C.: Inter-American Development Bank.

Love, Joseph. 2004. "Structuralism and Dependency in Peripheral Europe: Latin American Ideas in Spain and Portugal." *Latin American Research Review* 39 (2): 114–40.

———. 2005. "The Rise and Decline of Economic Structuralism in Latin America: New Dimensions." *Latin American Research Review* 40 (3): 100–125.

Luhnow, David. "Latin America's Left Takes Pragmatic Tack." *Wall Street Journal.* March 2, 2005, p. A15.

Lustig, Nora. 1988. "Del estructuralismo al neoestructuralismo: la búsqueda de un paradigma heterodojo." *Colección Estudios CIEPLAN* 23:34–50.

Machinea, José Luis, and Martin Hopenhayn. 2005. *La esquiva equidad en el desarrollo latinoamericano: una visión estructural, una aproximación multifacética, Informe y estudios especiales No. 14*. Santiago: Naciones Unidas.

Maloney, William F. 2004. "Informality Revisited." In *World Development* 32(7): 1159.

Mantega, Guido. 1989. "Celso Furtado e o pensamento econômico brasileiro." *Revista de Economia Politica* 9 (4): 29–37.

Marques-Pereira, Jaime. 2001. "Crisis financiera y regulación política en América Latina." *Comercio Exterior* 51 (9): 840–50.

Marcel, Mario, Marcelo Tokman, Rodrigo Valdés, and Silvia Benavides. 2001. Balance Estructural del Gobierno Central. Metodología y Estimaciones para Chile: 1987–2000. Santiago: Ministerio de Hacienda, Dirección de Presupuesto.

Martínez, Marcelo. 1999a. "Comprensión de la cultura no ciudadana en Chile." In *Ciudadanía en Chile: El desafío cultural del nuevo milenio*, ed. D. Farcas. Santiago: Ministerio Secretaría General de Gobierno. División de Organizaciones Sociales. Departamento de Estudios.

————. 1999b. "Modernización, modernidad y participación en Chile: Límites y perspectivas para una situación epocal." *Documento de Trabajo No. 3*. Santiago: Ministerio Secretaría General de Gobierno, División de Organizaciones Sociales.

————. 2000. "Nuevo trato: Alcances políticos y conceptuales para una política nacional y transversal de participación ciudadana." *Documentos para la Discusión No.2*. Santiago: Ministerio Secretaría General de Gobierno, División de Organizaciones Sociales.

————. 2001. "La Sociedad Civil en Chile: Precisiones Conceptuales y Rol de las Elites." *El Utopista Pragmático*. http://www.primeralinea.cl.

Mascarilla I Miró, Oscar. 2005. "El trilema económico y político-social de la globalización." *Comercio Exterior* 35 (6): 478–87.

McCloskey, Donald (Deidre). 1985. *The Rhetoric of Economics*. Madison: University of Wisconsin.

————. 1994. *Knowledge and Persuasion in Economics*. Cambridge: Cambridge University Press.

McNally, David. 1993. *Against the Market: Political Economy, Market Socialism and the Marxist Critique*. London: Verso.

Medina Echeverría, José. 1967. *Filosofía de la educación y desarrollo. Textos del Instituto Latinoamericano de Planificación Económica y Social (ILPES)*. Mexico, D.F.: Siglo XXI Editores.

Meller, Patricio, ed. 1992. *The Latin American Development Debate: Neostructuralism, Neomonetarism and Adjustment Processes*. Boulder, Colo.: Westview.

————. 1996. "La maldición de los recursos naturales y la segunda fase exportadora." Santiago: CIEPLAN.

Mendes, Constantino Cronemberger, and Joanílio Rodolpho Teixeira. 2004. "Desenvolvimento econômico brasileiro: Uma releitura das contribuições de Celso Furtado." In *Textos para Discussao No. 1051*. Brasilia: Instituto de Pesquisa Económica Aplicada (IPEA).

Michie, Jonathan, and Maura Sheehan. 2003. "Labour Market Deregulation, 'Flexibility' and Innovation." *Cambridge Journal of Economics* 27 (1): 123–43.

MIDEPLAN. 2000. "Posibilidades y limitaciones de las políticas económicas redistributivas: Perspectivas de largo plazo." Santiago: MIDEPLAN, Unidad de Estudios Prospectivos and Universidad de Chile, Departamento de Economía.

————. 2002. "Dinámica de la pobreza: Resultados de la encuesta panel 1996–2001." Santiago: MIDEPLAN, División Social. Departamento de Información Social.

————. 2004. Encuesta caracterización socio-económica nacional CASEN 2003: Principales resultados empleo. Santiago: MIDEPLAN.

Ministerio Secretaría General de Gobierno. 2001. "Plan para el fortalecimiento de las organizaciones sociales de la sociedad civil," Santiago: Departamento de Organizaciones Sociales, Ministerio Secretaría General de Gobierno.

Mirowski, Phillip. 1989. *More Heat Than Light: Economics as Social Physics, Physics as Nature's Economics*. Cambridge, U.K.: Cambridge University Press.

Moguillansky, Graciela. 2002. "Investment and Financial Volatility in Latin America." *CEPAL Review* 77:45–63.

Morley, Samuel A. 2001. *The Income Distribution Problem in Latin America and the Caribbean*, Libros de la CEPAL 65. Santiago: United Nations.

Mortimore, Michael. 2000. "Corporate Strategies for FDI in the Context of Latin America's New Economic Model." *World Development* 28 (9): 1611–26.

———. 2004. *FDI and TNC Activities in Latin America and the Caribbean*. Ottawa, Canada.

Mortimore, Michael, and Wilson Peres. 2001. "La competitividad empresarial en América Latina." *Revista de la CEPAL* 74:37–59.

Munck, Ronaldo and O'Hearn, Dennis, ed. 1999. *Critical Development Theory: Contributions to a New Paradigm*. London: Zed Books.

Muñoz, Oscar. 1992. "El crecimeinto exportador a largo plazo." *Foro 2000* 1 (4): 5–6.

Naim, Moises. 2002. "The Washington Consensus: A Damaged Brand." *Financial Times*. October 28, 2002. http://www.ceip.org/files/publications/2002-10-28-naim.asp.

Navarrete, Jorge. 2001. "Presentación." In *Confianza social en Chile: Desafíos y proyecciones*, ed. Ministerio Secretaría General de Gobierno. Santiago: Unidad de Investigación y Desarrollo, División de Organizaciones Sociales.

Nelson, Julie. 1990. "Gender Metaphor and the Definition of Economics." *Working Paper Series No. 350*, January. Department of Economics, University of California-Davis.

Neto, Alcino Ferreira Carara, and Matias Vernengo. 2002. "Uma releitura heterodoxa de Bresser-Nakano." *Revista de Economía Política* 22 (4 [84]): 152–55.

Novelo Urdanivia, Federico. 2001. "Un recorrido por las teorías de la integración regional." *Análisis Económico* 34:121–40.

Nuñez, Javier, and Cristina Risco. 2005. "Movilidad intergeneracional del ingreso en Chile." *En Foco 58*. Santiago: Corporación Expansiva.

Ocampo, José Antonio. 1998. *Rethinking the Development Agenda*. Santiago: United Nations Economic Commission for Latin America and the Caribbean.

Ominami, Carlos, and Roberto Madrid. 1990. "Chile: Elementos para la evaluacion del desarrollo exportador." *SUR Proposiciones* 18:120–58.

Öniş, Ziya, and Fikret Şenses. 2005. "Rethinking the Emerging Post-Washington Consensus Development." *Development and Change* 36 (2): 263–90.

Organización Internacional del Trabajo (OIT). 1998. *Chile: Crecimiento, empleo y el desafío de la justicia social*. Santiago: Organización Internacional del Trabajo.

———. 2003. *Políticas de empleo en Chile y América Latina: Seminario en honor de Victor E. Tokman*. Santiago: Organización Internacional del Trabajo.

Organization of American States (OAS). 1999. Guidelines for the Participation of Civil Society Organizations in OAS Activities [OEA/SER.G CP/RES.759(1217/99)]. December 15.

Osorio, Jaime. 2002. "Sobre las recetas para salir del subdesarrollo." *Política y Cultura* 17:69–98.

Ottone, Ernesto. 2000. "Algunas reflexiones sobre la tercera vía: A propósito de la reunión de Berlin." *Colección IDEAS* 1.

Ottone, Ernesto, and Ana Sojo. 2007. *Cohesión social: Inclusión y sentido de pertenencia en América Latina y el Caribe*. Santiago: Naciones Unidas.

Paley, Julia. 2001. *Marketing Democracy: Power and Social Movements in Post-dictatorship Chile*. Berkeley: University of California Press.

Palocci, Antonio. 2002. "Diretrizes do programa de governo do PT para Brasil. Perseu Abramo. http://www.fundacaoperseuabramo.org.br/sala_leitura/diretrizes2002.htm.

Paus, Eva. 1989. "The Political Economy of Manufactured Export Growth: Argentina and Brazil in the 1970." *Journal-of-Developing-Areas* 23 (2): 173–99.

———. 2004. "Productivity and Growth in Latin America: The Limits of Neoliberal Reforms." *World Development* 32 (3): 427–45.

Peres, Wilson. 1994. "Políticas de competitividad." *Revista de la CEPAL* (53): 49–58.

———. 2006. "El lento retorno de las políticas industriales en América Latina y el Caribe." *Revista de la CEPAL* 88:71–88.

Petkoff, Teodoro. 2005. "Las dos izquierdas." *Nueva Sociedad* 197:114–28.

Petras, James. 2005. "Six Myths About the Benefits of Foreign Investment: The Pretensions of Neoliberalism." *Counterpunch*. July 2 edition. http://www.counterpunch.org/petras07022005.html.

———. 2006. "Myth and Realities: Is Latin America Really Turning Left?" *Counterpunch*. June 4 edition. http://www.counterpunch.org/petras06032006.html.

———. 2007. "Between Insurrection and Reaction: Evo Morales' Pursuit of 'Normal Capitalism.'" Paper read at State Crises and Revolutionary Emergency, April 14, 2007, at La Paz, Bolivia.

Petras, James, and Fernando I. Leiva. 1994. *Democracy and Poverty in Chile: The Limits to Electoral Politics*. Boulder, Colo.: Westview.

Pinheiro, Armando Castelar. 2003. "Uma agenda pós-liberal de desenvolvimento para o Brasil." In *Textos para Discussao No. 989*. Rio de Janeiro: Instituto de Pesquisa Econômica Aplicada (IPEA).

Pinto S., Aníbal. 1961. "Los modelos de subdesarrollo: El impacto del capitalismo en América Latina." *Revista de la Universidad de Buenos Aires* VI (1): 5–48.

Piore, Michael J., and Charles F. Sabel. 1984. *The Second Industrial Divide: Possibilities for Prosperity*. New York: Basic Books.

Pollert, Anna. 1988. "Dismantling Flexibility." *Capital and Class* 34:42–75.

Poniachik, Karen. 2005a. "Chile, País Plataforma." Power Point presentation. http://www.foreigninvestment.cl/ pdf/chile_plataforma_de_servicios.ppt.

———. 2005b. "Chile, País Plataforma de Centros de Servicios Compartidos." Power Point presentation. http://www.foreigninvestment.cl/pdf/karen.shared.services.ppt.

Porter, Michael. 1990. *The Competitive Advantage of Nations*. New York: Free.

Power, Dorothy, Gerald Epstein, and Mathew Abrena. 2003. "Trends in Rentier Incomes in OECD Countries: Estimates, Data and Methods," ed. Political Economy Research Institute (PERI). Amherst, Mass.: University of Massachusetts-Amherst.

Prebisch, Raúl. 1976. "A Critique of Peripheral Capitalism." *ECLAC Review* 1:9–76.

———. 1980. "Towards a Theory of Change." *CEPAL Review* 10:155–208.

———. 1981a. "Dialogue on Friedman and Hayek from the Standpoint of the Periphery." *CEPAL Review* 15:153–74.

———. 1981b. *Capitalismo periférico: Crisis y transformación*. Mexico, D.F.: Fondo de Cultura Económica.

———. 1985. "La periferia latinoamericana en la crisis global del capitalismo." *Revista de la CEPAL* 26:65–90.

———. 1996. "Cinco etapas de mi pensamiento sobre el desarrollo." *El Trimestre Económico* LXIII (2) (50): 771–92.

Programa de Naciones Unidas para el Desarrollo (PNUD). 1998. *Informe de desarrollo humano en Chile, 1998*. Santiago: Naciones Unidas.

———. 2000. *Informe de desarrollo humano en Chile 2000*. Santiago: Naciones Unidas.

———. 2002. *Desarrollo Humano en Chile 2002. Nosotros los chilenos: un desafío cultural*. Santiago: Naciones Unidas.

Raczynski, Dagmar. 1989. "Apoyo a pequeñas unidades productivas en sectores pobres: Lecciones de políticas." *Notas Técnicas CIEPLAN* 133.

Raczynski, Dagmar, and Claudia Serrano. 2005. "Programas de superación de la pobreza y el capital social. Evidencias y aprendizajes de la experiencia en Chile." In *Aprendiendo de la experience: El capital social en la superación de la pobreza*, ed. I. Arriagada. Santiago: CEPAL-Cooperación Italiana.

Raghavan, Chakravarthi. 1999. "Development FDI, an Acronym of Yes, Maybe and Uncertainties." *SUNS South-North Development Monitor* 4513.

Rannie, Al. 1993. "The Reorganisation of Large Firm Subcontracting: Myth and Reality." *Capital and Class* 49:53–75.

Reinecke, Gerhard, and Jacobo Velasco. 2005. "Chile: Informe de empleo. Primer semestre de 2005." Santiago: Organización Internacional del Trabajo.

Report on the Special Unit for Technical Assistance among Developing Countries (SU/TCDC), UNDP Inter-Regional Workshop. 2005. *Social Protection in an Insecure Era: A South-South Exchange on Alternative Social Policy. Responses to Globalization*, May 14–17, 2002. http://www.cep.cl/sw2002/Informe_Final/SW2002_Exec_Summ.doc.

Reyes, Oscar. 2006. "Sobre el socialismo del siglo XXI en Venezuela." *Stockholm Review of Latin American Studies* 1:84–104.

Robinson, William I. 2003. *Transnational Conflicts: Central America, Social Change, and Globalization*. London and New York: Verso.

———. 2004. *A Theory of Global Capitalism: Production, Class, and State in a Transnational World*. Baltimore: Johns Hopkins University Press.

Rocha, Maria Geiss. 2002. "Neodependency in Brazil." *New Left Review* 16:5–33.

Rodríguez, Octavio. 2001. "Fundamentos del estructuralismo latinoamericano." *Comercio Exterior* 51 (2): 100–112.

Rodríguez Ostria, Gustavo. 2006. ¿Capitalismo andino-amazónico? *Los Tiempos. com*, February 19, 2006.

Rohter, Larry. 2004. "Learn English, Says Chile, Thinking Upwardly Global," *The New York Times*. December 29. http://www.nytimes.com/2004/12/29/international/americas/29letter.html.

Rojas Aravena, Francisco. 2006. "El nuevo mapa político latinoamericano." *Nueva Sociedad* 205:114–30.

Rosales, Osvaldo. 1988. "Balance y renovación en el paradigma estructuralista del desarrollo latinoamericano." *Revista de la CEPAL* 34:19–36.

———. 1991. "Posibilidades y desafíos de una estrategia de desarrollo alternativo." In *Chile: Problemas y perspectivas del actual modelo de desarrollo (II)*. Santiago: Sociedad Chilena de Economía Política (SOCHEP).

———. 1995. "Hacia una modernización solidaria: El debate entre progresismo y neoliberalismo." *Debates y Propuestas: Revista del Instituto Fernando Otorgués* 3:98–126.

Rosenthal, Gert. 2000. "Los años ochenta y noventa." In *La CEPAL en sus 50 años: notas de un seminario conmemorativo*, ed. CEPAL. Santiago: Naciones Unidas.

Ruccio, David. 1991. "When Failure Becomes Success: Class and the Debate Over Stabilization and Adjustment." *World Development* 19 (10): 1315–34.

Sader, Emir. 2001. "La izquierda latinoamericana en el siglo XXI." *Chiapas* 12:121–27.

Salama, Pierre. 2004. "Amérique latine, dettes et dépendance financière de l'Etat." In *Congrès Marx International IV*. September 29 and October 2, 2004, Paris. http://netx.u-paris10.fr/actuelmarx/m4salama.htm.

———. 2006. "Apertura y pobreza:¿qué clase de apertura?" *Comercio Exterior* 56 (1): 20–32.

Salzinger, Leslie. 2003. *Genders in Production. Genders in Production: Making Workers in Mexico's Global Factories*. Berkeley: University of California Press.

Sampaio Jr., Plinio de Arruda. 2005. *A dança imóvel e os impasses da transição: Por uma política de promoção do pleno emprego no Brasil*. http://www.desempregozero.org.br/ensaios/a_danca_imovel_e_os_impasses_da_transicao.php.

Samuels, Warren J., ed. 1990. *Economics as Discourse: An Analysis of the Language of Economists*. Boston: Kluwer Academic.

Sanchéz-Ancochea, Diego. 2004. "Capital Accumulation, Income Distribution and Exports in Economic Development. Applying the East-Asian Success to Small Latin American Countries." In *Latin American Economic Association (LACEA)*. San José, Costa Rica.

―――. 2005. "Anglo-Saxon Structuralism vs. Latin American Structuralism in Development Economics." *Paper delivered at the Conference of the Eastern Economic Association, New York, March 4–6, 2005*.

Santiago, Jayme Costa. 1990. *Memoria institucional da CEPAL/ILPES nos seus 30 anos de contribuiçao permanente no Brasil: setembro de 1960 a setembro de 1990*. LC/BRS/R.34. Brasilia: CEPAL.

Santiso, Javier. 2006. *Latin America's Political Economy of the Possible: Beyond Good Revolutionaries and Free-marketeers*. Cambridge, Mass.: The MIT Press.

Schatán, Jacobo. 2004. *Distribución del ingreso y pobreza en Chile*. Santiago: Fundación para la Superación de la Pobreza.

Schild, Verónica. 2000. "Neoliberalism's New Gendered Market Citizens: The 'Civilizing' Dimensions of Social Programmes in Chile." *Citizenship Studies* 4 (3): 275–305.

Schneider, Aaron. 2003. "The Politics of Brazilian Development Strategy." *Latin American Perspectives* 30 (4[131]): 92–97.

Schneider, Ben Ross. 1992. "A privatizaçao no governo Collor: triunfo de liberalismo ou colapso do Estado desenvolviment." *Revista de Economía Política* 12:5–18.

Schneider, Ben Ross, and Richard F Doner. 2000. "The New Institutional Economics, Business Associations, and Development." *Brazilian Journal of Political Economy* 20 (3[79]): 39–62.

Selowsky, Marcelo. 1990. "Stages in the Recovery of Latin America's Growth." *Finance and Development*: 28–31.

Serrano, Franklin, and Carlos Medeiros. 2004. "O desenvolvimiento económico e a retomada da abordagem classica do excedente." *Revista de Economía Política* 24 (2): 238–56.

Silva, Patricio. 1991. "Technocrats and Politics in Chile: From the Chicago Boys to the CIEPLAN Monks." *Journal of Latin American Studies* 23 (2): 393–98.

Smart, Alan, and James Lee. 2003. "Financialization and the Role of Real Estate in Hong Kong's Regime of Accumulation." *Economic Geography* 79 (2): 153–79.

Smith, Tony. 2000. *Technology and Capital in the Age of Lean Production: A Marxian Critique of the "New Economy."* Albany: State University of New York Press.

Sojo, Ana. 2003. "Social Vulnerability, Insurance and Risk Diversification in Latin America and the Caribbean." *CEPAL Review* 80:115–33.

Sojo, Carlos. 2002. "La noción de ciudadanía en el debate latinoamericano." *Revista de la CEPAL* 76:25–38.

Solimano, Andrés. 1999. "The Chilean Economy in the 1990s: On a "Golden Age" and Beyond." In *After Neoliberalism: What Next for Latin America*, ed. L. Taylor. Ann Arbor: University of Michigan Press.

———. 2005. "Hacia nuevas políticas sociales en América Latina: crecimiento, clases medias y derechos sociales." *Revista de la CEPAL* 87:45–60.

Solimano, Andrés, Eduardo Aninat, and Nancy Birdsall, eds. 2000. *Distributive Justice and Economic Development: The Case of Chile and Developing Countries*. Ann Arbor: University of Michigan Press.

Solíz Rada, Andrés. 2007. *La Nacionalización Arrodillada* Bolpress (April 1). http://www.bolpress.com/art.php?Cod=2007040103.

Somel, Cem. 2003. "Estimating the Surplus in the Periphery: An Application to Turkey." *Cambridge Journal of Economics 27* (6): 919–33.

———. 2004. "Commodity Chains, Unequal Exchange and Uneven Development." In *ERC Working Papers in Economics 04/11*, ed. Economics Research Center. Ankara: Middle East Technical University.

Soza, María Teresa. 1997. "José Ocampo: 'La CEPAL tiene mucho que vender.'" *Revista Qué Pasa*, December 30, 1997–5 January 1998.

Stallings, Barbara, and Wilson Peres. 2000. *Growth, Employment and Equity: The Impact of Economic Reforms in Latin America and the Caribbean*. Washington, D.C.: The Brookings Institution/Economic Commission for Latin America and the Caribbean (ECLAC).

Stefoni, Pablo. 2005. "Bolivia: 'The MAS Is Center-Left. An Interview with Alvaro García Linera, Bolivia's Recently Elected Vice-President.'" *IV Online magazine*: IV373—December 2005. http://www.internationalviewpoint.org/spip.php?article938.

Stockhammer, Engelbert. 2004. "Financialization and the Slowdown of Accumulation." *Cambridge Journal of Economics* 28 (5): 719–41.

Strassman, Diane. 1990. "Feminism and Economic Knowledge." In *Paper prepared for the American Economic Association, Annual Meetings in Washington DC.*

Summers, Lawrence, and Vinod Thomas. 1993. "Recent Lessons of Development." *The World Bank Research Observer* 8 (2): 241–54.

Sunkel, Osvaldo. 1967. "Marco histórico del proceso de desarrollo y subdesarrollo." In *Cuadernos del ILPES. Serie II. Anticipos de Investigación*. Santiago: CEPAL/ILPES.

———. 1990. "Reflections on Latin American Development." In *Progress toward Development in Latin America: From Prebisch to Technological Autonomy*, ed. James L. Dietz and Dimus D. James, 133–58. Boulder, Colo,: Lynne Rienner Publishers Inc.

Sunkel, Osvaldo, and Gustavo Zuleta. 1990. "Neostructuralism versus Neoliberalism in the 1990s." *CEPAL Review* 42:35–51.

Tavares, Maria da Conceiçao. 1996. "Homenagem a Anibal Pinto." *Revista de Economía Política* 16 (2 [62]): 5–6.

Tironi, Eugenio. 1999. *La Irrupción de las Masas y el Malestar de las Elites.* Santiago: Grijalbo.

Tokman, Victor E. 2003. "Consensos y disensos en las políticas de empleo." In *Políticas de empleo en Chile y América Latina: Seminario en honor de Victor E. Tokman,* ed. OIT. Santiago: Organización Internacional del Trabajo.

Torche, Florencia. 2005. "Desigual pero fluido: El patrón chileno de movilidad en perspectiva comparada." *En Foco 57.* Santiago: Corporación Expansiva.

Touraine, Alain. 2006. "Entre Bachelet y Morales, ¿existe una izquierda en América Latina?" *Nueva Sociedad* 205:46–55.

Treviño, Jesús. 2000. "Conversación con Osvaldo Sunkel." Internet interview. http://www.tamuk.edu/geo/urbana/sunkel.htm.

UNCTAD. 1997. *Trade and Development Report, 1997.* New York and Geneva: United Nations.

———. 2002. *Trade and Development Report, 2002.* New York and Geneva: United Nations.

———. 2004. *Trade and Development Report, 2004.* New York and Geneva: United Nations.

———. 2005a. Investment Policy Review Brazil United Nations Conference on Trade and Development.

———. 2005b. *Trade and Development Report, 2005.* New York and Geneva: United Nations.

———. 2005c. *World Investment Report 2005; Transnational Corporations and the Internationalization of R&D.* New York and Geneva: United Nations.

UNIDO. 2004. *Industrial Development Report 2004.* United Nations Indusrial Organization.

———. 2005. *Industrial Development Report 2005: Capability Building for Catching Up: Historical, Empirical and Policy Dimensions.* Vienna: United Nations Industrial Development Organization.

USAID. 1995. "From Cientelism to a 'Consumer-Service' Orientation." *Participatory Forum: Participation in Policy Reform* 12. Washington, D.C.: United States Agency for International Development.

———. 1997. "Rebuilding Infrastructure by Popular Demand: The Cabildos Abiertos Experience in El Salvador." Participatory Practices: Learning From Experience 9. Washington, D.C.: United States Agency for International Development.

van Deijk, Rivka. 2003. *Modernity, Regional Integration and the Victory of Lula Brazil on the High Road to Globalization?* http://www.agogo.nl/txtbrazil/txtlula/txtlula2.htm.

van der Borgh, Chris. 1995. "A Comparison of Four Development Models in Latin America." *The European Journal of Development Research* 7 (2): 276–96.

Vergara, Rodrigo. 2005. "Productividad en Chile: Determinantes y Desempeño." *Estudios Públicos* 99:23–62.

Vernengo, Matias. 2003a. "What's Next for Brazil After Neoliberalism?" *Challenge* 46 (5): 59–75.

———. 2003b. "Liberalización externa e inversión extranjera directa en Brasil, 1971–2000: una perspectiva neoestructuralista." *Investigación Económica* 62 (246): 125–47.

———. 2004. "Technology, Finance and Dependency: Latin American Radical Political Economy in Retrospect." In *Working Paper No: 2004-6*, ed. Department of Economics. Salt Lake City: University of Utah.

Villarzú, Juan. 2002. *Mínimos sociales e igualdad de oportunidades: Crecimiento con equidad.*

Walton, Michael. 2004. "Neoliberalism in Latin America: Good, Bad, or Incomplete?" *Latin American Research Review* 39 (3): 165–83.

Weiss, Linda. 1999. "Managed Opennesss: Beyond Neoliberal Globalism." *New Left Review* I (238): 126–37.

Welters, Angela. 2004. "Tecnologia, distribuição de renda e implicações para o crescimento: algumas notas sobre a visão da CEPAL nas décadas de 1970 e 1980 [The Effect of Technology and Income Distribution on Growth: Comments on the Perspective of ECLA, 1970-1990]." *Nova Economia* 14 (2): 111–24.

Weyland, Kurt. 2004. "Assesing Latin American Neoliberalism: Introduction to a Debate." *Latin American Research Review* 39 (3): 143–49.

Wilpert, Gregory. 2006. "The Meaning of 21st Century Socialism for Venezuela." *Venezuelanalaysis.com.* July 11. http://www.venezuelaanalysis.com/articles.php?artno=1776.

Woodmansee, Martha, and Osteen, Mark, ed. 1999. *The New Economic Criticism: Studies in the Intersection of Literature and Economics.* London and New York: Routledge.

Woolcock, Michael, and Deepa Narayan. 2000. "Social Capital: Implications for Development Theory, Research, and Policy." *World Bank Research Observer* 15 (2): 225–49.

World Bank. 1993. *Latin America and the Caribbean: A Decade After the Debt Crisis.* Washington, D.C.: World Bank.

———. 2006. "Equity Enhances The Power of Growth to Reduce Poverty: World Development Report 2006," Press Release No. 2006/054/S, September 20, 2005.

World Economic Forum. 2006. *The Global Competitiveness Report 2005–2006: Policies Underpinning Global Prosperity.* London: Palgrave MacMillan

Yamada, Gustavo. 2001. "Reducción de la pobreza y fortalecimiento del capital social y la participación: La acción reciente del Banco Interamericano de Desarrollo." In *Regional Conference on Social Capital and Poverty.* Santiago: ECLAC.

Zibechi, Raul. 2007. "Brasil no va a la izquierda: El segundo gobierno de Lula: Venía mal, sigue igual." *Rebelión/La Jornada.* January 14, 2007.

Zuege, Alan. 2000. "The Chimera of the Third Way." In *Necessary and Unnecessary Utopias: Socialist Register 2000,* ed. L. Panitch and C. Leys. New York: Monthly Review.

Zuleta, Gustavo. 1992. "El desarrollo desde dentro: Un enfoque neoestructuralista para América Latina." *Pensamiento Iberoaméricano* 21:304–13.

Index

FERNANDO IGNACIO LEIVA is associate professor and graduate studies director of the Department of Latin American, Caribbean, and U.S. Latino Studies at the University of Albany (State University of New York).